CABELL CEMETERIES

CABELL COUNTY, WEST VIRGINIA

VOLUME 3

Carrie Eldridge

Heritage Books
2024

There are certainly other cemeteries in Cabell County that have not yet been located. If you have additional information on any of the listed cemeteries or know of a site not listed, please get in touch with the author so she can add it to this material.

This project could not have been accomplished without the assistance of many of Cabell County residents. Those who wished have their names included as site readers. Thanks to everyone and special thanks to Colleen Eldridge, Betty Jameson, Clede Stephens and Rachel Harbour.

HERITAGE BOOKS
AN IMPRINT OF HERITAGE BOOKS, INC.

Books, CDs, and more—Worldwide

For our listing of thousands of titles see our website
at
www.HeritageBooks.com

A Facsimile Reprint
Published 2024 by
HERITAGE BOOKS, INC.
Publishing Division
5810 Ruatan Street
Berwyn Heights, MD 20740

International Standard Book Number
Paperbound: 978-0-7884-2785-5

CONTENTS

ILLUSTRATIONS

Dating Old Cemeteries is page 1
There are no pages 5-14

DATING OLD CEMETERIES

Case 1.William Merritt
Case 2.Spring Hill

      Cemteries are difficult to date for a number of reasons. There may be no markings at all to indicate site, all markings may be field stones, stones used may have been of sandstone with all marking obliberated by time, stones may have been damaged or finally burials may have been at varied periods of time which confuses the original date.

      If the cemetery is located only by word of mouth, dating is virtually impossible. If the informer can also provide a date you will have a time frame, not necessarily the orginal date. Most Cabell cemeteries that are unmarked were reported to be infants or plague victims buried rapidly.

      Field stone cemeteries are the oldest cemeteries in most cases.The burials were made early in the settlement of the area before a stone cutter was available or before the family had enough money to buy a cut stone. About the only way to date this group is an estimate from early settlements or reports from area residents.

      Damaged graveyards often have a few stones that can provide dates, but there is no way to determine the earlest burials. This also holds true for cemeteries with widely spaced burials. These usually contain separate and often unrelated families that have simpled used a common cemetery. The older burials can easily be overlooked because they may be overgrown or be field stones.

Case 1. William Merritt Cemetery located near Barboursvill NE of the junction of the Mud River and the Guyandotte River. The area was badly overgrown, stone were broken and buried. The Boy Scouts took this as project and we were able to clean this cemetery. A clean cemetery showed depressions of lost graves, but this information did not date the cemetery. The oldest marked stones are from the 1830 with one from 1821. They are made of marble (with a stonemakers mark), but there are a series of older cut stone from sandstone. These stones have flaked and broken. Several have designs remaining and one has a readable name, but none of these have a usable date.

Obviously, this cemetery predates 1820; but how do you date it. Historical information states Cabell County Court first met at William Merritt's house-Date 1809. Since people were in the county area before it was created, 1809 is not the earliest possible date, but probably close. The earliest burials are most often infants so if you can find a marriage date for the owner of the property you can estimate possible children.

Merritt owned a mill and was well to do, but are there field stone burials predateing the carved sandstone?? Do you have any genealogical information about the family? Finally, all of this information is fitted together like a puzzel that often has no answer. In the Merritt case we know that the cemetery predates 1820 only because there are a set of stones with older information(Sister Louisa died before 1820) and people who should be buried here have no readable stones. (William is unlocated although most members of his family are here.)

This Merritt Cemetery was simply a family cemetery. Most of the indentifiable graves can be connected to the immediate family. As the family expanded and moved to different areas, the cemetery ceased to be used. The last burial here was 1871, but it is 20 years after the majority of burials in the 1850',

16

Case 2. Spring Hill Cemetery is located in Huntington on 20th Street hill at Norway Avenue. This cemetery predates Huntington and the orginal location would have been on the hill south of Guyandotte and beside the James River Turnpike on a section of land from the Savage Grant orginally claimed by John Savage and transferred to William Holderby.

The Central Land Company (backed by Collis P.Huntington to purchase land to build a city)acquired its land from the orginal owners and in 1872 created a Huntington Park Board to oversee the sale of cemetery lots on the orginal 29acres of Spring Hill. The first map of Huntington(1874) shows the Spring Hill section already owned by the city with property owned by Buffington to the east and Holderby to the west. Since there are many early burials of both Buffington and Holderby,Spring Hill could have begun as either families' cemetery. It is more probable that it belong to the Holderby family because in 1870 William Holderby sold to these men (who would become the Central Land Company) a chapel that he built in the cemetery area.(Deed 16-540)

Thus we have a date of at least 1870. The Holderbys were here when Cabell was founded so burials here could have begun as early as 1800. These first burials would have been field stone and like the Merritt Cemetery followed by a sandstone that deteriorated.(The first marble stones came from Cincinnati or Marietta and usually had a stonemasons mark). WPA readings show 2 marked graves from 1834/5, but most of the readable stones that remain today bare dates from the 1850's.

Another dating aid is the Civil War Memorial Section. There are acutally two sections,one GAR and one CSA and although most of the stones have only names, it is possible to acquire dates from other sources. Several of the men buried here died during the war including General Jenkins.

Spring Hill was probably the community cemetery for most of Guyandotte considering its location on a hill south of the community and its proxcimity to the James River Turnpike.(The Guyandotte Cemetery was a plague cemetery.) There may have been a church here before Holderby's Chapel as indicated by the varied early burials and by the fact that the 1870 Holderby deed stated the the "church was to be used by both the Southern Methodists and the Southern Branch of the Presbyterians".

There have been reasonably good records kept at Spring Hill since it was incorporated in 1872, but these records contain few of the earlier burials. Once again we must use historical records,genealogial records and personal rememberances to date this cemetery. Historical records indicate there should be burials here from at least 1810. The WPA readings record 1834-5, but these stones have not been located.

Since this area was settled the same time as Barboursville, the same pattern of burials records should appear. This does not happen, possibly because it is a perpetual care facility and the grounds are kept clean. Stones damaged by vandals would have been removed if they could not be repaired and replaced correctly. Because this cemetery continues to be used, older stones and field stones have not been protected by being buried or overgrown.

After using all known information, the date of this cemetery remains unknown and the rescearher has discovered a period of 30 to 40 years with no records.

Sources: Cabell Cemeteries Volume I
        Cabell County Annals
        Cabell County Deeds
        Genealogical information/private sources.

INDEX TO CEMETERIES WITHIN HUNGTINGTON
from Russell Ck and R60 west to Cabell/Wayne line and N of I64

Source:
Universal Advertising
Associates Inc.

HUNTINGTON CEMETERIES
from Russel Creek on the East to the Wayne County line
and north of 16th Street Road(R10)

H1A-LAWSON/SLAVE-in Altizer near RR underpass on land used as police
shooting range-when dirt was moved skeltons were found and check of
court records indicate a Lawson family used this site to bury slaves.
No stones.(Source:Mrs.Reed.)Carrie Eldridge 10 sep 1990

H1-PETITE-R60 at mouth of Russell Ck-not located and reported destroyed
the is posibly same as My.Carmel on West Pea Ridge. Carrie Eldridge

H2--WRIGHT-former location Norway Avenue near Colored Home for Boys
 (Now Marshall Married Housing)DAR very poor condition
  /Kearns,Maggie E.Lee,w/o Dr.A.E. 29 Jan 1874 30y28d
  /Wright,Myrtie G. d/o WO & SE d 8 sep 1867
  /Wright,Mary H. d/o ED & E 7 oct 1853 6y11m6d
  /Wright,Edward s/o ED & E d 26 Jun 1851
  /McGinnis,Leon H.s/o AB & SE 5 Jun 1892-17 dec 1892
       Allen B. 23 dec 1866-4 apr 1893

#H3 EVERETTE,JR.- inside main gate at INCO just at end of bridge INCO
retains key(moved to Pats Branch Cem.in 1990)
Started John Everett Jr.fenced and maintained s/o cem #15
   /Everett,Sarah w/o Col.John   /Everett,Mary 19 nov 1816-9 aug 1836
         sep 1785-8 Jun 1855   /Everett,,Elizabeth P. w/o T W
      John 15 feb 1788-14 Jul 1871   d13 aug 1879
        Junior 83y   Talton W. 25 sep 1906   85y6m17d
        15 feb 1788-14 Jul 1871 /Everett,Amisetta w/o John S.
  /Everett,Henry Clay   28 nov 1828-24 apr 1851
      7 nov 1849-7 Jyl 1843   /Clark,Emma Everett
                                    1868-1888 d/o JS&A
John Everett Sr. is buried at Ona.

23

#H4-PAT'S BRANCH- location on INCO property back side-in 1940 was
considered in bad shape and DAR list was made at that time before
stones were down.(*-DAR) Read 1989:Brent Williams.

1 Bartlett,Sarah w/o WH
  5 dec 1854 25y3m6d
* Degraw, Isabella w/o Edward
  d/o J & M Baumgardner
  29 Jun 1855
* Downer, Eliza A.Flowers
  3 mar 1843-17 Jun 1874
* Elizabeth ?
7 Grose, Elizabeth w/o GW
  7 dec 1851 29y5m22d
9 Hite, John B.
  20 Jun 1805-9 mar 1880
  (wife at Guy.M.E.)
11 Jewell,Sally Ann w/o Benj.
  23 Jul 1854 64y6m26d
* Jewell,Louis A.
* Kise,Victoria d/o C & M
  21 Jul 1853-27 may 1872
13 Lester,Mary E. w/o RG
  3 dec 1854 21y
* McCorkle, Henrietta E.K.
  w/o Dr.AM-d/o Dr.Jacob
  Nancy Woltz of Fincastle,
  VA 5 aug 1844 27y4m22d
15 McCorkle,Sarah Ann d/o Dr.
17 McCorkle,Eglantine Jacinta
  30 aug 1848 7y10m12d
* McCorkle,Thomas Clinton
  s/o Dr. 23 aug 1851
  12y8m11d
* Walton, Anzina E. w/o Wm.A.
23 Wigner,John 3 Jul 1873
  47y6m24d of Gallia Co.
24 Wilson,Mary A. w/o Wm.
  30 Jul 1846-10 aug 1869
25 Wood,Don Carlos s/o James E.
  & Anna J. 24 Jan 1853
  3y9m1d
* Worden, Ida M.d/o W & H
  18 oct 1871 1y4m21d

2 Clark, Sarah L d/o AH & S 31 mar 1869
3 Douthit,William 28 Jan 1874 64y5m9d
4 Degraw,Martha E. d/o AC & E 31 Jan 1855
5 Duncan,Clarence D. s/o DL & Ida S.
  4 may 1872 25d
6 Fowler,Anna Eliza w/o WB
  4 feb 1851 2976m3d
* Mollie ?
* Hider, Harriet d/o H & J 1 dec 1832
8 Hite,James W. s/o JB & EA
  8 dec 1851-25 mar 1853
10 Hite,William Sr. 30 nov 1778-12 apr 1853
  (soldier of 1812)
* Jewell,Emma V. d/o DC & ME
  1 aug 1870 3m
12 Lagrange,Mary E. d/o WA & EV
  6 Jan 1881 23d
* Lagrange,Hally C. d/o WA & EV
  30 Jan 1880 7m10d
14 Matthews,Mary E. w/o James P.
  20 Jun 1854 24y25d
* Owens,William T. s/o GE & G
  14 aug 1873 12y8m10d
* Reid,Elizabeth J.F.d/o G & CW 22 apr 1881
16 Russell,Edward T. 26 dec 1854 21y10m26d
18 Shorter, Julis A. w/o WH
  3 dec 1878 39y10m15d
19 Shorter,d/o WH & JA 23 sep 1877 3d
20 Shorter,s/o WH & JA 24 nov 1878 1d
21 Shultz,Joseph 7 aug 1867 73y
22 Webb,Alice S.d/o T & A 23 mar 1864 2y11m
* Wheeler,Mary inf/o JG & Mary D.
  18 nov 1852-29 oct 1853
* Womeldorff,Anna Eliza w/o JW
  27 apr 1827-5 dec 1873
* Womeldorff,Jennie E.Lee d/o JW & AE
  1 nov 1869-17 oct 1870
* Worden,Leonard L.s/o J & ME
  13 aug 1876 1y7m
26 Winton,Sarah w/o Joseph
  20 may 1830 40y6m10d

#H5-Old St.JOSEPH'S Catholic-Guyandotte-Dietz hollow Rd. located in curve of road and has little upkeep-an area of vandalism.*=DAR--#=WPA

#Adkins,inf 1934
*Bean,Robert L.1873-1941
#Barry,Catherine E.10 nov 1932
/Bias,Larkin 1 feb 1900-27 Jul 1907
#Bias,Clarence 5-30?-1 Jun 1891
, Oliver 3 sep 1907-10 Jun 1925
#Bias,Edna 14 Jun 1918
/Bias,Hattie 17 nov 1891 41y w/o JL
#Birchill,inf 31 Jul 1872
/Blackwell,s/o WL&Pearl 8 dec 1919
/Birchill,James 30 Jul 1877 77y
#Blatt,Helen E.1909-1910
#Blevins,Charles 8 Jan 1931
#Blatt,Fredrick G.31 mar 1883-15 Jun 1912
#Blevins,Ida B.25 Jul 1938
#Blevins,Merith Louisa 21 sep 1936
#Bowden,Carl Mandell 14 apr 1936
/Brandenburg,Margert H.1861-1901
/Brown,Garnet 1908 inf
Ann Cain 1823-1884 grandmother
Mary 1910 ch/o JS&HS
Johanna A. 1873-1893
*Bueker,Hery C.1852-1914
Elizabeth R. 1879-1906
#Canty,John CoH 3rd NC Art
/Butcher,Ann F.29 sep 1871 w/oMH 57y10m16d
#Canty,mary 1842-1914
#Carroll,Annie 1885
#Carroll,Millard H.1946-1927
#Carroll,Minnie 17 Jun 1812-25 apr 1876
/Carroll,Thomas 66y10m8d
#Carroll,Elizabeth Downey 1854-1891
b.in Parrish of Mohill
/Carroll,Annie inf/o Tom&Mary sep-dec 1865
Letrin Co. Ireland
Catherine B.14 nov 1858-29 may 1903
17 Jun 1812-25 apr 1876
Ellen P.17 mar 1856-28 aug 1889
Mary Fee w/o Thomas Carroll
w/o James McLaughlin
b in Parish of Kiltubrett
Margaret A.17 feb 1848-10 Jun 1907
Letrum Co. Ireland
Charles F.27 Jul 1862-26 Jan 1933
25 Mar 1835-21 Jan 1928
/Chicatans,Frank 11 Jul 1876-19 Jul 1905
/Collins,Christine Fay 1930 inf
/Clanghton,Susan 16 feb 1882 WV CMEGS
#Coffman,Thomas Ashley 8-12-1934
/Connelly,Martin 11 Feb 1889 75y
/Colley,Lucy
*Connelly,Mary 17 feb 1889 67y
17 apr 1898-14 feb 1907
b Athlone Co.West Mead,IRE
/Debord,Catherine Amille
/Denore,Mary katherine1958-1959
1880 inf/o N&C
/Elkins,Archie CoB 5th Va Inf
#Eary
#Eary
#Fielder 1937
#Finley,James 18 apr 1925
/Fitzgerald,Joseph 1860-1907
#Fudge,John E.
/Gasner,Mary w/o George
/Ganty,Jno. 1835-1906 CoM 3rd Us Art
25 dec 1821-9 apr 1887
Mary 1842-1914
b Oxford,England
/Giola,Gerdlama Mamie Damego 1880-1910
/Harmon,Wm.Everett 1909-1962
w/o Francesco
/Haverly,Idonia C.
/Haverty,S.J.Tilden 2 dec 1877-21 oct 1891
1 may 1872-6 Jan 1900
/Henderson,Mary Eliz. 8 sep 1896-13 apr 1911
/Howard,Eliza 25 feb 1872wWH
/Hynes,Mary w/o M.17 may 1885 40y
/Inlow,Sarah J.1829-1908
Charles O.30 Jul 1887 27y21d s/oGS&KE
/Kain,Michael M. s/o M&M
(Mynes,Charles D. 1881)
1 feb 1888 30y7m24d
/Keen,Henry d 9 sep 1874
/Kain,Mary 9 Jul 1878 47y
/Keen,infant 1915- 1916
County Roscommon,IRE wMartin
/Keefe,Catherine 16 dec 1890 54y w/o PJ
/Kincaid,Margaret 1865-1936
*Legge,Milton 1907-1918
/Manley,Patrick 1842-1890
/Mattison 5 feb 1889 21y
Margaret 1845-1896
#McLaughlin,Ellen P.(Carroll)
Mary A. 1865-1895
17 mar 1856-10 Jun 1907
/Moruney,Edward Leo 1903-13EL&M
/Mulgahy,T. 2 sep 1882/59y6m7d
/Mulcany,Thomas Loyd s/oT&L
/O'Brien,John 1939-1916
20 may 1873 14y2m3d
/O'Brien,Louise 1842-1913
/O'Brien,Margaret 1809-1895
/O'Conner,Roger P. s/oT&S15 Jan 1910 23y

/O'Conner-father
/Parker,Jack R.1913 inf
#Quinlan,F.V. 1909
#Quinlan,Michael 1856-1935
*Rock,O.D.1815-1905
/Rottman,Rose S. 1871-1913
/Short,Hattie 1915-1917
#Sowards,Billie Lee 1937-8
#Stansill,Thomas H.
/Stender,Clarence Alloyicus
  6 feb 1881-16 aug 1898
  s/o Wendell
/Smith--22 feb 1843-1927
  w/o PS--d/o H&M Meade
/Wigal,John b 5 Jan 1832
  Mary A.25 apr 1835-18 aug 1901
/Witzgall,C.C. 1840-1902
 ,Kate w/o C.C. 1848-------

/O'Conner--mother
#Porter,John D.4 sep 1937
#Quinlan,Julia 1835-1871

/Roe,David S. 24 mar 1879 84y4m9d
#Romine,Hallie P. 12 nov 1953
/Shultz,Rose w/o Joseph 20 Jan 1881 75y
#Sprinkle,Cora Frances 1938
/Stewart,Robert 14 apr 1887 84y
/Stewart,Martha Ann d 24 nov 1885 67y
/Swann,B.F. 1854
  Sallie M. 1853-1902
/Swan,Lieut.Jno.T. Co G 5 WV Inf
/Welch,Ira Russell 1900-1905
#Whitt,George W.18 Jun 1938 54y9m4d
/Worden,William 19 feb 1884 41y father
/Worden,Rosa 11 nov 1876 d/o W&G
/Young,Ester Lee 12 dec 1933

Read 1989 Mary Swann & Kathy Kizzee 1988

#H6-GUYANDOTTE M.E. Church 5th Avenue at Floodwall in Guyandotte
fenced and maintained by park service.There is considerable empty
space which may have contained markers at one time,but this list is
the same as the 1945 list except for Erastus Wellington who is on back of
stone with his wife and missed by DAR. 1817-1886   CE 10 apr 1989
 /Adam-In memory of Edgar Athneil s/o Nathaniel S. & Pauline Adam d 13
   aug 1841 1y20d
 /Cooper-In memory of Jacob Cooper d in this place 1 sep 1829 37y6m
    a native of Washington Co.PA.
 /Cummings,Reuben d 4 Jan 1839 24y a brothers tribute
 /Gardner,Joseph 13may 1793-31 Jan 1846
 /Gardner,Frances I. d/o J & E Gardner 30 sep 1842-19 Jan 1849
 /Handley,Mary 4 dec 1829   84th year of her life
 /Handley,Lewis s/o S & S Handley who met with a atal accident,on board
  the Kanawha Steamboat with many of hos Fellow mortals Jun 24, & whilst
   his tender parents waited around him full of grief he expired
   25th 1829 aged 24y
 /Hite,Priscilla consort of John B.Hite d/o John & Elizabeth Wilson
   25 may 1815-18 feb 1839 23y8m24d
 /Hite,Elizabeth d/o JB & PW Hite d 30 oct 1860 24y11m22d
 /Hite,Isabella V. d/o F & M Hite 23 mar 1837 y711m
 /Holderby,Mrs.Ariana consort of James Holderby Esq.
   12 mar 1792-24 apr 1826
 /Lawson,Anthony Sr. of Logan Co.VA born Staunton Co *** of
   Northumberland,England 31 oct *** who on the return home from P***
   departed this life at Guyandotte 1768-1849   stone broken
 /Letulle,Mrs. Eleonor consort of Victor letulle 3 may 1763-27 Jan 1836
  A La Memoire D'Eleonor Gueulle Femme Letulle.Morte regrette de ses
  mombreux ames.Gette pierre est consacrie par son affectionne marie.
 /Mays,Josephine d/o JH & MC Mays 1 oct 1830 7y11m
 /Mears,George s/o F.Mears 30 Jul 1841 2y8m
 /Perkins,Protulous C.s/o Mrs.MK Perkins
  drowned 10 sep 1855
 /Peters s/o WL & MV Peters 2 Jun 1850

26

/Shaw,Silas 20 sep 1823   30y5m15d
/Smith,Dudley M.s/o DD & EC Smith 3 feb 1841
       Mary Bodue of Rouong,Kingdom of France 1811-5 Jul 1840   29y
/Wellington,Charles 6 Jun 1817 21710m
       Fredrick C. 27 Jun 1849   16y1m2d
/Wellington,Erastus 18 feb 1793-5 feb 1861
       Charlotte Webb w/o Erastus 10 feb 1802-24 mar 1886
Wellington-Walington
The following are collected in a section. According to DAR some have been
moved to this cemetery from other locations.
/Davis,Daniel 1759-1838 Pvt.Rev.War
       Betsey Stevenson 1756-1817
/Gellengwaters,Jas. 1756-1856 Pvt.Rev.War
/Love,Chas. 1753-1824 Pvt.Rev.War
       Susanna Childs 1756-1826
/Morris,Jno. d 1818 Capt.Rev.War
       Margaret d 1818
/Rece,Allen 1759-1831 Pvt.Rev.War
       Mary Climer 1873-1847

#H6A-Topping Court Norwood Rd completely destroyed in 1940's *(Henry miller*
   app. 70 graves (there was trial-plantiff-TRIPLETT)   *PROPERTY)*
   1 Luther Midkiff s/o James Lewis Midkiff 1912-1914
   2 Peyton l. Coffman d 2 nov 1880
Source:Virginia Midkiff Graham 25 apr 1989

H7-BETHEL Memorial Park- 100y E of X of Norway Ave. and Norwood Rd. Bethel
Rd dead ends in park.Orginally Negro/Black cemetery operated by McClain
Funeral Home(Their personal records were lost in a court case and funeral
home burned)-badly overgrown-some stones are visible but surrounded by
mulitiflora rose 5-10 acres).WPA=#(badly focused-some impossible)   Carrie
Eldridge 18 Jan 1990

/Atkins,Francis J.1932-1939   /Austin,Cornelius O.22 oct 1908-6 oct 1974
/Austin,William   /Austin,Mary
#Baldwin,Anna B.   #B------,Susie 16 aug 1934 46y
   22 aug 1911-20 nov 1931   #Be------,Fred 1 ma4 1935   36y
/Birchfield,Doshie   #Blair,Henrietta 25 apr 1936 40y
   29 mar 1904-27 oct 1963   /Bostick,Ed.26 mar 1890-18 feb 1945 WWII
/Briggs,Leslie 1885-1972   #Booker,William SpAm
   Agnes C.1892-1937   #Brown,Hazel Lillian 1934
/Brown,Jesse L.27 apr 1937 WWI #Burke,Mason 17 oct 1936 52y
/Carter,Theodore   #Clark,Wilmer B.30 sep 1886-12 nov 1927
/Carter,John Jr.   #Coleman,(--lin)dec 1934
   8 nov 1933-19 Jul 1944   /Dean,Tommy 22 mar 1893-9 aug 1938
#Dobson.Ella 1875-1927   #Ellis,John H.1884-1929
#Fain,John H.   /Fitzgerald,John 15 sep 1952
   11 dec 1880-17 Jan 1934   /Fleming,John calloway Jr.WWII
#Golden M.   #Franklin,Alice G.14 oct 1938 69y
/Goosly,Rev.John H.1872-1956/Garland,Ray E. 1899-1940
#Grays,Samuel 20 oct 1934 65y#Harmon,John 9 mar 1938 25y
#Harril,Salie 4 oct 1935 42y#Hill,Sylvia 14 may 1936 56y
#Holley,Edward 17 Jul 1934   /Holland,Harold 30 Jan 1892-25 dec 1966 WWI
#Jackson,James   /Johnson,Ned W.27 feb 1922-13 sep 1966 WWII
#Johnson,Mary E.1875-1927   #Johnson,Richard 14 apr 1932 70y

#Johnson,Mrs.   #Johnson,William nov 1937 56y
#Jones,D.M. 1926-1931   #Johnston,Rebecca 14 dec 1934 43y
#Jones,Frank 1906-1933   #Jones,Fletcher 21 jan 1936 47y
#Knight,Francis 1918-1927   /Jones,Saac 25 jun 1897-25 sep 1960 WWII
/Lee,Harvey 1897-1967 WWI   /Lockett,Sarah 1863-1928 w/o A.D.
/Londy,John   WWI   A.D. 1861
    25 dec 1893-18 sep 1959   #Martin,Robt C.4 apr 1934 62
#McFarland,Mrs.1932   /Moody,Rosetta E. 15 feb 1906-9 oct 1958
#Meadows,Rev.R.D.W. 1938   #Moore,Titus"Britt" 1902-1938
#Moore,Laura 12 mar 1937   #Morris,Joseph 1933
#Nash,Mattie 1861-1927   #Nichols,Finley 15 aug 1935 36y
#Owens,Oscar 9 oct 1926 80y   #Payn,Boble 12 jun 1934 inf
#Paynter,John N.11 may 1938   /Phillips,Elder R.16 may 1861-16 jan 1938
/Peters,Dianne Marie   /Phillips,Lula 1875-1939
    20 jun 1915-26 dec 1948   /Price,Edward C. 1881-1964
/Price,Thomas L.   Julia B.1879-1960
#Pogue,Jennie 29 apr 1937   #Pogue,Lucy 1845-1 jul 1930
#Pogue,Virgil 27 feb 1932WI   #Putts,Schorlotte 1938
#Qualls,Vesta Marie   #Raimey,Elizabeth A.14 aug -22 sep 1927
    14 nov 1932 5y8m9d   #Randalls,Clara 29 nov --
/Robinson,Charles M.1909-1942/Robinson,Rev.S.J. 1890-1948
#Shatterfield,Lucy   /Shatterfield,Joseph R.Sr.1879-1955
#Smith,Katherine 1934   /Smoot,Elvin C.1904-1968
/Stevenson,Will   WWI   Evelyn 1910--
    1 aug 1888-17 jun 1960   /Tatum,Emma 4 jul 1877-22 mar 1950
#Thompson,Chlora 1879-1936
/Turner,John 15 sep 1940 WII #Thornhill,Wesely 1 may 1932 37y
/Venable,Iona 1914-1959   /Venable,Patterson 6 sep 1911-17 aug 1959
#Washington, 1934   #Washington,Ora 1 jul 1936 29y
/Watkins,William 1940 WWII /Watson,Irvin 30 dec 1936
#Watson,Irvin 30 dec 1936WI #Whitehurst,Edward 20 dec 1887-9 may 1935
/Whithurst,M.B.1886-1944   #Williams
#Willis,Henrietta 20 dec 1934 28y   17 fs visible

#H7A--MARTIN,Mary-Norway Avenue to Bethel Rd,E side pt at Hibner Rd
under large trees/children's playarea,old fence.15 yd sq   CE 18 jan 1990
  /Ferguson,George H.1868-1943 (2 stones)
      Sarah Ann 1869-1948
  /Ferguson,Howard H. 1890-1936
  /Gibson,Grant   1877-1923
  /Martin,Mary 16 apr 183--10 apr 1909 w/o S (broken)
  /Pyles,Fannie L. 31 dec 1863-15 feb 1914 w/o J.L.
  /Taylor,Charles R. 11 may 1889-8 --n 194- h/o Georgia (broken)
  /Vernatt,Robert A. 1865-1932
4 fs and 5-10 unmarked

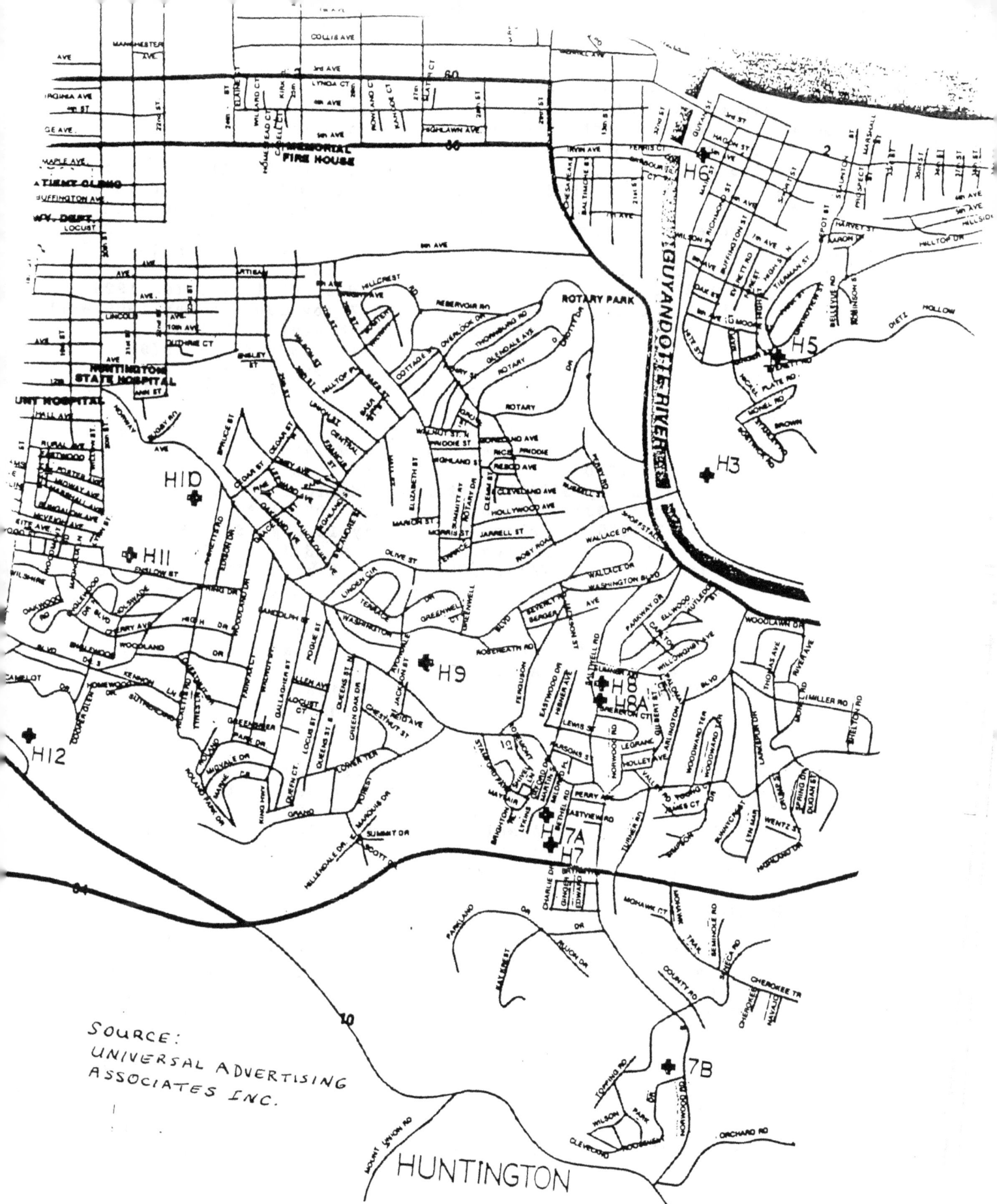

SOURCE:
UNIVERSAL ADVERTISING
ASSOCIATES INC.

HUNTINGTON

H8-HIGHLAND-R60 E to Washington Blvd rt 100y to Saltwell Rd-S 1/2m Just
past Summer Ave on lf. WPA=# Rachael Harbour mar 1990
This cemetery is part of Huntington Parks-records kept at Spring Hill.
WPA records list colored(Black)=c

/Abbott,Erskine R.1906-1971   /Abbott,Frank L.22 Jun 1902-26 mar 1981
  /Abbott,Hazel Napier 1910-1973/Abbott,Lonnie E.20 oct 1899-9 Jun 1968
  /Abbott,Norma A.1908-1952   /Adams,Theodore 15 Jan 1912-1 nov 1962 WII
    ch McComas,Rebecca L.1962   /Adams,Robert Lee 5 nov 1932-23 Jun 1981
  /Adams,Dorothy Mae Ballard   /Adams,Jack L.20 dec 1920-25 Jan 1976
    17 feb 1925-20 may 1983   /Adams,Nancy 1839-1903
  /Adams,Rosella 1836-1912   /Adkins,Raymond M.5 oct 1921-8 feb 1923
  /Adkins,Bruce B.1902-1967   /Adkins,Dewey R.7 nov 1901-28 may 1969 WWII
    Vitura 1896-1971   /Adkins,Garnett Stanley 1905-1937
  /Adkins,Roy 1899-1974   /Adkins,Jake 2 may 1896-15 mar 1979
  /Adkins,Vicki 1947-1952   J.Eva 28 Jan 1899-16 apr 1987
  /Adkins,Maggie 1880-15 mar 1936/Adkins,Ralph 21 dec 1917-18 may 1979 WWII
  /Adkins,Eugenie 1901-1952   Mary Ada 27 apr 1925
  /Adkins,Grover C.1886-1942   /Adkins,Georgia Mae 20 Jun 1899-9 feb 1936
    Kitty 1882-1951   /Agnew,Jeanette M.1889-1973
  /Alberts,Rosemary 1925-1980   Banks,E. 1887-1943
    Boyd L.15 Jan 1904-22 sep 88#Albright,Alice Harless 17 Jan 1935 49y10m
  /Algeo,Margaret E. 1911-1937   /Algeo,Robert Lee 1935 inf
  /Algeo,William H.1897-1935   /Allen,John Henry 12 aug 1932 WWI c
  /Allen,James E. 1938 inf   /Alley,Leonard Lee 23 Jul 1947 inf
  /Alley,Jeff Wm.1940-1942   /Alley,Charles W. 2 mar 1913-29 Jun 1982
  /Alley,Ella M.   #Anderson,Lizzie 4 Jun 1933 31y5m24d
      25 dec 1905-5 sep 1975
  /Angelo,Ronnie P.   #Anderson,Wm.Alexander 3 feb 1934 58y c
    1956-1976 gch/D&L Benedict   /Angles,James 1872-12 apr 1937 65y6m16d
  /Angles,Nina 1888-1954   /Anness,Grace may 8 mar 1878-24 aug 1954
  #Anness,John A.1861-1938   John A.15 sep 1881-29 apr 1938
  /Ansell,Lena 4 mar 1924   /Ansell,James P.Dennison 1931-33
    Rosalee 1921-1933   Ada Catherine 1897-1943
    Wilma 1920-22   Maxine 1921-1933
    Wilson,1920-1921   /Ansell,Lennie E.10 mar 1915-7 may 1980wII
  /Ansell,Abraham S.1871-1947   /Ansell,Luther W. 5 dec 1921
    Lillie R. 1875-1939   Gladys L.11 apr 1922-18 oct 1973
  /Ansell,George E.1899-1951   /Ansell,Myrtle J.16 Jul 1923 w/o Luther
    Eunice A.1903-1961   /Anthony,Andrew 1921-1984
  /Arthur,Eva Vivian 1938 inf   Mary C. 1928--
    Charles Otis 1917-1965 WWII/Arthur,Charles R. 1938 inf
    Althea Parsley 1919--   /Arthur,Kathryn Hussell 1923-1971
  #Atkinson,F.
  /Atkinson,Rev.Jos. 1847-1927   /Atkinson,Robert inf 29 nov 1918
  /Atkinson,Victoria 1853-1923   /Atkinson,John F.21 oct 1907-21 aug 1976
  /Atkinson,Effie L.1888-1981   /Atkinson,Alpha E. 1892-1953
    John P.1885-1963   Margaret T. 1894-1938
  /Atkinson,Wade C.1912-1933   /Atkinson,Hugh N.1881-1950
  /Atkinson,Virginia E. 1877-1946
  /Back,Granville M.1853-1940   /Bacorn,Mack A.4 sep 1861-29 Jan 1945 WWI
  /Bailey,Clotilda G.1902-1984   /Baker,May Stephenson 1871-1945
  /Baker,Mary 1850-1941   /Baker,Mildred M.27 apr 1924--
    H.P. 1845-1896   Christopher C.3 oct 1922-16 sep 1964WWII
  /Baker,Enoch 1842-1928   /Baker,Arnold Preston 28 Jul 1934 21y

Anne Bragg 1864-1937
/Barber,Sydney B.1851-1929
/Bare,J.S. 1880-1935
/Barnes,Charles 1868-1932
/Barnett,Rev.Laundle M.1904--
   Christine S.D> 1901-1982
/Bass,Ada Clark 1888-1931 c
/Bass,Ruth E. 1929-1977
/Bass,Sid Schrice 1969 inf
/Basenback,Jenni 1863-1933
/Bayes,William T.
    18 nov 1862-7 mar 1959
/Beale,John Morgan 1865-1944
    Margaret McGinnis 1863-1933
/Bellomy,C.Raymond 1912-1937
/Bellomy,Charles A.
    11 apr 1895-16 nov 1959
/Bellomy,Jerry Henderson
    25 may 1872-12 nov 1933
    Burcham,Alma Bellomy
   27 Jun 1875-21 dec 1964
/Benedick,Mary Eloise 1905-16
/Benedick,Robert S. 1907-1982
/Benedick,Edith Rose 1888-1946
/Benedick,Ernest H.1885-1959
/Bennett,Minnie C.1886-1940
    James G. 1881-1971
#Bennett,Gladys 28 mar 1936 16y
#Bennett,John W.3 dec 1936
    63y9m11d
/Berger,Martin 1858-1927
    Annie 1861-1930
/Bernstein,Mary 1880-1926
/Berry,Rheuben H.
    10 sep 1856-6 Jul 1933
/Berry,Sallie Rae 1929-1932
/Berry,Lillian D.
    4 apr 1867-3 mar 1940
/Bexfield,Elmer 1916 inf
    Thelma 1916 inf
/Bexfield,Marita Gail 1949-1952
/Bexfield,Drema Yvonne 1948-1953
/Bias,Riley M.1869-1925
/Bias,Elizabeth 1870-1940
/Bias,Lora B. 1894-1981
/Bias,Virgie lee 1888-1950
/Bias,Fred A.1890-1927
/Bias,Mabel 1902-1916
/Bias,Luther F.1899-1977
/Bias,Norman 1898 inf
#Bias,Ethel
#Bias,Millard B.28 Jun 1937 6y
#Bias,William 24 Jun 1894 36y
/Bills,Elbert L.25 apr 1941--

/Baker,Arnold P.1912-1934
/Bare,Ollie S.1872-19--
/Bare,J.T.1855-1942
/Barnett,Harold W.1913-1954
/Barnett,Laundle E. 1925-1981
    Eugenia M.1926--
/Bass,Thomas E. Sr.4 dec 1927-14 dec 1963
/Bass,Michael Augusta 9 Jun 1971
/Basenback,Martha 1871-1941
#Baumgardner,Edward 19 Jun 1937   29y
#Baumgardner,Margaret 16 dec 1937 26y
/Beckett,Frank 7 may 1889-18 dec 1984
/Bellomy,John Sam.11 dec 1906-30 Jun 1960
/Bellomy,Lillie A.18 apr 1900-10 sep 1938
/Bellomy,19 sep 1943-30 sep 1943
/Bellomy,Carl R.4 Jul 1924-3 Jun 1958WWII
/Bellomy,Henderson,28 mar 1902-19 sep 1974
/Bellomy,Leroy 5 Jul 1898-29 mar 1977 WWI
/Bellomy,Virginia C.8 nov 1902-27 Jul 1964
#Bellomy,Letlie A.19 sep 1918   38y4m25d
#Bellville,Glen Edward 4 sep 1936 inf
/Bendick,U.D."Dude"1881-1954
/Benedick,Lucy 1884-1969
/Benedick,Samuel M.1842--1904
/Benedick,Abigail 1847-1926
/Bennett,James E.10 feb 1872-31 oct 1975
    Minnie G.11 feb 1892-16 aug 1970
#Bennett,Verdie 25 sep 1936 inf
/Benson,Randolph W.1898-1978
    Edith Booth McDowell 1901-1967
/Berger,Charles S.2 sep 1886-27 Jul 1905
/Berry,Mary M.5 Jun 1858-2 dec 1941
/Berry,Nora B.21 oct 1900-8 aug 1985
/Berry,mary D. 27 may 1898-11 Jun 1914
/Berry,Charles E.29 nov 1861-21 Jun 1938
/Berry,J.Clarence 11 oct 1894-22 nov 1956
/Bexfield,Norman,F.1921-1976 WWII
/Bexfield,Charles H.1893-1955
    Flossie M. 1897-1982
/Bexfield,Etta B.10 nov 1894-22 Jan 1968
/Bias,William 24 Jun 1894   30y11m26d
/Bias,William Henry 1893-1980
/Bias,Harry W.31 may 1881-15 dec 1970
/Bias,Etta Diddle 1878-1951
/Bias,Walter J.1904-1952
/Bias,Allen G.1872-1915
/Bias,Andrew Carroll 11 nov 1856-30 dec 1895
/Bias,Eliza Lakeman 9 feb 1859-25 oct 1916
#Bias,inf 1938
#Bias,Erna Mrs. 14 dec 1937   37y1m20d
/Bias,sadie 10 apr 1931 26y12m23d
/Biehl,Nancy 1930-1952 (stone w/V.Adkins)
/Bills,Buddy Lee 3 Jan 1970-10 feb 1984E&S

Sharon K.13 oct 1949---
#Bird,Martin L.1910
/Black,Marcella 1918-1982
  Charles 1913-1980
/Black,Lloyd G.1956-1976
/Black,Virginia L.1909-1979
/Blair,Wilma Rose Childers
  21 dec 1916-14 aug 1987
/Blake,Chester O.1907-1963
  Hilda S.1907-1981
/Blake,Nora B.1889-1974
/Blake,A.L. Maxine 1902--
/Blake,Janet Lou 1941-1942
/Blankenship,Luisa L.1826-1895
/Blankenship,J.W.1845-1920
/Blankenship,E.M.
/Bledsoe,Grace
  5 nov 1900-10 oct 1961

#Boling,Mary Jane 3 sep 1930 59y
/Bostick,Richard 1897-1934
/Bostick,Edith H.1890-1981
/Bostick,Mattie 1867-1/11/1931
/Bowen,Oma Ferguson 1908-1982
/Bowen,Elizabeth L.1878-1902
/Bowen,Herman, E. 1915-16
/Bowen,Fisher 1880-1950
/Bowen,Dyke 1834-1909
  Sarah 1837-1903
/Boyd,Thelma Hazel 1909-1925
/Boyd,Mary Lee 1882-1958
/Boyd,James Harvey 1879-1967
/Briggs,Ophelia 1868-1940
#Britt,George L.1 Jan 1938 49y
/Browning,Hazel 1912-1963
/Brumfield,Marie W.1911--
  William F.1912-1978
/Burcham,Alma Bellomy
  27 Jun 1875-21 dec 1964
/Burge,Thelma Anna 1909-1946
/Burns,John H.1895-1978 WWI
/Bush,William B.1874-1937
/Bush,Ella B.1877-1955
/Callahan,Alice Turley 1869-1942
#Callicoat,Pearle mar 1932 16y
/Callicoat,Marguerite Kathleen
  1913-1980
/Campbell,Raymond 1930
  Mona 1933
/Canterbury,Tella Blanton 1884-1965
/Carlin,Georgia 1868-1938
/Carpenter,Nora 1886-1982
/Carr,Wm.Richard 1914-1936
/Carr,Minnie Lou 1934-37

/Bills,Ruby L.1895-1929
/Bills,Alexander J.1890-1976
/Black,George H.1891-1951
/Black,Florence 7 nov 1887-15---1929
/Black,Ruth F.5 nov 1923-5 Jun 1981
/Blair,George 22 dec 1890-18 Jul 1950
  Katherine R. 12 aug 1888-13 feb 1986
/Blair,Justine 1931-1940 d/o G&K
/Blair,Mary Catherine Kristine Owens 1986
/Blake,James Homer 11 aug 1896-7 oct 1971
/Blake,Ben T.1 dec 1901-7 sep 1979
  Mae E.11 oct 1912---
/Blake,Marie E.1928-29
/Blankenship,Wm.E.23 nov 1885-3 mar 1955
/Blankenship,Helen E.12 nov 1893-12 Jan 1955
/Blanton,Bennie 1919--
/Bledsoe,Garland 29 mar 1911-24 dec 1967II
/Bocook,Bertha Flora 29 sep 1907-1 dec 1962
/Booth,Clyde 14 aug 1894-31 mar 1966
/Bostick,June L.21 nov 1920-5 sep 1968
/Bostick,Guy R.1897-1927
/Bostick,Arnold 1893-1964
/Botto,Caroline 1836-29 may 1924
/Bowen,Rose 20 Jun 1883-3 apr 1921 w/E.J.
/Bowen,Luther F.1 Jan 1898-22 mar 1973
/Bowen,Golden H.9 feb 1889-29 Jul 1968 WI
/Bowen,Emma 1964
#Bowen,Ollie 26 Jan 1937 18y5m12d
/Bowen,Edgar J.26 dec 1892-30 nov 1955
/Bowman,Doris T. 1 oct 1909-12 Jul 1976
/Briggs,Roy E. 1886-1957
/Briggs,Mildred L.1884-1965
/Brookise,L.18 Jul 1911-8 sep 1980
/Brooks,Floyd T.21 Jun 1917-18 may 1979
/Brooks,Nellie Nance 6 nov 1904-26 Jun 1943
/Bryan,Marie 5 apr 1916-6 mar 1980
  Tommy 21 feb 1914-25 apr 1976 WWII
/Bryant,John Earl 15 sep 1937-29 aug 1981
/Burks,Cassey 1 Jun 1865 7y d/o BB&MW
/Burks,Martha W.22 Jun 1822-7 aug 1874
  B.B. 13 sep 1811-26 dec 1881
/Byrd,Morris,David Sr.1939-1980
/Byrd,Martin
/Callaghan,Laura Songer 1879-58
/Callicoat,Otha J.24 sep 1916-10 oct 1979
  Edith E.10 dec 1912--
/Callicoat,Beatrice 29 apr 1895-18 feb 1969
  Otha 6 feb 1888-23 Jan 19972
/Callicoat,Pauline 2 sep 1915-28 mar 1931
/Carey,Bert R.1898-1986
/Carey,Alva T. 1906--
#Carney,Harry 19y
#Carney,Sarah 1 Jan 1932
/Carr,Joseph B.9 nov 1928-3 Jun 1945

Martha Sue 23 may 1934 inf
/Carr,Wm.Jay 1890-1970
    Belle Wilson 1897-1971
/Carroll,P.E.1953-1980
/Carter,Curtis 1874-1950
/Carter,Alma F.1914-1978
    James H.1888-1943
/Carter,William K.1919-1957
/Carter,Shannon D.1883-1958
/Carter,James 1848-1934
/Carter,Lillie 1856-1928
#Chandler,Hiram J.19 may 1932
    73y9m22d
/Chambers,Mary M.23 dec 1901-14 apr 1968
/Chapman,B.Madelene 1906-19--
/Chapman,Francis C.1898-1966
/Chapman,Roy 1912-1975 wHelen
/Chapman,William E.1887-1936
/Chapman,Lucy Mae 1889-1966
/Charlton,Kenneth O.1901-1945
/Childers,Rosa M.1882-1968
/Childers,Wilbert E.1881-1947
/Childers,Goff 1889-1963
/Childers,Inf 1911
/Childers,1919 Inf

/Childress,Claude Franklin
    1 apr 1920-29 Jan 1976
/Christian,Delia 1855-1929
#Christian,Dillon 1855-1929
/Church,George A.1841-1885
/Church,Joseph J.1884-1939
/Clark,Inf 1919
/Clark,Irene 1900-1919
/Clark,Evie E. 1879-1959
/Clark,Lon S. 1889-1971
/Clark,Catherine 1863-1929
/Clark,John W. 1853-1944
/Clark,Hollace W.1902-1942
/Clark,Fonnie A.1883-1964
/Clark,Carlton C.Sr.1876-1953
/Clark,Richard 1897-1934
/Clark,Mabel 1909-1937
/Clark,A.H. 1824-1900
    Sarah Chambers 1834-1916
#Clark,Alma 10 mar 1937 82y10m10
/Clendenen,Julia 1876-1939
    Pleasant 1871-1945
/Clouse,John
    19 aug 1854-9 may 1951
/Cobbs,William
/Cochran,Lillian M.1869-1960
/Colburn,Amelia H.1880-1957
/Colburn,Howard 1908-1942

/Carr,Herbert Lee 18 mar 1926-6 aug 1944
/Carr,French Wilson 1914-1936
/Carson,Haskell H.1909-1970
    Georgia A. 1913-1989
/Carter,Mary 15 mar 1877-16 dec 1916
/Carter,James L.25 may 1910-23 Jul1949II
/Carter,Frances 1915-1971
    William 1911-1950
/Carter,Wm.L.24 may 1911-9 feb 1950
/Carter,Beulah B.1902-1988
#Carter,Judy 26 sep 1936
/Ceasar,Arzella I.7 aug 1928 18y c

/Chapman,Teddy 1907-1937
/Chapman,Dorothy 1910-1953
/Chapman,Ivan M.1908-1984
/Chapman,Antionete M.1925-1989
/Chapman,Robert P.1908-1909

/Childers,W.S.1843-1909 CoC 3rd WV Cal
/Childers,Victoria 1849-1915
/Childers,Jessie C.1890-1943
/Childers,Ellen V.1915-16
/Childress,Martha E.1888-1946
/Childress,William E.1880-1946
/Childress,W.E. 1915-1981
/Christian,Dorothy 7 dec 1907-10 nov 1978
/Christian,Jasper V.1874-1968
/Christian,Theodosia Earnest 1885-1968
#Church,Nahulda 18 apr 1935 64y6m2d
/Church,W.W. 1877-1949
/Clark,Charles 1874-1937
/Clark,Hazel Taylor 1907-1927
/Clark,Frank D. 1868-1935
/Clark,Jessie C.1878-1965
/Clark,Mildred M.1907-1920
/Clark,Harvey 1836-1921 CoH 9th VA Regt
    Emaline 22 aug 1837-5 mar 1901
/Clark,Carlton C.Jr.
    Ethel Honaker
/Clark,Walter M.1887-1927
    Walter B.1925-27 son
/Clark,Thomas J.1863-1925
/Clarke,Walter W.23 feb 1875-29 may 1906
#Clark,Goodin 31 may 1847-26 dec 1926
/Cloninger,Florence 1914-1988
    Arthur P.1909--
/Cobbs,Grace Napier 1899-1963
/Cobbs,Thomas David Sr.1894-1983
/Cobbs,Marietta 1930-34
/Cobbs,Carl Welch 1926-1940
/Colburn,Charles 1941-43
/Coleman,Alpha 1914-1927 c

33

/Collins,Robert 1909-1933
/Collins,Katie 1899-1930
/Collins,Donald WWII
    31 dec 1898-26 apr 1967
/Collins,William H.1941
/Collins,Harless 1913-1932
/Collins,Luther K.1880-1959
/Collins,Laura Alice 1876-1959
/Collins,Elizabeth 1860-1940
#Collins,Charles Lee 1936 inf
/Collins,John H.1852-1935
    Mallissie J.1878-1935
/Collins,James A.29 may 1925--
    Beulah M.12 oct 1931
/Cook,Willia 13 may 1943 WWII
/Cook,Harry 1886-1954
/Cook,Chloe A. 1881-1962
/Cook,Abner 1842-1914
    Nancy A.1851-1917
/Cooke,Charles L.1901-1952
/Cook,Lyle W.
    18 mar 1910-26 mar 1981
/Corum,James H.
    11 Jul 1897-21 dec 1986
/Cornwell,Mary Va.1844-1891
/Cosby,Thelma Calhoun
    5 mar 1906-6 aug 1938
/Coyle,Beulah DeVore 1902-1968
/Craft,Hugh A. 1873-1940
/Craig,Walter L.1875-1930
    Phoeba Ann 1876-1923
/Crawford,Gearld V.Rowsey 1917
/Cremeans,Herbert 1903-1953
/Cremeans,Sarah J.1859-1921
/Cremeans,Lewis F.1850-1913
/Cremeans,Paul E. 1932--
    Georgia B. 1911--
/Cremeans,Florida 1907-1970
/Cremeans,Manley 1909-1961
/Cremeans,Sarah Marie
    30 apr 1920-1 apr 1976
/Cremeans,Patsy Jane 1934 14y
#Cummins,Albert 23 sep 1937 69y
/Cummons,Walter Lee 1870-1968
    Bertha Marie 1883-1950
/Curtis,Henry C. 1868-1927
    Mary C.1868-1928
/Dabney,Sam 1877-1907
/Dabney,Louise Virginia
/Dabney,inf s/oSam
/Dabney,John Draper 1874-1893
/Darby,Ida F.
/Darling,Maggie I.1914-1957
/Damron,John 1898-19--

/Coleman,Flossie P.Peyton
    10 oct 1898-28 apr 1988
/Collins,Jerry L. 1943 -1974 WWII
/Collins,Elizabeth 1878-1931
/Collins,Lula J.1905--
    Loranzo D.2 oct 1899-18 dec 1971 WWII
/Collins,John T.4 mar 1897-15 oct 1970
/Collins,Cora B.1900-1914
/Collins,Shelby 1881-1969
/Collins,Willie K.1885-1954
#Collins,Sadie Alvina 3 Jan---13 sep---
/Collins,Luther P.1902-1953
/Combs,William Jr.1943-1944

/Cook,Sarah A. 1860-1925
    Henry J.1854-1928
/Cook,Gene B.31 oct 1932-28 nov 1986 K
/Cook,Cary B.3 Jun 1892-1 mar 1901 HJ&SA
#Cook,Mary E.2 Jul 1886-26 sep 1901
#Cook,Ronie I.15 Jun 1932
/Coon,James 28 feb 1895-20 dec 1950
/Cooper,Josephine Childers 1908-1934
/Corbitt,Beulah S.1903-1955
/Corum,Edgar E.3 nov 1894-3 Jan 1987
/Corum,Mary Alice 18 feb 1903-5 feb 1990
/Cox,Norman 1871-1950
    Trulaw 1874-1950
/Craddock,Jean Sharon 21 mar 1944 inf
    Jack Randall 21 mar 1944 inf
/Craig,Luther L.1896-1974
/Craig,Nellie G.1896-1949
/Craig,Elsie Ethel 2 mar 1895-27 mar 1899
/Cremeans,Marvin Lea 1918-20 s/oCW&SC
/Cremeans,Benjamin 13 Jun 1901 18y2m2d
/Cremeans,John F.4 mar 1881-29 aug 1945
    Emily V.22 nov 1881-22 nov 1962
/Cremeans,Wm.Louis 27 aug 1923-27 dec 1924
/Cremeans,Lewis 8 aug 1886-9 sep 1936
/Cremeans,Netie Porter 1881-1918
    Jack 1879-19--
/Crook,Pauline Charlton 1905-1953
/Cummings,William A.1865-1939
    Vinettie 1870-1944
/Cunningham,Evalyn Harrison 1905-1989
/Curtis,Martha E.1892-1973
/Dabney,Edward G.1876-1901
/Dabney,Stella B.1877-1951
/Dabney,William David 1836-1903
#Dabney,Mary Va.Cornwell
/Dailey,Lon 1899-19--
    Stella M.1895-1936
/Darden,Harriet E.Knox 1856-1935
/Damron,James S. 1929-1938 s/o J&Laura

/Damron, Anna Laura 1904-1963   /Daniels, Dennis M. 1 oct 1949-5 Jul 1969
/Daniels, James Alvin 1941 Inf   /Daniels, Patricia Ann 1943 Inf
/Davis, Ethel L. 1906-19 apr 1928   /Davis, Vivian Legg 1919-1949
/Davis, Adona F. 1896-1940   & inf son
#Davis, Henry B. 1878-1922   #Davis, Elizabeth M. 22 aug 1927 14y6m8d
#Davis   63y   #Davis, Myrtle May 3 sep 1931   57y1m3d
/Davis, Wm. Theodore 1888-1949   /Davis, Ira 24 Jun 1896-1 Jan 1949
/Davis, Oscar 1901-1975   /Davis, Thomas E. 27 apr 1915--
/Davis, Anna 1906-19--   Alberta Lee 26 may 1930-30 dec 1986
/Davis, Adrian Zoe 1878-1904   /Davis, Lucille W. 3 mar 1901-3 Jun 1976
/Davis, Henry B. 1878-1922   Paul H. 18 Jun 1900-2 sep 1980
/Dawson, George 1882-1969   /Day, Elsie M. 1892-1971
        Eva 1884-1961   William 1884-1963
/Deal, Isabella 18 apr 1936
/DeHart, Allen Clinton 1942 inf   /DeHart, Ezra Clyde 2 nov 1915-8 oct 1988
Dietz/Deitz   #Dietz. Minerva 1858-1938
/Dietz, Erma 1911--   /Dietz, Myrtle B. 1875-1966
/Deitz, Norman G. 1907-1964   /Dietz, Wm. G. 1867-1952
/Dietz, Jennie 1860-1938   /Deitz, Noah 1871-1950
/Dietz, Chas. 1856-1928   /Deitz, Lester D. 1873-1941
/Deitz, Rosana 1836-1912   /Deitzel, Dulcie Mitchell 1880-1956
/Deitz, Otto 1821-1895   #Dennison, James P. 4 Jul 1933 inf
/Dial, Edith R. 1904-1988   /Diamond, Mary Laney 1882-1957
/Dial, J. Harold 1903-1977   /Dick, Henry C. 1890-1960
/Dickel, Irene 1872-1958   /Dick, Beulah 1890-1970
        Henry 1862-1949   /Dickerson, Linnie Mae 1909-1943
/Diddle, J.M. 1838-1898   /Diddle, Thomas J. 1882-1906
        Mary F. 1845-1914   /Dillard, Mabel Perry 1900-1962 w/oHarry S.
        Charley F. 1875-1899 son   /Dillon, Nettie 1877-1915 w/o W.M.
/Dishman, Wm. Thomas 1869-1949   /Dishman, J.J. Co.B SW 5th WV Inf
    Orpha G. 1870-1948   /Dixon, Alice Crosby 5 Jul 1930 c
/Donathan, John 1903-1956   /Dorcas, Lydia 1883-1963
/Donathan, Tennie 1896-1985   #Dotson, Carolin Mae 15 oct 1934 7y3m22d
/Draper, John 1874-1983   /Dray, Gerturde 3 Jan 1899-9 sep 1939
/Drewry, Amanda M. 1855-1917   #Du Four, Paul 1850-1936
/Drewry, James W. 1894-1919   /Drummond, Hildred 1918--
/Drummond, Charles W. 1882-1973   James P. 1909-1986
        Jessie C. 1885-1925   /Duncan, John Lewis 19 Jun 1859-26 aug 1925
/Duncan, Brother 1909-1914   /Duncan, Eliza Fetty 8 may 1867-30 oct 1938
/Dunn, Dorothy 1912-1984   /Dunlap, Josephine 17 dec 1869-7 may 1896
/Eagan, Patrick 1870-1941   d/o G.Walker
        Hattie 1867-1952   /Edgington, Lester L.
/Earl, Grover C. 1892-1974   28 oct 1872-18 aug 1964
/Earl, Edith M. 1894-1933   /Edgington, Grace Olive
/Easthom, Norma Harvey 1910-1933   21 dec 1888-18 apr 1972
/Easthom, Orville M. 1900-1981
/Edwards, Bernice 1905-1980   /Edwards, Jon Stephen 1925 inf
/Edwards, Andy 1903-19961   /Effingham, Eunice P. 15 dec 1884-4 aug 1959
/Elkins, Carl E. 1912--   Jasper H. 8 oct 1877-15 may 1939
        Frances 1920-1973   /Elkins, Alexander 1847-1924
/Elkins, Oscar 1877-1935   Mary Elizabeth 1856-1928
/Elkins, Laura B. 1874-1945   /Elkins, Okey L. 22 Jan 1916-7 oct 1984
/Elkins, Lemuel T. 1873-1951   /Ellis, Gerturde 6 Jul 1894-13 may 1974
/England, Lillian A. 1917-1986   /Ellis, Gary Lee 1942-43 gdc/oT.M.DeVore

/England,Floyd W. 1911--   #Ensley,Mary C.15 nov 1929 12y7m14d
/Erwin,Virginia 1923-24
/Erwin,Cecil Earl 1916-1968   /Erwin,Albert M. 1889-1966
/Erwin,Norma L. 1930-1955   /Erwin,Zella E. 1899-1964
/Erwin,Nola Jane 1913--   /Erwin,Claud 18 Jan 1944 WWII
/Erwin,Donald E. 1927-29   /Erwin,Mable 3 Jan 1923--
/Eskew,Elizabeth J.1866-1956   Allen Eugene 20 feb 1929-19 aug 1984II
/Esque,Olive Oleta 1920 inf   /Esque,James Doliver 1874-1962
/Esque,Rose A. 1926-1980   Mary Jane 8 Jul 1879-10 feb 1972
/Esque,Alpha B. 1912-1980   /Esque,Leo F. 19 sep 1888-20 apr 1926
/Esque,Carrie Mae 1896-1969   /Esque,Donald,H.22 feb 1924-17 may 1982
    Ceron Sr.1891-1973   /Esque,Paul Austin 16 Jan 1931-21 oct 1951
/Esque,Ceron Jr. 1922-23   /Esque,Mattie 9 Jan 1870-30 Jul 1926
/Esque,Glen E.9 aug 1935   /Esque,Robert L.5 apr 1863-8 nov 1932
#Estep,Bernard 27 oct 1932 9y   /Esque,Leona Alvira Delilah 1910-1966
/Estep,Emery 1913-1948   /Estep,James C.1888-1940
/Estep,Golden Edward 1919-1945   Bertha Ann 1894-19--
#Estep,Betty Lee 4 apr 1935 inf/Evans,Thomas W,
/Evans,Michael Scott 1962 s/L&B/Evans,Dorothy White d 1971
/Fairfax,Pauline 1908-1987   /Fairfax,Lawrence E.27 may 1896-17 aug 1953
/Fairfax,Charles C.1900-1983WI /Fairfax,Myra E. 1897-1958
/Fairfax,Irma T.1898-1930 c   /Fairfax,Mathew L.Sr.1870-1933 c
/Fairfax,Norwood C.1893-1918 c /Fairfax,Maria E. 1874-1973
/Farley,Donald Edward 1946 inf /Fairfax,James A.12 oct 1912-17 Jan 1982
/Farley,Anna W.   #Fannin,John Stephen 6 mar 1925
    23 nov 1928-16 feb 1977   /Farren,F.W.
/Felix,Letha 1908-1971   /Felix,Paul E.1933-1983
/Felix,Willard F.1905-1966   #Ferguson,Curtis M.18 Jan 1926
/Ferguson,Clyde 1892-1926   /Ferguson,Virgie 1900--
/Ferguson,Elizabeth 1908-1936   /Ferguson,Irvin 24 nov 1941 WWII
/Ferguson,Riley A. 1863-1944   /Ferguson,Massie A.9 may 1906-9 mar 1983
/Ferguson,Samuel W. 1905-1950   /Ferguson,P.S.19 Jan 1886-11 oct 1903
/Ferguson,Richard 1872-1949   /Ferguson,Sameul W.29 may 1968-8 Jan 1975
    Pearl 1882-1953   /Ferguson,Walter 18 Jan 1895-15 apr 1962WI
/Ferguson,Buren 1859-1930   /Ferguson,Eliza Bell 9 Jun 1898-20 nov 1956
/Ferguson,Jack B.1916-1959   /Ferguson,Lola G.1895-1985
/Ferguson,L.C. 1855-1945   Colonel W. 1891-1960
/Ferguson,Merle W. 1916-1933   #Ferguson,Thomas 1918-1938
/Ferrell,Carrie M.1947-1980   /Fetty,Cecil Randolph 1913-1918
/Fetty,Jo Ann 1939-1989   /Fetty,Edith A. 22 Jan 1891-17 sep 1974
    Raymond G. 1930--   /Fetty,Elmer A. 6 may 1874-1 mar 1962
/Fetty,Gallin J.1863-1948   /Fetty,Alice Elizabeth 1915-1918
/Fetty,Connie Mac 1933 inf   /Fielder,Carrie G.1881-1947
/Fielder,Mary E. w/o Thomas   /Fielder,Homer H.1887-1936
    7 Jan 1859-29 apr 1902   /Fielder,Beulah Mae 1909-1941
#Fielder,Thomas d 7 Jan 1859
/Fielder,Maud 1889-1914   /Fillinger Frank 19 sep 1892-15 sep 1958WI
/Fillinger,Eliz.Ellen 1871-1934/Fillinger,Pearl 1900-1955
/Fillinger,James Phil.1868-1948/Fillinger,Stanley E.1898-1969
/Fitzwater,Mary A. 1878-1918   /Fitzwater,Stanley Ray 1904-1964
/Fitzwater,Carl L. 1910-1918   /Fletcher,Walker S.1885-1982
/Floyd,Hazel 1892-1947   #Flora,Robert A.29 sep 1937 51y6m
#Flora,Delbert 12 nov 1937 inf /Fogarty,Fredrick G.4 Jul 1890-16 dec 1939
/Forrest,Mary Va.1930-1937   /Fortune,Etta Fry 1870-1955

/Foster,Ada 1884-1938
/Fox,Russell Owen 1902-1933
/Fox,Leona T. 1871-1939
/Fox,John C.1873-1957
/Fox,Wm.S. 1864-1914
/Fox,Willie Mae 1914-15
/France,Daral E. 1858-1926
/France,Wm.1880-1949
   Nancy Noble 1883-1965
/Freeland,Mildred V.1907-1987
/Freeland,David A.1904-1963
/Fry,Olliebelle M.1908-1982
/Fuller,Ethel Dietz 1889-1974
/Fuller,James M.1884-1973
/Fuller,James O.1909--
/Gallaher,Cassie 1866-1948
/Gallaher,E.W. 1861-1949
/Gary,Henry 3 Jun 1926 65y c
/Gibson,John Henry 1898-1972
   Edith Bowen 1897-1972
#Gilbert,C.B. 16 feb 1934
/Gillenwater,larry E. 1944-1959
   Harry Bragg 1920-1975
#Gillenwater,--24 Jul 1924
/Gillette,Nora 1906-1960
/Gillette,Harry 1900-1964
/Gillispie,Annie 1884-1938
/Gilmore,Viola 1924-25
   Loretta Starkey 1918-1939
/Giola,Arizona 1875-1939
/Giola,John F.1865-1956
/Glass,Lucy A.1888-1928
/Glaspie,Mary 1894-1942
/Godby,Kate
#Goodmon,Lillie V.P>1898-1927
/Goodman,Addie 1884-26 apr 1935
/Goodman,Oscar 1899-1936
/Goodman,Pearl 1898-1927
   Sylvester 1882-1969
#Graham,R.C>1854-1926
/Graham,Noah F. 1894-1936
/Graham,Carl Martin 1938-42FM&AV
#Graham,Cynthia E.1858-1920
/Grant,Carlton Eugene 1909-1940
#Grubbs,inf 19 Jun 1934
/Gunnoe,Louis A.1912-1963
/Gunnoe,Orville F.1906-1957
/Gunnoe,Lowell 21 apr 1912
/Hackney,Joshua 1869-1940
/Hackney,Laura 1880-1943
/Hackney,Clayton 1903-1960
/Hager,Judith Ann 1940--
   Wm.Fredrick 1938-1988
/Hall,Lee G.1880-1922

/Fox,Ethel G.1896-1983 WWI nurse
   Leno E.19 aug 1894-15 nov 1961 WWI
/Fox,Joseph M.1899-1973
/Fox,Edna 1915--
/Fox,Erma Lee 18 aug 1914-17 Jun 1980
/France,Charles W.1892-1953
   Marie 1892-1958
/France,Homer 5 may 1896-27 apr 1936 WWI
#France,Sarah E. 1856-1926
/Fridley,Geneva 24 nov 1908-2 may 1977
/Fry,Rhoda 6 Jan 1833-20 oct 1927
   A.S.19 apr 1930-18 feb 1904
/Fudge,Wm.V.9 feb 1903-3 oct 19957WWII
/Fuller,Addie 1884-1946
/Fuller,James E.4 Jun 1878-6 may 1904
/Gallaher,Lavina F.22 oct 1866-30 dec 1943
/Gallaher,John 1837-1923
/Gallaher,Durcilla 1842-1913
#Gibson,Earl 20 Jun 1937 33y2m16d
#Gibson,Kenneth Neal 22 nov 1927 inf
#Gilbert,Dolores 17 Jan 1938 inf
/Gillenwater,Gladys Lony 1923
   Roy L. 1919-1958
/Gillenwaters,Clarence E.1892-1955
/Gillenwater,Frank22 mar 1893-17 Jun 1951
/Gillespie,Charle G.21 Jul 1900-6 Jul 1972
/Gillispie,Samuel 8 aug 1893-6 Jun 1940WI
/Gillispie,Anna Belle 10 aug 1875-5 may 1951
/Gilmore,Herod 1901-1955
   Verna 1900-1945
/Gladwell,W.Wheeler 1884-1968
/Gladwell,Bessie Bell 1882-1961
/Gladwell,Billie Gibson 1915-1924
/Godby,Muriel
#Godby,George W.26 apr 1936 74y1m28d
#Goodman,Morris 28 Jul 1907-3 oct 1926
/Goodman,Stella 20 Jun 1901 5 mar 1935 33y
/Goodman,Roger & Rodney apr 1946
/Goodmon,Susan 1857-1928
/Goodmon,Noah 1851-1934
/Graham,Lemuel T.Jr.17 apr 1921-31 oct 1988
   Virginia Ruth 21 mar 1927
/Graham,R.C. 1854-1925

/Grant,Edward 1880-1942
/Gundy,Ellis L.9 mar 1898-6 feb 1975
   Violet 4 Jun 1916
/Gunnoe,Gretchen 5 Jun 1914-23 sep 1988
/Hackney,W. 1906-1931
/Hackney,Euphal 1915-1925
#Hackney,Orville 4 feb 1906-20 oct 1931
/Hale,Samuel Lewis 1930-1933
/Hale,Lucinda 1886-1959
/Hale,Joe 1883-1953

/Hall,Lizzie E.1883-1969
/Hall,Mary
    Sarah
/Hall,Ethel 1910-1961w/oStrother
/Hall,Georgia Anna 1853-1919
/Hamm,Bert Edwin 1 sep 1937 WWI
/Hamm,Bert Edwin 1923-1936
/Hancock,Ora Peyton 1887-1954
/Hann,John R.1917-1940
/Hann,James E. 1912-1973
/Hanshaw,John W.1866-19--
    Minnie C. 1871-19--
/Harless,George D.1911-1972
/Harper,Ralph E.1915-1933
/Harper,Dana D.1873-1945
/Harper,Dana Jr.1912-1940
/Harris,Charles L.1909-1972

/Harrison,M.F.
/Harrison,Emma 1921--
/Harshbarger,Nan E 1880--
/Harshbarger,John E.1874-1932
/Harshbarger,Marie 1921--
    Hobert R.1908-1964
/Harshbarger,Earl 1920-21 BR&L
/Harshbarger,Sadie d/o WH&ME
    19 sep 1912-22 mar 1920
/Harvey,Robert 1858-1937
    Effie 1870-1949
/Harvey,Isabelle 1918-1981
/Harvey,Louvist L.1898-1973
    Hez 1891-1976
#Hatfield,America 1920 80y
#Hatfield--b 1848
/Hatfield,inf.CB&N 1913
/Hayden,John Henry 1881-1950
/Hayden,Jewel Lemley 1906-1927
/Hayes,Ruthie 1875-1950
/Hayes,James H.1868-1962
/Hayes,inf Payne 5 aug 1927
/Hayes,Imogene 1911-1912
/Hayslip,Vickletulle 1841-1912
/Hayslip,James L.1835-1878
/Hayslip.N.Louisa 1843-1927
/Hayslip,Samuel D.1838-1914
/Hayslip,Thomas J. 1808-1877
    Marjorie R. 1808-1889
    Richard 1851-1874 son
/Hazelett,family of Roscoe S.
/Hazlett,Haidee 1888-1967
/Hazlett,Robert A.
    21 nov 1884-5 dec 1964
/Henderson,J.Ernest 1888-1940
/Henderson,Georgia 1898-1952

/Hall,Raymond H.2 oct 1919-3 sep 1935
    Bud Clarence 21 Jul 1922-14 oct 1944WII
    Lenora N.1892-1958
/Hall,Wm.Tommy 22 sep 1953-9 feb 1963
/Hamlin,Helen L.
    20 may 1916-1 aug 1960
/Hamm,Laura Keenan 1885-1946
/Handley,George J.1907-1964
/Hann,James W. 1886-1947
/Hanshaw,Avenelle 27 feb 1923
    Raymond L.24 Jul 1924-10 aug 1986
/Hanshaw,Zella 1891-1936
/Harlan,Patsy Newman 1889-13 Jul 1937(0)
/Harper,Frances A. 1886-1974
/Harper,Charles F.1913-1985
/Harris,Rosa E.1876-1952
    William E. 1870-1968
/Harrison,Lucy C.25 sep 1865-29 Jul 1943
/Harrison,Julia 1885-16 Jun 1937 51y10m1d
/Harrison,Sylvia L.25 may 1912-27 Jul 1944
/Harshbarger,Chas.T.22 dec 1913-30 sep 1972
/Harshbarger,Cora Holland 1882-1965
/Harshbarger,Wm.Henry 1875-1954
    Minnie Ellen 1886-1952
    Benjamin R.1881-1966
    Lillie 1885-1924
/Harvey,Leslie Erwin 1899-1962
/Harvey,John W. 1848--
/Harvey,Sarah J.1855-1911
/Harvey,I.Bedford-Feller
    27 mar 1899-19 Jul 1987
/Hatfield,D.K. 1920 79y
/Hatfield,Marca 1920 81y
/Hatfield,Clinton B.1884-1937
    Nannie Wentz 1881-1960
/Havens,Wilbur Earl 26 feb 1910-24 apr 1982
/Hayes,Garland J.23 may 1907-22 may 1987
/Hayes,Harry E.7 may 1913-25 Jun 1987
    Thelma 9 aug 1917-
/Hayes,Barbara S. 1941-1943
/Hayslip,Carey B.22 dec 1841-21 Jul 1894
/Hayslip,Fannie Cochran 1875-1970
/Hayslip.George Victor 1867-1933
/Hayslip,Charles Halsey 1864-1931
/Hayslip,Harry Dunbar 1876-1949
/Hayslip,Minnie 1864-1905 d/o JL&V
/Hazelett,Ralph Vernon
    26 oct 1924-18 Jun 1979
/Hazelett,R.S. 29 arp 1895
/Hazelett,Zora 2 Jun 1899-4 sep 1954
/Hazlett,Robert A.25 aug 1916-4 oct 1946II
/Helwig,Katherine Tompert 1858-1936
/Henderson,Decater 1888-1927
    Leslie L, 1888-1932

#Henderson,Ezra Lee 1933 2y   #Henley,Nannie 20 may 1937 77y2m19d
/Hennen,Wm.Vernon 1860-1938   /Hennen,Perry 1840-1896
/Hennen,Mary Elma 1871-1950   /Hennen,Artemace 1834-1902
/Hennen,Ola 1856-1928   /Hennen,Blanche C.1872-1955
/Hennen,T.Jeff 1867-1938   /Hennen,Elijah 1869-1950
/Henry,Kenny Ray 1970-1971   /Hensley,Ira 26 feb 1883-7 oct 1951
/Hensley,Lucy 1881-1953   /Hensley,John T.27 Jul 1863-7 nov 1947
/Herbert,Robert F.1882-1954   /Henry,Hannah J.1893-1974
/Hicks,Paul 1911-1933
/Hicks,Russell J. 1925-1950   /Hicks,Robert Lee 1924
/Hicks,Thelma 1921-22   /Hicks,Blanche 1892-1937
/Hicks,Nellie E. 1921-1967   Marchant 1889-1978
/Hicks,Olive F.1914-1978   /Hicks,Destie Alice 1897-1973
/Hinchman,Stella Mae   /Hill,Donald Foster 6 aug 1899-25 apr 1981
    4 feb 1937 32y6m26d   /Hines,Katherine 1888-1951
/Hite,Sarah Malinda 1837-1895   /Hite,William 1807-1875
/Hite,Oggie L. 1898-1972   /Hite,Mary 1816-1894
    Paul W. 1905-1980   /Hite,Ann E. 1834-1855
#Hodges,George M.--54y1m6d   #Hodges,Thomas M.28 dec 1926 65y7m13d
/Holderby,W.R. 1847-1916   /Holderby Grace Richardson 1902-1927
/Holland,Hazel M. 1913--   /Holland,Charles H.1878-1907
    Jesse L. 1902-1956   /Holland,Frank E. 1900-1968
#Holland,Millard R.1919 inf   #Holland,Lorena 7 dec 1935 68y8m29d
#Holland,Stanley E.28 nov 1936   #Holland,Steve McKinley 21 Jan 1937 inf
#Holland,Wm.M.C. 25 nov 193-22y   #Holley,Charles Edward 23 apr 1938 29y14d
/Holley,James W. 5 oct 1944   /Holley,Sue A. 19 oct 1923--
    Kenneth O.6 Jun 1949   James H.Jr.25 feb 1921-4 feb 1975
/Holley,Manford 1880-1951   /Holley,Mable B.27 aug 1917(07)-26 Jul 1921
    Anna 1881-1919   /Holley,Mary A. 1890-19--
/Holley,James H.1891-1948   /Holley,Merlyn M.1923
/Holley,Pearl R.1897-1965   /Holley,Raymond M.21 Jan 1925-19 Jan 1945II
/Holley   /Holley,Berkley M.1910-1987
/Holley,George W.1882-1956   Iva Alice1922-1965
    Francie M.1885-1976   /Homer,Louie 1900-1941
/Horton,Rginald 1922-1930 c   /Howerton,Georgette R>13 Jul 1967 inf
/Howerton,Keith E.S. 1943--
    Patricia J. 1945 --   /Hubbard,Dorothy L.7 Jul 1935 7y
/Hubman,Elizabeth Ann 185-1941   /Hudson,Boyd S.15 oct 1922-21 nov 1977wII
/Huckelby,Wm.Chas. 1884-1938   /Huff,William J.17 aug 1906-31 oct 1975
/Huff,Ada B. 14 Jul 1983   /Huff,Kenneth Lee 31 aug 1950-1 feb 1968
/Huffman,R.Kaye 1925-1941   /Huffman,C.W.10 Jan 1901 37y5m
/Huffman,M.Inez 1891-1980   /Huffman,V.Alfreda 1916-1976
/Huffman,Evermont 1883-1957   /Huffman,Rosella 1918-1982
/Hughes,Jerome 1870-1950   /Hughes,Ora E.15 Jan 1915-4 Jun 1984
    Mary Bea 1893-19--   /Hughes,Evelyn Christie 24 Jun 1923-11 Jun 1988
/Hunt,Lottie F.   /Husk,E.Stanley 1919-1984 WWII
    28 sep 1877-6 feb 1936
/Huston,Dora Bell 1900-1945   /Hussell,John F.1890-1957
/Hysell,Wallace N.1848-1893   Bessie S.1893-1951
    Isabella 1851-1940   /Hysell,Gerturde 15 sep 1936 46y1m
/Hysell,John 1900-1985   /Hysell,Robert S.30 mar 1936 53y9m15d
/Hysell,Jessie 1906-1966   /Hysell,Elza E.1871-1946
/Jackson,Hazel H.1904-1984   /Jackson,Roland D.10 mar 1960-16 may 1973
    J.W. 1898-1985   /Jackson,Emma 26 may 1868-7 may 1926 c

/Jackson,Lucy H.1893-1943   w/o W.H.
/James,A.Jackson 1922-1941   /James,Minnnie 26 feb 1889-6 mar 1964
#Jarrell,Ramon E. 1937-38   /Jarrell,Nellie Wray 4 Jul 1901-15 dec 1950
/Jenkins,Philip E.1835-1913   /Johnson,James 12 Jul 1926 19y c
/Jenkins,Mary Hall 1837-1899   /Johnson,Matt 27 dec 1913-17 feb 1984
/Johnson,Walter W.1896-1983   Eva Marie 14 Jan 1919
    Myrtle L.1905-1976   /Johnson,James 1 mar 1840-13 Jan 1900 c
#Johnson,M.F. 6 feb 1900 76y   /Johnson,Wm.Edgar 1890-1950
#Johnson,Mrs.M.F. 75y
/Johnson,Cokey W. 1891-1960   /Johnson,Ida B.23 apr 1881-13 Jan 1957
    Mildred 1912-1982   Mary B.1 Jul 1917-13 Jan 1957
/Johnson,Millard 1856-1933   William H.19 Jun 1875-3 feb 1956
    Sarah 1856-1931   /Johnson,James W.1 oct 1910-29 dec 1989
/Johnson,Pamella 1958 inf   Marian F.24 apr 1913-2 may 1982
/Johnson,Thomas C. 1902-1977 /Jones,Earnest 1881-1924
/Jones,Mary V.1922-1970   Jennie 1882-1956
/Jones,Alfred T.1910-1965   /Jones,Virginia 23 may 1907-27 aug 1942
/Jones,L.F. 1854-1915   /Jones,Albert T.1865-1941
    Harry D.1887-1916   Adella 1867-1931
  s/Finley 5 Jan 1883-3/2/1906/Jones,Twylah Gibson 1927-1973
/Jones,Harry W.1903-1975   #Jones,John W.17 mar 1937
/Jopling.Cora Lee 1862-1945   /Joplin,James S.1856-1934
/Jopling,Nellie M.1892-1972   /Joplin,Rachel S. 1877-1965
    James A. 1893-1979   /Jordan,Frances Ward 1902-1965
/Judd,inf/s 1947   /Judd,Bert A. 1 Jun 1889-22 mar 1976
   inf/d 1944   Laura A. 11 Jun 1889-11 Jan 1958
   Donald 1913-1919   /Kaufman,Jennie B.21 Jun 1864-21 mar 1904
/Karriger,Laura Christian   /Keefer,Roy Earl 29 Jun 1936-8 Jun 1966
   1871-1957   #Keefer,Rosalee 30 Jul 1936 in
/Keffer,Joseph W. 1910-   /Keefer,Elmer E.1942-1959
   Ethel E. 1913-   /Keefer,John C.1913-1943
/Keenan,Ella   /Keenan,Felix 1853-1909 Sgt.
/Keenan,Ann   /Keenan,Walter 17 sep 1937 60y
/Keenan,Pat II   /Keenan,John
/Keenan,Jack   /Kelly,Sarah 1850-1935(2/7/34)
#Kelly,Levi 10 nov 1935 65y   #Kelly,Isaiah N.7 oct 1930 69y2m6d
#Kellogg,Esta 29 may 1936 22y /Kendle,James 1861-1939
/Kennedy,Betty G. 1924-27   Mary 18 may 1876-8 sep 1942
/Kennedy,Glayds 1902-1951   /Kessler,Cecil E.1901-1958
/Kennedy,Bascom R. 1896-1981 /Keyser,Mabel Smith 26 aug 1892-5 feb 1965
                    /Keyser,Lucian 21 mar 1876-15 sep 1953
/Kincaid,Arizona M.1889-1966 #Keyser,Maud Marie 16 mar 1936 25y7m24d
   Charles W. 1887-1953   /Kinnaird,Va.McWhorter 10 Jan 1930
/Kincaid,David Ovolo 1911-1930   Wm.Thurston 21 aug 1928-14 Jun 1985
/King,Justine   /King,Virginia B.25 sep 1869-29 aug 1948
  6 oct 1888-30 Jan 1925   David J.24 nov 1862-27 nov 1910
  (d/o.Caroline Walker)   /Kingery,Jeffery lynn 11 Jan 1952-12/9/72
/Knight,Willard Joseph 1939-51/Kyle,Alice A, 1852-1937
/LaFon,Mae Hann 1894-1975   George W. 1857-1931
/Lafon,Richard E. 1871-1937   /Lambert,Frances L.4 may 1908-21 mar 1988
    Maud F. 1885-1936   /Lane.Olive Hall 1910-1985
/Laney,Phoebe Bill 1926-1946   /Langdon,Mary Margaret 1914-1953
#Layne,Cary 19 Jul 1935 38y c /Leach,Mary 1887-1939
/Leach,Velma L.1916-1988   Charles 1880-1916

/Leffingwell,Frank 1908-1982   /Legg,Maxel 1921-1938
    elizabeth D.1911-1978   /Legge,Thomas Lee 1858-1933
/Legge,Fred 1886-1945   /Legge,Rhoda L.1885-1944
/Legge,Jessie M. 1885-1960   /Legge.Lula L. 1893-1976
/Legrand,Laura E. 1883-1940   /LeGrand,Claude Donald oct 1922-14 feb 1987
/Legrand,John R. 1877-1944   /LeGrand,Ollie 1883-16 aug 1916
/Legrand,Myrtle 1879-1958   Bessie E.Bias 4 Jan 1888-1 apr 1965
/Legrand,Allene 1893-1975   /LeGrand,Gordon Ray 14 aug 1927-26 aug 1977K
/Legrand,Albert W. 1892-1964   /LeGrand,Charles W.13 oct 1919-4 sep 1985wII
/Legrand Thomas W. 1923-1949   /LeGrand,Robert E.17 oct 1931-6 dec 1969
/Legrand,A.Wayne 1916-1921   /LeGrand,Ira J.10 mar 1896-16 Jul 1929WWI
/LeGrand,Mabel Jane 1925-1940   /LeGrand,Garnet 10 Jun 1903-8 mar 1971
/LeGrand,Robert 1865-1928   /LeGrand,Dalpha 16 oct 1899-3 Jan 1977
/LeGrand,Elvira 1860-1922   /LeGrand,Evan E.23 oct 1916-27 oct 1944wII
/LeGrand,Mable Jane 1925-1940
/LeGrand,Thelma Watts 1899-1932/LeGrand,Vinda L.1894-1977
/LeGrand,Claude 1899-1972   Walter E.1889-1946
    Loretta 1900-1971   /Leibee,Charles A.19 Jul 1899-14 Jun 1965I
/Leibee,Charles Donald 1965   /Leibee,Charles Wm.9 oct 1922-1 nov 1978K
    Charolte Ann 1965 inf tw   /Leport,William 6 aug 1863-5 dec 1942
/LeTulle,L.P. 1845-1920   /Lewis,Merritt(Merrill)E. 1880-1921
/LeTulle,Fannie V.1847-1900   Daisy 1885-1927
/Lewis,Charles W.1886-1969   /Lewis,Helen V.1903-1928
/Lewis,Della 1887-1945   /Lewis,Eliza J.1852-1910
/Lewis,Chas.E.Jr. 1945- 1949   Henry J.1846- CoF 1st OHA-
/Lewis,Gerturde 1874-1928 c   /Linkfield,Lora 1892-1978
/Linkfield,James Robt.1936 inf   Orville F.1892-1974
/Linkfield,Ida Ellen 1882-1962/Linville,Shirley Lee Balard 1887-1974
/Linkfield,Shelby L.1882-1947   /Long,Georgia A.6 oct 1890-27 may 1931
/Logan,Florence 1897-1943
/Losey,Ann 1858-1923   /Lowery,James S.10 Jul 1885-4 oct 1959
/Luther,Bernice M.1913-1985   /Lowery,Eunice 1900-1984
    William H.1905-1978   /Lykins,J.Thomas 1860-1931
#Lykens,James 29 aug 1926 42yc/Lykins,Minnie T. 1870-1951
#Lykins,Danny lee 17 mar 19--   /Lykins,John Jackson 1893-1959
/Lykins,Clymenia C.1897-1919   Mary Bea 1893--
/Lykins,Wm.Howard 1911-1964   #Lykins,Jas.Thos,1914-8/8/1931
    Riva Faye 1912--   #Lynch,Roy 28 aug 1936 inf
/Malcolm,Harry 1881-1966   /Malcolm,Robert B.24 nov 1843-29 dec 1904
    Alfa S. 1877-1949   Isabella H.1 dec 1843-5 aug 1903
#Mankin,Edward 25 may 1920   /Martin,Otis 14 oct 1895-5 may 1968 WWI
#Mankin,James G.18 sep 1934 16/Martin,Lieber Carl 12 aug 1893-2 mar 1964
/Martin,Milton 1872-1949   /Martin,Ruby E.29 dec 1898-17 aug 1978
    Lillie 1875--   Fred L.28 Jan 1897-19 sep 1978
/Martin,Mary C. 1883-1948   /Martin,Olevia McCorkle 1867-1937wFred McC
/Martin,Sherley A. 1939-40   /Martin,Madge Rollyson 1900-1950
#Martin,John C.6 sep 1932 30y /Martin,Edward 28 sep 1885-3 oct 1961
/Martin,Fannie b.1857   #Mathews,Nora 12 Jul 1931 23y1m12d
    McClelland 1863-1925   /Matthews,Mary Corrine 1896-1988
/Matnee,Alice 9 Jun 1926 c   /Maxwell,Mary Sedinger 1911--
/Maxwell,Robert L.1890-1967   /Maxwell,James Baker 1902-1969
    Easter J., 1893-1929   /Maxwell,Raymond O.19 Jun 1915-3 mar 1959
/Mayberry,George R.1846-1907   /Mayberry,Lizzie Thornburg 1855-1926
/Mayberry,Willia E. 1880-1940   /Mayenschien,Erskie Lee 13 Jul 1916 14y

/Maynard,Thelma Mae 1935 inf   Edwin Mitchell 13 Jul 1916 11y
/May,Ernest Irwin 1944-1947   /Mays,A.J. 1861-1935
/Mayse,Maud May 1884-1918   /Mayse,Tallahssee Handley
/Mays,Garrett R.1902-1942   7 feb 1905-22 feb 1987
/Mays,Evelyn Clark 1903-1968 /Mayse,Louise 18862-1927
/McCallister,Edgar 1888-1931 /McCallister,Clarence C.10/24/1918-12/17/83
   Erie 1889-1974   /McCallister,Lucinda
#McCallister &son 19 Jul 1933   29 Jul 185224 apr 1928
/McClain,W.C.Jr.1937-1941   /McClaskey,Melva Lee 17 mar 1932-4 dec 1944
/McClintock,John 1874-1957   /McClure,Donna G.1 oct 1947--
   Virgie May 1888-1974   Glenn L.II 19 Jan 1954-19 dec 1986
/McColgin,Alpha Gulliam 1894-1915
/McCorkle,Rury 1896-1899   /McCoy,D.B. 1882-1946
/McCorkle,B.Fred 1854-1900   /McDonie,Thos,Lee 27 feb 1897-8 mar 1963
/McGhee,E.W.1909-1978   /McGhee,Julius dale 21 sep 1921-8 Jul 1970II
/McGinnis,Dr.A.B. 1828-1898 /McGinnis,Ella Peyton 1879-1927
/McGinnis,Elizabeth 1840-1911 /McGinnis,Clay Warren 1872-1958
/McGinnis,Earl Peyton 1919-1972/McGinnis,Woodrow W.1913-1961
/McGinnis,Clay Jr.1920 inf   /McGuire,Wm.Joseph 8 feb 1883-19 mar 1937
/McGuire,Evelyn L.   /McGuire,Theresa R.13 Jun 1896
   13 Jun 1920-21 apr 1988 /McNeely,Dellifee D.30 Jun 1899-10 mar 1945
/McNeely,Eunice 1925 inf   /McNeely,Frank E.17 Jun 1894-17 Jan 1983
/McNeely,Charles M.1881-1919 /McNeely,Monte 14 Jul 1922-29 oct 1940
   Alice C.1877-1964   /McNeely,Verna L.11 sep 1894-19 aug 1972
                     /McNeer,Daniel E.CoF 4th WV Inf
/McWorter,Albert 1897-1955 /Meade,Lafe 12 Jun 1902-30 may 1960
   Edith 1905-1974   Georgia 2 Jun 1905-5 feb 1978
/Meabon,Fred D.8 sep 1961   /Meade,Archie 3 Jun 1940-30 Jun 1969
/Meabon,Ida Thayer 1882-1918   Bonnie Lou 18 sep 1938
/Meabon,Gay Alonzo 1912-1933 /Meadows,Grover C.23 sep 1892-15 nov 1965
/Meadows,T.E,1866-1932 /Meadows,Kate Gladys 20 may 1897-22 may 1984
   Ella 1867-1951   /Meadows,Carl E. 18 nov 1900-18 Jul 1988
   son 1899   /Meadows,Garnet 20 nov 1894--
/Meadows,William G.1919-1963 /Meadows,Bernard L.23 feb 1903-11 apr 1982
   Kathryn 1921--   /Meadows,Blanche kathleen
/Meadows,Lew Elza Jr.1924-1943   10 apr 1911-27 oct 1983
/Meadows,Luda 1884-1966   /Meadows,Lee G.9 Jun 1911-27 feb 1932
/Meadows,Robert K. 1883-1966 /Meadows,Nettie H.1886-1953
   Emma P. 1887-1966   /Meadows,Charley 29 aug 1878-14 aug 1952
/Meadows,Herschel H.1908-1977 /Melton,Jane Louise 4 oct 1931 inf
/Meddings,Ruby E.1914-1972   /Miller,Lulu B.1891-1946
/Miller,Idena C.1911-1975   /Miller,Alfred 1891-1954
/Miles,Hiram 1856-1912   /Minnick,Bernard C. 1889-1946
/Milner,Deboarh Jane 1958   Garnett E. 1898-19--
/Mildner,Clara 1873-1919
/Mitchell,Stella E.1899-1985   /Mitchell,Will E. 1882-1956
/Mitchell,Howard Joe 1899-1985 /Mitchell,Sarah E.1882-1946
/Mobley,Lizzie 1884-1963   /Moore,Truman 25 mar 1893-2 feb 1973
   James A. 1870-1941   /Moore,Cora Hood 1898-1945
/Moore,John A. 1905-1951   /Moore,Henry H.1906-06
/Moore,Pauline 1908--   /Moore,Nellie M.1901
/Moore,George W.1893-1962   /Moore,Myrtle Ellen 1866-1936
   Carrie E. 1897-1989   /Moore,William N.1864-1952
/Moore,Howard 1883-1917   /Moore,John B.1879-1937

Pansie 1893-1965
/Moore,Barney 1842-1925 CoI 67OH
    Rachel 1852-1927
    Sarah 1850-1931
/Moore,Arnold 1898-1957
    Goldie 1898-19--
/Moore,Elizabeth H.1875-1936
#Moore,Wayne Floyd 1932 inf
/Morris,Calvin R.1876-1946
/Morris,Hattie E. 1880-1950
/Morrison,Florence Gillenwater
    31 Jul 1897-15 feb 1976
/Mullens,Floyd 1858-1910
/Mullens,Zora 1870-1947
/Murphy,Lula 1894-1964
    William 1888-1948
/Murphy,Arthur 22 apr 1922
    Wanda L.
    19 oct 1930-27 may 1987
#Murphy,Elijah 7 mar 1935 82y4m
/Murray,Isabell 1859-1921
/Myers,Ruby Jean 1944-1960
    Mollie Howard 1902-1958
/Napier,Charles Benton 1889-1959
/Napeir,Mary Pierce 1918-1941
/Napier,Lillie 1 sep 1913
    Willie 1 sep 1913 twins
/Napier,Betty F. 1860-1934
/Nelson,Melvin 1868-1944
    Millie 1882-1959
    (Wentz,James 1876-1908)
/Newman,William Ed 1881-1928
/Newman,Marjorie 1911-1933
/Newman,Sarah ann 1887-1939
#Newman,Wm.1 nov 1932 76y7m26d
/Nichols,Edward J.1874-1945
    Ida M.1886-1925
/North,Mary F.1882-1967
/North,James R. 1871-1958
/North,Elvera S. 1916--
    Charles T.1905-1984
/Oldaker,James E. 1907-1979
    Georgia A. 1913-1980

/Ostrowski,Robert
    9 apr 1918-24 mar 1947 WWII
/Patterson,Bertha E.1891-1980
/Patterson,Walter J.1884-1949
#Paston,Georgia 25 nov 1930 18y
/Patrick,George W.   WWI
    3 feb 1895-3 Jul 1973
/Pemberton,Kathryn L.1888-1946
/Pemberton,Nellie M. 1903-1966
    William W.1901-1951

Thelma Eckart 1908-1981
    Dana 1910-1958
/Moore,Hazel R.16 Jun 1897-30 Jul 1980
/Moore,Ernest 3 feb 1896-21 apr 1956
/Moore,Wm.Franklin 7 aug 1890-4 mar 1917
/Moore,Guy C.1896-1968
    Gusta 1895-1951
/Morris,Fred C.1 feb 1915-25 nov 1987wII
/Morris,Elizabeth G.1909-1962
/Morrison,Alta M.27 Jan 1900-31 may 1985
#Moury,John 1846-1918 Civil War
/Mucklow,Betty F. 1918-1919
#Mullens,Mitchell 8 aug 1938 55y
/Murphy,Harmon L.23 sep 1872-1 feb 1956
    Julia Mae 11 may 1876-28 may 1931
/Murphy,Erthal Albert 4/8/1909-6/27/1974
/Murphy,Florence Mildred 2/5/1905-11/11/83
/Murphy,Admiral Dewey 9/30/1900-4/5/24
/Murphy,Edna Mae 22 aug 1916-11 Jun 1986
#Murphy,James F.9 mar 1937 57y (?)
/Murry,Evelyn V.27 feb 1903-25 feb 1985
/Myers,Clymenia Hall 1917-
/Myers,Kermit Lee 1909-1983
/Myers,William H.17 apr 1901-15 feb 1975
/Napier,Robert D.10 nov 1920-13 may 1966II
/Napier,Harry P.9 Jun 1919-9 aug 1988
    Delores A. 12 oct 1931--
/Napier,Clifford 12 dec 1897-25 nov 1942II
/Neal,Kenneth 27 may 1925-19 nov 1927
/Newman,James S.29 dec 1914-14 dec 1959
/Newman,Hazel Mae 7 mar 1920-13 aug 1987
/Newman,Lewis J.14 feb 1928-17 feb 1970wII
/Newman,Albert G.17 apr 1917-26 sep 1974II
/Newman,Garland W.1925-1945
/Noel,James M.19 Jan 1880-26 aug 1974
/Noel,Forrest J. 1916-1975wII
/Noel,Stella 27 Jan 1880-10 sep 1970
#Nohm,Otto John 14 sep 1937 64y10m4d
/O'Donnell,Sgt.Patrick 1851-1923
/O'Donnell,Mary 1855-1939
/Ohlinger,L.Harry 1885-1940
/Oldaker,Frank 1876-12 mar 1926
/Oldaker,Alpha L.9 Jul 1909-27 apr 1950II
/Oliver,Elizabeth Wentz 171 Jun 1912-20 Jan 1960
/Oxley,Evaline Jarrell
    11 oct 1871-21 Jan 1966
/Page,Hazel M.1923-1985
/Parsley,Paul R.10 dec 1947-20 feb 1968VN
    Wayne 1902-1967
    Bessie 1903-1981
    Cleo 1918-
/Pauley,Clifford E.9 dec 1923-9 apr 1986
/Pemberton,Merrill Leroy 1921-1932
/Pemberton,Edward 1877-1950

43

#Penuose, James Lewis 1937 inf
/Perkins, Frank 1896-1968
    Gladys M.1904-1930
    Robert 1930 inf

/Perry, Audrey M.1919-1987
    Herb B.1915-1987
/Perry, Mary E. 1877-19--
/Perry, Edward E.1927-1928
    Scott E. 1932-1934
/Perry, Stella M.1903-1976
/Perry, twin sons 21 apr 1944
/Perry, Lilliam L.1902-1985
/Petit, Garnettia R. 1900-1964
/Petrie, Solomon W.1915--
    Mildred M.1918-1984
/Pike, Howard W.3 sep 1907
    Ethel Boyd 14 oct 1911
#Poindexter, Hattie L. c
/Porter
/Poston, Georgia 1912-1930
/Poston, Freddie 1928-1943
/Powers, Velva 1900-1960
/Prichard, Edward R.   WWII
    27 Jun 1920-16 mar 1980
/Pulley, Ruth Hamlin 1903-1960
/Rairden, A.Byron 1897-1938
/Rairden, C.H.1871-1925
/Randall, Isabelle J.1877-1965
    Ira James 1868-1937
/Rardin, Wm.W.1913-1928
    Alberta 1916-1937
    Georgia A. 1908-1940
/Ratliff, L.Alan 20 apr 1920--

/Ray, Goldie Florence 1907-1936
/Ray, Aaron 1899-1930
/Ray, Edith 1910-1976
    Russell 1910-1976
/Ray, Edward 1877-1941
#Raynor, Arthur 5 Jan 1936 47y
/Rayborn, Edward D.1884-1953
/Reese, James D.10-903-1968
#Reynolds, Bertie 1900-1925
/Reynolds, Leona K.1893-1980
/Reynolds, Theodore F.1892-1930
/Reynolds, Nettie E. 1869-1969
    Alonzo 1869-1956
#Rice, Effie 30 Jun 1935 51y
/Rice, Richard A. 1952-1968
/Richardson, Ora E.1885-1971
/Richardson, Samuel Clinton
    1881-1963
/Richardson, R.F. 1858-1938

/Pemberton, Sarah 1883-1952
/Perkins, Benjamin F.10 Jul 1896-27 Jul 1968
/Perkins, James M.1878-1940
    Nancy L.1879-1959
/Perkins, Mickel 6 aug 1902-31 may 1964
    Millie 2 mar 1907-7 mar 1980
/Perry, Wm.S.20 apr 1903-10 mar 1968
/Perry, Mildred E. 1913--
    Yancy V.1911-1988
/Perry, Ray inf 5 Jan 1936
/Perry, Uba Myrtle 1878-1929
/Perry, Edgar 1880-1964
/Peters, Judith B.1926-1962
/Petit, Bernanrd E.26 Jan 1898-19 aug 1973
/Petrie, Ralph Lee 25 apr 1905-15 oct 1962II
/Petrie Billy Joe 2 nov 1936-16 Jan 1937
/Pickens, Augusta Hensley 3/6/1888/9/7/1967
/Pine, Isabelle K.1873-1936
/Poling, Martha 1874-1957
/Porter, Janet Lee 1940-41
#Poston, inf 29 dec 1929
/Potter, Brenda kay 31 Jan 1944=5 Jul 1973
    d/o Mat & Eva Boyd Johnson
/Prince, Nannie C.12 Jan 1913 70yw/oJ.M.
    Ocia B.17 oct 1882-3 aug 1903 d/oJM&NC
/Pullman, Pearl 1878-1938
/Rand, William W.28 Jul 1892-10 mar 1967
    Mattie P. 1898-1967
/Randant, Flossie Ensley 1890-1929
/Rangos, John 1880(Greece)-9 Jul 1940
/Rardin, Fredrick M.10 sep 1872-16 apr 1954
    Lutie D.23 oct 1883-2 apr 1955
/Rarden, Adam B.20 aug 1938 40y
/Ratliff, Sarah Saunders 1846-1931
/Ratliff, Lenora 11 oct 1921-8 nov 1898
/Ray, inf s 1936(on Perry twins stone)
/Ray, John 27 Jul 1890-24 nov 1965 WWI
/Ray, Elizabeth Alta 1894-1967
/Ray, Bertha Shelton 1886-1969
/Ray, Guy Herschel 1906-1972
#Ray, Eron Herschel 13 Jan 1936 inf
/Reed, Annie 20 aug 1875-30 Jul 1910 c
/Reed, Mary Louise 22 may 1922-11 Jun 1923
#Reeder, inf 7 Jan 1937
/Reynolds, Alva A 28 may 1893-27 Jun 1954
    Pearl M. 28 Jun 1899-5 nov 1946
/Reynolds, Denver 12 may 1919-5 Jan 1946
/Reynolds, Doris Jean 1931-34
/Reynolds, Denver 12 may 1919-5 Jan 1946
/Rhodes, Mabel 30 Jan 1900-18 feb 1961
    Russell 18 feb 19087-18 aug 1967
/Richardson, Mother 18 may 1818-28 dec 1896
/Richardson, Father 14 apr 1814-7 may 1902
/Richardson, Emma I.1865-1949

```
        Ella 1874-1905           /Richardson,Rev.George E. 1861-1927
/Ridenour,Pryce R.1906-1982       /Ridenour,Ross B.18 nov 1904-22 mar 1968
    Hazel H.1912-1967             /Riggs,Marion 1872-1932
/Riggs,Florence 1880-1956     /Riggs,Arizona Everett 7 aug 1884-27 Jan 1934
/Riggs,Edward R.1901-1980         /Riggs,Lona Frances 1913-1932
#Riggs,Tobe 71y                   /Rippel,Rose Collins 1911-1940
/Roach,Lawrence H.1901-1963       /Roberts,Clarence 1891-1983
/Roach,Creed 1873-1939                Stella Mae 1891-1978  m22 dec 1912
/Roberts,Lillian Geneva 1922-25#Roberts,Willie
/Robinson,William 1877-1940       /Robinson,Larry A.12 mar 1953-31 Jul 1986
/Robinson,Osceola 1876-1955       /Robinson,Michael David 8/11/1962-1/23/1989
/Rodefer,Annabelle 1919-1980      /Rogers,Emma D.27 dec 1880-3 may 1960
/Rodefer,Charles 1916-1963            Francis L.2 Jun 1876-12 Jan 1966
/Rollyson,C.Sherman 1870-1936 #Rogers,Fred A.1936 inf
    Emma Ryder 1875-1955          /Rollyson,Elmer C.9 Jun 1893-5 sep 1977wI
    Emily Marine 1914-1971        #Rollyson,Roy R.1904-05
/Romans,Dora E. 1879-1964         /Rood,Paul W.2 nov 1916-28 feb 1931
/Romans,Albert 1873-1939          /Rood,Sadie M.1896-1975
/Romans,Glen 1904-1918                Roy E. 1893-1945
/Rose,Robert W.1910-1959          /Rose,Georgia W.23 Jun 1917-12 may 1984
/Rose,Mary Ellen 1935-1938        /Rose,Wm.Thomas 6 Jun 1911-10 Jun 1959
/Rose,Charles W. 1886-1960        /Rose,Garfield 180-1943
/Rose,Roma Dement 1887-1976           Eva Jane 1891-1970 w/o Garfield
/Rose,Andrew J.1886-1899              Myrtle 1879-1910 w/o Garfield
/Rose,Charles H.1853-1940         /Rose,James G.30 may 1922-27 Jul 1968WWII
/Rose,Olive Vance 1858-1946       /Rose,Roy Ray 7 Jun 1926-12 aug 1959 WWII
/Rose,W.T. 1857-1908              /Rose,Gloria Lee 1930-1946
/Rose,Gratia 1864-1944            /Rose,John 1920-1921 s/o Garfield & Eva
/Rose,Pamela S.1978 inf           /Rose,James C.1885-1951
/Rose,Uriah 1858-1936             /Rose,Alice 1891-1970
/Rose,Louisa J.1861-1928          /Rose,Alfred 1880-1963
/Ross,Margaret Ann 1880-1945      #Rose,Opal Jan 1929 23y9m10d
    Betty Lee 1921-1943           #Rose,George V.23 mar 1897-19 aug 1916
    James H. 1881-1947            /Rose,George 23 mar 1897-19 aug 1916
#Roten,Dolores Jean 1934-5        /Rowsey,Minnie V.1888-1978
/Rowsey,Jack L. 1921-1964         /Rowsey,Fitzhugh L.1886-1960
/Roy,Callie L.Jr.1929-1930        /Rowsey,Betha F.5 Jul 1905-23 oct 1989
    Jackie D.1932-1932            /Rucker,Herbert R.1928-1986
/Rucker,Thurman D.1888-1959       /Rucker,Leslie M.30 apr 1903-22 aug 1967
/Rucker,Stella 1889-1966          /Rucker,Carson B.22 feb 1889-26 Jul 1965wI
/Rucker,Frances H.1923            /Runyon,Mary V.25 may 1903-15 sep 1976
    Loren Max 1921-1970           /Runyan,Robert Jr.1933-34
/Runyan,Dora E.1910               /Runyan,Thomas J.1881-1935
/Runyan,J.Ralph 1912-1986         /Runyon,Frances Lee 1940-41
/Russell,Mary Ella 1873-1945      /Russell,Rosa Deitz 1872-1955
/Rust,Lorraine 1892-1894          /Rust,George 1846-15 Jan 1932 86y11m5d
/Rye,D.M. 1853-1907               /Rust,Mary Elizabeth 1852-aug 1931
/Sabin,Helen Turner 1917-1958 /Salamon,Grace Meabon 1904-1935
/Samoles,John 1896-1946           /Sansom,Earl 30 Jun 1907-11 aug 1953
/Sargent,Treasure 1900-1947           Lora 17 may 1902--
    Frank 1867-1934               /Sargent,Freeman W.18 aug 1904-27 may 1965
    Grace 1866-1907               /Sargent,Bernard 6 Jul 1918-26 dec 1925
/Saunders,Ogle M.1893-1922        /Saunders,Helen Mary 11 feb 1910-12 nov 1986
/Saxton,Francis 1827-1901         /Saxton,B.W. 1868-1923
```

45

Malina J.1837-1909   Margaret M. 1878--
/Saxton,Jethroe 1898-1980 /Saxton,Carl E. 8 may 1922-17 Jul 1980
Rachael Rebecca 1903-1963 /Sacrberry,Barbara Isaacs 1935-1961
/Scarberry,Donald Albert 1956/Scarberry,Betty L.Esque 27 feb 1927-1 apr88
Franklin 1960 infs /Scott,Jeffery Alan 9 nov 1957-24 may 1973
/Schanek,John /Scheneberg,John Bluford 3/9/1921-4/23/79II
22 feb 1911-3 apr 1969 /Scheneberg,John B.20 nov 1887-26 sep 1950I
/Scheneberg,George P.1851-1894/Scheneberg,Beatrice M.4 Jul 1899-29 nov 57
/Scheneberg,Minnie B.1861-1931/Scheneberg,John B.1822-1897
/Sedinger,Agnes 1908-1973 /Scheneberg,Mary W.1821-1887
/Sedginer,Loren H.1895-1953 /Sedginer,James D.Jr.6 Jan 1871-25 apr 1941I
Sarah J.1896-1966 /Sedinger,Harry L.1868-1928
/Sedginer,Agnes D.1840-1932 Katie L.Holschuh 1873-1909
Col.James D.1838-1901 /Sedinger,James Lyle 1906-1973
1Lieut CoE 8th VA Cav CSA Virginia E.Burnes 1908-1972
/Seeley,William 1884-1929 /Selbee,Drusie Mae 25 oct 19--=15 aug 1979
/Seeley,Bessie 1890-1969 /Sexton,Nancy F.10 Jan 1963-27 sep 1966
/Shaffer,John M.1872-1948 /Shaffer,Violet L.15 oct 1926--
/Shaffer,Lelia T.1877-1953 Jackie Lee 26 oct 1935-15 may 1980
#Shaver,Paul Wm.4 apr 1937 inf/Sheets,Eddy E. 1928-29
/Shelton,Jerome M.1883-1961 /Shoemaker,Richard L.1883-1956
/Short,Homer M. Hastie S.1889-1984
29 apr 1900-13 oct 1945 /Shorter,W.E. 1870-1906
/Shuff,George 1872-1954 Jennie 1874-19--
/Shuff,Amanda Jane 1870-1946 Jack 1899-1928
/Shuff,Minnie Byrd 1896-1925 Emma 1902-03
/Shy,B.G. 1829-1914 /Shy,Chalmer E.13 Jun 1873-12 oct 1899
Mary Seamands 1833-1915 /Shy,Ruby Perry 1897-1984
/Shy,Benjamin G. 1867-1950 /Shy,Hugh Gorden 1900-1943
/Shy,Annie Thornburg 1873-1912/Shye,Richard E.1861-1927
/Sibrel,Lillie May 1923-1977 Ida Ella Jenkins 1870-1917
Harold Gordon 1914-1984 /Sikes,Bethal 13 feb 1913-12 feb 1949
/Simms,Joseph 16 aug 1936 /Silmon,albert L.15 apr 1918-2 may 1973
/Simpson,Frances Gayle 1949 inf/Simpson,Ruth Eleanor 1914-1979
/Simpson,Alta Marie 1892-1969 /Sites,Warren G.1920-1973
/Simpson,James Madison 1890-71/Slash,Elmo n.1909-1929
/Sizemore,David Clay.1871-1937#Slayton,Martha 1896-20 Jan 1937
/Sizemore,Mary Belle 1873-1950/Smith,Rev.V.S.31 Jan 1915 58y c
/Smith,Willa Jean 1932-1939 /Smith,Maude Erie 1885-1948
/Smith,Vincent H.1908-- /Smith,Violet Virginia 1917-1957
Irene E.1911-- /Smith,Georgia Lucille 1909-1980
/Smith,Burl H.1852-1951 /Smith,Madge 18 mar 1917-25 feb 1976
/Smith,Lovella J.1867-1937 /Smith,Ada B.1884-1944
/Smith,Clarence L.1888-1914 /Smith,James 17 dec 1810-12 nov 1898
/Smith,Minnie P.1906-1983 /Smith,James F.4 oct 1962-21 Jun 1975
Kenneth R.1906-1965 Corletta B.1940-1978
/Smith,Audley 1894-1976 /Smith,Diana 1932-1941
/Smith,Florence 1900-19-- /Songer,Wilda W.1905-1934
/Songer,Elmer L.1898-1976 /Songer,Rev.Ernest C.1903-1952
Gladys H.1905-- /Songer,Jacob E.1878-1943
/Spaulding,Ernest R.1882-1950 /Spaulding,Jack W.1925-1948 WWII
Hester A.1884-1971 /Spencer,Jack W.14 mar 1919-18 aug 1989
/Spradlin,Hazel 1911-1941 Lula M.21 sep 1935--
/Spurlock,Joyce June 1928-1970/Spurlock,Wm.G.24 apr 1843-30 aug 1930 WWI

/Spurlock,Sallie 1863-1940   /Spurlock,Eveline 1847-1919
/Spurlock,Jeffery Samuel 1964 /Stahl,Flo Keenan 20 oct 1908-9 sep 1986
#Stack,Darlene 1 sep 1934 Inf
/Stanley,Adaline S.   /Stapleton,Flora 25 mar 1910-24 sep 1970
   11 oct 1871-21 Jan 1966 /Staten,Dora Jenkins 1866-1993
/Stephenson,Charles L.1847-1911/Stephenson,Frank 9 mar 1890-7 nov 1945
/Stepp,Leona   /Stevenson,Nora 1894-1989
   20 Jul 1893-14 Jun 1979   Larry 1887-1953
/Stewart,E.McGinnis 1889-1955 /Stewart,Fletcher B.27 aug 1858-27 dec 1895
/Stewart,Willie M.1862-1898 /Stewart,Jennie McGinnis 1860-1936
/Stewart,D.Edwin 1852-1903   /Stewart,Ethel Mae 1879-1973
/Stewart,Sarah B.1861-1941   /Stewart,H.Carlisle 1892-1974
/Stewart,Maria Ann 1820-1904 /Stewart,Virginia K.1902-1983
/Stewart,Alice M.1859-1916   /Stewart,Hamilton W.1847-1913
/Stewart,William E. 1912-1959
#Stewart,Claude Leo 1897-1926 #Stickler,Calvin T.17 aug 1936 19y3m16d
/Stickler,Ethel Mae 1894-1958 /Stickler,Dewey 1898-1969
   Thomas L.1897-1953   Margaret 1901-1965
/Steed,Elisha B.1875-1962   /Steed,Clementine 1876-1949
/Stollings,Mont 1892-1972   #Stogden,Robert A.13 aug 1842-6 may 1932
/Stollings,Melvin   /Stone,Curtis L.1 may 1920 WWI
   2 Jan 1899-27 Jan 1974   /Storey,Blanch Asbury 3 feb 1884-4 Jan 1954
/Strum,Mary Alice 1883-1956 /Storey,Walter Ray 22 feb 1896-14 mar 1966
/Strum,Harold O.1879-1941   /Strum,Rev.C.9 oct 1860-14 apr 1927
/Strum,Sarah Cordella 1883-46 /Strum,L.I.21 apr 1856-10 Jan 1926
/Sudderth,Annie Beam 1896-1953/Sullivan,M.S.Martha L.1925-1926
/Sullivan,Richard D.1881-1945 /Sullivan,Vesta 2 may 1901-9 sep 1980
   Nellie 1899-1938   /Sullivan,Bessie Mae 29 nov 1917
/Swann,Ernest K.1908-1970   William C.24 may 1917
   Roxie C.1915   /Swann,Naomi L.1919-1920
/Swann,Walter C. 1878-1971   /Swann,Clarence E.1910-1925
   Roxie Lee 1887-1963   /Swann,Robert G. 1922
#Swann,Orval 1911 s/oW&Bertha #Swann,Robt Raymond 1923 2y10m
/Sweeney,Edna 1903-1983   /Swim,Heston 16 sep 1903-4 apr 1971
/Sydenstricker,Anna 1908-1983 /Sydenstricker,Margaret H.23 Jun 1917
/Sydenstricker,Wm.A.1885-1939   Forrest A.7 aug 1911-e sep 1982
   Letha M. 1885-1965   /Sydenstricker,John Andrew 1855-1917
/Sydenstricker,Curtis M.1894-1921   Charles A.1890-1916
/Tackett,Beulah B.1913-1956
/Taylor,Garland (Family)   /Taylor,Beatrice M.16 aug 1886-3 Jun 1965
/Taylor,Richard A.   William B.1 Jun 1884-7 apr 1965
   17 aug 1933-20 apr 1952 /Taylor,Wm.M.d 23 Jul 1948 h/oBeatrice M.?
/Taylor,Vernon D.1874-1955   /Taylor,Lawrence L.4 apr 1930-9 may 1981
   Marhta G.1882-1934   /Taylor,Katherine 9 dec 1897-30 Jul 1971
/Taylor,Mary E.1854-1949   /Taylor,Isabella A.29 apr 1831-14 aug 1903
/Templeton,Mary S.1902-1971 /Templeton,James F.1933-34
   Russell F.1902-1981   /Thacker,Alonzo L.1883-1966
/Thacker,Raymond H.1909-1922   Callie G.1892-1966
/Thomas,Mattie A. 1899-1978 /Thomas,Merrel Sue 1930-33
/Thomas,Maynard M.Sr.1901-1970/Thomas,William W. 1938-1983
/Thomas,Darrel C.1902-1965
/Thomason,J.O.1856-1911(Turner)/Thompson,John T.1880-1954
/Thompson,Sarah 186-1923   Stella A. 1881-1970
/Thompson,Lottie M.1882-1932 /Thompson,Elsie 1896-1959

```
        Anthony 1872-1948              #Thompson,Henrietta 1 Jan 1935 .77y77m6d
#Thompson,J.G. 1856-1911              #Thompson,America 25 dec 1936 46y
/Thornburg,Frank M. 1870-1935         /Thornton,George I.1894-1914
/Tomlinson,Guy 1890-1976              /Tomlinson,Ed.1879-1906
        Ora 1894-1975                 #Tomlinson,inf twins 28 Jul 1930
/Toney,Pearl M. 1876-1938             /Tompson,James Dee 18 mar 1923-10 sep 1943
/Toney,A.G. 1871-1942                 /Toney,Evelyn C.22 oct 1918-27 oct 1927
/Toney,Garnet F.1906--                /Toney,Robt.Clayton 22 mar 1929-5 Jul 1929
        Bernard C. 1905-1977          /Toney,Russell C.26 feb 1935 WWI
/Tooley,Norma M.27 apr 1923           /Tooley,Ira 3 Jan 1885-21 apr 1961
        Russell    WWII               /Tooley,Maude 26 oct 1888-24 Jun 1962
        28 apr 1918-3 Jun 1984        /Tooley,Kate Newman 23 nov 1884-14 sep 1978
/Tooley,Lyndle 1908-1909              /Tooley,Wilburn 23 aug 1883-17 Jul 1967
        Inf 8 mar 1912                /Tooley,Forrest G. 1909-1988
/Topping,C.M. 1856-1923               /Topping,Ida Lee 1887-1936
        Anna 1866-1941                #Trent,----192-    42y   c
/Trout,Nancy Frances 1937 3y          /Trent,Rev.H.L.1876-1931   c
/Triplett,Edward 1876-1945            /Triplett,Earnest V.20 aug 1898-8 Jun 1967
/Triplett,Ada T.1889-1958             /Triplett,Alma Bowen 26 sep 1901-11 feb 1985
/Turley,Charles E.1865-1925           /Turley,Clyde H.1902-1966
/Turner,Clara B.1862-1949             /Turley,Rosella 1901-1966
        Victor A.1846-1930            /Turner,Maywood Jr.1920-1976 WWII
/Turner,H.B.1858-1932                 #Turner,James M.1876-1930
/Turner,Dora 1871-1962                /Turner,Aaron H.1849-1926
#Turner,Maynard J.21 oct 1937             Sarah F.1855-1936
/Twyman,Violet M.1887-1959            /Turner,Clarence 1882-1968
        Alec C.1878-1967              /Tyler,Grace S.24 apr 1896-10 feb 1988
/Tyler,inf 9 may 1917                     Albert R.22 apr 1881-2 feb 1952
/Vance,Elizabeth K.1835-1901          /Vititoe,Kenneth R.20 mar 1927-13 mar 1977
/Vernatt,Lucy Louise 1917-1929/Wagner,Rosa Vernatt 1875-1959
/Walker,Vasco 1907-1980                   Charles P.1874-1956
        Mabel V.1907--                    Belle Vernatt 1910
/Walker,Caroline(m/Just.King) #Walling,Emma 8 Jan 1924 50y9m
        12 aug 1844-1 nov 1913        /Walton,Edith S. 1900
/Walton,Harry 1883-1930   c               Earl O.1900-1963
/Ward,Ernest G.1916-1988
/Ward,Ernest 1892-1957                /Ward,Evermont 16 may 1882 62y8m27d
        Thelma 1899-1968              /Ward,Ira N.1883-1948
/Ward,Clara B. 1896-1956              /Ward,Grace Shye 1888-1980
/Ward,Frank L.1894-19--               /Ward,Mary Louise 1873-29-may-1937 65y2m1d
/Watson,Charles J.1871-1933           /Ward,Grozy 1868-1949
        Kate 1872-1939                /Watson,Faye 14 Jul 1912-28 dec 1972
/Waugh,Warren 1908-1940               #Watson,Lyle E.14 may 1936 18y2m12d
        Georgia 1910-1957             /Wearty,Alice R. 1907-1970
/Weaver,Russell 17 apr 1944           /Weekley,Chad Edward oct-nov 1977
/Welch,Ernest B.1917--                /Wellington,Pansy P.1898-1987
        Lula B. 1917-1967             /Wellington,Bernard C.1897-1959
/Wellington,John R. 1861-1933         /Wellington,Leonard M.1903-1952
/Wellington,Myrtle W.1876-1934/Wellington,Erastus M.1831-1903
/Wells,Okey 1888-1973 WWI             /Wells,Charles S.15 may 1893-21 Jan 1972
/Wentz,Paul P.1903-1943               /Wentz,James Fred.24 sep 1907-24 Jan 1985
/Wentz,Effie M. 1868-1933             /Wentz,Sarah Janice 4 apr 1924-3 nov 1985
/Wentz,Anthony 1870-1952              /Wentz,Sarah Ina 10 mar 1895-1 dec 1983
/Wentz,Stella M.1894-1906             /Wentz,Charles Ray 11 dec 1920-11 apr 1962
```

48

/Wentz,Mary Ada 1884-1967   /Wentz,Henry C.1844-1922
/Wentz,Elizabeth 1892-1958   /Wentz,Susannah E. 1858-1910
/Wentz,Richard B. 1886-1952 /Wentz,Lulla B.20 aug 1877-6 oct 1901HC&SE
/Wentz,Susie R. 1895-1936   /Wentz,Henry Ervin 16 may 1938 WWI
#Wertz,Annie Losey 1858-1923 #Wentz,Howard 9 sep 1934 51y
#Wertz,Clara Mildred 1973-1919/Weser,Sylvia 1900-1958
/Wheeler,Cassie 1886-1972   Carl S.1894-1970
/Wheeler,H.K. 1883-1960   /Wheeler,Eliza 1869-1946
#Wheelor,inf 23 Jan 1934   #White.B.F. 29 oct 1925 c
/White,Henrietta 1859-1949   /White,Alma Ann 1896-1920
/White,Richard R. 1859-1944 /White,Golden Lee 1920-1928
/White,John Chester 1893-1949 /White,Wm.K.21 Jan 1916-24 Jun 1944
/White,Eunice B.1880-1961   /Whitt,Jeffery Brian 1973 inf
/White,Dr.Benjamin F. 1867-1925   Nathan Alan 1974 inf
/Whittington,G.W. 1852-1918 /Whittington,Dora M.14 apr 1877-13 sep 1909
     Lucy 1859--   /Whittington,Arthur G.4/10/1890-2/12/1966I
/Wilcox,Nora 1897-1953   /Wilcox,Charles 26 oct 1921-20 apr 1982
/Wiley,Mabel 1912-1917   Betty R.23 may 1927
/Wiley,Ruby I.   /Wiley,Margaret E.10 Jun 1893-5 nov 1979
     24 Jun 1914-17 nov 1941 /Wiley,Lonzo B.1 Jun 1886-2 may 1971
/Wilhoit,Doris Jean 1925-29 /Wilkes,Cora C.6 feb 1905-28 feb 1973
/Wilhoit,Olive 17 feb 1936   /Williams,Mae Day 23 Jul 1917--
/GWilliam,Harry H.1873-1926   James N.4 Jun 1913-8 oct 1977
     Phoeba Ann 1876-1923   /Williams,Nora 1870-1905
/Williamson,Earl 1908-1972
/Wilmink,C.Edward 1884-1945 /Wilkmink,Lois M. 1917-1929
     Mildred 1886-1977   /Wilson,Alvin E.16 apr 1916-22 feb 1985
/Wilson,Mary V.1862-1933   /Wilson,Pearl A.18 Jun 1909-25 apr 1975
/Wilson,Ruth Rose 1897-1947   Joseph C.1922-1984   WWII
/Winesky Eileen Blas 1911-- /Winters,Charley S.1869-1940
/Winesky,John S.   WWII   Maggie E. 1873-1950
     8 may 1913-30 Jun 1976 /Womeldorff,Daniel A. 1845-1873
/Wood,inf 1918   /Womeldorff,Jennie G.1844-1912
#Wood,Bert E.A.188-1912   #Wood,Mamie H.24 Jul 1935 49y7m29d
/Woodrum,Alice H.1876-1964   /Woodard,Dorothy L.5 nov 1943-23 Jan 1961
/Woods,Herbert L.1893-1955   /Woodard,Loretta 4 feb 1923-13 may 1981
     Wynamie 1890-1958   /Woods,Gregory allen 11 Jan 1952-29 aug 78
/Woods,Charles E.1922-1928   /Woods,Herbert L.13 Jul 1918-16 mar 1969II
/Woods,Ruth E. 1926-27   /Woods,William A. 1882-1932
/Woodson,Robert H.1868-1950 /Woody,Roxie L.1891-1977
/Worden,Harry D.1878-1918   William A. 1881-1933
/Worden,Lucy E. 1876-1925   /Workman,Lillie Marie 1919-1948
/Workman,Norma 1918-1940   /Workman,Charles L.28 mar 1926-30 Jul 1965
#Workman,Alice 9 Jan 1936 40y /Workman,Otis 1890-1945
#Workman,George L.15 nov 1937 /Wray,Samuel 1877--
/Wright,Ethel M.1879-1972   Catherine Nance 1881-1932
/Wright,Edward E.1864-1915   /Wright,Roy S. 1903-1972
#Wright,Arthur Earl 1937 42y   Charlotte M.1909--
/Wroten,James G. 1884-1951   /Wroten,S.Evelyn 31 dec 1907-23 oct 1986
/Wroten,Nannie 1902--   /Wroten,Ernest 19 aug 1906-26 Jul 1958 II
/Wroten,James David   /Wroten,Bethel 18 aug 1928-14 dec 1929
     27 Jun 1924-6 nov 1979   Brice 9 Jun 1924-18 Jun 1928
/Wyont,Bootie 1911-1933   /Wyant,Cecil Jr.9 Jul 1928-27 Jul 1939
/Wyont,Belva 1916-1927   #Wyont,Phyllis Marie 1 dec 1936

/Yates,Harry V.1884-1964   #Yates,Catherine 9 aug 1934 80y14d
     Mamie 1890-1972   #Yates,John Wesley 7 mar 1930
/Yates,Edgar Owen 1907 inf   /Young,Minnie V.1877-1918
/Young,Jessie 1894-1965   Phillip H.1863-1946
     May M.1887-1955   Mary Caverlee 1870-1963
/Young,Phyllis 1936-1987   /Young,Stella I.1893-1937
/Zihlmann,William G.   /Zirkle,Bertha L.19 jun 1924-7 feb 1972
     29 oct 1898-22 mar 1986   /Zirkle,Charles C.29 feb 1916-
     Dorothy Hensley 22 mar 1907   15 apr 1967   WWII
few unmarked graves and few inf

H8A-PAUPER-R60 E to Washington Blvd rt 100y to Saltwell Rd-directly
across Saltwell from Highland.   Rachael Harbour mar 1990

/Adkins,Ruby F.1930-1983 /Adkins,Mattie 8 aug 1869-10 apr 1958
/Angalett,James D. /Adkins,Robert Clyde 30 apr 1904-12 Jan 75
    4 nov 1927-27 Jun 1985 /Arbaugh,Josiah 1870-1942
/Bartrum,Shelby /Beckett,Sarah E.8 nov 1877-14 oct 1948
    3 Jan 1903-9 sep 1984 /Bell,Wm.E.14 dec 1921-21 nov 1986 WWII
/Berry,John H. /Blair,Maxine 1942-1968
    21 Jul 1914-28 sep 1981 /Bowling,Vicky Lynn 11 Jul 1979-20 mar 88
/Bradford,Jimmy H. /Brewer,Wm.Mathew 8 feb 1976-9 feb 1981
    11 may 1943-13 sep 1987 /Christman,Susie 16 Jun 1900-14 aug 1984
/Clampett,Wm.Roy Jr.1941-1986/Collins,Gary Lee 22 dec 1948-23 Jun 1976
/Cummings,Charles K.1905-1979/Dwornick,Flossie 31 mar 1906-11 apr 1970
/Debnar,George 1885-1974 /Ellis,Effie 4 may 1889-23 Jun 1973
/Ferguson,Virgil 1912-1965 /Fielder,Josephine 1918-1983
/Forth,Margaret F. /Fradd,John 22 may 1911-8 apr 1982
    18 Jan 1906-18 dec 1962 /George,James B.1897-1974
/Hall,Dayne Leon /Hesson,Edith A. 23 mar 1931-21 aug 1973
    5 sep 1920-21 may 1984 WWII/Himmongs,Emory A.1941-1983
/Holley,Samuel Delure 1913-'79/Horrocks,Reba V.26 oct 1921-7 nov 1984
/Huff,Friend C.1875-1954 /Janey,James John 1 Jul 1927-7 aug 1987 K
/Jones,Margaret 1923-1984 /Jones,Bertha 1880-1965
/Jonson,John 1871-1944 /Kelly,Joseph E.15 oct 1922-4 Jun 1975
/Keith,Rose Belle 1930-1974 /Leport,James.1882-1958
/LoveJoy,Rosalie 1916-1963 /Lyons,Anthony M.30 dec 1967-16 feb 1968
/Lyons,Doris,1934-1985 /Mattox,Eddie Lee 10 apr 1959-2 mar 1971
/Mason,Harry R.1388-1961 /Meade,Anthony Ray 1969 inf
/Newsome,John S. /Null,Wilda F.20 sep 1920-2 Jan 1958
    4 apr 1905-7 apr 1972 /Otten,John L.22 apr 1925-22 apr 1983
/Pack,Albert Hayes 1881-1968 /Parkmokuk,Wassell 18 mar 1884-31 aug 1974
/Partlow,Steve A. /Partlow,Loretta L.30 oct 1937-7 mar 1984
    19 aug 1960-7 apr 1984 /Pound,Thomas Edgar 16 oct 1882-5 Jul 1966
/Reynolds,Stacy Renea 1975inf/Reynolds,Anthy Thos 7 oct 1865-2 mar 1941
/Robinson,Charles Edgar /Salmons,Larry T.1921-1977
    31 Jul 1913-27 aug 1985 /Scarberry,James G.24 dec 1930-3 sep 1981K
/Slaughter,John H.   K /Sowards,Harold 1906-1966
    2 aug 1925-21 dec 1986 /Sowards,Anthony S.31 may 1917-6 mar 82II
/Spry,Mary /Stearns,Elmer 2 nov 1923-11 aug 1986
    4 may 1924-26 apr 1986 /Sykes,James A.12 aug 1919-11 aug 1983 WII
/Sykes,Mildrew 1905-1980 /Thacker,Steve W.Jr.1969 inf
/Tanis,Russell A.1970-1986 /Townes,Joe 4 Jul 1908-9 nov 1976
/Turvey,Billy Joe 1928-1970 /Walker,Richard L.15 mar 1968 inf
/Watkins,Blanche S.9 mar 1980/Watts,Arlie M.17 mar 1922-28 apr 1983
/Welch,William Y.   WWII /White,Alex 11 Jul 1898-19 apr 1968
    17 Jun 1911-24 Jan 1985 /Wickline,Ray 19 aug 1956-8 mar 1987
/Wellman,Chester   WWII /Wiggins,Arch F. 1882-1937
    18 apr 1893-2 dec 1985 /Wingfield,emma Jo 15 sep 1925-20 mar 1986
/Williams,Otto L.1906-1962 /Wilson,alfred S.14 apr 1948-19 dec 1978
/Wilson,Pearl /Zirkle,Clarence 16 Jun 1925-26 Jan 1983
    15 dec 1889-23 apr 1986

51

#H9-WOODMERE-E section of Huntington 2701 Washington Blvd.(one block
from Norway Avenue(James River Turnpike)Incorporated 1917-oldest stone
1885.Perpetual Care.WPA Gideon Dist.(same book as Spring Hill).
1801m-645unm. 1938 WPA readings only.
Carrie Eldridge 20 nov 1990 (COMPARE NUMBER UNMARKED IN SPRING HILL)

/Abbott,Harold Armin 1921-24 /Adams,Elizabeth 1847-1937
/Abott,John E. 1866-1927   /Adams,Floyd L. 1884-1925
/Adams,Billy 1924-26   /Adams,F.A. 1885-1933
/Adams,inf 1937   /Adams,Mary Josephine 24 Jan 1936 83y2m6d
/Adams,Jane 1922-26   /Adams,Walter B. 1896-1927 WWI
/Adkins,Margaret Lou 1914-1929/Adcock,Marguerite Anna 1895-1927 w/CM
/Adkins,Olivet 1898-1925   /Adkins,Ralph C. 1900-1937
/Adkins,Arnie C.1888-1962   /Adkins,Bertha May 16 may 1893-2 Jan 1944
   Ora Lee 1894-1965   /Adkins,Cline 28 Jan 1914-23 Jan 1955
/Adkins,Alton B. 1903-1986   /Adkins,Clarence D.1916-1944
   Sylvia M.1909--   /Adkins,Charles H.21 nov 1921-21 may 1978WII
/Adkins,Cain 1891-1972   Janice J. 1935--
   Lestie 1906-1986   /Adkins,Charles C.1923-1981 WWII
/Adkins,Cecil W.1890-1974   /Adkins,Connie Faye 1956-1959
   Grace H. 1897-1979   /Adkins,Florence 11 dec 1900-8 Jan 1961
/Adkins,Gallie 1882-1949   Jean Ann 22 sep 1943-18 Jan 1948
   Carrie L. 1881-1969   /Adkins,George O.22 mar 1893-8 oct 1958WII
/Adkins,Emm 1877-1955   /Adkins,Grover C.11 apr 1888-9 aug 1952
/Adkins,Fletcher T.1885-87   /Adkins,Garland H,1904-1964
   Florence 1893-1968   Hester 1910-1979
/Adkins,Earl Mosser 1913-1975   Curtis W.1964-66
   Dora Letha 1921--   /Adkins,Gladys M.6 Jun 1903-28 apr 1974WWII
/Adkins,Lilly 30 mar 1916   /Adkins,Golden 2 may 1893-21 feb 1951
/Adkins,Henry 1908-1988   /Adkins,Homer C.15 mar 1911-1 Jun 1985
   Eulala B. 1912-1980   Polly E.1921--
/Adkins,Hisel 1877-1964   /Adkins,Johnny 9 Jul 1898-2 Jun 1963
   Rosa 1884-1964   Bonnie A.1905--
/Adkins,James H.1935--   /Adkins,John Lincoln 30 may 1924-16 dec 79
   Sally R. 1932-1975   /Adkins,Jack T. Jr.12 sep 1970-9 Jul 1975
/Adkins,James H. 1893-1960   /Adkins,Leonard H.1919--
   Lettie 1897-1983   Betty G.1920-1971
/Adkins,Lyle 1908-1984   /Adkins,Kenneth M.11 oct 1953-20 nov 1987
   Eula Price--   /Adkins,kenneth Ray 31 oct 1895-19 dec 1967
   Roger Lewis 1929   Ora R. 1897--
/Adkins,Norman E. 1901-1962 /Adkins,Montague 17 aug 1903-15 Jan 1986
   Beulah V.1905-1947   /Adkins,Orville C.1914-1976
/Adkins,Opie E. 1910-1970   Fay O. 1915--
   Emma W.1913--   /Adkins,Myrtle 1889-1978
/Adkins,Ottie 1892-1959   /Adkins,Sherman 1895-1972
   Linda 1901--   Carrie 1889-1971
/Adkins,Vernon V. 1901-1949 /Adkins,Sylvester 1891-1976
   Lula May 1905-1977   Kitty K. 1899-1980
/Adkins,Ward 1907-1981   /Adkins,Stanley Sr.26 may 1910-12 apr 87
/Adkins,William H. 1925--   /Adkins,Neva Swinburn 3 sep 1901-9 apr88
   Dorothy F. 1925--   /Adkins,Stanley Jr.13 aug 1930-15 oct 65
/Adkins,Wilburn 1897-1945WI   /Adkins,Wm.E.22 Jul 1926-26 sep 1969
/Ainslie,Margareta 1874-1936 /Alberts,Sherman 17 sep 1938 44y3m3m
/Aldredge,Alta Hinds 1887-1923/Allen,Charles A.29 oct 1938 59y3m
/Alvis,Cornelius A. 1856-1933 /Altice,Edna 20 nov 1896-19 feb 1920w/CJ

/Archibald,Chas.Rhodes 1882-27
/Archibald,Fannie S.
    16 aug 1937 74y2m14d
/Arkell,Gohen 16 apr 1939 44y
/Arrington,Mary Ellen 1869-37
/Arthur,Marvin E. 1902-1933
/Arvis,Charles 1878-1921
/Arvis,Ival R. 1922-32
/Ashburn,Clarence M. 1883-1935
/Ashburn,Jean d1924
/Ashworth,Peter H,1867-1937
/Athey,Rev.T.H. 1870-1933
/Atkins,Tom D.1917-1978
    Joy W. 1929--
/Atkins,Jed Allen 1954-1978
/Aver,Henry 1869-1935
/Aver,Elizabeth 1871-1938
/Barber,George L. 1872-1929
/Back,Nellie 1897-1922
/Bailey,Clarence J, 1887-1929
/Bailey,Edward C. 1878-1936
/Bailey,Ella 1860-1932
/Bailey,George W. 1857-1922
/Bailey,Mary E. 1859-1929
/Ballard,A.M. 1891-1936
/Bane,Garry 1938 inf
/Banga,J.Charles 1914-1939
/Banks,V.Anise 1894-1929
/Barrett,John W. 1876-1935
/Barron,C.W. 1905-1934
/Barron,Mabel C. 1886-1919
/Bates,Willa 1902-1921
/Baysden,Wayne B.1858-1923
/Beardslea,Wm.Edgar 1870-1924
/Beckett,Glenn E., 1906-1926
/Beckett,Lucy 1853-31 mar 1938
/Beckett,Beulah 1901-1981
    Frances Marshall 1920-88
/Beckett,Frank M. 1869-1946
    Eliza C. 1871-1957
    Ada 1892-1967
    Claude T. 1896-1974
    Dovel 1907-1963
    Charles D.1913-1961
/Beckner,Nora J.1903-1928
/Beheler,Josephine 25 feb 1931
/Beller,Wm.Fredrick 1916-1921
/Belville,Samuel 1860-1935
/Benton,Anna Vest 1895-1924
/Berthold,James Ricd.1918-1925
/Beseler,Wilkelmine Sophia
    17 apr 1937 46y11m17d
/Bess,Frazier D. 1888-1931
/Bevan,Ada Lena 1898-1920

/Andrews,Marjorie Alice 1936 inf
/Arganbright,George A.1863-1936
/Armstrong,Charles C. 1874-1938
/Armstrong,Mary C. 1876-1928
/Armstrong,Nellie Alexander
    14 oct 1937 67y5m26d
/Armstrong,Richard D. 1869-1935
/Ash,Bertha D. 1866-1936
/Ash,Rev.David L.23 oct 1855-9 feb 1925
/Ash,Dora B.Hammond 27feb 1861-8 sep 1931
/Ash,Rev.J.M.1869-1930
/Atkins,James G.24 may 1912-26 oct 1982
/Atkins,Tom David 1 seo 1881-8 apr 1962
    Ada H.30 Jul 1886-23 oct 1969
/Atkinson,A.Hale 1914-1925
/Atkinson,Mary Mabel 13 mar 1930 38y3d
/Auvil,Mary Edna 1879-1925 w/o S.Harry
/Backus,Rev.R.G>16 mar 1867-19 Jun 1931
/Baer,Teckla Jane 14 feb 1939
/Baisden,Walter W. 1876-1929
/Baker,Drussia O. 1910-1927
/Baker,Elizabeth L.6 nov 1936 95y5m16d
/Baker,Willaerd P. Jr.1909-1935
/Ball,Charlie 1876-1923
/Ball,Ivan H.1904-1923
/Ball,Joseph S.1858-1929
/Banfield,Dr.James C. 1859-1934
/Barbour,Rachel Dillon 1892-1922
/Barnhart,Vina Glenola 9 oct 1935 46y11m
/Bartley,Isaac Albert 25 nov 1933 61y5m27
/Baum,Villa Merle 1902-1922 d/o NJ&Louise
/Bayliss,Melissa E.1865-1932
/Beard,Flora E. 1856-1932
/Beazley,Phillip A. 2 feb 1937 72y9m9d
/Beckett,L:illian E. 1911-1929
/Beckett,Reese J.1869-1924
/Beckett,Everett J.1908-1984
    Josephine M. 1922--
/Beckett,James E. 1871-1949
    Cora Inez 1883-1970
    Valka C. 1898-1972
    Grace W. 1903-1988
    Emma S. 1900--
/Beckner,P.E.1887-1930
/Beckner,Ruth 1898-1925 w/o Delbert
/Beidenmiller,Chas.Henry 1892-1928
/Bentley,Colby Charles 28 mar 1938 inf
/Berisford,John Elliott 1928-1930
/Berry,Elbert T.16 dec 1937 44y9m23d
/Berry,Frances Baker 8 mar 1939 59y4m13d
/Berry,John W. 1847-1927
/Beswick,Augusta 15 may 1851-8 oct 1924
    Samuel 14 may 1855-2 dec 1921

/Bevan,Fred Carl 1885-1935
/Bevan,M.M. 1863-1922
   Mrs.M.M. 1864-1938
/Bevan,Ray F.1921-1938
/Bias,James K. 1845-1923
/Bias,Joe 1878-1902
/Bias,Lucy C. 1854-1937
/Bias,Martha R. 1920-1925
/Bias,Liddie E.1882-1923
/Bick,Thomas 1878-1928
/Billus,Martha A. 1839-1923
/Black,Charles S. 1909-1928
/Black,Mary H. 1865-1921
/Black,Walter 1904-1923
/Blair,J.W. 21 mar 1929
/Blair,Walter Gary 1932-38L&R
/Blake,James N, 1878-1937
/Blake,Leland Lee
   23 dec 1938 25y1m27d
/Bledsoe,Louise 1842-1925
/Bledsoe,Champ C.1911-1971
   Hazel S.1915--
/Bledsoe,Luther E.1903-1987
   Edith W. 1904-1976
/Bloss,Susie K. 1870-1922
/Blosser,E.E. 1862-1925

/Body,Richard F. 1870-1932
/Boley,Lelia A.1874-1934
/Bolling,Julian E. 1876-1927
/Bondurant,Emma H.1880-1929
/Booten,Mary Ann 1926-27
/Boothby,Viretta 1888-1925
/Boothe,Madia 1892-1929
/Boster,Alvin Ed.Jr.1928-36
/Bostic,Charles M. 1866-1918
/Bostic,Sophronia J.1869-1931
/Bostic,Charles M. 1866-1918
   Sophronia 1869-1931
   Bernice E. 1897-1945

/Bowen,Alderson 1872-1930
/Bowen,Bascum 1869-1928
/Bowen,Dorothy Eloise 1921
/Bower,Giles M. 1891-1936
/Bowman, Joseph C.1872-1935
/Boyd,Bertha A. 1896-1924
/Boyd,John C.1877-1920
/Boyd,Robert P. 1864-1924
/Brewer,Arthur M. 1889-1927
/Brewer,Evelyn Ruby d 1920
/Brinker,Annie E. 1859-1937
/Brinker,A.G.W. 1853-1926
/Brinker,D.H. 1859-1922

/Beswick,Clark M. 1885-1886
/Bevins,inf d 1939
/Bias,Calvin A. 20 Jun 1854-5 aug 1937
/Bias,Gussie 27 apr 1935 25y1m20d
/Bias,Jacob B.31 mar 1934 73y
   Miriam A.Bledsoe 1864-1937d/o Moses
/Bias,Mary Grace 1 Jan 1938
/Bias,R.A. 1850-1912
/Billups,Emma McComas 1858-1952
/Billups,John S. 1880-1936
/Bishop,Thomas Jr.1888-1919
/Black,Glenn Giles 31 aug 1934 4y
/Black,Susie 8 mar 1934 33y6m10d
/Blackwell,J.S. 1884-1928
/Blain,Gerturde Duke 1910-1931
/Blankenship,E.G. 5 may 1855-2 Jan 1934
/Blankenship,Louise Caroline
   16 mar 1933 71y7m1d
/Blake,May 6 mar 1902-2 nov 1923
/Blake,Richard Alex 1918 inf
/Bledsoe,Sadie Johnson 1897-1941 w/Homer
/Bledsoe,James Ed.20 mar 1921-5 oct 1972
/Blevins,Ellen 1872-1930
/Blood,Edith 13 feb 1939 60y3m9d
/Blower,Verkin 1917-1935
/Boecker,K.Edward 4 oct 1917-11 apr 1984
   Mildred L.Fellure ---2 may 1985
/Bolin,Melissa Amm 4 dec 1937 73y8m3d
/Bolin,Charles L.1895-1930
/Bond,A.F. 1867-1924
/Booth,Charles J. 1861-1936
/Booth,Jack Richard 1927-1929
/Booth,Mamie Ellis 1898-1929
/Booth,Paul 22 mar 1936 WWI
/Booth,Victoria 1859-1929
/Bourner,Eva 18 Jan 1936 40y27d
/Bostic,John Sherman-23 nov 1883-5/27/52
   Mayme Heizer 12 Jan 1892-4 may 1970
/Bostic,Edsel A. 1931-1979
/Bostic,Lola Me 14 may 1901-20 sep 1968
/Bowe,James Hughes 18 Jun 1924 WWI
/Bowe,LaFayette 1854-1921
/Bowen,Alpha 17 dec 1878-17 Jan 1928
/Bowen,Herbert C. 3 mar 1937 41y7m18d
/Bowles,Oscar N. 1841-1924
/Bowles,Veronica Winona 1904-1936
/Boyce,James Herbert 3 feb 1936 76y5m29
/Braden,Ruth Bryant 1908-1928
/Brammer,Bertha 1901-1936
/Brammer,George W. 1850-1926
/Brammer,Nancy Sue 21 aug 1938 7y
/Bridge,Nannie V. 1873-1935
/Bromley 25 aug 1938 inf
/Bronson,Dorothy Kendle 1910-1928

/Brinker,Edward E. 1863-1929
/Brothers,W.Frank 1898-1936
/Brown,Della M. 1869-1937
/Brown,Nettie V. 1874-1931
/Brown,Ollie 28 feb 1939 61y
/Brown,Sanford 1875-1926
/Brown,R.L. 1885-1927
/Bruce,Nancy J. 1845-1933
/Bryan,Alice 1861-1934
/Bryan,Bettie E. 1863-1935
/Bryan,Denver C. 1906-1932
/Bryan,Dr.H.H. 1852-1924
/Bryan,Julia Ann 1850-1929
/Bryan,W.Pickney 1846-1925
/Bryant,Mattie 10 apr 1934 56y
/Bryant,Ora Frances 1897-1935
/Buchanan,Charles H.1866-1933
    Rilla 1864-1924
/Bugg,C.W. 1875-1928
/Burgess,Alfred B. 1848-1927
/Burgess,Maria L. 1854-1931
/Burk,Rebecca 4 Jan 1934 85y
/Burke,James L. 1889-1929
/Burke,Sallie M. 1853-1928
/Burlew,Rena B. 1911-1935
/Bush,Betty Embry 1858-1924
/Bush,mary E. 27 nov 1934 66y
/Bush,Oliver Floyd
    12 Jul 1935   55y7m28d
/Butcher,Etta 1883-1926
/Byus,Jennie 1865-1937
/Cadle,John V. 1857-1931
/Cadle,Sarah V. 1847-1939
/Callihan,M.E. 1868-1936
/Cardwell,Henry C. 1857-1925
/Cardwell,Margaret S. 1855-38
/Carpenter,Oscar A. 1887-1938
/Carper,Hollis M.d 1937
/Casto,Herman, G. 1875-1924
/Carter,Harriett E. 1846-1936
/Carter,John G. 1859-1923
/Carter,Thomas H.1882-1927
/Carter,Sapho Bryan 1890-1977
/Carver,Robert L. 1875-1929
/Chafin,Esther 1859-1930
/Chafin,F.Marian 1855-1903
/Chafin,James A. 1890-1903
/Chafin,John B. 1879-1899
/Chapman,Alice M. 1860-1939
/Chapman,Alma T. 1883-1924
/Chapman,Benjamin H. 1857-1935
/Chapman,C.Linnville 1896-84
    Irene J.1898-1970
/Chapman,Bonnie Mathes 1913-

/Brooks,Alice Roberson 1879-1922
/Brooks,Thomas H. 1879-1938
/Broughman,Joseph A.1904-1967
    Sarah M.1880-1976
/Broughman,Sue 1905-1983
/Browning,Essie 30 sep 1937 29y2m20d
/Brumfield,James Mitchell 1891-1931
/Brumfield,Eunice M. 1918-1932

/Bryan,Cora May 26 aug 1938 43y3m4d
/Bryan,Dr.George E. 9 feb 1860-21 Jul 34
/Bryan,Judge T.J. 1854-1923
/Bryan,Martha A. 1872-1927
/Bryan,Susan Blain 14 feb 1855-14 aug 38
/Bryan,William Pickney 1846-1925
    Julia Ann 1850-1929
/Buckner,Charles McVea 1885-1936
/Buffington,Peter Cline II 1868-1938
/Bunch,Norvell Floyd 1877-1929
/Bunch,Zachariah A. 1848-1926
/Burger,E.E. 12 apr 1898-23 Jan 1924
/Burger,Merle Ena 1886-1938
/Burgin,Frank H. 10 Jun 1938 77y3m27d
/Burns,Elmer V. 1862-1924
/Burns,Ruth Violet M. 1926-1933
/Burton,Edith E. 2 apr 1936 52y9m27d
/Bussell,Elmer 1853-1938
/Butler,Biddie Isabel 30 may 1933 553y2m2
/Butler,Charles 1864-1923
/Butler,Clara Myers 1884-1932
/Butler,Homer F. 1882-1920
/Cain,Robert Dunn 1912-1922
/Caldwell,Margaret 1899-1922
/Camp,Gustie Elizabeth 1889-1939
/Campbell,Charles Wm. 1856-1935
/Carico,John W. 1858-1931
/Carico,Mary F. 1857-1920
/Castle,Charles E. 1866-1922
/Castle,John A. 1879-1936
/Cartmill,James A. 31 dec 1931 88y2m10d
/Cartmill,James L. 1871-1922
/Cartmill,Lucy A. 9 nov 1935 88y

/Catron,Pau. 1907-1931
/Chalmers,Sidney E. 1858-1922
/Chambers,David 1855-1924
/Chambers,Emma A. 1861-1926
/Chambers,Martha Ann 1867-1939
/Chambers,Okey 1884-1932
/Chapman,Mary E. 14 Jun 1880-31 may 1937
/Chapman,T.J. 1885-1934

/Chapman,Allie 30 dec 1866-6 oct 1941
/Chapman,Chalsy L. 24 oct 1906-1989

55

/Chapman,Bill F. 1927-1969   Opal R. 1 sep 1908--
/Chapman,Earl B. 1919-1963 /Chapman,Charles A. 27 mar 1864-27 apr 1940
/Chapman,Emery H. 1892-1964 /Chapman,David S.16 nov 1928-20 sep 1977
 Hattie E. 1895-1976 /Chapman,Forrest R.10 sep 1903-22 oct 1973
/Chapman,Eugene O. 1912--   Glayds M. 17 Jan 1904-31 Jul 1955
 Ruth M. 1911--   /Chapman.Henry L.28 may 1926-24 may 1969
/Chapman,Frank 1885-1953   Erna 1921--
 Isabel H., 1883-1964 /Chapman,Hurshel R. 1904-1977 WWII
 Lola B. 1908-1987   Guy Melvin 22 dec 1910-6 aug 1973
/Chapman,Jack D. 1922--   /Chapman,Isaac M. 1875-1944 s/oHL&SJ
 Flona L. 1896-1976   Ethel Sanders 1880-1937
 Joyce M. 1929--   Nina Grace 29 Jan 1884-24 apr 1958
/Chapman,J.Walker 1874-1960 /Chapman,Parker W. 8 sep 1904-17 may 1958
/Chapman,Madelyn 1918-1979 /Chapman,Oliver K. 1901-1981
/Chapman,T.J. 1885-1934   Letha Rowsey 1900-1989
 Fem G. 1891-1981   /Chapman,William M. 1899-1980
           Eva Jane 1908--

/Charles,George D. 1898-1929 /Childers,Zilpha Marie 1906-1922
/Charles,John G. 1917-1923 /Childers,Nevada B.1876-1938
/Charles,Mary Catherine 1938 /Chipps,Richard 7 mar 1939 6y
/Charles,J.Lundy 1882-1931 /Christy,Elizabeth E. 1874-1937
/Church,alex Austin 1882-1938 /Clagg,Ida 24 aug 1938
/Church,George L. 1898-1918 /Clark,Adah Lee 1872-1936
/Church,John W. 1842-1898 /Clark,Frank 1859-1935
/Clay,Elizabeth B.1873-1937 /Clark,F.Hampton 1925-28
/Clay,Mary Jane 1864-1934 /Clark,John E. 1881-1925
/Claypool,Garnet Sheets 1882-21/Clark,Louie W. 1883-1934
/Clements,Amelia L,   /Clendennin,Lottie M. 1878-1920
 25 mar 1881-3 aug 1936 /Cliness,George W. 1852-1926
/Clements,Clarence W.1909-1934/Clingenpeel,Josepine 1878-1925 w/CC
/Clements,Walter J. 1890-1934 /Clutts,James Standard 1917-1925
/Cobb,George W. 1881-1922 /Cofer,Charity A. 1881-1926
/Coleman,Maggie E. 1859-1936 /Cogar,Thomas F. 2 oct 1938 48y11m9d
/Coleman,Paul N. 1922-26   /Colliflower,B.F. 1872-1935
/Coleman,Ruth Cooper 1906-1932/Colliflower,Emma 1872-1924
/Coleman,Sadie Davis   /Colvin,William Thomas 1872-1932
 26 feb 1939 47y4m12d   /Cometto,James A. 28 mar 1881-8 feb 1937
/Connelly,Everrett M. 1862-23 /Conrad,Jessie Lee 1924 Inf
/Cook,Eugene B. 1903-1918 /Cook,Ethel Allene 14 sep 1879-24 apr 25
/Cook,Florence 1872-1934   /Cook,John Jay Jr. 1909-1931
/Cook,Martha Amm 1870-1923 /Cook,Mary C. 1870-1923
/Cook,Mildred F. 1859-1936 /Cook,Mary Oliva Thacher
/Cook,William 1862-1929   24 Jul 1856-28 apr 1926
/Cooper,Sarah E. 1873-1934 /Copeland,Mary F. 1861-1935
/Cooper,T.R. 1842-1922   /Copenhaver,Harry S. d1923
/Corns,Mary J. 1860-1927   /Copenhaver,Margaret E. 1925-26
/Cort,Belle E. 1868-1921   /Coryell,Blanche E. 1881-1933 w/oCE
/Cort,Lewis H. 1853-1924   /Cowdin,Althea Elizabeth 1884-1926wCW
/Cort,Lewis H.Jr.1893-1929 /Cowles,Ruby Pearl 1903-1938
/Courts,L.S. 1859-1938   /Cowles, Inf 1938 s/o VJ&Ruby
/Cox,Andrew Jackson 1855-1921 /Crabtree,Rev.A.M. 1869-1933
/Cox,Nelson C.Jr.1922-23   /Craft,Willie 1875-1937 w/o James
/Craner,Matilda S. 1860-1924 /Craig,Lola Mae 16 nov 1897-6 sep 1939
/Crawford,Bernard Neal 1897-35/Crane,Lora May Smith 1887-1933 w/oBert

/Crawford,Genoa Vivian 1903-20
/Crawford,John C. 1861-1934
/Crow,Edgar C. 1861-1929
/Crow,Edgar Garred 1900-1939
/Cundiff,John T. 1855-1927
/Cunningham,Alma G.1889-1930
/Cunningham,Jack 1918-1939
/Cunningham,R.E. 1879-1930
/Curry,Arnold H. Jr.1921-23
/Curry,Nannie J.1869-1930
/Dakin,Elizabeth C. d 1934
/Damron,Sallie C. 1887-1937
/Davidson,Emily 1854-1922
/Davidson,James A. 1854-1939
/Davidson,Vinson R. 1900-1922
/Davis,Bertha 1846-1921
/Davis,Charles D. 1845-1924
/Davis,Garnet 1891-1935
/Davis,Nellie 1887-1933
/Davis,Ona 1896-1936
/Davis,Otis 1867-1925
/Davis,Richard A. 1915-1924
/Davis,Robert Gene 1927-1931
/Day,George W. 1861-1931
/Deal,Ralph R. 1872-1919
/Dean,James W.A. 1856-1936
/Dean,Leonidas T. 1872-1931
/Denney,Stella A. 1881-1931
/Derwacter,John S. 1854-1925
/Derwacter,Mary L. 1855-1934
/Dial,A.Gallie 1868-1934
/Dial,John Ward d1925
/Dial,W.Verlin 1894-1918 WWI
/Dickinson,Albert H.1893-1936
/Diddle,Ernest B. 1898-1920
/Diddle,James A. 1871-1935
/Dillon,Polly A. 1845-1926
/Dills,Mollie G. 1867-1926
/Dingess,John G.4 may 1934 29y
/Dixon,Beulah Catron 1894-1917
/Dodds,C.E. 1853-1932
/Dodds,Homer F. 1889-1921 WWI
/Donovan,Martha R.1879-1936wCP
/Douglas,Robt.Winfield 1922-36
/Douglas,Wm.McClelland 1888-28
/Draper,Lola Louise 1918-1922
/Duke,Milton S. 1867-1924
/Duncan,Cordie 1890-1932
/Duncan,Fredrick A. 1889-1918
/Duncan,Henry C.1843-1932
/Duncan,Sidney A. 1863-1929
/Durea,Charles A. 1900-1938
/Durea,Charles E. 1866-1930
/Durea,Jennie 1869-1924

/Crites,Rev.John W. 1857-1933
/Crouse,C.W. 1860-1920
/Crummett,Martin J. 1858-1925
/Cummings,Emma E. 1858-1923
/Cummings,William R. 1850-1918
/Cummings,George F. 1886-1937
/Cunningham,.Mary A. 1873-1919
/Cunningham,Mere McDowell 1885-1938
/Cyrus,Louise M. 1914-1920
/Dailey,John T. 1923 inf
/Dallis,Charles Jr. 1920-23
/Daniels,F.M. 1852-1924
/Daniels,Herman C. 1887-1932
/Daniels,Lewis Andres 1860-1927
/Davin,Charles Ashley 1879-1881
/Davin,John 1848-1912
    Mary Montgomery 1858-1920
/Davin,Katherine Bidgood 1886-1935w/Harlo
/Davis,John Love 18 sep 1933 70y7m25d
/Davis,Lena 12 Jan 1939
/Davis,Louise Kathryn 1920 inf
/Davis,Susan Venora 1936-38
/Dawson,Alex C. 1881-1919
/Dawson,Helen B. 1 dec 1934
/Dawson,Justine 1909-1930
/Dearing,Virginia E. 1853-1922
/Deegans,Kathryn E.Morrison
    20 Jan 1914-7 Jun 1982
/Derbyshire,Charles Edward 1880-1935
/DeSilvey,Isabelle 1866-1925
/Dick,Lee S. 1854-1925
/Dickey,Elsie May 1857-1930
/Dickey,John Clifford 1852-1936
/Dickey,W.R. 1880-1936
/Diehl,Abraham 1857-1932
/Diehl,Bertha O'Dell 1888-1926
/Diehl,Elizabeth M.1860-1930
/Diehl,inf 1922 s/o Louis & Ann
/Diehl,Mary Ann 1915-1926
/Diehl,Wm.Francis 1890-1938
/Donahue,Bessie 1908-1932
/Donnally,J.H.1873-1931
/Dowdy,Charles E.31 mar 1938 54y9m7d
/Dowdy,Leslie Thomas 21 Jul 1882-23 Jul34
/Dowdy,Reba Meek 10 nov 1889-21 apr 1939
/Druen,Lindsey Lucille 1907-1926
/Duling,Mary Bayne 1896-1933
/Duncan,Martha J. 1845-1932
/Duncan,Michael L 1852-1924
/Duncan,William F. 24 Jun 1938 63y1m27d
/Dunfee,Gladys L. 1905-1926
/Dunfee,Henry O. Jr.1917-1933
/Dunlap,Wm.Henry 6 nov 1938 63y7m29d
/Durrett,Alma Beatrice 8 sep 1939 39y9m10d

/Durfee,Harry H. 1865-1929 /Durrett,James Franklin 1860-1934
/Dyer,Irvin Dutch 1899-1939 /Dye,Caledonia Gilfelen 1858-1925
/Eakin,John B. 1872-1936 /Easley,Jack Hatcher 1919-1921
/Earl,Mary Lou 1930-1938 /Easley,Mary L.17 apr 1937
/Earle,Billie Bert 1921-1930 /Easterling,Patricia Ann 7 oct 1937 12y
/Eaves,Lola L. 13 dec 1935 16y /Elliot,Julien P.1903-1934
/Eblin,Clark A. 1875-1933 /Elliot,Kate Shepard 27 oct 1845-1 may 32
/Elam,Charles 30 Jun 1934 inf /Ellis,Kendall D.1892--
/Ellis,John F. 1858-1925 Anna Rowsey 1896-1987
/Ellis,Clara B. 1886-1924 /Ellis,Maria 1870-1938
/Ellis,Cora H. 1899-1925 William 8 Jun 1938 79y8m3d
/Elswick,Anthony C. 1885-1920 /Enoch,Oliver C. 1852-1928
/Enslow,George W. 1866-1920 /Erskine,Clayton H.22 nov 1934 45y
/Esque,Hamlin 1893-1922 /Erskine,Bernard Eldon 1908-1923
/Esque,Leah Louise 1922-23 /Erwin,Carl Edwin 17 dec 1931 inf
/Evans,Mary Ida 4 may 1936 50y /Evendoll,Peter 16 mar 1933 63y8m12d
/Evans,William 1898-1935 /Ewen,Ida Taylor 1869-1927
/Farley,Edward G. 1866-1934 /Farah,Mabiha Facorey 1 Jan 02-14 apr 35
/Farley,Elizabeth M. 1859-1924 w/o David
 James Wm.1857-1928 /Farr,John S.Sr.18 mar 1862-21 mar 1936
/Farley,Thomas J.1867-1928 /Farrish,Maurine Morrison
/Farrar,Amine L. 1860-1936 30 dec 1910-26 Jun 1982
/Faulconer,A.W. 1845-1927 /Farris,Anna 1867-1936
/Faust,Fred L. 1885-1929 /Faulkner,Cecily Margaret 1887-1938
/Faust,Fred Rowland 1914-19 /Faulkner,John 1856-1929
/Ferrell,W.C. 1904-1929 /Fellure,Bert 1884-1955 s/oWashington
/Ferguson,Clara 10 feb 1936 62y Lula J.Johnson 1893-1964 d/oHJ&C
/Ferguson,Richard C.1873-1939 /Fillinger,Robert 1912-1923
/Fink,Hugh Crockett 1871-1926 /Field,Linda Smith 10 oct 1880-27 aug 39
/Fisher,Bert E. 1898-1929 /Fizer,Edward E. 1910-1936
/Fisher,Morris 1869-1936 /Fleshman,H.H. 1866-1933
/Fisher,Rosena F. 1887-1925 /Flory,Cora Lee 1885-1921
/Flower,Rosalie 1930-1936 /Floyd,Garnet Elaine 1913-1938
/Follrod,Nellie C 1902-1935 /Floyd,Mollie May 1901-1926
/Forbes,Archie 1889-1931 /Floyd,Wilson 27 sep 1938
/Foster,Alice 1866-1935 /Foard,Mary Morgan 1921-1929 d/o D&O
/Foster,John A. 1865-1937 /Fragulis,Marie 23 sep 1938 30y4m29d
/Fowler,Elinor Fay 1929-30 /Fraley,G.H.1899-1925
/Fowler,Roy 1899-1931 /Frampton,Lee Wilson 1897-1928
/France,Dosha 1864-1936 /Frampton,Peyton G. 1891-1936
/France,Margaret L. 1898-1925 /Franklin,marvin G.1900-1930
/France,William H. 1902-1939 /Francis,John Elliot 1911-1934 s/oJD&PE
/Frew,mary 2 apr 1935 68y11m28 /Freeman,Aubrey Raymond 24 mar 1923 18y
/Fry,Margaret E. 1906-1922 /Freeman,Charles Hughes 3 Jul 1920 66y
/Fry,Mary Wilcox 28 oct 1936 /Freeman,Fay M.4 mar 1891-3 may 1931
/Fulks,John W. 1863-1922 /Fuller,Arnold 1872-1932
/Fullerton,Earl S. 1899-1936 /Fuller,Gorden P.1874-1922
/Fulton,Josph W. 1887-1930 /Fuller,Jean 24 Jul 1923-9 Jan 1935
/Fulton,Mary Kathryn 1925-26
/Gallaher,John T. 1862-1923 /Gang,Charles 24 sep 1913-12 Jul 1934
/Galloway,Dorothy A.1931-1968 /Gamer,Virginia Midkiff 1902-21
/Garland,Daniel R. 1857-1937 /Gardner,martha Ellis 22 Jan 1931 7y
/Garland,Loma B. 1883-1933 /Garner,Va.Midkiff 1902-1921
/Garred,Lou E. 1857-1938 /Garrison,John F. 1868-1928

/Garred,Owen D. 1852-1933
/Geiger,John C. 1877-1924
/George,William L. 1924-1931
/George,Hoe Kissinger
    27 apr 1931
/Gerrald,Perlina 1859-1918
/Gibson,Allyn Farl 1887-1937
/Gibson,Era 1880-1932
/Gibson,James T. 1857-1923
/Gibson,Menerva 1850-1939
/Gibson,Minnie C.1880-1929
/Gill,Ray 1896-1963
    Maude 1896-1974
/Gillespie,George W.1869-1932
/Gillispie,Melba S.1903-1938
/Gilliland,Stanley L.1908-1929
/Ginn,Drusilla E. 1926 inf
/Givens,Emmet E.1899-1925
/Givens,Okey E. 1907-1927
/Glover,Ida mae 1869-1938
/Goekemeyer,Henry 1862-1927
/Golden,Sarah A.1864-1927
/Gooch,James W. 1864-1924
/Gore,A.W. 1854-1924
/Gore,Jennie 4 aug 1933 60y
/Gottshall,C.H. 1874-1929
/Gould,Earl M. 1895-1938
/Graham,Daisy R. 1895-1933
/Graham,Jonathan Thomas
    1865-1938
/Graham,Mary Louisa 1865-1932
/Grate,W.M. 1878-1937
/Gray,George B.1855-1929
/Gray,Julia Butler 1864-1911
/Grimmett,Robt.Kilgore1949-195-
/Griffith,Myrtle Bowen 1906-29
/Grizzell,Patsy Ann 9/8/1939
/Grogan,Jesse H. 1880-1925
/Grose,Mary C. 1896-1932
/Grose,Mary V.1855-1922
/Grose,T.W. 1840-1933
/Gwinn,John T. 1879-1927
/Haddox,Hannah Catherine
    17 nov 1938 80y10m4d
/Haddox,Lathrop Latrobe
    1 feb 1939 84y7m16d
/Hall,Charles H. 1836-1921
/Hall,Eliza E. 1855-1939
/Hall,Ella Vansant 1855-1926
/Hall,Harriet M. 1840-1922
/Hall,Samuel B.1855-1937
/Hall,William T. 1859-1928
/Hall,William H. 1880-1926
/Hamer,John M. 1859-1930

/Garvin,Audryn Duncan 1902-1932
/Gebhardt,John B. 1849-1932
    Caroline Von Burg-1856-1935
/Gerlach,H.Martin 1879-28(Dr.)
    Amy G.Hamilton 4 sep 1859-9 oct 1926
/Gerlach,George W.25 jan 1937 62y4m10d
/Gibson,Charles R. 1885-1929
/Gibson,David Burger d1929
/Gibson,Sarah Ellen 1859-1935
/Gibson,Wm.Bailey d1928
/Gill,James Benton 1931 inf
/Gill,Orville G.1891-1956
    Islea R. 1894-1989
/Gillette,Emmett E.1918-1921
/Gillette,Willie Mae 27 nov 1937 55y7m14d
/Gillmore,Elizabeth J.1846-1920
/Gilmore,Lena Combs 1892-1931
/Gilmore,Thomas B.1841-1928
/Glenn,Don Oliver 1920-1929
/Godwin,A.Maude 1931
/Godwin,William H. 1909-1931
/Goff,T.N. 1 nov 1876-30 apr 1939
/Gordon,Minnie L.24 aug 1889-8 feb 1937
/Gosnay,Alice B.1858-1919
/Gosnay,Thomas J. 1841-1920
/Goucher,Frank A. 3 dec 1936 61y
/Goulding,Ellen E. 1890-1919
/Goulding,George C.1881-1885
/Goulding,Oscar J. 1910-1920
/Grant,Eldridge 1889-1924
/Grant,Rosie B.1892-1938
/Graves,George W. 1848-1927
/Green,Mildred E.Mosier 1907-1925wBW
/Greenwell,Owen W. 1881-1937
/Grimmett,Ralph E.22 jul 1906-7 nov 1985
/Gregory,Jean Alexander 1871-1932
/Gregory,Peter 1841-1937
/Gregory,Rachael Josephine 1848-1920
/Grubb,James H.1866-1936
/Grubbs,Columbia Ann 17 jan 1937 69y10m2d
/Grubbs,Leon Claude 10 sep 1931 66y4m1d

/Hagen,Kathryn Wyant 21 aug 1937 21y3m28d
/Hagen,Mary F. 1897-1925
/Hager,William A. 20 feb 1936 54y7m23d
/Hager,W.C. 1874-1939
/Hall,Daisy 1896-1926
/Hall,Elinor Franklin 1919-1924
/Hall,Henry P. 4 jan 1927 62y8m25d
/Hall,James P. 1844-1926
/Hall,Rhoda 26 jan 1932 69y9m16d
/Hall,William A. 1924-27
/Halstead,Fannie M. 1864-1936
/Halstead,J.Bert 1872-1924

/Hamill,Roy H. 1884-1927 /Halstead,Wellington G. 1859-1936
/Hamilton,A.A.Jr.1887-1929 /Hamlin,B.F. 1877-1929
/Hamilton,Charles H. 1922-1936/Hamlin,Charles 1865-1921
/Hamilton,James O. 1903-1921 /Hamlin,Mack T. 1877-1920
/Hamilton,Martha H.1853-1927 /Hamlin,Walter 1882-1921
/Hamm,Charles M. 1864-1930 /Hammock,E.S. 3 mar 1938
/Hamrick,Dorcas Adari 192-13 /Hammock,S.Wilson 1893-1933
/Handley,Fred G. 1849-1935 /Handley,Charles Morris 1886-1924
/Handley,George C. 1873-1922 /Handley,Mary R. Morris 1847-1929
/Handley,Shelton G. 1897-1923 /Handley,Stella 1875-1923
/Hanley,Patricia Ann 1933 inf /Hannan,Russell H.15 oct 1894-5 Jun 1922
/Hannoon,Hadgia 1859-1927 /Hanshaw,Elizabeth Oakes 1909-1936
/Harbour,D.Curtis 1893-1929 /Harbour,Jennie 1863-1930
/Harbour,Mack F. 1878-1928 /Harbour,Robert 1864-1932
/Hardin,J.H. 1872-1929 /Hardy,Tenia A. 1863-1929
/Harlan,Louisa 1915-1919 /Harless,Albert M. 1873-1936
/Harold,George P. 1883-1937 /Harless,Allen R. 1893-1937
/Harpold,Elizabeth 1876-1933 /Harper,Roland Algerman 1896-1924
/Harpold,George W. 1865-1930 /Harper,Roland A.Jr.1923 inf
/Harris,Emma S.1855-1938 /Harrison,Mozelle Swann 1915-1974
/Harris,E.W. 1888-1936 /Hartenbach,Katherine 1854-1939
/Harris,W.O. 1887-1930 /Hartenbach,Hnery 1853-1935
/Harvey,Hary Hagen 1887-1939 /Haskell,Homer 1863-1930
/Hastings,Herman Waldo 1923-26 /Hatfield,Don 8 apr 19115-4 mar 1959
/Hatfield,William A. 1919-1989   Esthel 20 Jul 1893-15 sep 1961
   Toka A. 1922-- /Hatfield,Howard D.1909-1985
/Hatfield,Leander 1868-1939   Launa W. 1912--
/Hatten,Virginia Ruth 1916-1923/Hatfield,W.Michael 1951-1968
/Hawes,John Henry d14 apr 1937 /Hay,Strother 1866-1931
/Hawes,Lucy E. 1866-1929 /Hay,Virginia Jeffers 1913-1951
/Hayes,Enoch E, 1867-1937
/Hazard,C.J. 1853-1926 /Haynes,Dr.A.F. 1860-1923
/Hazlett,James Hoyt 1931 inf /Heatherman,James 1860-1935
/Heck,Stephen Elmer 1870-1935 /Heiner,E.Ellen 1848-1926
/Henkle,Eva 1866-1921 /Henderson,Emma Bandum 1860-1928
/Henkle,George 1856-1929 /Henderson,Vela Bowen 4 aug 1902-21dec31
/Hensley,Edward C. Jr. 1921-22 /Henritze,Ernestiine Stump 1898-1927
/Hensley,Johnson Selbee 1916-19/Hensley,Edward C.1896-1929
/Hensley,Fredrick E. 1920-21 /Hensley,J.R. 6 Jan 1873-5 aug 1935
/Hensley,Henrietta 1924-26 /Hensley,Jennie Barnes 1879-1935
/Hensley,Paul Lambert Jr.1936inf/Hensley,Johnson 1857-1932
/Hensley,Victoria 1865-1902 /Hensley,William Henry 1889-1933
/Hensley,Emery S.1891-1958
   Sarah W. 1890-1972 /Hensley,Bernie E. 1895
/Hensley,Bob 1943--   Sarah E.1898-1975
   Becky 1943-1983 /Hensley,Claude C.Jr 22 nov 1929-25 seo 77
/Hensley,Wm.V.1931-1945 /Hensley,Ella 28 apr 1897-10 may 1969
/Hensley,Edward C. Jr.1921-2/Hensley,Edmund D.1911-1965
/Hensley,Fredrick E.1920-1 /Hensley,Henrietta 1924-26
/Hensley,John L. 1909-1978 /Hensley,Morris L. 1928-1980
   Nina L. 1910-1969   Jane E. 1927--
/Hensley,Gordon W. 1922 /Hensley,Norman, M. 1919-1980
   Phyllis M.1925--   Naomi 1920--
/Hensley,Rufus P.1903-1980 /Hensley,Thomas 1911-1979

```
        Gamie 1903--              Burley 1911-1980
/Hensley,Myron B. 1912-1976 /Hensley,William M.1880-1972
      Eleanor 1917--            Lula M. 1892-1975
/Henson,E.1858-1932           /Herren,Clara Virginia 1917-1920
/Hetyer,A.R. 1863-1930        /Hewitt,Daniel Elmer 23 may 1865-1dec21
/Hibner,Edward Wayne 1884-1936 /Hicks, Joseph S. d9 dec 1934
/Hidy,Charles G. 1866-1925    /Hicks,William F. 1860-1932
                              /Hicks,Roxie 22 Jul 1987
/Hidy,Daisy M. 1873-1924      /Higgans,James Blanton 1933-1938
/Higgins,Lucy H.1857-1927     /Hill,D.L. 1878-1922
/Himes,K. Hurbert 1893-1935   /Hinchman,William M. 1878-1934
/Hinerman,Alta M. 1897-1926   /Hinerman,Archie W. 1922-1924
/Hinerman,Charlotte 1871-1934 /Hinerman,Maggie M. 1868-1938
/Hinerman,Walker 1861-1922    /Hines,Constance N. d10 feb 1939
/Hite,Charles G. 1860-1885    /Hite,Frank W. 1819-1891
/Hite,Henry Clay 1857-1938    /Hite,Mary F. 1826-1889
/Hix,Aubury Russell,Jr.1907-30 /Hoback,Claude J. 1880-1929
/Hobgood,Lizzie               /Hoff,Isabelle C. 6 Jul1892-7 mar1937
   12 Jul 1862-12 Jun 1939    /Hoff,Richard 19 aug 1913-13 mar 1938
/Hobgood,L.P.1854-1927        /Hoffman,Hervey C. 1869-1936
/Hogg,Lucian M. 1867-1924     /Holderby,Elizabeth 1865-1914
/Hogg,Rosa 1871-1929          /Holderby,Elsie M. 1894-1921
/Holley,Mary F. 1852-1936     /Holley,Levitus 4 may 1938 68y3m20y
/Holley,Parthenia 1875-1930   /Holley,T.A. 1848-1929
/Holliday,Elmer N. 1917-1926  /Holm,William 1920-1936
/Holliday,William A. 1860-1934 /Holton,Elma G. 1910-1921
/Holton,George Thos d30 Jun 34 /Holton,June d27 Jan 1938
/Holtzworth,Charles J.1881-1929/Honaker,Halcie M. 1918-1935
/Holtzworth,Jacob J.1856-1924 /Hood,John .1854-1928
/Holtzworth,John Ed d9 dec 1922/Hood,thomas Bryon 1907-1933
/Hopkins,Euler 1881-1938      /Hooper,Ella M. 23 feb 1891-18 Jan 1928
/Horner,Seldon 1868-1933      /Hooper,Ira W.30 sep 1848-16 sep 1924
/Horner,Firman R. 1898-1926   /Hooper,Tandy H. 1878-1929
/Howard,Catherine 1854-1929   /Howard,Edgar M.Sr.17 Jul 1890-10 Jan 37
/Howard,Osee M.  1893-1926    /Howard,Jack Harmon 2 dec 1936
/Howell,P.L. 1850-1923        /Huddleston,Ray C. 1896-1919
/Howell,Fanny D. 1882-1926    /Huddleston,Robert B. 1868-1938
/Huffman,Flora Louise 1907-1923/Humphreys,Juanita 1915-1920
/Hughes,George Henry 1902-1932 /Humphreys,Richard D. 1859-1937
/Hughes,Margaret 1907-1929    /Hundley,Dosha B.1882-1923
/Hughes,W.H. 1881-1923        /Hundley,Henry T. 1859-1934
/Hurst,alma Louise 1915-1928  /Hundley,Leonard R. 1920-1931
/Hurst,Janie C. 1885-1912     /Hundly,Lillie 22 Jan 1901-28 Jun 1930
/Hutchinson,Anna Laura 1873-34 /Hunt,Leona Bethel 1894-1935 w/oWm.A.
/Hutchinson,J.Howard 1877-1925 /Hutchinson,Charles E. 1919-1960
/Hutchinson,Stanley 1899-1979 /Hysell,Fannie H. 1848-1920
/Ingram,James P. 1867-1928    /Innis,Edward Wingett 2 may 1938 36y7m
/Insco,Frances Mae 1893-1936  /Inscoe,Joseph 1839-1921
/Isaacs,Martha 1858-1936          Sarah 1849-1924
/Isaacs,Rev.Ruben R.1853-1936 /Inscoe,Virginia Fay 1901-1926
/Isbell,Lewis Daniel 1848-1931 /Ison,Spencer 1864-1937
/Isbell,Mary Elzabeth 1850-1936
```

/Jackson,Julia Yantus w/oNaaman   23 feb 1883-8 Jul 1937
/James,Sarah Alvis 1888-1920   /Jackson,Evelyn Frances 1914-1930
/Jarvis,Tom Pat s/oTH&M   /Jackson,John Henry 1852-1938
    6 nov 1917-31 Jul 1934   /Jackson,Mary Susan 1857-1932
/Jeffers,Inf 1921 s/oGH&E   /Jenkins,Ida Holt Crotty 1899-1932
/Jeffers,Paul E. 1904-1937   /Jenkins,Jean Marian 1926-1934 d/oJ&K
/Jefferson,Donald N. 1923   /Jesse,Cora May 1871-1925
/Jefferson,Ida 1899-1923   /Johnson,Kathie Catherine 1866-1934
/Johnston,James Edmond d1931   /Johnson,Lucinda White 1850-1923
/Johnston,James E. 1852-1927   /Johnson,Mary 29 apr 1933 33y6m3d
/Johnston,Lyda V.1863-1934   /Johnson,M.C. 14 Jun 1937 59y2m10
/Jones,F.W. 1874-1934   /Johnson,Nath J. 1881-1938
/Jones,Henry W. 1924-35   /Jones,Wm Trunnell 15 may 1889-15 mar 37
/Jones,Paul R. 1904-1934   /Jones,William T. 1890-1928
/Jones,Robert A. 1871-1934   /Jordan,William Thomas 18 Jul 1934 57y
/Jordon,Morris F. 1936-38   /Jukovich,Steve 28 mar 1939 47y4m13d
/Justice,John E. 1891-1928   /Justice,Saralie 1922-1928
/Kane,Florence J. 1868-1933   /Karnes,Lola 1910-1935
/Kayes,Thelma Eves 1907-1932   /Keathley,Mollie 1874-1925
/Keeler,Esther Headley 1856-37   /Keathley,William T. 1866-1929
/Kelley,Effie A. 18651931   /Kellerman,Effa T. 1894-1920
/Kelly,Edward J.1871-1924   /Kendle,Eva Doddridge 10 dec 1936
/Kershner,Crosby C. 1884-1938   /Keyser,Henry B.1863-1939
/Kershner,Montie 3 nov 1933   /Keyser,Walter,1883-1917   WWI
    56y8m11d   /Kidd,Donald Lee d1932
/Kilgore,Rosena F. 1853-1927   /Kincaid,Arthur O. 8 Jul 1873-19 mar 31
/King,Alma M. 1896-1937   /Kincaid,John Lewis 14 dec 1936 78y5m4d
/King,Blanche E.1893-1921   /Kincaid,Martha Ann 19 Jan 1938 79y6m15d
/King,Daisy D. 1890-1937   /Kingrey,Annie Hufford 1903-1924
/King,Eloise Neal 1909-1938   /Kingsbury,Bernie 1 oct 1939 46y1m5d
/Kinney,H.E. 1883-1920   /Kipp,John D. 1876-1927
/Kirk,Nelie G. 1861-1920   /Kirtley,Ella Louise 1921-1928
/Kirk,Richard 7 may 1939   /Kiser,Ethel M. 1878-1905
/Kittle,Elizabeth 1879-1936   /Kiser,Jesse W. 1873-1939
/Klinebell,Wanda M. 1911-1928   /Kiser,Ruby F. 1899-1935
/Knapp,Jennie V.1871-1932   /Knight,Fred A. 10 sep 1883-2 apr 1928
/Knowlton,Josephine 1863-1939   /Knight,Idella D.1860-1925
/Knootz,James M. 1854-1926   /Kounse,John W. 1851-1927
/Knootz,Ocea V. 1852-1925   /Kreil,Charles 1868-1930
/Knootz,Clara D. 1875-1919   /Krueger,Ethel Mae 1905-1927
/Kuhn,Lemuel P. 1868-1929
/LaFollette,Alice d1930   /Lake,Mary E. 1847-1934
/Landers,James T. 1892-1923   /Lake,Sarah J. 1859-1937
/Langdon,Marie 14 aug 1939   /Langfitt,Dr.S.F.1869-1939
/Lapole,James R. 1937 inf   /Lawhorn,Ada lee 13 Jun 1939 59y6m16d
/Lapole,Lindsay L. 1892-1934   /Lawter,Benjamin H.13 nov 1867-19 nov 24
/Lay,William Olen 1888-1930   /Layman,Inez M. Noble 1913-1932
/Leake,Robert O.Jr.1926-1931   /Layman,Nellie M. 1878-1935
/Legge,Medora Cavender 1864-35   /Leckie,Doanld Jr.16 oct 1937
/Leighton,Minnie S. 1872-1936   /Leckie,Jerry E. 1903-1937
/Lemings,Otis 1908-1931   /Leckie,Margaret 1877-1923
/Lemley,Adaline 1847-1926   /Lenahan,John M. 1882-1935
/Lemley,John F.1858-1922   /Lenz,George A. 1876-1931
/Leppert,Caroline 1869-1937   /Leroy,Harry C. 1884-1936

/Leppert,Howard E. 1898-1939 /Leslie,Rev.L.E. 1845-1930
/Lewis,Addie S. 1865-1936 /Lewis,B.H. 1887-1938
/Lewis,Earl L. 1897-1934 /Lewis,Julian H. 1889-1929
/Lewis,L.P. 1857-1928 /Lewis,Kingsbee 4 Jul 1939 79y5m12d
/Lewis,Mary A, 1854-1936 /Lewis,May B.1873-1928
/Lewis,S.D. /Lindemood,J.W. 1854-1926
/Lipton,C.C. /Lindewood,Rachael J. 1848-1915
/Lively,Cora E. 1883-1933 /Locke,William R. 1875-1933
/Lively,Marian Douglas 1916-21 /Long,Chas Beale Morgan 29 sep 1939 68y
/Losee,W.Ray 1905-1927 /Long,Charles Louis 1923-25
/Louden,Jessie M.1877-1935wCS /Long,Flora 1898-1922
/Louden,Mary Gerturde /Long,Laura 8 sep 1937 37y2m15d
   25 mar 1938 75y7m /Long,William E. 1887-1931
/Lucas,J.Ezra 1892-1934 /Lowery,Jessica 29 dec 1931 56y1m6d
/Lumpp,Etta 1869-1927 /Lowry,James W. 1858-1925
/Lurch,Fred 1861-1936 /Lusk,Blondine 1895-1932
/Luthe,Mary 1867-1923 /Lynn,Bertha Lee 1916-20 d/o JA&V
/Lynd,Ira W. 1877-1934 /Lynn,Edwin 1921 s/o JA&V
/Lyons,Major W.H. 1857-1930 /Lynn,Harry G. 1885-1938
/Lyons,Victoria B. 1858-1933 /Lynn,Velva 1896-1927
/Madge,Edward A. 1910-1937 /Maddy,Emma R.Betts w/o Homer B.
/Magoon,Claudia   22 mar 1885-21 feb 1936
/Magoon,W.W. 1862-1921 /Mahan,Edward Kenna 1878-1934
/Mallory,Mamie S. 1867-1920 /Malcolm,Clarence Bruce 11 aug 1939 35y
/Mallory,Samuel H. 1865-1925 /Malcolm,Jack Morris 1918-1927
/Malloy,Howard Malcolm 1897-35 /Marcum,James Overton 1865-1938
/Mann,Frank W. 1861-1936 /Marks,Wandall R. 1906-1937
/Martin,C.A. 1879-1939 /Marrs,G.S. 23 dec 1854-3 Jan 1933
/Martin,Geroge T. 1887-1921 /Martin,Alice Winifred 20 nov 1937 29y7m
/Martin,Hiram B. 1881-1938 /Martin,Anna Lee 1882-1928 w/o HB
/Martin,J.E. 1866-1929 /Martin,Irene A. 10 apr 1939 33y3m12d
/Martin,Lydia B. 1898-1934 /Martin,James Daniel 22 jun 1934 35y10m
/Martin,W.McTyeire 1895-1925 /Martin,William Ernest 1900-1929
/Massey,J.Summers 1873-1928 /Masterson,John T. 1864-1927
/Massie,Evan 1876-1923 /Masterson,Mary A. 1860-1932
/Massie,Josie OP. 1879-1939 /Mathews,Charles H. 15 may 1892-13Jun38
/Maynard,Darwood 15 oct 1939 47y/Mathews,W.L. 1861-1922
/McAlister,Dallis 1889-1927 /McCaffery,C.J. 1863-1939
/McAlister,James Monroe 1938 /McCallister,Bessie M. 30 aug 1938 51y5m
/McAlister,Mary 1861-1936 /McCarthy,Rev.John 1856-1934
/McClaren,Phillip D. 6 feb 1938/McCarthy,Samuel N.1874-1930
/McClarey,Charles L. 1853-1937 /McClure,Alice Burgess 1854-1928
/McClarey,martha A. 1860-1937 /McColm,Frank C. 8 aug 1863-11 feb 1934
/McComas,Emily 4 dec 1937 /McColm,Ida Varner 28 apr 1868-22 sep 34
/McComas,Eva 1889-1932 /McComas,Elizabeth Barker 1857-1937
/McComas,Jobe 1856-1928 /McComas,William Edwin 1902-1937
/McComas,L.M. 1887-1918 /McCoy,Chilton A. 1917-1935
/McDaniel,Homer F. 1892-1919 /McCoy,R.C. 1897-1921
/McDaniel,Mary Louise /McGinnis,Benjamin F.25 oct 1871-22Jul34
   17 apr 1937 50y11m5d /McGinnis,Dorothy R. 1917-1921
/McGougan,L.M. 1866-1938 /McGinnis,James D. 1867-1933
/McKee,Willie A. 22 nov 1938 /McIntosh,Colin R. 24 aug 1934 35y
   74y3m8d /McIntosh,George C. 20 Jan 1936 69y
/McKelvey,John A. /McIntosh,Wilton Randolph 1895-1928

19 mar 1937 65y3m9d
/McLaughlin,J.F. 1862-1921
/McLaughlin,Lewis E.1869-1938
/McMahon,Joseph Rolla 1876-1922
/McNelly,Jane Beard 1907-1936
/McVey,John A. 1873-1938
/McVey,S.A. 1875-1936
/Meadows,Ellis Rudolph 1894-38
/Meadows,J.W. 1866-1926
/Meadows,Kenneth M. 1891-1918
/Meek,Edmin V.1921 inf
/Meek,Edward C. 1888-1937
/Meek,Gerald C. 1905-1935
/Meyers,August H. 1864-1931
/Michael,Charles E. 1874-1923
/Michael,Joseph F.1926-1938
/Michael,Mary C. 1853-1937
/Miller,Anna M. 1864-1934
/Miller,Charles V. 1870-1927
/Miller,Cyrus Neal 1875-1935
/Miller,Glenn Fenton 1902-1936
/Miller,Louise 1917-1926
/Miller,Ora Frances 7 oct 1933
/Miller,Mayme B.1883-1934
/Miller,R.H. 1857-1920
/Mitchell,C.W.1889-1918
/Mitchell,Harold F.1912-1937
/Mitchell,Mary Bloss 1863-1930
/Moore,Herman 1869-1924
/Moore,Robert C. 1908-1935
/Moreland,Alonza 1885-1937
/Moreland,Dorothy Luci 1920-23
/Morris,Claude G. 1874-1928SpAm
/Morris,Jessa A. 1891-1921
/Morris,J.Corbett 1901-1935
/Morris,Charles R.
   4 sep 1935 76y10m25d
/Morris,Mary lou 15 nov 1935inf
/Morris,Wm.Edgar 1883-1920
/Mosby,Fred 1892-1936
/Mosby,Ruth L. 1912-1930
/Mosier,John S. 1858-1939
/Muller,Blanche 1891-1935
/Munsell,Myrtle L.6 Jan 1935 36y
/Myers,Carolyn 1905-1918
/Myers,Emmet E. 1867-1937
/Nash,Howard B.1897-1918
/Nash,Robert A.1879-1925
/Nash,Winifred 1872-1925
/Neely,Verna Knight 1893-1929
/Neff,Oscar R. 1867-1933
/Neff,Sylvia Mae 1882-1937
/Newman,Eliza Jane 28 feb 1936
   72y6m25y

/McLaughlin,Gerturde 15 apr 1939 65y3m9d
/McLaughlin,Ida Mae 2 may 1939 69y8m2d
/McLaughlin,M.Alice 1872-1931
/McMillan,Charles 3 Jan 1939 23y3d
/McNeely,Morgan E. 1867-1935
/Meabon,Mary Francis 16 dec 1937 22y11m
/Meadows,Clara B. 4 Jun 1884-22 apr 1886
/Meadows,Esom H. 6 oct 1859-17 feb 1908
/Meadows,Roe 22 may 1889-16 oct 1918 WI
/Meadows,Virginia L. 1912-1933
/Meldahl,Alex 1855-1916
/Meldahl,William 1900-1927
/Mengert,Elizabeth O. 1887-1927
/Middleton,A.L. 17 aug 1939 64y6m28d
/Midkiff,Agnes 1861-1932
/Midkiff,Hampton,1894-1924
/Millender,Irene Fowble 1868-1938
/Miller,Cecil S.25 aug 1894-3 Jul 1920
/Miller,Cora L. 17 sep 1903-4 aug 1938
/Miller,Daisy 1897-1932
/Miller,Harry L. 1881-1924
/Miller,John Craig 24 aug 1858-17 Jan 26
   Sallie Rutherford Tinsley
   d24 Jul 1939
/Miller,John H. 14 apr 1931 66y2m16d
/Mitchell,Donald E. 1914-1931
/Mitchell,John W. 1864-1931
/Mitchell,Richard Lee d 1931
/Molter,Adolph 8 sep 1939 90y9m28d
/Molter,Elizabeth Moaty 1858-1932
/Morgan,John Paul 5 feb 1907-6 Jul 1927
   s.o WS&Mary E.
/Morgan,Lunicia 1856-1938
/Morgan,Paris Edward 1881-1928
/Morgan,Thomas F.1883-1923
/Morrison,Darell D. 1896-1938
/Morrison,Edgar G. 1883-1924
/Morrison,Granville Price 1839-1932
/Morrison,Homer A. 1873-1927
/Morrison,Mary L. 1882-1937
/Moses,Rosa Evans 1872-1934
/Moss,Hubert 4 sep 1843-8 sep 1926
/Mossman,America Davis 9/14/1861-9/20/37
/Murphy,Wm.J.14 feb 1879-11 nov 1936
/Mynes,Pauline N.1895-1925

/Neal,James Alfred 1837-39
/Neal,Olive Mae 1891-1927
/Neal,Samuel B.16 sep 1853-14 may 1939
/Neal,Shelby R. 1903-1930
/Neighorgall,Chas.W.1932-1935
/Neutzling,Cola 3 feb 1939 62y9m17d
/Newman,Joseph R.26 dec 1938 78y6m23d
/Newman,Lydia Eugenia

/Newman,Elizabeth 1894-1918   25 dec 1847-15 Jan 1919
    w/o Pearl S.   /Newman,Myme Bell 20 Jan 1893-28 mar 17
/Nicol,Alexander 2 mar 1932   /Newman,Rilla Dennison 1875-1929
/Nickel,Charles M. 1888-1929   /Nihiser,Estel M. 1896-1933
/Nimon,Nellie F.1877-1921   /Noble,Eliza Jane 1842-1927
/Noonan,Elizabeth 1857-1939   /Noble,inf 30 Jan 1933
/Norman,Charles W.1929 inf   /Northcott,Nathaniel D.1881-1935
/Notter,Jesse M. 1856-1933   /Nuckels,Ferry H. 1890-1923
/Nugent,Anna M. 1880-1932   /Null,Donald Lee 1899-1934
/Nurnberger,Belle Kyle 1859-38   /Null,Thomas Allen 13 feb 1937 72y8m29d
/Oakes,George A.1873-1922   /Obenshain,Thurston Allen 13 nov 1938 59y
/O'Brien,Lewis W.S.1867-1939   /Oberholtzer,Jessie A. 1865-1933
/Odell,Bertha Chambers 1873-31   /Ogg,David Lewis 19 may 1856-9 feb 1935
/Odell,Mary Va.1909-1929   /Ogg,Ginevea Wyatt 11 nov 1860-27 mar 36
/Oksnee,Emma V.1877-1935   /Oliver,Fannie J.1856-1939
/Oksnee,Svend H.1877-1929   /Oneill,Bessie V.
/Oney,Xina Womack 1887-1935   /Oppenheim,Augusta 1852-1928
/Osborne,Guy S. 1870-1927   Simon 1839-1930
/Osborne,Ola Parsley   /Osburn,Ida L. 29 aug 1875-24 Jan 1937
    16 apr 1898-25 aug 1928   /O'Shea,William S. 1917-1936
/Oswald,Lilly Elma 1908-1923   /Owens,Amos 11 may 1934 26y6m24d
/Oxley,Dixie L. 1909-1929   /Owens,Hobart G. 1896-1926
/Oxley,Francis A.1880-1933   /Owens,Mary 1 feb 1935 55y10m26d
/Pack,Susie 1885-1926   /Owens,Mary V.22 dec 1868-25 Jul 1937
/Pack,Theodore 1882-1926   /Palmer,John P. 1856-1926
/Pancake,Daniel J.1862-1928   /Panson,Patricia Jean 3 mar 1933 inf
/Parker,William H. 1889-1927   /Parsons,Betty Jo 1924-27
/Patterson Carl Albert 1911-34   /Parsons,E.A.F.4 dec 1865-16 Jul 1931
/Patterson,Mary C. 1870-1932   /Parsons,Henrietta 25 jul 1896-15 Jun 28
/Patterson,,Samuel W. 1863-1932 /Parsons,Murriell 27 apr 1892-8 dec 1920
/Patterson,Thomas C.1904-1932   /Patton,Edward 1884-1936
/Paul,John T. 1875-1935   /Pauley,Edgar S. 1863-1933
/Paul,Lydia Belle 1873-1937   /Payne,Harry D. 21 oct 1938 WWI
/Peck,William G. 1869-1923   /Payne,John W. 1916-18
/Pennington,Merton 1905-1938   /Payne,William W. 17 aug 1872-19 oct 26
/Perdue,A.R. 1873-1933   /Perry,Alice Maxine 1925
/Perdue,Cass 1859-1929   /Perry,Emmett D.1 apr 1935 31y10m19d
/Perdue,Nelson   /Perry,Gillie 2 dec 1938 87y11m21d
    23 feb 1930 73y10m2d   /Perry,J.W. 25 dec 1863-13 nov 1937
/Peters,Donald Ray 1929-1930   /Petry,Billie T. 26 dec 1934 inf
/Petty,Wm.Walton 1886-1927   /Petry,Florence G. feb 1935 inf
/Pfeiffer,George S.1884-1935   /Petry,Raymond J.11 feb 1935 inf
/Pfelfer,Lillie M. 1900-1934   /Phillips,Homer M. 1889-1923
/Pifer,Dock S.1855-1918   /Phillips,John H. 1972-1929
/Pifer,Madalyn 1918-1924   /Phillips,Mary F.1850-1926
/Pilcher,Ernest L. 1887-1938   /Pine,A.G.6 apr 1938 73y6m7d
/Pilcher,Roy 1890-1930   /Pitzer,Bertha Lee 1873-1926
/Plaster,Lucile Williams 1906-31 /Plymale,Albert G.30 nov 1934 63y17d
/Plunkett,John Berkley 1905-32   /Plymale,Daisy W.18 oct 1933 63y9m17d
/Pollard,Ira C.1884-1934   /Plymale,Mary Louise 1885-1924
/Porter,A.V.1880-1930   /Pool,James W.31 oct 1871-4 may 1933
/Porter,David Le 1937 inf   /Porter,Clyde Clarence 21 mar 1938 WWI
/Porter,Edwin H.Jr.1926-29   /Porter,Flossie May 1891-1919
/Porter,Ellis 1893-1924   /Porter,Pamelia V.1862-1938

/Porter,Ruth Cremeans 1912-1937 /Porter,Sallie Tinsley 3 sep 1916-1920
/Porter,S.R. 1851-1918 /Porter,W.W. 1857-1934
/Powell,Lester C.d1918 /Powers,Ben F.1888-1925
/Powell,William F.1907-1934 /Powers,Ruth Arlene 1920-1926
/Pratt,Frank 1871-1928 /Preston,John W. 1847-1922
/Price,James 1880-1936 /Preston,Mary 1. 1847-1931
/Priddy,Gorden 1923-25 /Prichard,Elizabeth G.1912-1937
/Proudfoot,J.M.1855-1925 /Pryor,Earl B.Jr.d1922
/Proudfoot,Theodosia 1861-1933 /Pyler,Golden C.3 sep 1939 8y
/Qualls,Annabell Kingery 1880-31
/Raines,Elverna 1.1915-1930 /Ramsey,Allen Earl 1879-1927
/Ratliff,George F.1837-1909 /Ray,Alonza 1866-1930
/Ratliff,Nancy Ann 1839-1909 /Ray,Arrahanna 1863-1925
/Ratlieff,Lillian G.1883-1936 /Ray,Dora Bell 20 mar 1873-13 Jun 1935
/Radcliffe,Floyd Jr.1927-32 /Ray,Hnery S.1891-1928
/Rayburn,Carl James 1901-1936 /Ray,Mollie 1901-1935
/Reatherford,H.R.1866-1934 /Ray,Sarah E. 1843-1920wJoseph M.
/Reckard,G.Homer 1884-1928 /Reed,Fred E.Jr.1879-1934
/Reeder,Emily L.1 mar 1934 /Reese,A.Sidney 1867-1926
/Rees,Emma Bentz 1881-1967 /Reese,Edwin Cassius 26 oct 1938 WWI
/Reid,Ora Louise 1867-1922 /Reese,Margaret 1861-1925
/Reiley,Barrie F.1873-1934 /Reiley,Sarah Ann 1855-1933
/Renner,Ella Eliza 1867-1935 /Reynolds,Anita Gwinn 1923-1931
/Renner,Frederick J.C.1865-1935 /Reynolds,Harry T.14 mar 1937 51y11m26d
/Rhodes,Alberta G.1867-1938 /Reynolds,Harry T.Jr.1922-23
/Richardson,Neil Howard 1875-27 /Richey,Mary D. 1861-1929
/Richardson,T.H. 1852-1927 /Richey,William C.1852-1925
/Rickard,Dr.C.M.1873-1934 /Rider,Barbara 1862-1935
/Rickard,henry 1859-1933 /Rider,Melville B.1859-1926
/Rickard,Laurean 1856-1934 /Riggs,Nancy J.1858-1926
/Ripley,Amos 1846-1919 /Ritter,Mabel Virginia 1930-38 d/WM&M
/Ripley,Rena Morrison 13 oct 32 /Roach,Percy P.1907-1928
/Roberson,Dr.G.C.1884-1920 WWI /Roach,Samuel T.1876-1937
/Roberson,Lov.1853-1938 /Robertson,William H.1872-1939
/Roberts,Brnjamin B.1929-1930 /Robinson,Meta Elizabeth 2 feb 1935 19y
/Roberts,Dorothy M.1917-1920 /Robinson,William A.1892-1930
/Roberts,Francelia V.1881-1923 /Robson,Morris J.1912-1936
/Roberts,Inf 1922 /Rochefort,Robert M.28 Jun 1939 75y2m19d
/Roby,Phillip D.1913-1932 /Roe,Bertha A.1893-1919
/Rolph,Noami 1862-1931 /Roe,Kenneth M. 1917-1918
/Rolph,Wm.Frank 1859-1930 /Roe,Luther M. 1876-1938
/Romine,Clifford 1887-1917TS&MC /Rood,Daniel 16 apr 1937 71y
/Romine,Mary C.1854-1923 /Rood,Maryland 1868-1926 w/oMC
/Rose,Isabella 1875-1934 /Rood,Mary M.1878-1929
/Rose,Jasper C.1869-1927 /Rosenheim,Cora Robson 1868-1930
/Ross,Cora Bell 1878-1900 /Row,Dr.W.D. 1861-1923
/Ross,C.Albert 1891-1930 /Royce,Jack Herbert 3 feb 1936 76y5m29d
/Ross,William A.1863-1936 /Russell,Edward 1886-1936
/Russell,George G.1913-1931
/Sadler,J.B.1868-1923 /Sanders,Arthur H.1848-1922
/Safford,Earl 1904-1927 /Sanders,Mary E.1874-1918
/Salmon,Edward B.1863-1931 /Sandrock,Minnie E.1874-1918
/Sansom,Glenoma Hope d1923 /Sanks,Barten 20 feb 1895-11 Jun 1938
/Saunders,Charles B.1857-1936 /Saunders,Levi 28 sep 1930 68y1m

/Saunders,Ella M. 1876-1929   /Saunders,Marvena Mae 1929-1933
/Saunders,John C. 1874-1930   /Saunders,S.E. 1852-1933
/Saver,J.Phillip 1863-1928   /Sawyer,Mary A. 1853-1923
/Sayre,Anna I.1856-1928   /Schmidt,Margaret Hester 13 mar 1939 41y
/Schieffelin,Lav.1893-1937   /Schmitz,Theodore S.1878-1938
/Schrote,Mary E. 1857-1937   /Schoew,Fred.Leonard 10 mar 1866-20Jan39
/Seal,Fred K. 1849-1937   /Schulze Margaret Rebennak 1868-1936
/Seal,Margaret P. 1849-1930   /Seaman,Roy L. 1896-1935
/Sebaugh,Celia P. 1881-1935   /Secrest,Harry R. 1871-1937
/Sellards,Wm.D. 1861-1924   /Sexton,Charles 1862-1924
/Shackleford,Leon 1892-1933   /Shafer,Della Lenora 1871-1937
/Shamblin,James D. 1885-1930   /Shafer,James Samuel 1866-1937
/Shamblin,Roy W.1893-1927   /Shanklin,Charles W. 5 Jan 1934 inf
/Shank,Blanche Darrah 1886-1934/Shannon,Wm.A.8 dec 1899-23 oct 1938
/Shank,Thos.Walter 1866-1932   /Shaw,Elizabeth E. 21 feb 1934 73y
/Sharitz,Claude H. 1885-1929   /Shaw,Mary Margaret 1903-1926
/Shelton,America V. 1841-1923   /Shepard,John Claudius 1843-1927
/Sheppard,C.H. 1909-1922   /Shepard,John Mannen 1886-1898
/Sheppard,John S. 1881-1939   /Sheperd,Hattie 22 aug 1939 73y11m24d
/Sheppard,Rev.Wm.F. 1848-1930   /Sheperd,Wm.R. 1853-1928
/Shmonoff,Harry 1900-1923   /Shore,George L. 1865-1929
/Short,Howard E. 1925 inf   /Shouen,Anna May 8 mar 1939   55y9m4d
/Short,Noel Douglas 1918-1922   /Shumaker,Paul F. 1915-1922
/Shumway,Ira 1852-1923   /Shumaker,Sadie M.1892-1934
/Shumway,Louesa 1852-1921   /Sidebottom,G.W.1868-1934
/Siers,William A.1894-1928   /Sidebottom,Myrtle 1894-1927
/Silvers,O.Hailey 1891-1928   /Simmins,Bernie 1895-1935
/Simms,Alice M. 1858-1926   /Simpson,Arah E.18 oct 1860-11 dec 1938
/Simms,Belle 1871-1926   /Sinsell,Henrietta 13 mar 1873-26 sep 34
/Simons,Eliza 1847-1937   /Sites,Laura 1863-1921
/Simons,Bryan 1870-1925   /Skaggs,Grover C.25 nov 1934 48y5m15d
/Simons,Wm.H. 1869-1922   /Slater,Florence Jane 27 Jun 1937 70y11m
/Smeltzer,Elmer E. 1861-1936   /Slater,Harrison 1859-1934
/Smeltzer,Emma 1874-1938   /Slaughter,Betty Garland 1855-1923
/Smith,Alice M. 1863-1938   /Slaughter,Eliza 1849-1926
/Smith,Bertha E. 1883-1923   /Slaughter,Wm.P. 1869-1932
/Smith,Fannie J. 1869-1921   /Smith,Bess T. 1914-1920
/Smith,Earl 1882-1922   /Smith,Conrad T. 1905-1936
/Smith,Hattie G.1862-1927   /Smith,Hattie 19 Jun 1928 66y11m24d
/Smith,James L. 1866-1923   /Smith,Henry S. 7 Jan 1933 73y6m28d
/Smith,Jo Retta 1934 inf   /Smith,L.R. 1913-27 s/o L.Roy&Gerturde
/Smith,Lusta Jane 1874-1939   /Smith,Margaret E.16 mar 1933 80y4m12d
/Smith,Maggie 1871-1927   /Smith,Minnie E. 1871-1928
/Smith,O.F. 1873-1935   /Smith,Reba Robertson 1913-1937
/Smith,Phillip S. 1866-1933   /Smith,Rhoeba Jane 1865-1925
/Smith,Roy 1891-1939   W.A. 1849-1937
/Smith,V.Evelyn 1915-1923   /Smith,Walter C.Jr.1908-1929
/Smithson,Inf 1931   /Smoot,Thelma Louisa 1929-1934 s/o JE&B
/Snyder,Dr.J.E.1876-1926   /Snedegar,Mary Ann 7 oct 1936 76y8d
/Snyder,Marcus R. 1873-1924   /Sowards,Leonard Winter 1869-1933
/Sovine,Barbara Lou 1938 inf   /Sowards,Stella May 1882-1925
/Sparks,W.G. 1868-1919   /Sowards,James 1857-1927
/Spaulding,Minnie M.1877-1937   /Sowards,Rebecca I. 1861-19937
/Spears,John Wesley 1908-1936   /Spurlock,Donna Shyrene 1931-1937

/Spencer,Eliza J.1856-1921
/Sperry,Martin R. 1873-1929
/Sprouse,Hattie L. 1897-1922
/Stackhouse,Mary 1871-1928
/Stafford,Elizabeth C.1866-1925
/Stalnaker,Randall H.1918-1939
/Starkey,John W. 1856-1938
/Starkey,Walter W. 1888-1937
/Stephenson,John L. 1866-1935
/Stevens,Betty Jo 1936 8y2m3d
/Stolings,Jack 1924-27
/Stone,Harry Lee 1855-1938
/Stone,James E.Jr.1919-1920
/Stone,Maggie M. 1871-1924
/Stone,Velma H. 1917-1920
/Strachan,Mary 1888-1938
/Stratten,A.W. 1857-1926
/Stuart,John T. 1855-1937
/Stump,John F. 1850-1927
/Sturm,Gordon B.1858-1922
/Strum,Louise B.1863-1926
/Swan,Permelia Barcus 1863-1928
/Swan,Till A. 1860-1936
/Sweetsir,Cora L.1871-1931
/Sweney,Mary A. 1860-1931
/Sweney,William W.1853-1920
/Swezey,Dr.A.J.1869-1924

/Talip,H,M,1868-1923
/Talip,John H.I. 1890-1927
/Taylor,Chs.Wm.23 feb 1935 44y
/Taylor,Earley C.1901-1932
/Taylor,Elizabeth M. 1880-1930
/Taylor,Georgia A. 1872-1930
/Taylor,Harry C.1869-1934
/Taylor,Harvey W.1862-2934
/Taylor,W.H.1859-1920
/Thacker,Inez Evlyn 1902-1928
/Thomas,Howe O.1886-1923
/Thomas,Orville 1912-1937
/Thornton,Joseph B.1895-1927
/Thornton,Laura A. 1861-1931
/Thornton,Sadie 1898-1923
/Todd,Ruth R. 1886-1925
/Tinsley,L.B.1875-1929
/Tomlinson,Bernard T.1893-1938
/Tompkins,Katherine E.1871-1933
/Tompkins,Noah P/1871-1939
/Torbert,Charles A.1861-1930
/Trainor,Amos 1869-1933
/Trent,Ervin E.1867-1935
/Trout,Bess Newman 1890-1922
/Turley,Wm.11 Jan 1938 83y7m2d
/Turner,Matilda 1862-1939

/Spurlock,Aresus 1876-1927
/Spurlock,Edward P. 12 aug 1884-22 oct36
/Spurlock,Martha A. 1865-1938
/Spurlock,Marvin B.1879-1929
/Spurlock,Myrtle E. 18 feb 1888-19 sep22
/Stanley,Laura B.1863-1921
/Stanley,Virginia C. 1865-1928
/StarcherLillian Smith 1885-1926
/Sterling,Mary Jane 1870-1924
/Stewart,Avery Jr.1929-1932
/Stewart,Charles A. 1890-1918
/Stewart,George E. 1875-1930
/Stork,John A. 1884-1930
/Stover,M.Marco 1903-1919
/Strader,Bernice Bennett 1897-1932
/Straughan,Daisy McKnight 1876-1923
/Stricker,William A. 1871-1929
/Strickling,James H. 1865-1934
/Stutler,Jack lee 1939 inf
/Sullivan,Charles 1879-1936
/Summers,James M. 1872-1924
/Swann,Bessie 19 Jun 1933 46y
/Swann,Lee 1921-1939
/Swann,Lizzie 1884-1924
/Swann,Patrick H, 1858-1927
/Swentzel,Lyda helen 1922
/Swisher,Howard A. 29 oct 1933 17y7m28d
/Swisher,Lula Light 23 mar 1939 51y7m18d
/Tarbutton,Carroll Quinley 1875-1938
/Tarbutton,Laura Morris 1871-1935
/Taylor,Corydon R.1889-1932
/Taylor,Flora Mae 23 apr 1893-10 mar 34
/Taylor,Malcolm C.17 apr 1876-1 apr 1937
/Taylor,Orville 1 may 1939 77y10m20d
/Taylor,Josephine Augusta 9 dec 1937
    81y9m27y
/Taylor,O.H.30 oct 1895-3 Jun 1939
/Templeton,Chas.Foster 1879-1930
/Thompson,Edward A.25 mar 1934 59y
/Thompson,Walter L.1887-1934
/Thompson,Wanda Mae 1938 inf
/Thompson,William A. 1868-1938
/Thuma,John H.1861-1938
/Tignor,Hatton S.11 apr 1930 41y9m14d
/Tingley,Walter Pendleton 11 aug 1933
/Tompson,Sarah 30 apr 1933 47y6m16d
/Topp,Amy Shorten 22 sep 1936 65y2m5d
/Traylor,Jeanette Marg. 23 feb 1929 72y
/Traylor,Wm.Wesley 8 aug 1916-31 mar 35
/Trimble,Anna Mary 6 may 1884-13 Jan 38
/Trimble,John 1877-1936
/Trimble,Louise 1883-1935
/Tucker,Edward 31 mar 1917-12 may 1939
/Tucker,H.B.18 nov 1893-31 Jul 1932

/Turner,Ruby Morris
    21 oct 1937 32y7m7d
/Tyree,Frank H.1873-1933
/Uhles Emma C. 1881-1927
    Harry A. 1869-1924
/Vaden,John H. 1860-1935
/Valentine,Catherine 1867-1939
/Van Voorhls,Ruth 1900-1925
/Vaughn,Rosa Ellixson 1895-1931
/Vest,Bessie Workman 1902-1924
/Vest,Crawford E.1842-1929
    Co M 3rd WV Cav
/Vest,Harry C.1891-1929
/Vest,Sarah F.1844-1935
/Vines,A.A.
    15 oct 1892-18 may 1934
/Vines,Mattie L.
    15 nov 1854-29 oct 1935
/Wagoner,John 1884-1919
/Walker,Charles H.1894-1933
/Walker,Effie 26 nov 1929 25y4m
/Walker,Thomas Edgar 1856-1936
/Wallace,Bessie M.1886-1934
/Wallace,Elizabeth Warth 1900-26
/Wallace,Hannah Fulks d1930
/Wallace,James V. 1881-1935
/Warren,James Ed.1928 inf
/Warth,Ruth H.1869-1927w/H.Clay
/Watkins,Beulah Hill 1880-1932
/Watts,Alvas 1890-1928
/Watts,Ellis 1874-1924
/Watts,Frankie B.1875-1930
/Watts,Louisa 1872-1937
/Watts,Richard A. 1920-21
/Watts,Wm H.9 mar 1939 66y1m24d
/Webb,Eugene C.1889-1930
/Webb.Laura Kinder 1854-1933
/Webb,Marie 3 dec 1934 32y
/Weese,Parker C.1900-1926
/Wellman,Robert L. 1866-1939
/West,George W.1853-1928
/Wetzel,Paul 12 apr 1939 18y11m
/Whalen,William J. 1895-1933
/Wheeler,Luther L. 1881-1936
/White,Charles F. 1876-1931
/White,Edward C.1897-1935
/White,Grace May
    4 dec 1934   67y6m14d
/White,James Ballard 1924-25
/White,Norvill W.19 Jul 1934 23y
/Whittenberg,A.R.1872-1928
/Whittenberg,K.J.1912-1934
/Wiegel,Charles E.1898-1924
/Wilcox,Inez Davis 1878-1937

/Tucker,Kenneth P. d1923
/Tweel,Lucile B.5 aug 1911-22 apr 1933
/Tyree,Elspeth Bennett 1923 inf
/Ullom,Pearl Bellamy 1906-1925
/Utterback,Ruby 25 Jun 1938 61y10m24d
/Van Faussien,Pauline 1919-20
/Van Fleet,Eva Wheeler 1893-1927
/Van Fleet,Homer R.1891-1929
/Varner,Chas.Damarin 14 nov 1937
/Varner,David Naif 8 nov 1936 5y
/Vickers,Dorothy Nannette 1935 inf
/Vickers,Floyd 26 feb 1864-8 feb 1936
/Vickers,Norman Lee Jr.1929-1934
/Vickers,Rena Alice 1907-1921
/Vickers,Viola J.13 may 1863-7 nov 1937

/Waldeck,Eleanor J.4 oct 1929 10y6m22
/Waldeck,Dr.George N.1872-1939
/Waldeck,William G.H. 1922-31
/Wall,Sherman 28 mar 1932 28y
/Walton,Frank 1880-1938
/Ward,Aleck 11 oct 1933 74y9m
/Ward,Billy Joe 23 feb 1939 14y5m2d
/Ward,Cebren 28 feb 1937 36y
/Ward,Charles Lee inf
/Wass,Donald Lee 1929-1932
/Wass,Ida 1869-1922
/Wass,John A. 1865-1935
/Waugh,Albert F.1881-1925
/Waugh,Bertha May 1896-1937
/Waugh,Rebecca 1877-1934
/Waybright,Vaught 8 Jan 1933 43y6m25d
/Weaver,Emma Kathryn 13 Jul 1881-3 dec34
/Weber,Earl F.1886-1939
/Wedgwood,George C.1902-1929
/Weekly,John S. 1894-1925
/Welker,Verner E. 1892-1934
/Wells,Alexander 16 mar 1939 WWI
/Wells,Ben 1849-1922
/Wells,Ruth 1923 inf d/oJA&Nannie
/Whipple,Gerturde Hatten 1869-1937
/Whitaker,LollieV. 1865-1930
/Whitaker,Marie Dupont 1855-1923
/Whitaker,S.C. 1866-1926
/Whitley,M.L. 1858-1918
/Whitley,Naomi 1854-1925
/Whitney,Elizabeth Heatherman
        w/o Dr.L.L.
/Whitney,Emma T.1849-1939
/Whitten,John L.5 feb 1861-17 nov 1933
/Whitten,Mary G.31 mar 1863-9 may 1936
/Wilcoxen,Harriet Josephine 1869-1936

w/o Isrel S.
/Wilcox, James R. 19 dec 1936 35y
/Wilcox, Malissa B. 1862-1921
/Wilkes, Charles Henry 1926-27
/Wilkes, Minnie 1866-1934
/Wilkins, Rhoda Lawton 1900-1930
/Wilkinson, Edith 1882-1921
/Wilkinson, James P. 1879-1939
/Wilkinson, Joseph L. 1902-1922
/Wilkinson, Olive G. 1864-1924
/Williamson, H.L. 1878-1934
/Wilson, Claude N. 1890-1908
/Wilson, Dixie Madeline 1912-29
/Wilson, Frank H. 1892-1936
/Winters, Addie 1865-1936
/Winters, Belle E. Gibson
    w/o George Loyd Winters
/Winters, maymie E. 1894-1925
/Wolfe, Clark 1873-1929
/Womack, Lydia Biggs 1867-1935
/Wood, Artis Verlin 1923-33
/Wood, Lucy H. 9 sep 1938
/Wood, Newman, J. 1890-1921
/Woods, Harry Thomas 1859-1924
/Workman, Amos, 1895-1931
/Workman, Cleo 6 sep 1939 42y
/Workman, Wm. Taylor 1852-1927
/Worley, John J. 1846-1927
/Worley, Sarah G. 1864-1916
/Worley, Thomas J. 1906-1934
/Wren, Rev. C.E. 1853-1922
/Wright, Freda Faye 1907-1937
/Wright, Margaret 1870-1938
/Wright, Martha Ann 1921-1926
/Wroten, Cora C. 1889-1927
/Wroten, Jesse J. 1889-1928
/Yates, Bertha M. 1881-1900
/Yates, Charlotte S. 1856-1922
/Yates, Sallie B. 1876-1935
/Yates, William P. 1854-1928
/Young, Ginevra 1877-1923
/Young, Macil B. 1913-1920
/Young, Ollie V. 1885-1919
/Zimmerman, Carter P. 1894-1929
/Zimmerman, John E. 1859-1925

/Wilcoxen, Harriet Warth 1843-1924
/Wild, Marjorie Taylor 1883-1935
/Wildoner, Charles E. 1878-1935
/Wiley, Belma Dora 1870-1934
/Wiley, Hugh H, 19 Jun 1886-21 apr 1921
/Wiley, Ray 21 mar 1917-16 apr 1938
/Williams, Charles 16 apr 1931 54y11m26d
/Williams, Ellis Alfred 1874-1931
/Williams, John M. 1911-1920
/Williams, Rosa H. 1862-1934
/Williams, Samuel Vinson 20 apr 1930 55y
/Windsor, Charles L. d 1931
/Winter, Gabriella Roby 1863-1930
/Winter, H.V. 1863-1930
/Wiswell, Meredith Price
    23 Jun 1880-28 Jul 1939
/Withers, Anna M. 1901-1936
/Witten, George W. 19 mar 1929   75y3m
/Witten, Mary 25 nov 1933 79y8m
/Womeldorff, John Ed. 1859-1933
/Woodcock, Loretta Hager 16 feb 1937 22y7m
/Woodford, Cleophas 28 may 1929 74y4m18d
/Woodson, G.T. 1865-1921
/Wooten, Enoch 1864-1923
/Workman, Effie 5 aug 1893-13 mar 1935
/Workman, Virginia B. 28 dec 1935 70y
/Workman, Wm. L. 29 may 1935 77y6m22d
/Wormser, Samuel 1875-1928
/Worth, H.R. 1883-1921
/Wotring, Minerva E. Ross 1876-1922
/Wright, Carrie E. 1883-1936
/Wright, Carrol Monroe 1927-1934
/Wright, Mollie Josephine 1919-20
/Wright, Thomas B. 1860-1936
/Wulfman, Thomas Henry 1927-28
/Wyant, Sam
/York, Sallie 1857-1936
/Yost, Charles G. 1879-1935
/Young, Annie L. 1911-1920
/Young, A.B.H. 1837-1918
/Young, Loreen E. Smallridge 1905-1937
/Young, Nora B. 1883-1920
/Zaferlov, Nick 1882-1939
/Zihlman, Dorothy Joan 12 feb 1934 inf

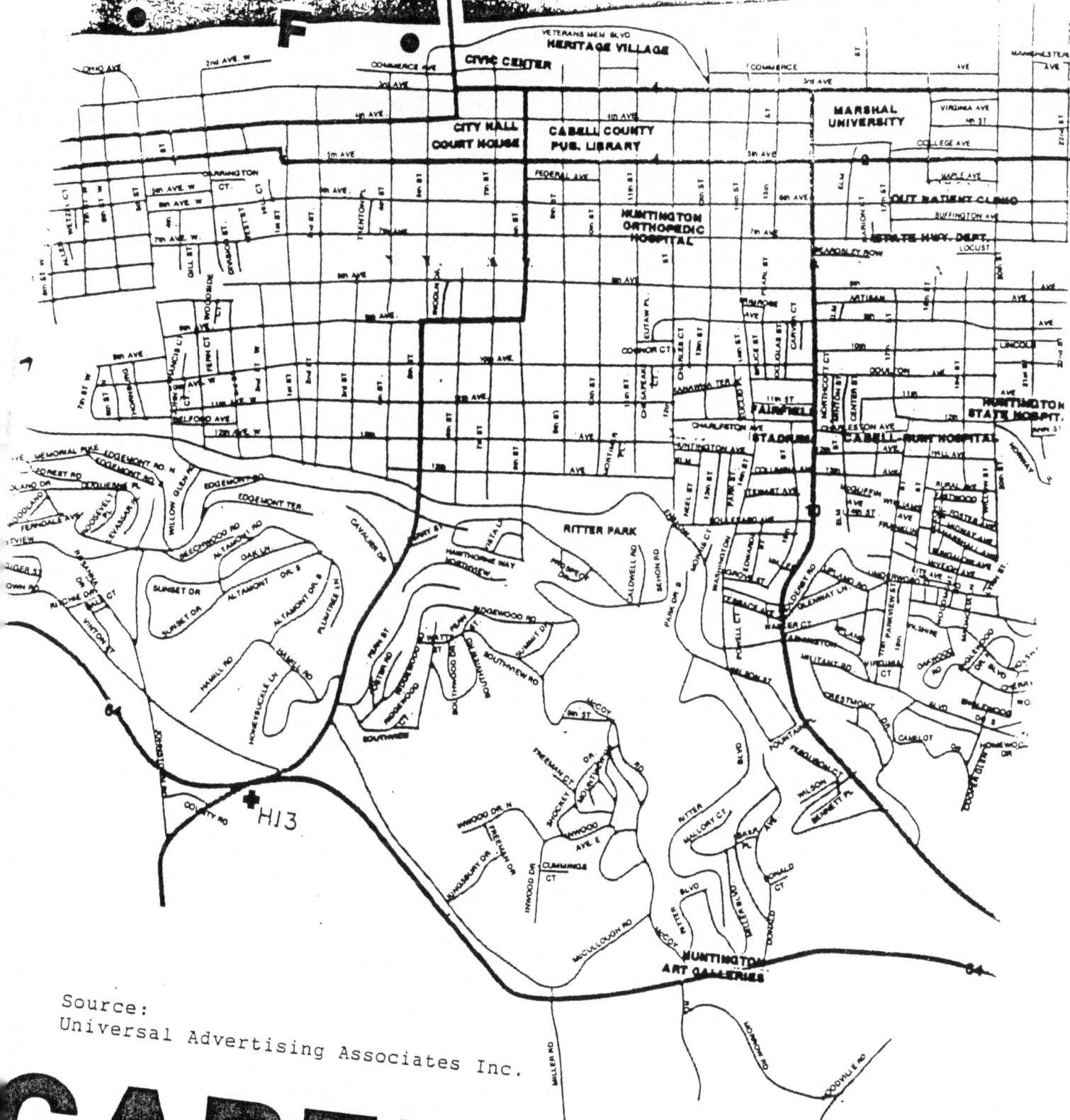

OHIO RIVER

CABELL

Source:
Universal Advertising Associates Inc.

71

H10-SPRING HILL- hill section south of Htng at 20th St.-very old-
following this section indexed by itself

H11-FORESTLAWN- located adjacent to Spring Hill-at Wiltshire Blvd.
and Washington Blvd. modern -unread

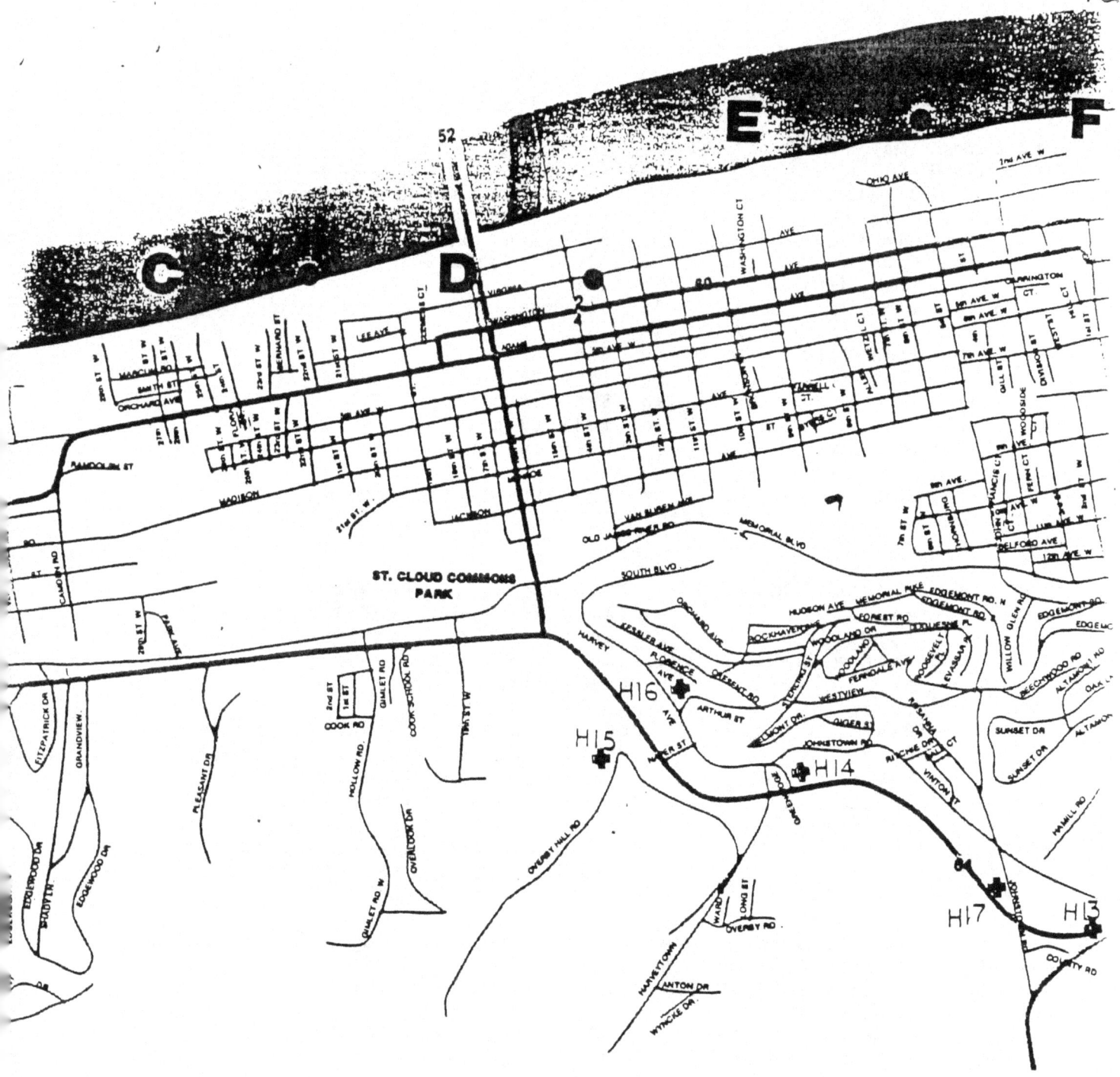

H12-PAINE/Stephenson-located E side 16th St Rd addtion just before I64 X
    DAR reading 1945 lists many more graves than are evident today
    update 1988 Anna Bryant   *=DAR
   *1 Carter,Mary E. 9 oct 1920 64y3m
   *2 Fuller,Elizabeth w/o Sylvester 8 oct 1852   26y2m13d
    3 Paine,Dr.William 22 aug 1865 80y6m21d   (home by cemetery)
    4 Paine,Frances d/o Wm.& E.B. 9 mar 1955   22y8m24d
    5 Paine,Harry 16 sep 1821-25 Jun 1912(no DAR)
    6 Russell,Sarah w/o A.G. 23 aug 1866   38y2m15d
    7 Stephenson,Mary 16 mar 1860 66y
    8 Stephenson,Mark 14 mar 1876   80y8m8d
    9 Stephenson,Francis A. 13 sep 1852   10m
   10 Stephenson,Calvary M. 9 aug 1859 42y3m11d
  *11 Stephenson,Mary Paine 16 sep 1821-25 Jun 1912 d/o Dr.Wm
  *12 Stephenson,Sidney B. 25 Jan 1882 23y11m21d
   13 Stephenson,William P. 26 oct 1849-19 nov 1926
   14 Stephenson,Thomas M 29 aug 1858-9 dec 1927

H13-PINKERMAN-W side of R52 S of Htgn city limits DAR only
    /Pinkerman,John W. 1847-1929
        Josie E. 1861-1926

H14-Childry-3 1/2m S Htng 1500ft N of Harveytown Rd WPA=#
    #Canterberry inf   #Canterberry,May 1890-1912
    #Canterberry,Daisy   #Canterberry,George 1888-1913
    #Canterberry,Rev.G.W.1851-1901 #Canterberry,Sam
        Tennessee 1860-1906   #Canterberry,James
    /Childry,Bessie   /Childry,Walter
        25 nov 1884-31 nov 1886   /Childry,Ed 12 sep 1861-7 sep 1888
    /Childry,Henry   /Childry,Sam W.24 sep 1835-2 feb 1900
        25 dec 1805-30 sep 1887   Sarah 13 Jul 1838-12 oct 1874
    #Crockett,Stella Bell   #Hutchinson,inf 11 dec 1934
        28 sep 1938   60y   #Hutchinson,William 1880-1927
    #Ross,Hannie   #Hutchinson,Stella Anna May 16 Jul 1930
        9 dec 1869-17 oct 1923   #Ross,G.P. 11 feb 1866-23 dec 1929
    #Ross,inf 8 apr 1929

H15-Huxham-Harveytown Rd to Overby Rd t-h turn rt 100yd fenced and well
kept(WPA=#) Carrie Eldridge 15 nov 1989
    #Dillon,William H.1852-1934? /Duckworth,Irnea S.1916--
    /Dixon,William H.1852-19--   Swanson G. 1906-1970
        Elizabeth Huxham 1853-1933 /Grubb,Bertha Frances 1922 inf
    /Grubb,Mary C.1899-1969   /Grubb,Claude Vernon 15 mar 1927-14 Jun 77
        Claude W.1901-1966   /Grubb,Victoria A. 1862-1908
    #Grubb,Howard E.1894-1895w/oWm   Will H.1862-1901
    /Grubb,Evelene 1928-1933   /Hatten,Charlotta L.1855-1936
    /Grubb,Carroll J.1931 inf   Wiley Jr.1859-1946
    /Huxham,Henry C. 1828-1918 born in England
    /Huxham,Sarah Ann Hughes 1831-1908 born in Ireland
        w/o H.C.-d/o Mary Hickey Hughes
    /Huxham,Florence V. 8 sep 1903-28 Jun 1906 d/o Claude W. & L.W.
        granddaughter of Henry & Sarah Ann Huxham
    /Huxham,Harry F. 1870-1918 s/o Henry C. & Sarah Ann
    /Huxham,John H. 1866 inf s/o H.C. & S.A.

/Huxham,John L. 1819-1898 bro/o Henry C.
     2nd Hus/o Mary Hickey Hughes Huxham
/Huxham,Mary Hickey Hughes 1812-1897 mother of Sarah Ann Hughes Huxham
/Huxham,Samuel C.1869 inf s/o HC & SA
/Huxham,Lula W.1883-1954   /Huxham,Howard W.26 apr 1903-29 apr 1946
/Huxham,Claude W.1875-1954   /Huxham,inf 23 apr 1911
/Huxham,Arletta V.1907-1978   /Huxham inf Jan 1957
     Stuart H.1907-1963   /Sanford,Sadie D. 1889-1955
                                     Louis R. 1882-6 dec 1937 s/o H&Eliz.

H16-Hull/Harveytown-turn E on Harveytown Rd at 5th St and I64 1/2m E
  on small rise N of rd mowed,many overturned stones.DAR=/ WPA=# Stones=x
  Begun by the Hull family.   Carrie Eldridge 18 nov 1989
  (The number of missing markers indicates that this cemetery is either
   smaller than it used to be or double buried.There is a school against
   one side.Present area is about 1/2 football field)
xAdkins,Henry L.1887-1962   xAdkins,Edward 16 feb 1889-20 feb 1975
/Adkins,Enos 1847-1926   xAdkins,Lawrence Edward 1911-1924
/Adkins,Mary Jane 1853-   xAdkins,George B. 1861--
     4 feb 1942 88y10m3d   Lucinda Walls 1861-1917
#Adkins,P.L.Jr.1925 inf   #Adkins,Pleasant 11 may 1889-27 sep 1934
xAdkins,Pleasant Jr.1925 inf   Della Mae 1899-1955 m16 jun 1916
xArthur,Willard M.1900-1978   xArrington,Jimmie H.s/o NH&Alah N.1931-32
/Arthur,Herbert & Hurshel 1907xArthur,Lee 21 sep 1877-26 jan 1964
xArthur,Wilda B. and son   Linnie M.3 jun 1880-14 dec 1952
     26 may 1881-2 jun 1903   xArthur,Jennie 22 sep 1853-6 jul 1913
xArthur,J.Dee 1882-1961(Nora)xArthur,Victoria 1903-1926
xArthur,Lonnie 1884-1941   xArthur,Nora Bell 29 jan 1940 55y6m13d
     Laure   1884--   #Arthur,Sterling Morris 5 jul 1933 10y9m17d
/Arthur,Lillian 1905-1908   #Artrip,Georgia B.1872-1932
xBond,Ezra Earl 1912-24 JE&B xBond,Leonard s/o John 1918-1931
xBond,Eugene 1915-1921   xBond,Ada Pinkerman 12 sep 1895-22 jan 1969
xBond,Joseph   xBond,Henry 23 jan 1889-7 jul 1969
xBond,Caroline   xBond,Temperance
xBond,Inos R. 1892 inf   xBond,Anna Lee 1894 inf
xBond,S.Luke 1858-1894   xBond,Lemueal R.15 oct 1920-15 apr 1962WII
xBond,John 1890-1946   xBond,Johnny Leonard 27 jun 1918-7 jun 31
/Boster,F.M.1845-1918   xBoster,Elizabeth 1882-1918
     Susan 1849   xBoster,Thomas 1879-1959
xBenedict,Caroline   /Brown,Alfred CoH 9th WV Inf
xBenedict,Henry Jas 1837-1905   Pheobe 1844-1919
xBrown,Ethell 1882-1916   xBrowningGlayds Opal 29 aug 1907-30 aug 81
xBruce,Sylvester O.1860-1923 xBruce,Roscoe E.1903-1906 s/o SO&A
     Arratentia 1860-1944   Rebecca M.16 may 1898-5 dec 1918
     Dewey M.1898 s/o SO&A   xBruce,Nancy Thompson 5 nov 1819-8 sep 1903
xBrumfield,Lewis Earl 1931-81xBush,Jewel P.15 jul 1916-1 apr 1981
xBush,H.Nye 1914-1932   xBush,James N.10 nov 1883-5 feb 1931
xBush,Wetzel W.   xJosie N.23 sep 1884-12 apr 1956
     10 apr 1910-22 dec 1960   xBush,Roy R.29 may 1908-11 nov 1967
/Callicoat,Rosy Lee 1888-1905xCassell,Laura E.1877-1928
xCanterberry,Frank 1895-1920IxCassell,James R.1872-1950
xChain,Elijah 1872-1936   #Chatterton,Dora E.3-3-1933 47y
/Clonch,B.E. 1880-1920   xChildrey,Isia D. w/o SW 1861-1920
xCloniger,Gladys 1908-1974   xCloniger,Elmer S.25 aug 1905-15 jul 1958

75

xColiflower,Minnie Wall
    1854-1919
xColley,Caroline 1882-1951
/Cox,William
xCox,George H.J. 1818-1882
    Stella J. 1877-1880
#Cyrus,June 6 Jun 1923 inf
xCyrus inf 1938
xCyrus,Ardyth 1912-1969
xCyrus,Blanch M.1918--
xCyrus,Mattie 1887-1965
xCyrus,Pete 1888-1959
xDefoe,Lindorf 1885-1955
xDefoe,Rachael M.1902-1966
xDuncan,Jerrol D.1918-1922
xEarl,Hattie J.
    10 Jul 1893-22 nov 1976
xEarl,Shelby P.
    2 nov 1892-10 aug 1955
/Earl,Henry 1871-1935
xEarl,Alfred H.
    2 feb 1868-30 aug 1963
/Etling,Ralph 1868-1938
xFlowers,Olive B.1884-1971
xFlowers,Simeon 1873-1948
xFloyd,Mollie H.1891-1971
xGibbs,Frank 1894-1957
    Mabel 1894-1973
xGraham,Anna May 1896-1936
    30 mar-13-may
xGreen Sarah 1876-1953
xGreen,Effie 1901-1905
xGreen,Alfred 1907-1912
xGrubb,John W. 1920 inf
xGrubb,Harry I.
    10 oct 1891-27 Jan 1963
xGwinn,Chester G.1881-1978
xHawes,Freddie H.s/o WC&AH
    15 sep 1896-14 nov 1902
xHazelett,C.D. 1900-1936
xHetzer,Tressie Marie 1904inf
xHetzer,Anna Bell 1906 inf
xHite,Roy 12 apr 1909
    Russell 28 Jul 1917
xHowell,inf s/oJA&FD 1909
xHuffman,Matilda Jane 1847-1929
xHuffman,Catherine 1812-1896
    W.M. 1805-1896
    Thomas 1852-1896 s/oWM&C
1 xHull
/Insco,William
    8 Jan 1830-7 apr 1870
xJarrell,inf 1925
xJeffers,Jos.CoD 5th VA Inf

xCole,Olive 1895-1918
xCole,Lawrence W.4 apr 1940 47y8m28d
xCook,James H.nov 1937-17 Jun 1962
xCox,Bessie & Jessie 1881 inf
    Winifred 1874-1886
    Horace A. 1879-1880
/Cyrus,Matilda Marie 13 aug 1901 13y
/Cyrus,Myrtle Blanche 19 Jan 1889-4/8/1891
xCyrus,Nuna 8 dec 1932   63y5m29d
    Joseph S. 1864-1938
xCyrus,Clarence 1 dec 1891-12 dec 1964 WWI
#Defoe,Charles L 14 dec 1937 63y8m29d
xDefoe,William 3 Jan 1910-20 dec 1967
xDotson,dennis C.7 sep 1907-1 mar 1974 WII
xDuncan,Mattie A.#Mollie 16 Jan 1869-8/3/29
    Wm.Harvey 3 apr 1943   83y5m26d
/Earl,Capt.Alton Chester s/o Shelby
    &Hattie 1914-1941 b Ayrshire,Scotland
/Earl,Caroline Marie 11 aug 1942 31d
xEarl,Tempa 28 Jan 1870-24 feb 1948
xEarl,J.Hughey 17 oct 1887-23 feb 1957
xEarl,Anna B.1873-1946
/Etling,N.D. 1833-1901
xFlowers,H.T.19 apr 1912-12 Jul 1937
xFlowers,Howard Emil 1906-1963
/Gibbs,Garland B.19 oct 1893 32y11m5d
/Gibbs,Vernie Ethel 17 mar 1934 32y11m5d
/Gibbs,Creed E.8 mar 1907-25 Jan 1948 WWII
xGilmore,Lawrence   1910-1911s/o WW&N
/Green,Arch 1870-6 Jun 1935   63y2m6d
xGreen,Nora 1892-1905
xGreen,James 1898-1936
xGrimmett,Lorene Sullivan 1909-1956
xGugel,Lester B.3 apr 1896-18 Jan 1976 WWI
xGwinn,Bessie Bond 6 oct 1893-25 feb 1965
#Hann,Earl 1914-1918 s/o James & May
/Hill,Cola F. 2 aug 1934   66y6m10d
xHazelett,Ross 29 apr 1940   49y2m11d
xHazelett,Ethel Earl 1903-1986
xHetzer,John 9 apr 1885-12 aug 1912
xHite,Louise 1913-1916 d/o Florence
xHite,Clerona 1866-1940
xHowell,inf d/o JA & FD 22 apr 1918
xHuffman,James W. 1874-1922
xHuffman,A.J. 29 apr 1842-10 nov 1906
/Huffman,Lucrecy d/o AJ & M 14 Jan 1883 7d
xHull,Hiram D. 15 may 1850 42y1m2d
xHull,Ann 19 Jun 1894 84yw/o Martin
#(Irby,George W. 1861)
#(Irby,George W.Jr. 1899 73y Civil War)
xJarrell,W.B.1868-1953
xJarrell,Mary 1866-1924
xJeffers,Ann 1841-1955

xJohnson, David T.
    1 dec 1839-14 dec 1914
      Sarah J. w/o D. 4 may 1876
#Jones, W.D.
xJordan, F.F.1852-1929
      S.E. 1853-1916
#Lindimood, Mary Duncan
xLindemood, Mrs.May 1892-1914
/Long, Mattie 10 jul 1931 70y
/Long, James E. 1880-1927
xLyons, Sarah
    17 apr 1850-13 sep 1932
      Wm.B.3 aug 1850-22 oct 1939
#Mays, J.M.
xMayo, Mollie 1882-1952
    Thomas J.1876-1946
xMayo, Myrtle 1907-1923
xMcDaniel, Rebecca M.
    2 may 1886-12 aug 1927
xMcDonald, Harley Allan 1891-13
xMiller, Edleweise 1924-1925
xMiller, Gardner 1895-1916
xMontague, Jeanne 1920-1921
#Mustin, inf 1907 d/o WJ&RP
/Norris, P.R.
    24 feb 1843-20 jan 1918
      Lydia A.
        25 dec 1849-10 apr 1924
xO'Dell, John 1881-1956
xOverby, John 1822-1913
      Elizabeth 1837-1909
xOverby, Olevia Ann 1879-1954
xOverby, Edith 1904 inf
/Overby, W.18 jul 1908 inf
xOverby, Robert Hall 1898-1947
xOverby, Dyke B.1874-1961
      Lenora M.1883-1933
xOverby, Garnet Mae
        27 may 1910-27 dec 1937
xOverby, Joseph H.
      13 dec 1909-11 may 1968
/Owens, Earnest S.
      25 sep 1889-11 feb 1929
xPagett, Fannie 1887-1912
xPinkerman, Burtie 1888-1969
      Rev.I.Frank 1881-1985
xPlaster, Ezburn L.1894-1973
      Dora).1903-1986
#Polhamus, Willie J s/o E&R
      15 mar 1886-4 jan 1908
xPyles, Hiram 1861-1946
xQuerry, Ruby E.1892-1944
xQuerry, Oliver 1853-1934
xQuerry, Emma 1864-1946

xJohnson, Bessie F.d/oSW&Isa Childry
      14 mar 1899-6 nov 1915
xJohnson, Cordelia L. 20 jan 1874-26 mar 06
      Edna T. 19 may 1906-21 sep 1911
#Kessick, Harry H.1885-1909
xKnight, George W.1837-1893
      Amanda 1853-1895
xLong, Cecil 1888-1975
      Jessie 1895-1979
#Long, William 17 feb 1938 77y2m13d
xLong, Edith d/oWM&ML26 dec 1891-2 nov 1894
#Markin, Roy Clyde 6 may 1933 17y3m
xMathes, Virginia Dare 1909-1959
xMayo, Phyllis Ann 15 may 1943-19 sep 1958
xMayo, Rema S. 11 nov 1914-28 feb 1976
      Leslie 9 dec 1910-30 jul 1965
xMayo, John Henry 1884-1947
xMcConnell, albert 1857-1937
      Sallie 1857-1913

xMitchel, Paralee Bond 1871-1939
xMitchel, John 25 mar 1938 43y7m7d
xMorris, Donald K.19 aug 1935-1 apr 1977
xNewton, Alma S.7 may 1916-26 jun 1965
/Norris, Rosella May 17 aug 1892 27y2m-PR&L
/Norris, Bettie N. d/o PR&LA 2 mar 1906 18y
xO'Dell, Frank E.18 dec 1910-23 dec 1961
xO'Dell, D.Louise 23 jul 1913-15 dec 1963
xO'Dell, Robert D.8 oct 1924-9 jan 1980
xOverby, John S.1863-1943
/Overby, Charlotte Fay 1935-1936
/Overby, Garnet May 27 dec 1937   27y7m6d
/Overby, Nora 10 oct 1933   50y3m2d
xOverby, Charles Henry 1878-1942
xOverby, Ike 17 apr 1909-27 apr 1980
xOverby, Cecil Arthur 30 oct 1907--
      Anna Weeze 16 may 1909--
xOverby, Lillian 6 jan 1918-16 may 1921
xOverby, Delia A.22 dec 1898-5 oct 1980
xOverby, Claude J.7 sep 189610 oct 1971
xOsborne, Pauline 1915 inf
      Cecil Jr 1916 inf
/Owens, inf dau
/Partlow, Clara M.w/o M.O.1889-1920
xPartlow, Durward C.1913-1944
xPlaster, Charles J.1869-28 jul 1937
      Mary R.1859-1946
xPlaster, Richard Lincoln 1950-1951
xPlaster, Ernestine 1 may 1926=27 aug 1928
xPolhamus, Tressie J.1870-1917
xPyles, Cynthia 1867-1951
xQuerry, Mabel Claire 1883-1893
xQuerry, Lily 9 may 1899-27 may 1974
xRay, Jefferson 1853-1924

xRay,Emma 1893-1897   xRay,Eliza C.1858-1903
xRay,Georgia 1892-1909   xRece,J.Lou 1862-1947
xRichards,John W. 1921-1985 xReynolds,C.S.5 sep 1875-14 feb 1909
xRose,Betty Maude 1897-1930 xRose,Jeff D. 1890-1926
xRutherford,Michael L 1947infxSadler,Parasade Bond
xSansom,Frances L.1894-1937 xShepard
#Shepard,John E.14 Jan 1935 69yxShepard,Frank 1891-1955
xShepard,Ernest R.1903-1965 /Shuff,Bertha 13 sep 1888-11 Jul 1907
    Marie E. 1906-1985   /Shuff,Lola Dove 11 mar 1940 46y6m21d
xShuff,Donald Ray   xShuff,Lester Sr.7 aug 1890-25 may 1972
    13 sep 1926-14 sep 1976 xShuff,Henry 13 Jul 1896-1 dec 1938 WWI
xShumaker,Charles W.   xSimmons,Mayme 1893-1919
    CoG 7th WV Cav   xSizemore,Simon H.8 Jun 1850-17 may 1913
xSmith,Opal Earl 1906-1931   xSizemore,Amanda 15 nov 1935 70y8m29d
xSmoot,Dewit C.Co F 1st OH HA#Stafford,Anna 2 mar 1934 31y7m2d
#Stephenson,Harry W.1890-1926xStaley,Helen F.1952-1978
xStephenson,Harry W.1890-1926xStephenson,Alfred Jr.16 apr 1911--
xStephenson,Eva G.1890-1933   Argusta 31 mar 1908-15 feb 1989
xStephenson,Alfred 1881-1979 xStephenson,Frank 1887-1981
    Fannie 1885-1974   xStephenson,Hattie F.7 mar 1901-3 noc 1918
xStephenson,Wm.Lee 1891-1969 xStephenson,Josephine 1 aug 1869-21 mar 57
    Maude E. 1896-1983   xStephenson,Henry Col 9th WV Inf
xSullivan,Ira L,3 aug 1941 38y   Sarah J.7 may 1844-28 dec 1903
xSullivan,Elgie 1889-1960   xSullivan,James 1914-1985
    Ruth M.1891-1948   xSullivan,Marie 1915-1948
xTeschler,Jacob 1894-1938   xTaylor,Robert F.26 mar 1920-29 nov 1968
xTeschler,Bobby 1923 son   xTechler,Georganna 1902-1987
#Thompson,J.N.27 Jun 1927   #Thompson,Nancy 5 nov 1819-8 sep 1903
    xFlorida 1866-1924   xThompson,James N.1866-1927
xThornburg,Thomas Q.1860-1918xThornburg,Liela M.23 feb 1892-14 may 1950
    Levorn 1862--   xThornburg,Beatrice 1913-1919
xTiller,John 1885-1964   xTiller,Marion Marie 2 may 1915-4 feb 1972
xTiller,Rebecca 1885-1971   xTrosper,Elmer Azle 8 Jun 1905 infs/o BD&ME
xTrosper,Oren Lessie 1892 inf/Trosper,Ballard D.23 Jan 1864-28 feb 64y
xTurner,Lee Roy WWI   Minite E.19 feb 1867-3 oct 1904
    10 oct 1890-27 feb 1973 xVannewkirk,G.Paul 1917-1919
xWalker,Mathew C.1875-1911   xVia,John J.13 aug 1884-13 feb 1980
xWalker,Daniel L.2 Jan 1930 48/Via,Bertha Mabel 5 nov 1911-11 Jan 1919
xWalker,Catherine 1838-1925 xWalker,Dora E.6 aug 1885-21 mar 1933
    Mathew 1839-1895   /Warren,Henry 5 apr 1942 73y1m9d
xWether,Louisa 1881-1918   xWhite,Henrietta 8 Jan 1921
#Wilks,Benjamin F.11 mar 1855/Wilks,George W. 26 Jul 1870 29y5m9d
#Wilson,Anna 30 oct 1938 57y xWilliam,Xilphia 27dec 1903-24 Jan 1908
xWright,Charles   xWright,Thomas M. 1857-1913
    18 dec 1833-21 sep 1926   Mary E. 1867-- w/o T.
    Martha 25 oct 1841--   Edna M. 1906-07 d/o
xZihlman,Arnold G.   xWright,Richard E.1889-1954
    3 feb 1894-3 apr 1967 WWI   stones fallen--8
                                fs---------- 25
                                illegible---- 8
                                unmarked----- 30

H18-Johnson-mouth of Johnson Hollow off James River Turnpike at 15 St.W
begun by James D. Johnson,many unmarked graves DAR(Moved by interstate 64

78

construction to Wayne County.Only DAR=/1944 or #= WPA 1938 listed)

#Adkins,Roy C.24 nov 1935 22y11m24d #Aliff,inf 1938
/Adkins,Matheas /Aliff,Ettie 4 apr 1920 5y
/Akers,John 16 feb 1935 54y /Aliff,Susan 17 apr 1920 4y
/Avis,Samuel 21 apr 1937 inf#Bartram,Mrs.James F.30 Jun 1933 81y7m10d
/Bartram,Wedington /Bartram,Thos.2 aug 1888-11 mar 1926
   Mary B. /Bartram,Maudie Jul aug 1902
     27 may 1867-29 may 1928   McFeele,Robert D.1925-1927
/Bartram,Nora 20y8m2d /Beatty,Everett Roy
    7 oct 1889-9 Jun 1910 #Belcher,Roy C.1904-1929
#Bentley,Mrs.C.C. 1938 29y? /Bentley,C.Curtis 1909-1938
/Bentley,Julius 23 feb 1943 3y/Bentley,Jarvey 29 oct 1865-28 Jul 1927
/Bentley,Delma Jean sep 1937 #Billups,Arett 29 sep 1931 69y8m17d
/Blair,Ernest /Blankenship,William B.2 feb 1942-27y9m17d
#Bruce,Inf 5 oct 1932 #Bryan,William 23 sep 1923 6y8m15d
/Burgess,John A. 1867-1936 /Burtner,Maude 1877-1941
/Bush,James W.bBotetourt Co./Byrom,Susie inf 26 feb 1916
   18 apr 1850-16 sep 1915 /Carter,Mahala 18 nov 1932 74y7m
/Carnell,Jaunita 2 feb 1923 /Carnell,Richard 28 mar 1924
/Carnell,J.L.1865-19-- /Caudill,mary J. 9 sep 1938 inf
   Sarah J.1859-1928 #Chaffin,Phylis Emogene 21 oct 1938 inf
#Chaffin,Helen Fay 1933 inf /Chandler,Gaberiel S. 13 Jan 1934 72y7m26d
/Chandler,Stella 7 apr 1934 /Chandler,Elmer Lee 18 Jan 1938 43y11m23d
   56y5m29d /Chapman,William M.30 may 1936 61y1m21d
/Claxon,Bell 1897-1936 /Cobin,John R. 19 apr 1939 81y8m14d
/Coburn,Mary E.8 oct 1932 /Collins,Manuel 9 mar 1941 60y7m7d
   74y1m26d /Conner,Peter E.11 mar 1941 79y4m12d
/Conner,Elizabeth 1872-1938 /Connock,Wilbert 24 mar 1929 13y10m5d
#Cook,Nancy 93y /Cook,Marinda 1855-1921
#Cornett #Cornett,Richard 28 mar 1924 inf
#Cornett,Waunita 2 feb 1923 #Sarah J. 1859-1928 w/o J.L.
#Crager,John W. /Crager,Jarvie 10 Jul 1902-30 sep 1931
   4 dec 1935 79y3m24d #Crager,Jane 2 apr 1866-4 Jul 1931
/Crager,Jennie 13 dec 1931 /Crager,lawrence D.15 oct 1940 36y9m17d
/Crawford,Mary E.
   12 may 1935 63y4m13d /Curnell,William Co F 1st OH HA
/Cyrus,James Golden 1923-4 /Curnell,Elizabeth 17 mar 1857-13 mar 1938
/Cyrus,Eileen Marie 1920-23 /Diamond,Frank 17 Jum 1935 68y3m1d
#Daniels,Manley 30 may 1937 #Duncan,inf 1932
   19y10m5d /Dunkle,Harry Lee 10 dec 1932 1y4m29d
#Earls,Harrison #Elkins,Icy 14 nov 1906-4 feb 1917
   5 oct 1933 54y1m29d /Elkins,Virgie L.22 Jun 1908-2 feb 1917
/Elkins,Thelmer 1911- 1917 /Elkins,Joy 14 nov 1906-4 feb 1917
/Elkins,Walter H. /Elkins,Thurman 14 Jan 1905-17 sep 1927
   6 apr 1942 64y11m23d /Elkins,Virginia L. 14 dec 1935 4y1m18d
/Elkins,James W. /Elkins,Inez 1907-1934
/Estep,Meredith Edward #Estep,Mary M. 4 oct 1938 70y6m17d
#Estep,Albert /Farmer,William Jr. 13 aug 1927-5 nov 1939
#Fannin,Ray C.11/24/1935 22y#Farrell,Nancy E.2 sep 1935 53y11m18d
/Furguson,mat /Ferguson,Edmond T.28 apr 1932 78y8m4d
/Ferguson,Vance 1905-1936 /Ferguson,Ply--- 8 Jun 1934 64y4m9d
#Ferguson,Mary #Ferguson,Edna Marie 5 aug 1938 inf
#Ferguson,Lizzie 1/25/1935 23y/Fitzgerald,J.31y10m3d
/Flowers,Auzley 12/11/193-50y#Flowers,Paul 10 Jun 1922 6y88m15d

/Freeman,Lizie 1888-1921 /Fuller,Sylvester B.CoB 5th WV Inf
/Fuller,Lora Luella /Fuller,Virginia Lee 14 nov 1932 7y11m14d
   11 Jul 1932 59y1m26d /Fuller,Ray B.30 may 1935 31
/Gibson,Charles E. /Gifford,William S. 1866-1933
   16 jan 1933 2y9m /Gilkerson,Leander 5 aug 1939 77y11m17d
/Gibson,Dorothy J. /Griffith,Thomas 22 oct 1941
   1 mar 1936 2y4m /Griffith,Earl 27 Jul 1941 27y9m17d
/Gunnoe,Elizabeth 1847-1940 /Grizzell,Prudence 11 feb 1929 67y
/Gunnoe,Isaac V. 1874-1940 #Haines,Norma 21 apr 1932 55y10m10d
#Han,Bert C. 19y9m10d /Hancock,James G. 22 dec 1940 WWII
/Hancock,Edith May 1923-1924/Hancock,Eddie F.1919-1940
/Harless,Calvin 1860-1926 /Hancock,Theodore 28 feb 1934
   Missouri 1871-1922 /Hatten,Hildreth M. 11 aug 1929 inf
#Hatten,Florence 33y #Heyton,Rev,hence 3 dec 1888-14 Jan 1931
/Hodge,Shirley Jean 1939 inf/Holbrook,Peggy Lou 23 oct 1932 inf
/Hoos,Cleo 5oct1934 9y4m11d /Houck,Florence 1894-1940
/Hoose,Charles #Hudeburgh,Gladys 10 Jul 1932
   21 nov 1932 69y5m30d /Hutchinson,Mary F. sep 1935 2y1m23d
#Hysell,Alexander /Hutchinson,Ben H.29 may 1890-31 oct 1908
   4 dec 1933 64y /Irby,Lucy 1872-1928 w/o R.T.
/Hysell,Ora /Irby,George W. 15 Jul 1897-17 oct 1911
/Johnson,Cpl.Jas,D.1843-1928#Jeffers,inf 3 Jun 1934
   Co D 10th WV Inf /Johnson,Charles E. 1847-20 may 1914
/Johnson,Naomi   Nora E. 8 Jun 1908 28y
   8 may 1904-11 aug 1913 /Johnson (all on same stone)
/Johnson,J.D. Jr. 1880-1914   William 31 aug 1872
   Madeline   Anna w/o William 1874-1916 42y
   4 mar 1843-28 Jan 1901   Hattie--Francis--Willard--Myrtle
/Johnson,Edward F.   Paul--Edith--Aulden--Ester--Delmer
   24 nov 1910-10 dec 1925   Madaline--Waunnetta
#Kazee,W.J.3 nov 1928 46y9m /Johnson,Germany 28 feb 1935 65y11m4d
/Lafferty,Bert 1 sep 1940 52y#Lampert,Elizabeth 10 aug 1936 62y11m28d
#Looe,Olive 28 oct 1937 29y #Lucas,Louis 14 mar 1932 73y11m27d
#Marrs,Edward 23 apr 1933 84y#Martin,inf 1933
#McCaffery,Guy Ray 1938 inf #McCaffery,Jackie Lee 1935 inf
#McCloud,Robert 1932 inf /McCloud,Virgil 8 Jun 1900-30 Jun 1914
/McCloud,Edna Mae 1942 inf /McCloud,P.V.T.Maryland
#McCloud,James 22 sep 1933   22 may 1896-10 oct 1918
   43y7m7d /McCloud,Elijah W. 15 dec 1922 77y
/McCloud,Annie #McCloud,Mary 16 Jan 1854-19 apr 1923 w/oJH
   20 Apr 1881-24 mar 1931 /McCloud,May w/o A.H.
/McCloud,Dora 24 dec 1932   15 aug 1874-19 apr 1928
   43y1m23d /McCloud,Rinda 20 sep 1939 82y11m20d
/McCoy,Willie 1908-1936 #McFreeley,Robert D.17 apr 1925-12 aug 38
#McWorther,Otho M.11 Jan 1930/Meadows,Charles F. 1935 inf
#Meadows,Christine 1937-38 #Mossburg,inf 4 oct 1933
#Murphy,inf 3 oct 1933 /Nease,Edith Mae 25 nov 1900-3 Jan 1937
#Nicely,James Charles /Nease,Raymond 4 nov 1925-13 sep 1928
/Nichols,Dallas Carley /Noble,Vina 3 sep 1932 66y4m11d
   18 oct 1933 inf #Pinkerton,Fredrick 2 may 1923 inf
#Pinkerton,Leroy #Pinkerton,Maxine
#Pinson,Melvina Marie 1937 8y/Pyles,Herman S. 29 Jun 1913-8 aug 1938
#Pyles,Janet Sue 28 Jan 1937/Pyles,boyd Sherdian 11 aug 1941
/Riggs,marie 189-=1925 /Riggs,Fred 22 Jan 1932 39y4m2d

#Robinson,Jeff 25 sep 193   /Robertson,Elizabeth Virginia
#Romine,Eliza Alice 1928-38   2 feb 1942   31y1d
/Romine,A.C.   /Salyers,Gladys 1909-1922
#Sarten,Joe,Jr.17 dec 1936   Catherine 1915-6
#Silvey,Ethel 1922-23   /Silvey,Martha E. 1920-21
/Simmons,Helen10/14/1933 44y#Simmons,Alexander 17 dec 1928 48y
/Simmons,Harold 31 oct 1934 #Simmons,Anna 30 jan 1938 27y10m9d
/Skaggs,Tim 10 Jan 1935(33) /Smith,Betty Lou 1927
#Smith,Betty Lou 1927   /Smith,Calvin 17 Jun 1940   86y3m
#Smith,Dan   #Smith,Dorothy Alice
#Smith,Mary M.   #Smith,Pearle 22 sep 1933 3y
/Spence,Tinza Lee 29 Jan 1940/Spencer,William C. 6 Jun 1940 39y7m16d
#Stambrouk,-28 nov 1931   /Stapleton,Mrs.Sidney Jane 20 oct 1942 39y4m
     82y2m14d   #Stille,Inf 29 may 1934
/Stump,Ulysses 1 may 1923 47y#Swim,Richd.Ray 9 oct 1933 61y2m11d
/Swim,Wm.Robert 1888-1940   /Thomas,H.E. 1924-1927
/Thomas,Wm.R. 1922-1924   /Thompson,Helen Mae 1928-1930
#Thornton,Jasel R.   /Thompson,Mrs.Levina 2 oct 1933   53y
    21 sep 1930   4y   /Turley,James M. 1857-1929
#Walker,Inf   Nannie P. 1852--
#Walker,Inf 1 Jan 1932   /Walker,Nannie 30 Jan 1939   28y7m19d
#Walker,Louis E.   #Walker,Katherine 11 sep 1932
#Walker,Norma Lee 1932-1933   81y9m   d/o Donald&J.W.
#Wells,Leonard   #Wedington,Mary Bartram
   10 oct 1935   50y6m   27 may 1867-29 dec 1928
/Wells,John 1866-1936   /White,Oucy 17 feb 1932
/Wheeler,Ida Fay 8 may 1939 /Williams,mattie 26 nov 1938 44y
#Wills,John 1899-1936   /Wood,Benjamin F. 2 mar 1940 71y9m8d
#Willert,Ann E. inf

#H18-Small Pox Cemetery-referred to in literature-seems to be old
Guyandotte Cemetery-It was in a flood area and main burials probably
moved to Spring Hill quite early.Victor Letulle is buried a t Spring
Hill although 1st wife is at Guyandotte.

81

#H19-MAYO hilltop above X of Spring valley and Sherwood Rd
(Wayne County)dense underbrush probably 10 unmarked
-Brent Williams 20 nov 1988
   /Adams,A.Vernon 30 may 1900-13 may 1900 ??
   /Adams,John H.22 may 1867-23 sep 1957
      Cora E. 20 mar 1875-23 dec 1943
   /Carey,Clarence E.5 oct 1895-12 Jun 1951
   /Carey,Michael 1942
      Linda 1946
   /Carey,H.Maxwel 1917 inf/o B.F.& Lenonae
   /Carey,Elizabeth 15 Jun 1845-8 nov 1913
   /Carey,Henry E. 1837-1925
   /Carey,Bernice 23 Jul ---37 broken
   /Carey,Everett 1900-1901 s/o B.F.& Adia
   /Ellington,Edsel 26 Jun 1922-23 nov 1968 WWII
   /Hatten,Charles H.1885-1900
   /Hatten Loyd 6 may 1884-24 Jun 1892 s/o M&M
   /Hatten,Marion F.1852-1913
   /Hatten,Henson B.1887-1918
   /Johnson,Nancy H. d 21 Jul 1902 32y
   /Johnson,James M. 1903-1975
      EmmaJean 1910-1977
   /Johnson,Lon
   /Longfellow,Zella B.6 aug 1894-27 mar 1914
   /Mayo,Richard 9 feb 1915 inf
   /Mayo,John T. Co.H 13th WV Inf. Civil War Union
   /Payne,Herman E. 1906-1923
   /Smith,Newton 17 may 1882-30 sep 1983
      Cynthia Mayo 24 mar 1885-14 Jan 1964
   /Toney,Wife 20 nov 1820-10 nov 1876 w/o William

Callicoat-32,75,   Claxton-79   Craft-34,56   Derbyshire-57
Callihan-55   Clay-56   Crager-79   Derwacter-57
Camp-55   Claypool-56   Craig-34,56   DeSilvey-57
Campbell-32,55   Clements-56   Crane-56   Dial-35,57
Canterberry-74,   Clendennin-33,56   Craner-56   Diamond-35,79
  75   Cliness-56   Crawford-34,56,   Dick-35,57
Canterbury-32   Clingenpeel-56   57,79   Dickel-35
Canty-25   Clonch-75   Cremeans-34   Dickerson-35
Cardwell-55   Cloniger-33,75   Crites-57   Dickey-57
Carey-32,82   Clouse-33   Crockett-74   Dickinson-57
Carico-55   Clutts-56   Crook-34   Diddle-35,57
Carlin-32   Cobb(s)-33,56   Crouse-57   Diehl-57
Carnell-79   Cobin-79   Crow-57   Dietz-35
Carney-32   Cochran-33   Crummett-57   Dillard-35
Carpenter-32,55   Cofer-56   Cummins-34   Dillon-35,57,74
Carper-55   Coffman-25,27   Cummings-26,34,   Dills-57
Carr-32,33   Cogar-56   51,57   Dingess-57
Carroll-25,33   Colburn-33   Cummons-34   Dishman-35
Carson-33   Cole-76   Cundiff-57   Dixon-35,57,74
Carter-27,33,   Coleman-27,33,   Cunningham-34,   Dodds-57
  55,74,79   34,56   57   Dodson-27
Cartmill-55   Colliflower-56,   Curnell-79   Donahue-57
Carver-55   76   Curry-57   Donathan-35
Cassell-75   Colley-25,76   Curtis-34   Donnally-35
Castle-55   Collins-25,34,   Cyrus-57,76,79   Donovan-57
Casto-55   51,79   Dorcas-35
Catron-55   Colvin-56   Dabeney-34   Dotson-35,76
Caudill-79   Combs-34   Dailey-34,57   Douglas-57
Ceasar-33   Cometto-56   Dallis-57   Douthit-24
Chaffin-55,79   Connelly-25,56   Damron-34,35,57   Downer-24
Chain-75   Conner-79   Dankin-57   Dowdy-57
Chalmers-55   Conock-79   Daniels-35,57,79   Draper-35,57
Chambers-33,55   Conrad-56   Darby-34   Dray-35
Chandler-33,79   Cook-34,56,76,   Darden-34   Drewry-35
Chapman-33,55,   79   Darling-34   Druen-57
  56,79   Coon-34   David-57   Drummond-35
Charles-56   Cooper-26,34,56   Davidson-57   Duckworth-74
Charlton-33   Copeland-56   Davin-57   Dufour-35
Chatterton-75   Copenhaver-56   Davis-27,35,57   Duke-57
Chicatans-25   Corbitt-34   Dawson-35,57   Duling-57
Childers-33,56   Cornett-79   Day-25,57   Duncan-23,35,57
Childress-33   Corns-56   Deal-35,57   76,79
Childr(e)y-74,   Cornwell-34   Dean-27,57   Dunfee-57
  75   Cort-56   Dearing-57   Dunkle-79
Chipps-56   Coryell-56   Debar-51   Dunlap-35,57
Christian-33   Corum-34   Debord-25   Dunn-35
Christman-51   Cosby-34   Deegans-57   Durea-57
Christy-56   Courts-56   Defoe-76   Durfee-58
Church-33,56   Cowdin-56   Degraw-23   Durrett-57,58
Clagg-56   Cowles-56   DeHart-35   Dwornick-51
Clampett-51   Cox-34,56,76   Deitz-35   Dye-58
Clanghton-25   Coyle-34   Denney-57   Dyer-58
Clark-24,27,   Crabtree-56   Dennison-35
  33,56   Craddock-34   Denore-25

Eagan-35
Eakin-58
Earl(s)-35,
   58,76,79
Eary-25
Easley-58
Easter-58
Easterling-58
Easthom-35
Eaves-58
Eblin-58
Edgington-35
Edwards-35
Effingham-35
Elam-58
Elkins-25,35,
   79
Ellington-82
Elliot-58
Ellis-27,35,
   51,58
Elswick-58
England-35,36
Enoch-58
Ensley-36
Enslow-58
Erskine-58
Erwin-36,58
Eskew-36
Estep-36,79
Esque-36,58
Etling-76
Evans-36,58
Evendoll-58
Everett-23
Ewen-58
Fain-27
Fairfax-36
Fannin-36,79
Farmer-79
Farah-58
Farley-36,58
Farrell-79
Farr-58
Farrar-58
Farren-36
Farris-58
Farrish-58
Faulconer-58
Faulkner-58
Faust-58
Felix-36
Fellure-58
Ferguson-28,36,
   58,51,79

Ferrell-36,58
Fetty-36,58
Field-58
Fielder-25,36,51
Fillinger-36,58
Fink-58
Finley-25
Fisher-58
Fitzgerald-25,
   27,79
Fitzwater-36
Fizer-58
Fleming-27
Fleshman-58
Fletcher-36
Flora-36
Flory-58
Flowers-58,76,
   79
Floyd-36,58,76
Foard-58
Fogarty-36
Follrod-58
Forbes-58
Forrest-36
Fortune-36
Forth-51
Foster-37,58
Fowler-24,58
Fox-37
Fradd-51
Fragulis-58
Fraley-58
Frampton-58
France-37,58
Francis-58
Franklin-27,58
Freeland-37
Freeman-58,80
Frew-58
Fridley-37
Fry-37,58
Fudge-25,37
Fulks-58
Fuller-37,58,74
   76,80
Fullerton-58
Fulton-58

Gallaher-37,58
Galloway-58
Gamer-58
Gang-58
Ganty-25
Gardner-26,58

Garland-27,58
Garner-26,58
Garred-58,59
Garrison-58
Garvin-59
Gary-37
Gasner-25
Gebbarht-59
Geiger-59
Gellengwater-27
George-51,59
Gerlach59
Gerrald-59
Gibbs-76
Gibson-28,37,
   59,80
Gifford-80
Gilbert-37
Gilkerson-80
Gill-59
Gillenwater-37
Gillespie-37,59
Gillett-37,59
Gilliland-59
Gilmore-37,59,76
Ginn-59
Gioia-25,37
Givens-59
Gladwell-37
Glaspie-37
Glass-37
Glen-59
Glover-59
Godby-37
Godwin-59
Goekemeyer-59
Goff-59
Golden-27,59
Gooch-59
Goodman-37
Goosley-27
Gordon-59
Gore-59
Gosnay-59
Gottshall-59
Goucher-59
Gould-59
Goulding-59
Graham-37,59,76
Grant-37,59
Grate-59
Graves-59
Gray(s)-27,59
Green-59,76
Greenwall-59

Gregory-59
Griffith-59,79
Grimmett-59,76
Grizzell-59,80
Grogan-59
Grose-24,59
Grubb(s)-37,59
   74,76
Gugel-76
Gundy-37
Gunnoe-37,80
Gwinn-59,76
Hackney-37
Haddox-59
Hagen-59
Hager-37,59
Haines-80
Hale-37
Hall-37,38,51,59
Hallstead-59,60
Hamer-59
Hamill-60
Hamlin-38,60
Hamilton-60
Hamm-38,60
Hammock-60
Hamrick-60
Han-80
Hancock-38,80
Handley-26,38,60
Hanley-60
Hann-38,76
Hannan-60
Hannoon-60
Hanshaw-38,60
Harbour-60
Hardlin-60
Hardy-60
Harlan-38,60
Harless-38,60,80
Harmon-25,27
Harold-60
Harril-27
Harris-38,60
Harrison-38,60
Harshbarger-38,39
Hartenbach-60
Harvey-38,60
Haskell-60
Hastings-60
Hatfield-38,60
Hatten-60,74,76
   80,82
Havens-38
Haverly-25

Haverty-25
Hawes-60,76
Hay-60
Hayden-38
Hayes-38,60
Haynes-60
Hayslip-38
Hazard-60
Hazelett-38,
  60,76
Heatherman-60
Heck-60
Heiner-60
Helwig-38
Henderson-25,
  38,39,60
Henkle-60
Henley-39
Hennen-39
Henritze-60
Henry-39
Hensley-39,
  60,61
Henson-61
Herbert-39
Herren-61
Hesson-51
Hetzer-76
Hetyer-61
Hewitt-61
Hibner-61
Hicks-39,61
Hidy-61
Hider-24
Higgins-61
Hill-27,39,
  61,76
Himes-61
Himmongs-51
Hinchman-39,61
Hinerman-61
Hines-39,61
Hite-24,26,
  39,61,76
Hix-61
Hoback-61
Hobgood-61
Hodge(s)-39,80
Hoff-61
Hogg-61
Holderby-26,
  39,61
Holland-27,39
Holley-27,39,
  51,61

Holliday-61
Holm-61
Holton-61
Holtzworth-61
Homer-39
Honaker-61
Hood-61
Hooper-61
Hoos(e)-80
Hopkins-61
Horner-61
Horocks-51
Horton-39
Howard-25,61
Howell-61,76
Howerton-39
Hubbard-39
Hubman-39
Huckelby-39
Huddleston-61
Hudeburgh-80
Hudson-39
Huff-39,51
Huffman-39,61,76
Hughes-39,61
Hull-76
Humphreys-61
Hundley-61
Hunt-39,61
Hurst-61
Husk-39
Hutchinson-61,74
  80
Hussell-39
Huston-39
Huxman-74,75,76
Hynes-25
Hysell-39,61,80

Ingram-61
Inlow-25
Innis-61
Insco(e)-61,76
Irby-76,80
Isaacs-61
Isbell-61
Ison-61

Jackson-27,39,
  40,62
James-40,62
Janey-51
Jarrell-40,76
Jarvis-62
Jeffers-62,71a,76

Jefferson-62
Jesse-62
Jenkins-40,62
Jewell-24
Johnson-27,28,40,
  51,62,77,80,82
Johnston-28,62,
  71A
Jones-28,40,51,
  62,77
Joplin-40
Jordan-40,62,77
Judd-40
Jukovich-62
Justice-62

Kane-62
Kain-25
Karnes-62
Karriger-40
Kaufman-40,62
Kayes-62
Kazee-80
Kearns-23
Keathley-62
Keefe-25
Keefer-40
Keeler-62
Keen-25
Keenan-40
Keffer-40
Keith-51
Kellerman-62
Kellogg-40
Kelly-40,51,62
Kendle-40,62
Kennedy-40
Kershner-62
Kessick-77
Keyser-40,62,71A
Kidd-62
Kilgore-62,71A
Kincaid-25,40,62
King-40,62
Kingery-40,62
Kingsbury-62
Kinney-62
Kipp-62
Kirk-62
Kirtley-62
Kise-24
Kiser-62
Kittle-62
Klinebell-62
Knapp-62

Knight-28,40,62,
  71A,77
Knootz-62
Knowlton-62
Kouse-62
Kreil-62
Krugher-62
Kuhn-62
Kyle-40
LaBelle-71A
LaFollette-62
LaFon-40
Lagrange-24
Lafferty-80
Lake-62
Lambert-40
Lampert-80
Landers-62
Lane-40
Laney-40
Langdon-40,62
Langfitt-62
LaPole-62
Lawhorn-62
Lawson-23,26
Lawter-62
Lay-62
Layman-62
Layne-40
Leach-40
Leake-62
Leckie-62
Lee-28
Leffington-41
Legge-25,41,62
LeGrand-41
Leibee-41
Leighton-62
Lemley-62
Lemings-62
Lenahan-62
Lenz-62
Leport-41,51
Leppert-62,63
Leroy-62
Leslie-63
Lester-24
Letulle-26,41
Lewis-41,63
Lindemood,63,77
Linkfield-41
Linville-41
Lipton-63
Lively-63
Locke-63

Lockett-28
Logan-41
Londy-28
Long-41,63,77
Longfellow-82
Looe-80
Losee-63
Losey-41
Louden-63
Love-26
Lovejoy-51
Lowery-41,63
Lucas-63,80
Lump-63
Lurch-63
Lusher-71A
Lusk-63
Luthe-63
Luther-41
Lykins-41
Lynch-41
Lynn-63
Lyons-51,63,77

Madge-63
Maddy-63
Magoon-63
Mahan-63
Mallory-63
Malloy-63
Malcolm-41,63
Mankin-41
Manley-25
Mann-63
Marcum-63
Markin-77
Marks-63
Marrs-63,80
Marshall-71A
Martin-28,41,
   63,80
Mason-51
Massey-63
Massie-63
Masterson-63
Mathes-77
Matnee-41
Mat(t)hews-24,
   41,63
Mattison-25
Mattox-51
Maxwell-41
Mayberry-41
Mayenschein-41
Maynard-42,63

May-42
Mayo-77,82
Mays-26,42,77
Mayse-42
McAlister-63
McCaffery-63
McCafferty-80
McCallister-42,
   63,71A
McCarthy-63
McClain-42
McClaren-63
McClarey-63
McClaskey-42
McClintock-42
McCloud-80
McClure-42,63
McClogin-42
McColm-63
McComas-63,71A
McConnell-77
McCorkle-24,42
McCoy-42,63,80
McDaniel-63,77
McDonald-77
McDonie-42
McFarland-28
McFreeley-80
McGhee-42
McGinnis-23,42,63
McGougan-63
McGuire-42
McIntosh-63
McKee-63
McKelvey-63
McLaughlin-25,64
McMahan-64
McMillan-64
McNeeley-42,64
McNelly-64
McNeer-42
McVey-64
McWorther-42,80
Meabon-42,64
Meade-42,51
Meadows-28,42,64,
   80
Mears-26
Meddings-42
Meek-64
Meldahl-64
Melton-42
Mengert-64
Meyers-64
Michael-64

Middleton-64
Midkiff-27,64,71A
Miles-42
Mildner-42
Millender-64
Miller-42,64,77
Milner-42
Minnick-42
Minton-71A
Mitchell-42,64
   77
Mobley-42
Molter-64
Montague-77
Moody-28
Moore-28,34,42
   43
Moreland-64
Morgan-64
Morris-27,28,43
   64,77
Morrison-43,64,
   71A
Moruney-25
Mosby-64
Moses-64
Mosier-64
Moss-64
Mossburg-80
Mossman-64
Moury-43
Mucklow-43
Mulcany-25
Mulgahy-25
Mullens-43
Muller-64
Munsell-64
Murphy-43,64,80
Murray-43
Murry-43
Mustin-77
Myers-64

Napier-43
Nash-28,64,71A
Neal-43,64
Nease-80
Neely-64,71A
Neff-64
Neighorgall-64
Nelson-43
Neutzling-64
Newman-43,64,65
Newsome-51
Newton-77

Nichols-28,43,80
Nicol-65
Nickel-65
Nida-71A
Nihiser-65
Nimon-65
Noble-65,80
Noel-43
Nohm-43
Noonan-65
Noris-77
Norman-65
North-43
Northcott-65
Notter-65
Nuckels-65
Nugent-65
Null-51,65
Nurnberger-65

Oakes-65,71B
Obenshain-65
Oberholtzer-65
O'Brien-25,65
O'Conner-25
O'Dell 65,77
O'Donnell-43
Ogg-65
Ohlinger-43
Oksnee-65
Oldaker-43
Oliver-43,65
Oneill-65
Oney-65
Oppenheim-65
Osborne-65,77
Osburn-65
O'Shea-65
Ostrowski-43
Oswald-65
Otten-51
Overby-77
Owens-24,28,65,77
Oxley-43,65

Pack-51,65
Page-43,71B
Pagett-77
Paine-74
Palmer-65
Pancake-65
Panson-65
Parker-26,65
Parkmokuk-51
Parsley-43

Parsons-65
Partlow-51,77
Paston-43
Patterson-43,65
Patton-65
Patrick-43
Paul-65
Pauley-43,65
Payn-28
Payne-82,65
Paynter-28
Peck-65
Pemberton-43
Pennington-65
Penuose-44
Perdue-65
Perkins-26,44
Perry-44,65
Peters-26,28,
   44,65
Petit-44
Petrie-44
Petry-65
Petite-23
Petty-65
Peyton-71B
Pfeifer-65
Phillips-28,65
Pickens-44
Pifer-65
Pike-44
Pilcher-65
Pine-44,65
Pinkerman-74,77
Pinkerton-80
Pinson-80
Pitzer-65
Plaster-65,77
Plunkett-65
Plymale-65
Pogue-28
Polhamus-77
Poindexter-44
Poling-44
Pollard-65
Pool-65
Porter-26,44,
   265,66
Poston-44
Potter-44
Pound-51
Powell-66
Powers-44,66
Pratt-66
Preston-66

Price-28,66
Prichard-44,66
Priddy-66
Prince-44
Proudfoot-66
Pryor-66
Pulley-44
Pullman-44
Putts-28
Pyler-66
Pyles-28,77,80

Qualls-28,66
Querry-77
Quinlan-26

Radcliffe-66
Raimey-28
Raines-66
Rairden-44
Ramsey-66,71C
Rand-44
Randalls-28,44,
   71C
Randant-44
Rangos-44
Radin-44
Ratliff-44,66,
Ray-44,66,71C,
   77,78,87
Rayborn-44
Rayburn-66
Raynor-44
Reatherford-66
Rece-27,78
Reckard-66
Reed-44,66
Reeder-44,66
Rees-66
Reese-44,66
Reggel-71C
Reid-24,66
Reiley-66
Rener-66
Reynolds-44,51,
   66,71C,78
Rhodes-44,66
Rice-44
Richards-78
Richardson-44,
   45,66
Richey-66
Rickard-66
Ridenour-45
Rider-66

Riggs-45,66,80
Ripley-66,71C
Ripple-45
Ritter-66
Roach-66
Roberson-66
Roberts-66
Robertson-66,81
Robinson-28,51,
   66,81
Roby-66
Rochefort-66
Rock-26
Rodefer-45
Roe-26,66
Rogers-45
Rolph-66
Rollyson-45
Romine(s)-26,45
   66,81
Rood-66
Rose-66,78
Rosenheim-66
Ross-66,74
Roten-45
Rottman-26
Row-66
Rowsey(u)-45,71C
Roy-45
Royce-66
Rucker-45
Runyan(o)-45
Russell-26,45,
   66,74
Rust-45
Rutherford-78
Rye-45

Sabin-45
Sadler-66,78
Safford-66
Salamon-45
Salmons-51,66
Salyers-81
Samoles-45
Sanders-66
Sandrock-66
Sandford-75
Sanks-66
Sansom-45,66,78
Sargent-45
Sarten-81
Saunders-45,66,67
Saver-67
Sawyer-67

Saxton-45,46
Sayre-67
Scarberry-46,51
Scott-46
Schanek-46
Scheneberg-46
Schieffelin-67
Schmidt-67
Schmitz-66,67
Schoew-67
Schrote-67
Schulze-67
Seal-67
Seaman-67
Sebaugh-67
Secrest-67
Sedginer-46
Seeley-46
Selbee-46
Sellards-67
Sexton-46,67
Shackleford-67
Shaffer-46,67
Shank-67
Shanklin-67
Shannon-67
Sharitz-67
Shatterfield-28
Shaver-46
Shaw-27,67
Sheets-46
Shelton-46,67
Shepard-67,78
Shmonoff-67
Shoemaker-46
Shore-67
Short-26,46,67
Shorter-24,46
Shouen-67
Shuff-67,78
Shumaker-67
Shumway-67
Shultz-24,26
Shy-46
Sibrel-46
Sidebottom-67
Siers-67
Sikes-46
Silmon-46
Silvers-67
Silvey-80
Simmons-67,78,81
Simms-46,67,71C
Simpson-46,67,71C
Sinsell-67

Sites-46,67
Sizemore-46,78
Skaggs-67,81
Slash-67
Slater-67
Slaughter-51,67
Slayton-46
Smeltzer-67
Smith-27,28,46,
  67,78,81,82
Smithson-67
Smoot-28,67,78
Snedegar-67
Snyder-67
Songer-46
Sovine-67
Sowards-26,51,67
Sparks-67
Spaulding-46,67
Spears-67
Spencer-46,
  68,81
Sperry-68
Sprinkle-26
Sprouse-68
Spurlock-46,
  47,67,68
Spry-51
Stack-47
Stackhouse-68
Stafford-68,78
Stahl-47
Staley-78
Stalnaker-68
Stambrouk-81
Stanley-47,68
Stansill-26
Stapleton-47,81
Starcher-68
Starkey-68
Staten-47
Steans-51
Steed-47
Stender-26
Stephenson-47,
  68,74,78
Stepp-47
Sterling-68
Stevens-68
Stevenson-28,47
Stewart-26,
  47,68
Stickler-47
Stille-81
Stogden-47

Stollings-47,68
Stone-47,68
Storey-47
Stork-68
Stover-68
Strachan-68
Strader-68
Stratten-68
Straughan-68
Stricker-68
Strickling-68
Strum-47,68
Stuart-68
Stump-68,81
Sturm-68
Stutler-68
Sudderth-47
Sullivan-68,78
Summers-68
Swann-26,47,68,
  71C
Sweeney-47,68
Sweetsir-68
Swentzel-68
Swezey-68
Swisher-68
Swim-47,81
Sydenstricker-47
Sykes-51
Tabor-71D
Tackett-47
Talip-68
Tanis-51
Tarbutton-68
Tatum-28
Taylor-28,47,68,
  78
Templeton-47,68
Tescher-78
Thacker-47,51,68
Thomas-47,68,81
Thompson-28,47
  48,68,78,81
Thornburg-48,78
Thornhill-28
Thornton-48,68,81
Thuma-68
Tignor-68
Tiller-78
Tinsley-68
Todd-68
Tomlinson-48,68
Tompkins-68
Tompson-68
Toney-48,82

Tooley-48
Topp-68
Topping-48
Torbert-68
Townes-51
Trainor-68
Traylor-68
Trent-48,68
Trimble-68
Triplett-48
Trosper-78
Trout-48,68
Tucker-68,69
Turley-48,68,81
Turner-28,48,68,
  69,78
Turvey-51
Tweel-69
Twyman-48
Tyler-48
Tyree-69

Uhles-69
Ullom-69
Utterback-69

Vaden-69
Valentine-69
Vance-48
Van Faussien-69
Van Fleet-69
Van Voorhis-69
Vannewkirk-78
Varner-69
Vaughn-69
Venable-28
Vernatt-28,48
Vest-69
Via-78
Vickers-69
Vines-69
Vitatoe-69

Wagner-48
Wagoner-69
Waldeck-69
Walker-48,51,69
  78,81
Wall-69
Wallace-69
Walling-48
Walton-24,48,69
Ward-48,69
Warren-69,78
Warth-69

Washington-28
Wass-69
Watkins-28,51,69
Watson-28
Watts-51,69
Waugh-48,69
Waybright-69
Wearty-48
Weaver-48,69
Webb-24,69
Weber-69
Wedgwood-69
Wedington-81
Weekly-48,69
Weese-69
Welch-26,48,51
Welker-69
Wellington-27,48
Wellman-51,69
Wells-48,69,81
Wentz-48,49
Wertz-48
Weser-49
West-69
Wether-78
Wetzel-69
Whalen-69
Wheeler-24,48,69,81
Whipple-69
Whitaker-69
White-48,69,78,81
Whitehurst-28
Whitley-69
Whitney-69
Whitt-26
Whitten-69
Whittenberg-69
Wittington-48
Wickline-51
Wiegel-69
Wigal-26
Wiggins-51
Wigner-24
Wilcox-48,69,70
Wilcoxen-69,70
Wild-70
Wildoner-70
Wiley-49,70
Wilhoit-49
Wilks-49,70,71D,78
Wilkins-70
Wilkinson-70
Wilkmink-49
Willert-81

Suppliment #1-
        JOHNSON CEMETERY -formerly in the west end of Huntington at the
mouth of Johnson Hollow. REMOVED BY I-64 construction
Reinterment at several sites in both Cabell and Wayne Counties.
no dates given on the Removal Sheets
####Burials on this page and not on H18 would be buried after 1945.
Graves were numbered 1-734 begining count NE corner
            unknown graves.(180 or 25%)
Alphabetical list given not orginal numbers.
All in first section moved to DOCK'S CREEK Cemetery-Wayne Co.WV

Adams,James L.	Blankenship,Susie	Cook,twins/Carl
Adkins,George W.	Blankenship,Hiram M.	Cook,Delbert
Adkins,Virginia	Blankenship,William E.	Cook,twins
Adkins,Walter	Bungard,Harry	Cook,Bobby
Adkins,Thurmond	Burgess,Mollie	Corns,Orville
Adkins,Edith	*Burgess,John A.	Cornwell,Wiley
Adkins,A.	Burns,Joyce,	Craft,inf
Adkins,Halie Marie	Burtner,Maud	Craft,inf
*Akers,John	*Bush,James W.	*Crager,Lawrence
Aliff,Georgia	Bryan,inf/Susie	Crager,Flossie
*Aliff,Susie	Bryan,Elizabeth	*Crager,Jarvie
*Aliff,Effie	Bryan,Ida M.	Cremeans,Edith M
Aliff,Alson	*Bryan,William D.	Cremeans,2 inf
Artrip,Leonard	Bryan,Nora A.	Crockett,Georga
Artrip,Leonard	Bryan,Duncan	Curnell,Sarah
Artrip,inf	Bryan,James	Curnell,twins
Artrip,Mable	Bryan,inf/Susan	*Curnell,Wanda
*Arvis,Samuel	Bryan,Hassel Lee	Curnell,W.M.
Babcock,Donald	Chandler,Elmer Lee	Curnell,Ella.
Babcock,John	Chandler	*Curnell,J.L.
*Bartram,Maddy	*Chandler,Stella	Curnell,Richard.
*Bartram,Mary B.	*Chandler,Gabriel	*Daniels,Nanley W.
*Bartram,Wed	Christian,inf	Daniels,Minnie Bell.
*Bartram,Thomas	Cheek,John W.Sr.	Daniels,Wm.H.
*Bartram,Nora	Cliff,inf	Davis,Theodore
Bartram,Nina R.	*Clason,Bell	Davis,Theodore Wm.
Basenback,Anna Lee	Clason,Ina L.	Dean,Dorothy
Beckner,inf	Claxon,Mary Bell	Dean,inf
*Belcher,Roy G.	Cobull,John	Deskin,R.E.
Belcher,James	Cobun,Bob	*Diamond,Frank
Belcher,James	*Cobun,Ellen	Dower,inf/Lee
Belcher,John	Coffman,inf	Earl,Callie
Belcher,Anna	Cogur,Eliza	Earl,Harrison
Belvin,Catherine	Collins,Wanda	Earl,Lemuel
*Bentley,C.Curtis	Collins,Cleatis	Eggleston,inf
Bentley,Dallas	Conley,Debra Kay	Eggleston,inf
Bentley,Dallas	Conley,James	Ekers,Patsy
*Bentley,Jarvis	Conley,Dolly Jane	Ekers,Floyd
*Bentley,Delmas	*Conner,Elizabeth	Elkins,Charles E.
*Bentley,Julius	*Conner,Peter	*Elkins,Va.Lucille
Bentley,Susie	*Cook,Marinda	*Elkins,James W.
Billips,James Perry	Cook,Wm.R.	*Elkins,Inez
Billips,inf	Cook,Rossella	*Elkins,Thelmer
Black,Walter	Cook,Anna Louisa	*Elkins,Icy

Elkins,William	*Gibson,Dorothy	Johnson,Stella B.
Elkins,inf	*Gibson,inf/Chas	Johnson,Mother
Elkins,Luro	Gibson,Eunice G.	Johnson,Shirley
*Elkins,	Gibson,Elizabeth	Johnson,Thomas B.
*Elkins,	Gibson,Pierce Isaac	Johnson,Georgie L.
*Elkins,Virgie	Gifford,Mary	2/Johnson
Elkins,Frank	Gillett,inf/America	Johnson,Fannie
Elkins,Emma	Grizzell,Mattie	Johnson,Anna
Elkins,Roba	*Grizzell,Prudence	*Johnson,William
Elkins,Josephine	Grizzell,Charles	*Johnson,Madeline
*Elkins,Walter	Grizzell,Robert	*Johnson,J.D.
Ellis,William	Gunn,Isaac	Johnson,Julious
Estep,Harvey	*Gunnoe,Isaac	*Johnson,Jas.D
Estep,Herbert	*Gunnoe,Elizabeth	Johnson,Wmma K.J.
*Estep,Albert	Gunnoe	Johnson,John
Estep,James	Haberlin,John	3/Johnson,inf
Estep,Mary E.	*Hancock,Eddie	*Johnson,Edward F.
Fannin,Ronnie	*Hancock,Theodore	*Johnson,Norma
*Fannin,Roy Clyde	*Hancock,James G.	*Johnson,Charles E.
*Farmer,Junior	*Hancock,,Edith May	Johnson,Nettie
Felix,Jane	*Hancock,Eddie	Johnson,Ray J.Thomas
Ferguson,Geo.Ralph	Hancock,Lana	Johnson,Bud
Ferguson,Everett H.	Hancock,Charles	Johnson,Ben
Ferguson,Madison	Harber,inf	Johnson,Lester
Ferguson,Franklin	Harkins,Joseph	*Johnson,Germany
Ferguson	*Harless,Calvin	*Keese,W.J.
Ferguson,Vince	*Harless,Missouri	Lambert,Larry
Fitzgerald,J.	Harless,W.M.	Lambert,inf
*Flowers,Raul U.	Harmon,Judy Ann	Lambert,Mary E.
Flowers,Lemuel	Harmon,Va.Carol	Laverty,Samuel S.
*Flowers,Auize	Harris,inf	Laverty,J.A.
Flowers,Florence	*Hayton,Hence	Laverty,M.S.
Flowers,Jeoard	Hicks,Nora	Laverty,V.T.
Francis,Mary	Hicks,Menace	Lewis,Archie C.
Freeman,Elizabeth	Hicks,inf	Lowe,Grant
*Freeman,Lizzie	*Hoose,C.A.	Lowe,inf
Freeman	*Hoose,Cleo	Lowe,Shelby
Fritz,George Wm.	Houck,Carl	Lowe,Marie
Fritz,George	Howe,Anna	Luther,Andy
Fritz,George Kr.	Howe,Ruby	Maddings,Mammie E.
*Fuller,Laura	Howe,G.W.	Madding,Bill
Fuller,Charles	Hughes,Junior	Madding,Walter
Fuller,Laura	Hughes,C.M.	Madding,Darlene
Fuller,George	Hutchinson,inf HB	*Martin,inf
*Fuller,Virginia	*Hutchinson,Ben H.	Martin,Elliot
*Fuller,Roy	Hutchinson,Paul D.	Martin,Ronald E.
Fuller,Harold	Hutchinson	May,Emma
F	Irby,R.L.	May,Dora
F	Irby,Victoria Harris	Maynard,inf
F	*Irby George W.	Maynard,Mary D.
Gibson,Carol	*Irby,Lucy	McClanahan,Adolph
Gibson,Alvin C.	Isom,Sam	McClanahan,Harold
Gibson,George	Johnson,Wm.Oliver	McClanahan,Mildred

McClanahan,Lillian	Perkins,Robert	Stump,Ollie
McClanahan,Fredrick	Perkins,Myrtle K.	Stump,Maggie
McClanahan,Fannie	Pinkerton,Anna	Starr,2 inf/John
McClanahan,Clarance	Pinkerton,Charles	Stender,Hiram
McCloud,George	*Pinson,Melvina	Sublett,Martha
*McCloud,Rinda	Powell,John H.	Sweeney,Herbert
McCloud,Va.Rutha	*Pyles,Herman Sr.	Sweeney,Nettie
McCloud,Joe	Pyles,Effie	Sweeney,Lana
*McCloud,Dora	*Pyles,Boyd,Sherdian	Swim,Jerome
McCloud,John B.	Pyles,inf	Swim,Jerrs
McCloud,Lavern	Reed,Harry	Swim,Maybell
McCloud,Wilburn	Reed,Della	*Swim,Robert
McDaniels,Alma	Rice,Glenn	*Swim,Richard
McDaniels,Ailene	Rice,Larry	Swim,Christina
McDaniels,Anna Bell	Rice,Jerry	Swim,Hawkins
McDaniels,Margaret M.	Richard,Glen	Swim,Phillip S.
*McFreeley,Robert D.	Riggs,Elsie	Thomas
McGuire,Belva	*Riggs,Fred M.	Thomas,Paul
McKee,Ethel	*Riggs,Marie	*Thomas,H.E.
McWhorter,Fred	Robuon,Elizabeth	*Thomas Wm.A.
McWhorter,Grace	Rose,Betty Maynard	Thompson,Ada
McWhorter,Jacob	Ross,Marguerite	Thompson,Lon
McQuarter,Billy	Runyon,Charles	*Thompson,Helen Mae
*McWhorter,Otha	Runyon,Junite	Thompson,inf
McWhorter,May E.	Runyon,Hadie	*Thompson,Levina
*Moble,Villa	Runyon,Sidney	Varney,Ray
Moore,Simon Jr.	*Salyers,Catherine	Vance,Della
Moore,Nellie	*Scaggs,Tim	Taylor,inf
Moore,Emma J.	Shafer,inf	Terrell,Thelma
Moore,simon	Shepperd,Martha	Terrell,Nellie
Moore,Louisa	Shuff,Arvil	Terrell,Samantia
Moore,Hattie	Shuff,Charles	Terrell,Wm.G.
Moore,Simon Jr.	Shuff,Irene	Terrell,Myrtle
Morrison,Bill	Shuff,inf	Terrell,Nicholas G.
Moore,Va.Stumper	Sifford,William S.	Terrell,Nancy
Mooney,James	Singer,Glayds	Terrell,Robert J.
Mooney,Thomas	*Simmons,Helen	Turley,Edna
Mooney,Ellis	*Simmons,Harold	*Turley,James M.
Mooney,mary	Simmons,Virginia	Turner,Eloise
Money,Mary N.	Simmons,Dian	Walker,Delores
*Murphey,Barbara G.	Simmons,Nannie	*Walker,Lucian
Neal,Henry	*Smith,Betty Lou	*Walker,Norma Lee
*Nease,Raymond	Smith,Nasira	Walker,Charles
Nease,Charles	Smith,Geneva	Ward, Lee Ander
Nease,J.B.	Smith,inf	Ward,Mary Jane
Nease,Nellie Ruth	*Smith,Dan Lee	Ward,M.Sidney
Nease,Edith	*Smith,Dorothy Alice	*Wells,John
Neff,Stella	Spaulding,Algord Lee	Wells,Lona
*Nicely,inf	Spencer,L.E.	Wells,Della
*Nicholas,inf	Spence,inf	Webb,Zuia
Owens,inf	Spencer,Mima	Wheeler,Lloyd G.
Pennington,Ina B.	Spencer,William	*Wheeler,Ila Fay
Perkins,Frona	*Stump,Eullicus G.	*White,Lucy

Whitney, inf
Wilburn, inf
Williams, inf d/Henry
William, inf Hoggie
Williams, Henry
Williams, Mattie
Williams, Albert S.
Winkler, Nora Lee
Wray, Jennie

BAYLOUS CEMETERY
*Lowe, Olive
Maynard, William H.
McCloud, Vina
McCloud, Everett
McCloud, Edna Mae
McCloud, Minnie
Patrick inf

CROOKS CEMETERY
*Curnell, Elizabeth
Ferguson, Edward
*Ferguson, Plymule
Harman, Floyd
Hutchinson, Richard Ray
*Hysell, Ora
Hysell, Roberta Lynn
Martin, Otho
*Martin, inf
*Mossburg, inf
Ross, Park
*Silvey, Ethel
Silvey, S.B.
*Silvey, Martha E.
Smith, Mabel Perdue
Spears, Juanita
Spears, Edward
Workman, William
Workman, Marrell
Workman, Alta
Workman, Edward
Workman, Mary Ellen
Workman, Jiles
Workman, Margaret

CYRUS CEMETERY
*Cyrus, Eilen Marie
*Cyrus, James Golden

DONAHUE
Donahue, Granville

EARLS CEMETERY
Simmons, Pearlie

WOODMERE CEMETERY
Moore, Elwood
Moore, Sharlene
Marrs, Edward F.
Pinkerton, Fredrick L.
Pinkerton, Jas Francis
*Pinkerton, Leroy
Pinkeron, Mary M.F.
Rodefer, Judith Ann
White, Charles
White, Leonard

WYANT CEMETERY
Romine, Walker R.
Romine, Dora Margaret
Romine, Mabel
Romine, Charles Abner
Romine, Otis Erwin
Romine, Madeling
Romine, Pauline
Romine, Dortha

SUSIE CHAPEL CMEMTERY
Jack, Napoleon
Jack, Nancy
Jack, Luther Moore
Smith, Margaret

MOUNT VERNON CEM.
Reed, Effie B.

SPRING HILL CEMETERY
Meadows, inf

CRESCENT HILL CEMETERY
*Blair, Earnest W.
*Chaffin, Phillis
*Chaffin, Helen
Dillon, Velva Louise
Farley, Adeline
Farley, Russell
Farley, Earl Russell
Farley, inf
Ferguson, Ford
*Ferguson, Matt
*Fuller, Sylvester B.
Fuller, Georgie
Gardner, Billie
Jack, inf
Jack, Loren
McCloud, Mary w/o J.H.
McCloud, Clenia
McCloud, Wirchester
*McCloud, Anna
McCloud, Tommy Jr.
McCloud
McCloud, Velva Louise
*McCloud, Jim
McCloud, Everett
McCloud, Morland
*McCloud, Elijah
*McCloud, Robert
*McCloud, Virgil
Taylor, Randal
Snider, William
Snider, Sarah
Ross, Albert
Ross, Betty
Ross, James M.

HILL CREST CEMETERY
Haines, Norma
Haines, William F.
McKenzie, Fannie
McKenzie, Ida
McKezie, inf

25% of the reinturned graves are marked unknown
The WPA/DAR list 243 graves, but only 131 are
listed among the reinturned.
This leaves 112 unaccounted for, which are
probably part of the 25%(180). If this is the
case then there are still 68 unidentified.

SPRING HILL CEMETERY

Please accept my appolgy for an incomplete reading of Spring Hill. The size of this cemetery is simply beyond one person. I decided to complete the 1938 WPA reading and even that has required many, many hours.

The 1938 survey was printed in book form and listed 5,318 names with an additional 2353 unmarked. My assumption was finding the unmarked cards in the cemetery files would not take much time and would make the 1938 survey complete. After all 2300 names would take only half as long as the first 5300. The completed survey to 1939 contains more than 20,000 names.

NOTE: The readings added to the orginal survey are taken from the registration cards that are on file in the cemetery office and not from headstones. Some markers were added after the orginal survey, but many of the burials were and are unmarked.

Spring Hill was either an area with several family cemeteries or a church cemetery for there are many graves that predate the "official" opening of 1872. Although I have found nothing to "prove" an earlier date, the WPA reading include several from the 1840's and there is one stone 1838. (see Case #2 Dating Cemeteries)

The orginal WPA survey does not seem to have included the "Black" section. I do not know about Potters Field. (Many cards have the name of the mortuary.)

Burials at Spring Hill from the State Mental Hospital (located across the street) were made by number not name, although some have markers.

Spring Hill encompasses an area of one hundred acres, of which fifty have been developed. In 1911 there were about 300 burials a year, today about 200. The population of Huntington was the largest in the 1950's and 60's.

H#10-Spring Hill X of 20th St and Norway Ave.in Huntington.Very large
1938 WPA readings only.(Published in book form)
Cemetery incorporated in 1874,fire destroyed some records in 1915.Area
was probably earlier cemetery,as oldest stone is 1842.This is prepetual
care and several small grave yards have been moved here from throughout
the city and county.(Buffington-Jenkins-and others.)
1938-WPA-Gideon Dist.-5,318m-2,353um graves(same % today)
WPA list used.(It was alphabetized with no indications for dual stones-
except w/o()in some cases. *= Many markers were added after 1938 reading.
x=date of burial from office records(card gives date and location
NOTE: Orginally there was a separate Black section which was apparently
      not included in 1938 WPA readings.
NOTE: There are many family mausoleums which were not included 1938.
NOTE: Misspelled names included as separate listing with correct spelling.
Carrie Eldridge- 13 nov 1990

/Abbott,Angeline 1828-1916	/Abatt,Mamie E.7 aug 1908-10 sep 1912
/Abbott,Mason D. 1824-1889	xAbbott,Albert 11 apr 1910
/Abbott,Elizabeth B.1862-1924	/Ackerman,Andrew Wm.1854-1925
/Abdo,Ollie 22 feb 1911 42y	xAbrahams,inf 24 aug 1911
xAdams,H.H. inf 21 apr 1910	xAbshire,Llucretia
xAdams,Mrs.A.H.26 nov 1911	xAbshire,Willian 6 may 1913
xAdams,infs 1912-14-15-20-22	xAdams,infs 1925-28
xAdams,Arthur 11 jun 1909	xAdams,Asa 1898-99
xAdams,Andrew J.11 jan 1934	/Adams,Alta 1874-1929
/Adams,Arthur H. 1879-1927	/Adams,A.J. 4 may 1855-8 jun 1934
xAdams,Della 6 nov 1927	/Adams,Asa 18 jan 1936 55y2m10d
/Adams,D.P. 1824-1920	/Adams,Blanche 1872-1911
/Adams,Ernest B. 1901	W.W. 1867-1926
xAdams,Elova 27 aug 1923	xAdams,Betty Joe 20 feb 1934
/Adams,Frank E. 1869-1936	xAdams,Fannie 8 nov 1911
/Adams,Hamlin M. 1840-1905	xAdams,Edward W.3 mar 1909
/Adams,Edward Co L 1st OH LA	Elizabeth 18 nov 1835-29 aug 1901
/Adams,Henry W. 1877-1914	/Adams,Eloise Magee 21 apr 1937 29y4m14d
/Adams,Hubert S.20 feb 1936	/Adams,Emily J. 13 mar 1882 26y w/o FK
/Adams,inf 20 feb 1933	/Adams,George D. 1846-29 oct 1890
/Adams,Jenkie V.14 dec 1915	/Adams,Helen Margaret 21 jun 1916-18 dec18
xAdams,James C.9 nov 1927	xAdams,James k.P.21 mar 1926
/Adams,Jennie S.1852-1938	/Adams,Jane 3 mar 1844-29 may 1905 w/o EW
/Adams,Joel T. 1861-1907	/Adams,Jimmie inf 1900 s/o MA&JV
Kate C. 1867-1924	/Adams,J.C. 7 nov 1927 76y /
xAdams,Kate C.28 oct 1923	xAdams,Loulah S.8 mar 1929
/Adams,Lou V. 1849-1909	/Adams,Letta 8 jan 1860-26 apr 1911
/Adams,Maebelle F.1897-1930	/Adams,Malinda 24 sep 1878 25y2m4d
/Adams,Margaret 1835-1922	/Adams,Mary M.23 nov 1878 54y w/o E.W.
/Adams,Morley 19 feb 1911	/Adams,N.A. 17 jun 1853-21 may 1926
xAdams,P.A.23 jan 1918	xAdams,Paul Edward 6 feb 1919
/Adams,Robert F. 1874-1934	/Adams,Ray 1902-28 may 1930
xAdams,Roberta 13 apr 1937	xAdams,Ruth 27 feb 1919
/Adams,Sarah J, 1840-1894	/Adams,William 27 aug 1822-24 nov 1894
/Adams,Virginia 1899-1936	/Adams,William G.29 nov 1848-19 mar 1895
/Adams,William S.1833-1913	xAdams,William H.10 oct 1932
xAdams,William S.12 nov 1931	xAdams,William W. 18 dec 1926
xAdkins,America 4 dec 1939	
xAdkins,Beatrice 5 feb 1914	xAdkins,Bascum Waynor 31 jan 1931
xAdkins,Charles 19 aug 1912	/Adkins,Anna Louise 1906-1908

/Adkins,Charles 1881-1934   xAdkins,Ella 20 sep 1926
xAdkins,Elisha 19 Jul 1911   xAdkins,Elmer V.20 apr 1934
/Adkins,Geneva 1894-1903   xAdkins,Frances 27 Jan 1917
xAdkins,George M.8 aug 1925   /Adkins,Florence Louise 6 nov 1935 22y1m6d
/Adkins,Inf 24 nov 1938   /Adkins,Glane 24 may 1937 3y4m4d
/Adkins,Josephine 1861-1922   /Adkins,James L. 8 mar 1934 81y10m29d
xAdkins,James Oliver 17 mar 15   Frances 3 feb 1919 w/o J.L.
xAdkins,John 20 dec 1913   xAdkins,John Lewis 9 aug 1935
xAdkins,John C.18 aug 1925   xAdkins,Mary Etta 13 may 1938
/Adkins,Lillian 1884-1886   xAdkins,Minnie 28 feb 1920
/Adkins,Noah 1834-1907   xAdkins,Nonia Bell 8 dec 1936
/Adkins,M.J. 1854-1922   /Adkins,Octavia Ann 1841-1922
/Adkins,Nancy J. 1863-1921   xAdkins,Orin E.27 may 1939
xAdkins,R.C.13 mar 1924   /Adkins,Robert E. 1887-1912 s/o EE & Jose
xAdkins,Riley 22 apr 1917   /Adkins,Sherman 16 mar 1938 73y9m4d
xAdkins,Rosa 6 jun 1922   xAdkins,Sarah Arthur 13 nov 1936
xAdkins,Virginia 13 apr 1910   xAdkins,Walter 25 Jul 1913
xAdkins,many infs
xAgnew,Thomas 1 Jun 1932   xAgazio,Gregomici 6 sep 1912
/Agnew,Frank 1870-1937   xAhern,Daniel 9 dec 1931
   Viola Durant 1868-1916   xAhern,Roland 5 feb 1929
/Akers,Anna Jenkins 1893-1916   /Akers,Isabelle 1898-1923 w/o EB
xAkers,Cynthia 28 jun 1934   xAkers,D.H. 21 mar 192
xAkers,Ellis 24 feb 1916   xAkers,Hobert 13 may 1931
xAkers,John E.1 jun 1932   xAkers,James O. 14 feb 1925
/Akers,Luviney 1861-1917   /Akers,William Robert 27 jun 1936 42y7m17d
/Akers,Nathan 1858-1937   /Akers,Zora Anna 1891-1923 w/o Robert
/Akers,Walter W.1882-1916   xAkers,Z.Z. 25 oct 1910
xAkers,Walter 10 nov 1918   xAlberts,Josephine 1918-1936
xAlbright,Alice H.2 mar 1925   xAlderman,Anderson 1903
xAlden,Allie 22 feb 1911   xAlderman,J.B. 6 jan 1924
/Alderson,Rosa M.1876-1936   xAlderman,Donald inf 9 apr 1921
   Mandy McDowell   /Alderson,Overton D.1853-1932
xAlderson,Mirian 1906   /Alderson,Thomas G. 1880-1924
xAlexander,George 1 may 1912   xAlexander,Mary F. 22 may 1932
/Alexander,Edward L 1885-1907   xAlexander,Mrs.Miner 24 mar 1910
/Alexander,Edrige 1885-1926   /Alexander,Vera C.17 Jul 1890-3 aug 1914HP
/Alexander Rita A.29 aug 1938   /Alger,Newman S.23 Jul 1903-12 aug 1911
xAliff,inf 18 aug 1923   /Alger,Edwin N, 1870-1919
/Allen,Amos 1835-1917   xAlger,Samuel 29 nov 1931
   Hannah 1837-1963   /Allen,Georgia Bryant 1877-1923
xAllen,Clara 21 sep 1935   xAllen,David L. 28 nov 1921
xAllen,Elsie 11 nov 1924   xAllen,George 27 Jul 1923
xAllen,Mary 19 sep 1913   xAllen,James Martin 28 sep 1929
xAllen,Robt.12 apr 1914   xAllen,Ruth A. 26 may 1916
xAllen,Victor Lee 13 nov 1934   xAllen,Virgie King 12 nov 1933
xAllen,Walter lee 16 nov 1939   xAllen,Winnie 5 Jan 1937
/Alley,Orville 18 nov 1934 64y   xAlley,Clara 15 apr 1926
/Alley,Christine 1899-1937   xAlley,Gypsey M.20 Jun 1921
/Alley,Sallie 1855-1912   xAlley,Jacob 8 dec 1915
xAlley,J.E. 18 oct 1918   xAllie,inf/John 22 dec 1931
xAllison,Frank 27 dec 1930   xAltizer, inf 5 apr 1919
xAllison,J.E. 30 may 1924   /Altizer,S.S. 26 oct 1844-17 Jul 1907
xAmos,Agnes 20 aug 1910   xAmsden,Harriet E. 26 apr 1928
xAmos,Willie C.28 aug 1910   xAnderson,Bill 3 mar 1925

xAnderson,Blanche 22 apr 1926xAnderson,Damond C.22 may 1918
xAnderson,Dora 20 feb 1912   xAnderson,F.W. 29 jan 1923
/Anderson,Juanita V.1926-7   /Anderson,Carrol 19 dec 1910-2 feb 1935
xAnderosn,inf/oDam C.22 may18xAnderson,Isabell 1 nov 1938
/Anderson,Rena 1888-1919   /Anderson,Claudette 6 oct 1937 4y6m
xAnderson,J.M. 20 jan 1923   xAnderson,inf/o James 31 oct 1912
/Anderson,J.W. 7 apr 1868
xAnderson,Louise 3 aug 1926   /Anderson,J.L.6 apr 1934-6 dec 1901
xAnderson,Luna 4 oct 1920   xAnderson,Maggie 23 jan 1916
/Anderson,Lucile   /Anderson,Mary E.4 jan 1878-5 jun 1918
    15 jul 1893-4 feb 1911   xAnderson,Marie 18 sep 1913
xAnderson,Mary 28 nov 1922   xAnderson,Mary Francis 26 aug 1913
xAnderson,Paul W.jul 1916inf xAnderson,Rena 22 jul 1924
xAnderson,Rebecca 16 apr 1913xAnderson,Sam 8 apr 1917
xAnderson,Sidney J.2 jan 1929/Anderson,S.J. mar 1865-11 apr 1904
/Anderson,William C.1887-1926/Anderson,Thelma 7 oct 1935 23y4m25d
/Anderson,William H.1866-1937/Andre,Augustus 2 jun 1838-24 feb 1907
xAndre,Almira C.5 feb 1916   xAndre Paul 20 apr 1906
/Andrews,Paul Fearing 1882-14/Andre,Fred I.29 mar 1875-16 dec 1936
xAndrew,Lula 4 jun 1937   /Andrews,Virginia Huddleston 1899-1928
xAngle--1910-1921   /Angles,Clemantine H. 1861-1932
/Angles,Rev.P.C.1854-1928   /Angles,Paul 7 apr 1886 inf s/oPC&CH
xAntean,Mary Ann 10 feb 1937 /Appenzellar,Charles F.1882-1923
xArberson.Isabell 1 nov 1938 xArcher,G.Fern 6 nov 1927
/Archer,John Q.1851-1918   /Archer,Frances Mather 1833-1917
/Archer,Virginia A.1849-1920 /Archer,James Lester 1923-1928
/Archer,Va.Ruth 1920-21   xArcher,R.R. 15 feb 1932
/Arlington,Rich.D. 1939 inf xArmontrout,George jun 1903
/Armstrong,Bertie 1876-1933   /Armstrong,Freddie D. 1933-1936
/Armstrong,Mildred 1899-1921 /Armstrong,George L. 1870-1935
xArmstrong,inf/JE 1913   xArmstrong,Paul Leroy 5 jul 1911
xArmstrong,Robt Hall 9feb1935xArriean,Ruby H. 19 apr 1917
xArrington,Henry 23 apr 1923 /Arrington,Caroline 1891-1921w/o Geo.E.
xArthur,Alice 24 dec 1931   /Arnold,John W. 4 aug 1859-6 aug 1902
xArthur,Calla L.5 jan 1927   /Arthur,Dimmie F. 1878-1920 w/o Oda C.
xArthur,Emily--   xArthur,Elizabeth 12 mar 1926
/Arthur,George W.1855-1906   xArthur,Hilda M.18 sep 1926
xArthur,George 24 oct 1918   xArthur,James 20 apr 1923 inf
xArthur,Joe 20 apr 1923inf   /Arthur,Jenkie 1879-15 jun 1891   11y11m6d
/Arthur,Leo Frank 1907-1936   xArthur,Lewis 1892
/Arthur,Margaret 1859-1933   xArthur,Marion 19 feb 1924
xArthur,Virginia 11 sep 1920 xArthur,William J.4 dec 1909
/Asbury,Adam 1812-1889   xAsbury,Adam C.4 may 1932   71y7m24d
xAsbury,Anna 1891   /Asbury,Ernest A. 1883-1905
xAsbury,Junmie 1891   xAsbury,H.W. 11 feb 1911
xAsbury,John A. 1894   xAsbury,John 18 apr 1930
/Asbury,Isaac A.1853-1906   /Asbury,Martha O.D. 1842-1897
xAsbury,mary R.1909   xAsbury,Sally 13 feb 1910
/Asbury,William F. 1844-1888 xAshley,John 23 jan 1936
xAshworth,Albert P.14 feb 1932xAshworth,Pensy 17 jan 1927
/Ashworth,Fannie 1860-1894   /Ashworth,Ellen Louise 12 feb 1931 8m18d
/Ashworth,L.J. 1851-1920   /Ashworth,Hattie Louise 1887-1888 d/o FJ&F
/Ashworth,Wilson 3 jun 1936   /Ashworth,Pearl Jackson 1883-1894 s/o FJ&F
    21y6m19d   /Ater,Media 1898-1919
/Atkins,Arthur A.1908-1931   /Atkins,Leonard C. 1883-1934

xAtkins,ella 30 mar 1937   xAtkins,Florence King 9 nov 1935
/Atkins,Germa Benton 1888-1913/Atkins,Oren E. 27 may 1939   WWI
/Atkins,James P.1894-1905   /Atkins,Walter G. 1903-1911
/Atkins,Walter J.1887-1913   /Atkins,William L. 1861-1929
/Atkins,W.P. 1869-1931   xAtkinson,Carrie 1887-1939
xAtten,J.W. 16 oct 1912   xAtkinson,Wade C.8 Jan 1933
xAugustine,Anna 27 Jan 1924   /Ault,Frank M. 3 mar 1931
xAurten,Clara B.4 Jun 1917   /Ault,Julia E.1856-1926 w/oH.C.Greenwell Sr.
/Austin,Charles E.Jr.1923-33 xAult,Charles 6 Jan 1936
xAustin,Eliza 29 aug 1918   /Avery,Margaret 12 nov 1923
xAustin,Marian 17 feb 1921   /Avery,Robert CoA 4th WV Inf
/Ayers,A.2 oct 1909   xAylesworth,D.F. 28 apr 1930
xAylor,Annie 21 may 1915   xAylesworth,Martha 20 apr 1917
xBaber,Betty Warner 3/19/1925xBacado,Josa 12 mar 1933
xBachi,Alex 1 nov 1918   /Bacook,Ella 1898-1931
xBackus,G.E.20 Jan 1925   /Bacchus,Morgan V. 8 sep 1872-21 Jan 1934
xBackus,W.B> 7 mar 1920   xBackus,James H.22 aug 1980
/Badgley,Fredrick F.1851-1919xBaer,James P.1936 inf
/Bagby,A.W. 1856-1929   /Bagby,Carrie Mahan 1894-1918w/JE
xBagby,inf/Jessie E. 1912/1919/Bagby,Leo F.28 aug 1888-30 Jan 1889
xBagby,inf/John 1918/1919   xBagby,Mary J. 12 Jan 1913
/Bagby,Mary L. 1854-1917   /Bagley,Lizzie J. 30 dec 1938 58y4m17d
xBagby,Mollie W.1913   xBagley,Martin L.8 apr 1988
xBailey,Edith 25 may 1921   xBailey,Evans 12 feb 1923
xBailey,inf/Harold 1917   xBailey,inf/J.E. 13 may 1914
xBailey,Jennie 26 may 1919   xBailey,L.B.14 dec 1939
xBailey,Matilda 27 Jan 1917   xBailey,Ora M17 apr 1910
/Bailey,Ralph 24 apr 1937 60y/Bailey,Robert 17 Jul 1935   WWI
xBailey,S.E. 25 aug 1922   xBailey,Winton E. 14 dec 1939
/Baily,Melvin s/oEG&LB 1908-9xBaisden,Vivian 10 dec 1936
xBaise,Opal 26 oct 1915   /Baker,Adeline 1828-1912
/Baker,Annie Marcum 1855-1923xBaker,Edgar 1914-1934
/Baker,Alfred R. 1886-1918   /Baker,Elizabeth A. 1851-1910
      Cyntha C.1868-1918   /Baker,G.Truehart 1898-1901
/Baker,inf/oJO&EF10/23/1914   xBaker,John Robert 14 nov 1930
/Baker,Lena V. 1902-1936   xBaker,R.M. 1 mar 1919
/Baker,Dr.Morgan 1851-1916   /Baker,Rowlins M. 1871-1919
/Baker,R.Emmett 1848-1914   /Baker,William Pope 1920-1928 s/o JE&LR
/Baker,Virginia M.1882-1937   xBaker,Vivian Noel 7 may 1922
/Baldwin,Stephen M.1851-1926 xBaldwin,Fannie 31 aug 1910
      Melissa A. 1861-1830   xBaldwin,Jennie 11 Jan 1932
xBales,Ethel 4 Jul 1923   /Ball,Elizabeth Liza 1873-1935
xBall,Gallie 14 Jan 1919   xBall,inf/o Lynch 1914
xBall,James 7 sep 1923   xBall,Martha 27 Jan 1923
xBall,Margaret 1 oct 1934   /Ball,Rosco 3 dec 1877-7 Jun 1915
/Ball,William H.1855-1924   /Ballangee,Austin 21 Jun 1909-23 oct 1911
/Ballangee,Jerry 25 Jun 1911   /Ballangee,Edwin 14 sep 1906-20 oct 1911
      Annie 14 may 1900 63y   xBallangee,Mary Louise 10 aug 1931
xBallangee,Lute 26 Jul 1920   /Ballard,Louise Smith 1884-1931
xBane,inf 14 oct 1921   xBanes,Annie 4 Jan 1919
xBangon,Joe 2 aug 1918   xBank,inf/o Paul M 3 Jul 1930
/Banks,Laura M.1856-1938   /Bank,William 1867-1931
      Major W.H. 1856-1927   xBanks,Edgar 12 mar 1911
/Barber,Alice V.1902-1917   xBarber,inf 18 oct 1923
xBarber,Sadie 25 oct 1922   /Barbour,Elisha CoA 5th WV Inf

/Barbour,Nettie
   18 mar 1846-13 apr 1916
     Sp Am Co M 27th Reg
xBarcklow,Nannie 24 Jan 1930
xBare,Juanita Jun 1918 inf
xBarkley,Mary 5 Jul 1918
xBarlow,Inf 17 Jun 1925
xBarnes,Claude 29 Jan 1921
xBarnes,W.M. 17 may 1923
/Barnett,Bernard Lee 1901-1925
xBarnett,B.L. 23 feb 1910
/Barnett,Clinton C. 1869-1935
xBarnett,George 19 may 1937
xBarnett,Isabell 15 Jun 1932
/Barnett,Mary J. 1856-1929
xBarnett,Thomas P.30 Jun 1934
/Barney,Jackson Allen 1927-30
/Barrack,John 1851-1929
    Emma L. 27 Jun 1953
xBarrett,John S.5 mar 1915
xBarrett,Louisa 13 dec 1915
xBarrit,Ann 8 mar 1936
xBarron,Maud 19 Jun 1919
/Barrows,Millard A.1852-1911
/Barth,John 1868-1921
   Jessie 1878-1936
xBarth-- 10 dec 1923
/Barton,Juliet 4y
/Basden,Vivian 1907-1936
xBasenback,Cora 12 mar 1930
/Basenback,G.L. 1872-1924
xBasenback,George 21 aug 1924
/Basenback,J.C.1887-1919
/Basenback,J.M.1850-1914
/Bastianelli,Adrain L
   1886-1928
xBass,Harold Z.24 Jul 1916
xBaugh,Henriette 23 oct 1918
xBaumgardner,Isabell 25 Jul1931
/Baumgardner,Henry
  Co E 8th VA Cav CSA
/Baumgardner,Rebecca 1824-1897
xBaxter,H.K.18 Jun 1927
xBaxter,Joe 31 oct 1918
xBaxter,W.M. 2 nov 1918
xBayes,Columbia J.3 nov 1939
/Bayes,Harry 23 oct 1933 WWI
xBayes,Helen 14 Jun 1926
xBayes,Peggy Tyem 16 nov 1931
xBays,Eleanor Velma 15 Jan 1929
/Beal,Peter 1862-1900
/Beal,Elizabeth 1838-1914
/Beal,Joseph 1829-1909
xBeale,Charles M. 3 Jun 1930
/Beales,David M.1828-1910

xBarbour,Etta L. 25 oct 1918
xBarbour,Frank 9 mar 1919
xBarbour,Mary A. 25 aug 1921
/Barkla,Carolina Potts 1836-1917
/Barkla,William 21 dec 1835-27 sep 1902
/Barkla,Clarence S.27 feb 1875-12 Jan 1900
xBarnes,Cathryn 27 dec 1919
xBarnes,Ocie 19 aug 1918
/Barnett,Betty 1845-1911
    Rev.Nelson 1846-1909
xBarnett,Carter 6 aug 1921
xBarnett,Hattie 26 apr 1916
xBarnett,Ouida A. 1928
/Barnette,John Charles 1849-1894
/Barnette,John H. 1874-1905
xBarnett,Wm.F. 13 feb 1924
xBarnhouse,Charles 30 oct 1914
/Barr,Margaret Ann 23 aug 1935 74y1m7d
/Barrett,Charles M. 7 sep 1928 WWI
xBarrett,Lizzie 20 Jan 1922
/Barringer,Asa 1856-1921
    Katie 1860-1918
xBarringer,John Hughes 26 sep 1926
xBartlett,Charles 29 may 1934
xBarley,Inf 6 feb 1922
/Barton,Charles D. 36y
/Barton,Dewey 1898-1918
/Barton,William 1870-1921
xBartram,Van 16 sep 1928
xBasenback,Inf/o F.B.16 Jul 1916
/Basenback,Carl 16 nov 1933 7y10m10d
xBasenback,Inf/o Geo. 8 may 1920
/Basenback,Juanita 9 dec 1934 11m27d
/Basenback,Victoria 1849-1931
/Bastianelli,John Howell-19 nov 1915Inf
/Bastianelli,Louise A.24 Jan 1939 48y4m2d
xBatts,Ethel 27 dec 1938
xBaulech,G.W.29 sep 1911
/Baumgardner,Edna 1893-1918 w/o JA
/Baumgardner,James M. 1830-1914
/Baumgardner,Lucinda 1843-1926
/Baumgardner,J.L.13 mar 1839-18 may 1911
    Elizabeth 27 may 1833-8 Jun 1895
/Baxter,Arthur Judd 25 Jul 1936 65y11m17d
xBaxter,Inf 26 mar 1914
/Bayes,Cecil C.10 mar 1939 31y
xBayes,Inf/oJ.M. 29 Jun 1910
xBayes,James M. 8 apr 1931
xBayes,Effie 10 oct 1912
/Baysden,John M.1862-1893
/Baysden,John M. 1894-1938
xBeal,George 21 apr 1924
/Beale,Ella Ausgusta 31 aug 1870-13Jul1892
/Beale,Robert W.1867-1910
/Bealoff,Hazel 26 sep 1923

/Beales,Eva 1832-1907   /Beamer,Thomas D. 4 mar 1834-18 dec 1906
xBeamond,inf/o OW 4 oct 1915   xBeamer,Mary J. 1836-1907
xBeard,Charles 14 may 1926   /Beardsley,Lucy C. 1849-1904
/Beauchamp,Ann M.   /Beardsley,Andrew J. 1844-1921
   1844-1915w/o Granville WellsxBearman,Bertha 24 may 1913
xBeaver,Anice L. 11 apr 1915   xBearman,Jacob 2 mar 1917
xBeaverly,John P.27 mar 1925   xBeavers,James F. 29 apr 1917
/Beck,Myrtle L.27 dec 1932   /Beavers,Mary Alice 1870-1912
/Beck,Murlie L.Davis 1895-1932xBecklhemier,inf 6 feb 1924
/Beckerman,Isadore L.1911-22/Becklheimer,Myrna Louise 17 jul 1939 10m20d
/Beckett,Frank M.1874-191 8   xBecket,Aldon inf 5 may 1916
xBeckett,Lula 5 apr 1910   xBeckett,Lucretia Addline 8 mar 1926
xBeckett,Mary E 1859-6feb1915   xBeckett,Sarah Almedia 11 dec 1930
/Beckett,Saddie 1868-1934   xBeckett,William 8 jul 1910
xBeckett,Wm.E. 3 Jun 1930   xBeckman,Sarah L.Pollock 2 mar 1914
xBeckner,George 19 apr 1917   xBeckner,Ernest L. 18 dec 1921
/Beckner,J.C. 1854-1929
xBeckner,Iva B.1884-1939   xBeckner,John O.7 sep 1927
xBeckner,Louise 3 may 1914   /Beckner,Leonidas R. 1862-1934
xBeckner,Ruth 18 nov 1927   xBeckner,Rena Anderson 6 feb 1919
/Beckner,Van Lear 1860-1937   xBeckner,Sarah 29 aug 1930
xBeckner,Zalissa 5 mar 1920   xBeddow,James 1904
/Bee,Gus 1887-1918 John A.   /Beddow,Sallie M. 21 jan 1939 73y1m22d
/Beebee,Fanny Louise 1863-1939xBeen,Altha 8 jan 1923 inf
xBeen,Clara Ann 20 Jan 1924   xBeen,Margary E.4 Jan 1926 inf
xBeen,Ruth M.11 jan 1926 inf   xBeen,inf 28 feb 1919
xBeincampen,Islem 30 mar 1936 /Behrend,inf 1910 d/o Harry & Hattie
   Minnie 2 feb 1931   /Bekeck,Louis 23 nov 1934 53y
xBelcher,Denver 25 oct 1932   /Belcher,Laura 18 aug 1860-10 mar 1930
xBelcher,Fred 16 jul 1922   /Belcher,Lucy 13 may 1890-13 dec 1923
xBelcher,Inez 10 dec 1919   /Belcher,Wm M.23 aug 1890-23 oct 1918
/Belcher,Norman E.inf 1917   xBelcher,inf/o James R. 29 nov 1915
xBelcher,Ollie F.31 may 1919   xBelcher,Wayne E. 19 feb 1925
xBelknap,Cora 5 mar 1935   /Bellman,Samuel 1881-1930
xBell,inf 20 oct 1921   /Bell,Charles Buford Jr.1935 inf
xBell,Peter 10 sep 1918
/Bell,Homer 1868-1922   /Bellamy,Sarah F.16 nov,1884 59y1m6d
/Bell,Maria V.1839-1927   xBellomy,H.C. 7 mar 1912
/Bellissimo,Frank 1879-1937   xBellomy,Josephine 27 apr 1910
/Bellville,Charley 1923 5y   xBelveal,Earl Ray 5 dec 1914
/Bender,Gilbert 1884-1924   xBelveal,Elonzo A. 27 may 1939
xBender,S.G. 8 Jul 1924   xBelveal,Therma 9 oct 1927
xBennett,America 1872-1920   xBelville,Jacob 17 aug 1924
xBennett,Betty B.6 may 1930   xBelville,Jennie 18 aug 1919
xBennett,E.A.5 sep 1915   /Benedict,George E. 1863-1909
   Laura 5 sep 1915   /Benedict,Emma Jane 23 mar 1932 65y1m4d
/Bennett,Mildred Haller 1880-15xBentley,inf/o ES 7 dec 1913
xBennett,Hall 16 jan 1928   xBentley,inf 28 jul 1917
/Bennett,inf 27 jun 1930   /Bentley,Hyacintha inf 1913
xBennett,Mrs.M.H.1 aug 1915   /Bentley,Judith Ann 14 feb 1935
/Bennett,Clifford 1902-1923   /Bentley,Pearley May 1910-1913
/Bennett,Francis 1919-1922   /Bentley,E.L. 1888-1916
/Bennett,Lewis 1862-1903   /Benton,John 19 jan 1892
xBerger--23 may 1925   xBenton,Aliee 9 mar 1919
xBerlt,Guy Wright 1932   xBenton,Chapman 13 jul 1913

/Bernelce,Hilda 1915-1919 /Berrege,William L. 1 Jan 1933 60y6m18d
/Berry,John M. 1841-1922 /Berry,Bettle 11 sep 1891-20 Jun 1892
/Berry,Lavina 1829-1914 xBerry,Floria Ann 1 may 1925
xBerry,Judith 25 apr 1924 xBerry,Paul Wilson 4 oct 1937
xBerys,Elinor 15 Jan 1929 inf xBess,Anna 30 oct 1912
xBess,H.C. 30 Jul 1936 /Bess,Lillian 22 feb 1882-2 Jan 1906
/Bess,Isaac N.1849-1909 /Bess,Henry Clay 70y2m23d
xBess,Harriet 14 may 1910 xBess,inf/o Mattle 6 apr 1911
/Bess,James A. 1854-1920 /Bess,Ida 5 aug 1861-6 oct 1916
/Bess,Mary A. 1851-1923 /Bess,Mary E. 1860-1930
xBetts,Isaac J.16 Jul 1912 /Beswick,Clark M.1885-86
xBetts,Mary A. 15 feb 1912 /Beswick,Katie Norton 1880-1909
/Beuhring,Lee Davis 1867-1935/Beuhring,Fredrick G.L.27 Jun 1859 67y2m27d
    Mamie M. 1859-1911   Frances Eleanor 1797-16 Jun 1841 44y16d
/Beuhring,Harold Henry /Beuhring,Fredrick Donenberg 1828-1903/FGL
   1860-1884 s/o FD&FE   Frances E. 1838-12 oct 1882 44y7m9d
/Beuhring,Edgar Francis 1870 /Beuhring,Fredrick Alexander
   s/o FD & FE   1865-1887 s/o FG & FE
xBeuhring,Martha E.13 apr 1914xBeuhring,Walter D. 18 apr 1932
xBeuhring,Ora Peyton 1863-1941xBiagi,Andia 20 mar 1940
xBevan,John H.1 apr 1920 /Biagi,Peter J. 1864-1935
xBevan,Mrs.P. 22 may 1909 /Biagi,Raffalello 1855-1928
xBevan,R.C.2 may 1910 /Bias,Beatrice 5 may 1916 inf
xBias,Douglas lee 22 Jul 1938 /Bias,Ed 13 apr 1918 inf
/Bias,Charles F. 1882-1919 /Bias,David A. 1855-1927
/Bias,D.Vickers 1901-1931 xBias,Eugenia 24 feb 1934
xBias,Everette 14 may 1914 xBias,Herman G.4 apr 1936
xBias,Hayes 2 aug 1918 inf xBias,Lucy 15 may 1935
/Bias,Martha 1894-1925 xBias,Mathew 2 mar 1925
/Bias,Mary F. 1904-1908 /Bias,Martha R.6 Jul 1846-28 nov 1932
/Bias,Theodore 1879-1925 /Bias,Roy Woodrow 1914-1926
xBias,Vickers 17 Jan 1913 xBias,W.A.Jr 28 sep 1911
/Bibb,Mary Lambert 1897-1925 /Bias,W.A.30 oct 1841-15 aug 1903
/Bibb,William D.1858-1911 /Bicker,Margaret 1829-1911
/Bibb,Martha E. 1904-1925 xBickers, inf 1 may 1923
xBick,Arthur 1876-1893 xBick,Charles 19 feb 1913
xBick,Sarah 2 sep 1911 xBick,John Edwin 23 Jul 1939
/Biederman,Louis 1844-1918 xBiederman,Helen Icie 19 dec 1938
/Biederman,Yettie 1857-1895 /Bienderman,Jacob 1889-1912
/Bienbaum,Joseph 1849-1925 /Biern,Arhtur L. 13 Jun 1886-17 mar 1928
/Bienelan,Eliza 28 dec 1921 /Biern,Emmanuel 28 Jan 1851-12 mar 1925
/Biggs,Anie M. 1880-1919 xBiggs,Alice W. 3 nov 1920
/Biggs,Elizabeth Jane 1850-13 xBiggs,George Nicholas 13 Jan 1903
/Biggs,W.Davis 1880-1908 /Biggs,George N. 1846-1926
/Biggs,Helen R. d 1915 xBiggs,Misouve Bell 7 Jul 1925
xBillups,George M.19 nov 1932 /Billups,Maggie F. 15 nov 1937 34y1m9d
/Billups,Elsie 14 mar 1917 /Billups,Mary Imigene 9 sep 1937
xBillups,Merrill 4 nov 1931 xBillups,Paul 7 aug 1924
xBingham,Jack M. 11 Jul 1912 xBirch,Isiah Lee 31 Jan 1938
/Birchhill,William A.1858-1917/Birchhill,Thomas 22 aug 1876 50y
xBirchhill,Caroline 31 oct 1910xBird,Forrest 30 apr 1930
xBischoff,Bernard F.7 Jun 1939xBischoff,Elizabeth R. 7 sep 1931
/Bishop,Anna D.1855-1918 xBishop,Emmitt L.1883-1939
xBishop,Georgia Ellen 7/19/1935/Bishop,George W. 24 aug 1880 36y7m
/Bishop,Hallie K.1889-1931 /Bishop,H.C.6 aug 1857-23 aug 1909

/Bishop,James 1848-1934   /Bishop,Jane 9 Jan 1820-18 may 1901
xBishop,Lon 20 mar 1918   xBishop,Thas.Jr.28 apr 1919
/Bishop,Neal 1874-1918   /Bishop,Nancy J. 30 Jul 1886 18y10m
/Bishop,Ople 12 oct 1881 1y7m/Bishop,W.A.6 sep 1820-1 nov 1903
xBishop,William 29 Jan 1911   xBlark,Bertha May 7 may 1926
/Black,Annie M.1851-1922   xBlack,Charles M.17 may 1918
/Black,Dora 1875-1926   xBlack,Eddie 1 oct 1923
/Black,E.Lowell 1857-1917   xBlack,Elizabeth 11 feb 1927
xBlack,Ezery 24 dec 1923   xBlack,Florence 28 Jul 1914 inf
xBlack,Florina 14 aug 1917inf/Black,Hazel H.9 mar 1880-15 aug 1890
xBlack,James 16 Jun 1928   xBlack,Henry Jr.14 mar 1922inf
/Black,James W.1850-1908   /Black,James W.1895-1933
/Black,J.Walter 1888-1923   xBlack,Lloyd Loremy 24 mar 1931
xBlack,L.E. 11 Jul 1917   xBlack,Lois 24 apr 1919
xBlack,Mary A.6 nov 1932   xBlack,Victoria 23 Jan 1917
xBlack,William 24 nov 1915   /Blackburn,J.L.12 may 1834-26 Jul 1905
xBlackburn,Henrietta 5 sep 1935/Blackburn,George B.may 1883 25y
/Blackburn,M.C.1860-1909   xBlackburn,Mrs.J.F. 29 nov 1913
xBlackeney,James C.1886   xBlackwell,Emma E.4 apr 1913 inf
/Blackwell,Susie E.1851-1921 xBlackwell,H.C.15 feb 1916
/Blackwell,Sidney B.1849-1916xBlackwell,Mrs.S.B. 8 Jul 1921
/Blackwood,Sarah C.1850-1918 /Blackwood,J.Harvey 1836-1917
xBlaier,Miliaed 5 aug 1923   /Blair,Charles Willard 1867-1934
xBlair,James 18 oct 1920   xBlair,Mary 3 apr 1928
/Blake,Aline 1908-1910   /Blake,Captola B. 1864-1919
xBlake,Carrie May 12 may 1931xBlake,Catherine 20 dec 1914
xBlake,Mrs.Clyde 24 oct 1914 xBlake,Clarence J.18 dec 1914
/Blake,Clyde 1888-1938   /Blake,Edith Mae 30 Jan 1885-3 Jan 1905
xBlake,Goldie 30 nov 1915inf xBlake,James 4 apr 1914
/Blake,G.Frank 1872-1921   /Blake,James N. 1837-1906
/Blake,John W. 1876-1926   M.Jane 1840-1918
/Blake,L.Edward 1858-1922   /Blake,Mary 1841-1909
xBlake,Marjorie J.16 apr 1918xBlake,Thurmond L.23 dec 1930
/Blaker,Eva M. 1901-1922   /Blaker,Franklin Edgar 17 feb 1937 26y5m2d
/Blaker,L.E. 1897-1919   /Blaker,Wm.H. 1871-1932
/Blanchard,James E.1860-1893 xBlaker,N.B.1882-19--
xBlanchard,Beulah 1902   xBlanchard,Ella 17 oct 1934
xBlanchard,Hester 1889   xBlanchard,James 1898
xBlanchard,Wanda 1905   xBlanchard,Victoria W.1857-1945
xBland,Ada 16 nov 1910
xBland,Dondana 24 dec 1924   /Bland,Emma V. 1848-1904
/Blank,C.C.1871-1932   /Bland,Eliza 1870-1923
/Blank,H.H. 1882-1935   /Bland,John H. 1853-1932
xBlankenship,Adeline 11/3/18 /Bland,James E. 15 Jun 1939 89y9m5d
/Blankenship,Allen 1856-1913 /Blankenship,Amanda E. 1858-1917 w/oRD
xBlankenship,Arminda 12/5/32 xBlankenship,Clara E.3 sep 1930
xBlankenship,Cyrus 11/23/22   xBlankenship,Jefferson 26 may 1928
/Blankenship,Fenton 1853-1938/Blankenship,Edger 3 Jun 1876-16 dec 1915
/Blankenship,inf 24 may 1935 /Blankenship,Edith 5 Jan 1937 84y9m10d
/Blankenship,Joseph 1883-1911/Blankenship,Elizabeth C. 1854-1930
xBlankenship,H.H. 1 apr 1920 xBlankenship,tws Paul & Arthur feb 1937
xBlankenship,Reuben D.6/21/25xBlankenship,William C.12 mar 1917
/Blanton,James F. 1859-1932   /Blanton,E.Lynwood 1893-1899 s/o JF&AL
/Blatt,Katharina 1856-1916   xBlatt,Anthony
xBlatt,Katherine 25 may 1921 xBlatt,Etha 28 Jun 1922

xBlazer,inf/o MP 21 oct 1925 xBldidge,inf 19 nov 1923
xBledsoe,Mrs.C.B. 15 Jul 1916/Bledsoe,Chester Raymond 1909-1910 HC&G
/Bledsoe,Cleadeth 1908-1909 xBledsoe,Gerturde 1 Jun 1920
xBledsoe,Louie 12 dec 1922   /Bledsoe,Thomas 1877-1938
/Bledsoe,Dorothy L.1938 inf xBlevans,inf/Wm.T.14 sep 1917
xBlevans,John B.17 nov 1920 xBlevans,Thomas 22 may 1921
/Blevin,Lotta Bell 1893-1919 /Blevins,T.A.1887-1921
/Blevins,Clarissa 1877-1938 /Blevins,Wm.Thomas 9 mar-12 sep 1912
/Blizzard,William L.1861-1917xBloss,Mollie 1 mar 1930
/Bloss,Isaac 1832-1897   /Bloss,Garnett Coleman d 1930
/Bloss,Sarah A.McClure1830-25/Bloss,W.M. 1859-1902
xBoase,Opal 26 oct 1915   /Bobbitt,Osee Anna 1895-1913
/Bockway,Charles W.1913-1918 /Bobbitt,Nellie Maxwell 1869-1936
/Bockway,Minnie Henderson   xBocck,George 25 aug 1909
    1879-1915   /Bocook,Ella 1898-1931
xBodley,Charles 2 feb 1926   xBocook,Rudolph 5 nov 1908
xBoggess,Norman T.1878-1901 /Boggess,Mary Cory 3 aug 1851-31 dec 1927
/Boggess,Harry Julien 1884-98/Boggess,Taylor N. 10 dec 1848-18 aug 1913
/Boggs,J.Edward 1866-1923   xBoggs,Lettie 1842-1872
xBoggs,Mary M.24 Jul 1927   xBoggs,Nancy 1820-1895
xBoggs,Wm.A. 1815-1899   xBoldie,Eugene 15 may 1920
xBohlin,James P. 30 nov 1923 xBolding,Mary 5 aug 1922
xBoling,John 20 Jun 1915   /Boley,Lawrence 14 sep 1933 3y7m11d
xBoling,Mary E.7 oct 1924   xBolling,Robert Edward 5 may 1926
xBolling,inf 11 aug 1919   xBolt,Mrs.E.E. 19 dec 1918
/Bolt,M.M. 1852-1925   /Bolt,Grace 1879-1911 w/o W.H.
/Bolt,M.M. 1846-1912   xBolwing,Benjamin 23 mar 1936
xBond,Alex J,3 dec 1922   xBone,Martha 20 dec 1932
xBond,Violet 16 mar 1922   /Bonecutter,Everett 3 aug 1909-14 oct 1910
xBonecutter,Jane 27 feb 1920 xBonecutter,inf/Wm.&Liz. 23 feb 1920
xBonesetter,Mary E.1906-08   /Bonham,Charles A. 1882-1888
/Bonham,John A.1844-1922   /Bonner,J.W. 1827-1 may 1891 64y
    Mary L.1847-1904   xBooe,Helena F.1 may 1917
/Booker,John 1833-1898   /Booker,Lucy 1851-1920 w/o John
/Booker,Mary 1885-1936w/o WH xBooker,Isaac 1 sep 1933
/Boolley,A.B.15 apr 1915   xBooker,Mary A. 19 aug 1914
/Boone,John William 1840-1901xBoone,Flora 10 aug 1914
/Boone,Ella 1886-7d/oWalter /Boone,Rachael Price 1855-1923
/Boone,John W. 1883-1935   /Boone,Walter 1886 inf
/Booten,Mack 1848-1929   /Booten Mary 26 dec 1936 54y7m4d
/Booth,Archie 1895-1934   /Booth,Absolom P. 1868-1938
xBooth,Abigal 9 Jun 1928   xBooth,Betty C.28 Jun 1926
/Booth,Charles C. 1885-1918 /Booth,Bertha M. Ferrell 1893-1926
xBooth,Carrie 26 nov 1926   xBooth,Elizabeth 16 feb 1939
/Booth,Dave Elden 1913-1937 /Booth,Ethel 13 apr 1894 d/o DW&MM
/Booth,Mary Hannah 1923-4   xBooth,Herbert 22 Jul 1938
xBoothe,Mary 1 sep 1916   /Booth,Virginia Frances 1918-1920
xBoothe,William   xBooton,Henry 6 sep 1918
/Born,Gustave 1853-1926   xBosland,inf 11 nov 1926
/Bossinger,Henry C.1837-1914/Bossinger,Chauncey I.5-20-1872/6-9-1887HC&RE
/Bossinger,Rachael 1843-1916/Bossinger,Myrtle M.5-19-1876/3-4-1881 HC&RE
xBoster,Emory 16 mar 1924   xBoster,Charles Owen 1927 inf
/Boster,Julia Ann 1873-1938 /Boster,Effie 19 oct 1938 69y10m
/Boster,Eunice Mandell d1895 /Boster,Louise Gilbert 1859-1895
xBoster,Luther 3 mar 1926   /Boster,Major McKinley 22 oct 1922 WWI

/Boster,Ray 1896-1923   /Boster,Viola 25 aug 1916 inf
/Boster,Ruby M. 1904-1918   /Boster,Wm.Curtis 1886-1925
xBoster,W.S.30 Jan 1924   xBoston,Lucy 13 oct 1926
/Botkin,E.H.Jr.1925 inf   xBowden,Ramon R.12 feb 1927
                             /Boswell,Edith Van meter 1876-1934
/Bowels,Guy A.26 dec 1935 58y/Bouren,Sarah 14 sep 1929 69y4m15d
/Bowen,Bertha 1886-1907   /Bowen,Florence Delma 1898-1936
xBowen,Ezra J.1874-1897   xBowen,F.O. 2 nov 1923
/Bowen,Fred 1837-1908   xBowen,Glen 23 apr 1923 inf
/Bowen,Isabella 1854-1918   xBowen,Harriet 13 may 1920
xBowen,Lake S.10 Jun 1922   xBowen,Lowery D.11 mar 1928
xBowen,Mira Jean 20 Jun 1928 /Bowen,Pinkey E.3 Jan 1936 63y13d
/Bowen,Rufas 18 oct 1937 WWI xBowen,Sarah 14 sep 1929
xBowen,Zaze 1886   /Bowers,America V.1855-1919
xBowers,James 30 Jan 1917   /Bowher,John 16 oct 1879 28y2m22d
/Bowers,Walter J, 1850-1917 xBowles,Daisy 1 apr 1917
xBowles,Gladys 5 dec 1936   xBowles,Guy A. 26 dec 1935
xBowles,Richard V.1915 inf   /Bowles,Eva F. 1880-1927
xBowles,inf/o HE 19 oct 1916 xBowles,inf/o Mary M 12 may 1914
xBowles,W.M. 27 apr 1926   xBowling,C.L. 4 apr 1918
/Bowling,B.B. 1858-1937   xBowling,C.A. 1904-1933
xBowling,Grace M.29 aug 1933 xBowling,Chas.A. 13 may 1933 inf
xBowling,J.L. 6 aug 1920   xBowling,Susan R.1 feb 1917
xBowling,Wm.R. 28 Jun 1937   xBowman,Fannie 28 aug 1920
xBowman,Ada 15 dec 1926   Lizzie 25 Jun 1930
xBowyer,Helen Louise 1926 inf/Boxley,Anna R. 7 Jul 1890 26y
xBoyd,Mrs.A.R. 2 nov 1909   Charles Ascham 14 dec 1935
/Boyd,Charles A. 1894-1930   /Boxley,inf d/o CA& Anna 2 Jun 1890
xBoyd,Alexander R.2 may 1928 xBoyd,Blanche 5 sep 1926
xBoyd,Charity A. 17 apr 1919 xBoyd,Clare E. 25 Jan 1916
xBoyd,Eliza 19 apr 1922   xBoyd,George 18 apr 1917
xBoyd,Eliza 1850-1913   xBoyd,John 1 nov 1920
/Boyd,Peter 1830-1917   /Boyd,Sarah 24 Jun 1935 70y1m16d
xBoyd,William 19 apr 1922   /Boyd,Zoe Shafer 1899-1919
/Boyd,William 1848-1920   xBoyd,William P.16 dec 1935
/Boyer,Cornelia Ann 1841-1927xBoyer,Eliza Ann 3 nov 1938
/Boyer,Lillian D.1903-1935   /Boyer,Frisley D. 1839-1911
/Boyer,Phillip 14 Jun 1938 70yxBoyse,inf 18 oct 1915
xBradbury,Rosa Lee 18 aug 39 xBraden,Alice 30 Jul 1923
xBradburg,Wm.J. 10 oct 1926 /Brackman,James W.1872-1937
/Bradley,T.O.9/9/1884-9/10/11/Brackman,Mary Louise 1899-1938
/Bradley,Chester1/14/1935 28y/Brackman,Randolph S. 1858-1932
/Bradley,Anna Marie 23 dec 27/Bradley,inf/o JO 22 Jun 1911
/Bradley,J.T. 1855-1926   /Bradley,Thomas J.21 feb 1926
  Grace 1 nov 1869-11 mar 1938/Bradley,William F.9 aug 1923
/Brady,Bridget C.1854-1891   xBrady,James 22 dec 1938
/Brady,Catherine 1885-1905   /Brady,Patrick S. 1853-1915
/Bragg,August 29 mar 1926   /Brady,William A. 1873-1930
/Bragg,Arsula   /Bragg,Grover C. 1 dec 1891-14 oct 1893
  29 mar 1852-4 apr 1883   /Bragg,Hazel J. 11 nov 1893 inf
xBragg,Charlie 29 aug 1920   /Bragg,James H.22 feb 1847-18 Jul 1928
xBragg,Clinton 26 Jun 1909   Sarah L.27 apr 1863-26 mar 1926
xBragg,Sterling Woodrow 10/5/17/Bragg,Llewellyn 5/6/1881-5/24/1914 SpAm
xBragg,Walter 2 oct 1925   /Bragg,Mary A. 21 oct 1889-4 nov 1890
/Braley,E.W. 1880-1938   xBraley,Florence Hall 9 nov 1939

xBrammer,M.R. 13 mar 1926 /Brammer,Hezekia D.8 Jul 1857-23 may 1880
/Brammer,C.K. 1831-1904 /Brammer,Joseph 1827-27 dec 1881 56y3m19d
/Brammer,George Lee 1861-1939/Brammer,Orin Lawson 1896-1931
/Brammer,Matilda M.1837-1867 /Brammer,Sarah P. 1835-1906
/Brammer,R.F. 1856-1931 /Brammer,Willie 1864-1887
/Brandenburg,John 1852-1935 /Brandenburg,Henry Andrew 1856-1935
/Brandenburg,Eliz.1855-1929 /Brandenburg,Ida Haning 1860-1904
xBrandenburg,Kate 2 nov 1933 xBrandenburg,Margaret 17 sep 1901
xBranham,Hudson 6 may 1939 /Branham,Oscar E.24 apr 1933 WWI
xBranham,Thomas 16 mar 1913 /Brashears,Hamilton Howard Jr.
xBranlon,John 10 mar 1920   19 dec 1938 29y6m5d
xBreager,William 21 dec 1907 xBreauz,Joseph 29 aug 1916
xBreeden,D.H. 22 Jan 1924 xBricker,Myrtle 28 oct 1927
/Brewer,James2 sep 1890 31y10m/Bricker,Lillian R. 5 dec 1935 50y8m4d
/Bridge Aubrey K. 1903-1916 /Bridgewater,Irvin 1875-1931
xBright,Charles W. 1875-1931 xBright,Irene 22 feb 1939
/Bright,Frank S. 1883-1918 /Bright,Emma J, 30 mar 1937 83y6m18d
/Bright,Florence M.1880-1918 xBright,R.D.1903
xBrightwell,inf/o Grace 1928 xBrisco,Mattie 25 Jan 1927
/Brindley,Thomas 1860-1932 /Brittain,Alma Sullings 1843-1915
    Louisa 1864-1916 xBrittingham,Cary 12 sep 1913
xBritt,Carrie 10 may 1923 xBrittingham,John 2 Jul 1911
xBritt,Alma 2 Jan 1915 xBrittingham,Nellie 13 apr 1911
xBritton,Maxine 25 apr 1921 /Broaddus,John Albert 25 nov 1933 57y8m2d
xBrockett,Luther 22 apr 1927 /Broadhurst,Maria 1827-17 Jun 1881 53y11m13
/Brockmeyer,C.A.1888-1931 /Brockmeyer,Carrie F. 25 apr 1931 w/o WA
/Brockmeyer,Edna M.1886-1931 /Brockmeyer,Charles A. 1830-1883 Civil War
/Brockmeyer,Clarice E. /Brockmeyer,James A.1905-6s/o Chas & Folsom
   1861-1925 /Brockmeyer,Katherine 1834-1923
xBrockway,James H.28 oct 1921xBroh Julius 2 Jan 1941
/Broh,Adolph /Broh,Fannie M.6 mar 1874-2 apr 1920 Julius
   17 dec 1840-13 dec 1923 /Broh,Harry,L.16 feb 1882-1 mar 1920
/Broh,Jetta Rose /Broh,Herman Lester 27 nov 1888-19 aug 1907
   24 mar 1844-5 aug 1911 /Broh,Mike 14 Jun 1864-29 aug 1931
xBromley,William C.8 nov 1939xBroh,Lucy 1860-1938
/Bromley,Josephine /Brooking,Albert W. 1901-1939
  1862-1885 d/o SS&Mary VinsonxBrooks,Charlotte 27 Jan 1918
xBrooks,Charlotte 23 apr 1922xBrooks,inf/W.E.16 feb 1916
xBrooks,Joseph 13 Jun 1915 xBrooks,inf/W.E. 30 apr 1919
xBrooks,Henry 7 dec 1917 /Brooks,Richard H.2/5/11 CoL 4th VA Inf CSA
/Brooks,Va.Mayme 1911-12 /Brooks,Thomas W.1899 CoA 33th VA Reg CSA
/Brooks,V.Verne 1907-1932 /Brooks,Will E. 1871-1936
xBrooks,Nannie J.1874-1898 xBroom,Mary C.1924-1933
/Broomhall,George C. /Broskie,Lulu G.25 may 1840-19 feb 1932
    9 dec 1848-23 nov 1927 xBroskie,Charles C. 10 dec 1942
/Broomhall,Louise D. /Brown,Albert G.1847-1930
   16 dec 1854-19 feb 1932 xBrown,Alex D. 4 Jan 1929
/Brown,Anna 1857-1904 xBrown,Alexander 2 apr 1914
xBrown,Alice Lee 21 Jan 1928 xBrown,Almira 12 apr 1910
xBrown,Anna 15 may 1927 xBrown,Anna 20 sep 1920
xBrown,Bernice 28 Jan 1922 xBrown,Bessie Smith 10 Jun 1936
/Brown,Benjamin 1874-1938 /Brown,Corbett R.2 may 1881-18 Jun 1937
xBrown,C.E. 9 mar 1923 inf /Brown,Corinne 6 apr 1919-4 may 1919
/Brown,Charles Cosby d1923 xBrown,Carol Louise 1925
/Brown,Charles A. 1847-1932 /Brown,Clara B.24 aug 1870-4 sep 1912

xBrown,Cora 2 feb 1927   xBrown,Cynthia 6 may 1919
/Brown,Douglas W.1877-1936 /Brown,Drussie 7 nov 1892-19 oct 1896
xBrown,Dorothy Louise 3/2/32 xBrown,Edgar 3 apr 1912
/Brown,Edgar S. 1864-1923 /Brown,Ernest 1884-1885 s/o RG&ME
/Brown,Elizabeth 1848-1909 /Brown,Ethel 15 jan 1890-31 oct 1917wChalmer
xBrown,Elizabeth 27 Jan 1920 xBrown,Effie 28 aug 1919
xBrown,E.S.1889   xBrwon,Etta 25 oct 1935
/Brown,Francis 1916-1921 xBrown,George 17 sep 1937
xBrown,Henrietta 26 sep 1925 xBrown,George L. 30 Jul 1930
/Brown,Howard E. 1870-1929 xBrown,Horace 10 jun 1915
xBrown,James 5 Jun 1923   xBrown,James H.16 apr 1931
xBrown,James 11 nov 1916 xBrown,Janice 6 mar 1920
/Brown,J.H.1861-3 mar 1939 /Brown,Jessel 1895-1937 41y11m12d
/Brown,Joe 1868-1925   /Brown,Jennie 15 may 1930 50y9m
xBrown,John N.14 sep 1917 xBrown,John P.14 dec 1919
/Brown,John W. 1848-1909 /Brown,R.17 feb 1917 inf
/Brown,Katie 1875-1925   xBrown,Laura 27 Jan 1911
xBrown,Kathleen B.29 mar 1938/Brown,Libbie Z. 1863-1931 w/o David
xBrown,Lennie 8 Jan 1935 xBrown,Louiza M.26 apr 1917
xBrown,Lula 14 Jun 1926   xBrown,Lucille 8 nov 1925
xBrown,Margaret 16 Jun 1921 xBrown,Martha B.1858-1895
/Brown,Mary C. 1879-1938 /Brown,Mary C.1929-1933
xBrown.Mary 12 may 1927   xBrown,Nellie 4 oct 1916
/Brown,Mordecai 1838-1907 /Brown,Robert G.31 mar 1852-10 Jun 1911
/Brown,Overton A. 1849-1924 xBrown,P.P.7 Jul 1920
xBrown,Paul 5 may 1922   xBrown,Perly 23 aug 1924
/Brown,Richard F. 1938 inf xBrown,Ray 23 may 1916
xBrown,Robert G. 11 Jun 1911 xBrown,S.K. 1 apr 1918
/Brown,R.R.Jr. 1870-1912 /Brown,S.S. 1879-1931
/Brown,Thomas 9 apr 1923 WWI /Brown,Thomas J.Jr.20 mar 1918-15 mar 1920
/Brown,Thomas 22 Jun 1935 /Brown,V.A.15 aug 1921
/Brown,Unie 1872-1920 w/oJW /Brown,Virginia Myrth 1885-1923
/Brown,Victoria 1856-1921 xBrown,Virginia 4 aug 1911
xBrown,W.L. 25 apr 1925   /Brown,Walter Jr.1934 inf s/o Walter & Dot
/Brown,William 1886-1923 /Brown,William W. 1860-28 apr 1931 71y8m6d
/Brown,Wirt 1878-1915   /Brown,Woolf D.4 aug 1895-8 oct 1932 Lib&D
/Brown,Kathleen B.Brady   /Brown,Onida A.Barnett 1900-1928 w/o A.H.
 1870-1938 w/o JG Brown   /Browning,Wanda Marie 11 mar 1934 1m1d
/Brownrigg,Wm.Henry 1868-1906xBrownell,Jacqueline 15 Jun 1922
/Brownrigg,John Joseph Sr. /Brownrigg,John Joseph Jr. 1866-1923
   1830-1875   /Brownrigg,Margaret E. 1862-1933
/Brownstein,Rosalee 1924-1929/Browsky,Stanley 4 Jul 1923
/Brownstein,Oscar 1881-1924 /Broyles,Margaret A. 1877-1911
/Brownstein,Rebecca 1882-1925/Bruce,Rebecca L.6 Jun 1834-29 may 06wJohn
/Bruce,Annie M. 1849-1926 /Bruce,Edgar F. 31 oct 1841-14 Jul 1895
/Bruce,Helen 1902 inf   xBruce,Catherine Rich 1 Jun 1935
xBrunefield,inf 17 Jan 1912 xBrunt,inf 1 aug 1921
xBrunefield,inf/WmM.1/5/1913 xBrunt,inf 13 may 1917
xBryan,Harry Jr,8 apr 1929 xBryant,A.J.4 may 1922
/Bryant,John T. 1862-1925 /Bryan,Wesley 1907-1913 s/o HA&LB
/Bryant,May J. 1851-1924 xBryant,Atta May 13 sep 1902
xBryant,inf/Wm. 15 Jun 1911 xBryant,Susan 24 may 1912
xBryant,Virginia 3 Jul 1926 xBryant,William 28 aug 1922
xBuck,Mrs.C.M. 18 may 1951 /Buchanan,Charles B. 1868-1913
/Buck,Charles M, 1861-1935 xBucher,Lawrence Lowell 13 Jun 1935

/Buckey,Evaline L. 1821-1906 /Buckley,Dr.T.L.H.1817-7 Jan 1892 75y7d
/Budgewater,Irvin L.1875-1931/Buffington,Eliza J.1811-6 sep 1862
xBuffington,Georgia 9/22/1921xBuffington,Margaret G. 1865-1929
/Buffington,Garland 1865-1919/Buffington,Edward Standard (Dr.)
/Buffington,W.H. 1818-1899   11 aug 1847-24 feb 1929
/Buffington,William Henry   Nannie Lyell 8 oct 1851-23 dec 1925
    25 feb 1787-28 Jun 1858 /Buffington,Louise Garland 1841-1918
  Nancy Scales   /   /Buffington,Peter Cline 1814-1875
    11 nov 1795-24 sep 1882 xBuffins,inf/o Maude 7 may 1920
/Buford,Frances M.1891-1920 /Bull,Annie 1849-1921
/Bull,Clara 1882-1905   /Bull,W.H. 1840-1918
/Bull,Melvina 1879-1909   /Bullock,Viola E. 1906-1926
/Bullock,Ollie T.1880-1913 xBullock,Viola E. 1858-1957
xBullio,Robert 25 Jun 1924 /Bullock,Thomas J. 1852-1910
xBunch,Clarissa A.3 apr 1917 xBunch, inf/o J.P.10 mar 1913
xBunch,inf/o Effie 2/4/1914 xBunch,Virgil A. 26 dec 1921
xBunch,Lewis 17 sep 1911   /Bunch,Macey G.29 apr 1907 28y w/o W.F.
xBunch,Nancy 1907   /Bunch,Walter Franklin 26 apr 1907 1m1d
/Bundrant,Leonard B.1911-1921/Burcham,Alice Marlene 27 feb 1938 inf
/Burchette,Andrew J.1869-1928xBurcham.W.C. 13 Jan 1920
     Helen Geiger 1874-1914 xBurchfield,Marie inf 18 mar 1915
xBurdett,Emma 21 aug 1922   inf/o Walter 8 dec 1915
xBurdett,Leo 27 Jul 1919   /Burdette,Charles Linwood 1904-5
/Burdette,Osie L.1860-1923 /Burdette,George Marden 1931-8
/Burdette,Elliot V. 1859-1917/Burdette,Hazel Ann 1928 inf
/Burdette,Helen 1912-1918   /Burdette,Standley G. 1938 inf
xBurge,Richard 17 Jan 1927 /Burgess,Elizabeth Ann Harmon 1840-1921
/Burgess,Annie L.--   /Burgess,Adelaia Margaret 9 sep 1937
xBurgess,Ademan 7 aug 1935 /Burgess,Ellen Scott 1869-1933
xBurgess,Julia 1854-1908   /Burgess,Minnie E. 1873-1903
xBurgess,Nora 19 oct 1913   /Burgess,James Washington 1837-1904
xBurgess,Ona 1935   xBurgess,W.H. 4 apr 1924
xBurgett,Leo 27 Jul 1919 inf xBurke,Henry 2 mar 1910
/Burke,Henry W. 1842-1911   xBurkett,Michael C. 10 Jul 1935
xBurks,Elizabeth 6 oct 1908 /Burkheimer,Henrietta 1844-1925
/Burks,Creede C.1861-1925   /Burkheimer,Henry William d 1892
/Burks,George E.1851-1906   xBurkheimer,William 15 feb 1914
xBurks,Alberta M.1940   xBurks,Elizabeth 1899-1908
xBurks,Donald 24 aug 1926   xBurks,Georgia J.1 apr 1933
xBurks,Grace 3 dec 1930   xBurks,Helen 23 may 1920
/Burks,Irvin D.3 sep 1890 7y /Burks,Henry Albert 24 Jun 1884 s/oLH&HM
/Burks,Edna d 20 nov 1887Inf /Burks,Lennis B.apr-oct 1883 s/o GE&AM
/Burks,Mary E. 1865-1924   /Burks,Lewis Henry 26 may 1840-26 may 1906
/Burks,Recta 11 Jun 1889 8y5m/Burks,Theodore Sidney 1884 Inf/oLH&HM
xBurks,Henry W. 28 may 1911 xBurks,Eunice Adella 1894-1914
xBurner,C.R. inf 2 Jun 1930
xBurnett,Charles E.9apr 1926 /Burns,Albert 1848-1921
xBurnett,inf/o C.E. 2/21/1917xBurns,Mrs.Albert 15 sep 1912
/Burns,Alex Co E 13th WV Inf xBurns,clover 29 feb 1909
/Burns,Dr.A.C.1848-1907   /Burns,Blanch B.26 sep 1868-4 feb 1891WA&PJ
/Burns,Charles 1871-1910   /Burns,Daisy Campbell 1873-1914
/Burns,David 1855-1925   /Burns,Douglas 1902-03
xBurns,David henry 1878-1939 xBurns,Diana 23 feb 1937
/Burns,George 1879-1909   /Burns,Elmo Elizabeth 1920-22
/Burns,Henry Dudley 1883-1936/Burns,Henry Samuel 1841-1882

xBurns,Imogene 1870-1910   /Burns,Howard Beauchamp 1880-1900
/Burns,James 1884-1937   xBurns,Mrs.J.H. 12 feb 1910
/Burns,James F. 1883-1912   /Burns,Rev.James H. 1832-1913
xBunrs,Jeff 9 Jan 1938   xBurns,John A. 18 apr 1923
/Burns,John 1874-1893   xBurns,John P. 30 jun 1925
/Burns,John P.Jr. 1852-1890   xBurns,Margaret 6 oct 1919
/Burns,Mary E. 1853-1913   /Burns,Lydia Margaret 1852-1929
/Burns,Mary K. 1839-1919   /Burns,Nell D. 1877-1912
/Burns,Mary L. 1835-1910   /Burns,Osceola 1847-1908
/Burns,M.L.1840-1912   xBurns,O.G. 25 mar 1935
/Burns,Peter E. 1895-1934   xBurns,Pamelia 30 nov 1910
xBurns,Richard inf 5/24/1915   xBurns,Rosela 27 nov 1910
xBurns,Susan 1887-1939   /Burrows,Ida 1873-1934
xBurton,Caroline 19 feb 1921   /Burton,Mabel 20 may 1939 58y10m17d
xBurton,Samuel F. 15 feb 1934   /Burton,Samuel Doyle 1906-1916
xBusby,James A. 1 oct 1936   xBush,Carl Edward 17 dec 1924
xBush,Donald 26 feb 1930   xBush,Francis Bell 8 mar 1937
xBush,John O.2 dec 1915   xBush,John O. 9 Jan 1931
xBush,Lemuel 31 may 1936   xBush,infs/o John 1915 & 1916
/Bush,Mary J.1858-1922   xBush,Paul 21 sep 1923
xBush,Virginia 13 apr 1915   /Bush,W.H.17 apr 1844-21 feb 1918
xBuskirk,Joseph C. 1 Jun 1937   /Buskirk,Melda nov 1867-nov 1916
xButler,Eliza M. 1908-1877   Robert Ward 1867-1918
/Butler,Benjamin F.1837-1907   /Butler,C.Harry 1867-1902
/Butler,Kathleen R.1899-1918   /Butler,Charles Freeman 1915-1932
xButler,Houston C.2 mar 1928   /Butler,Julia Ann 1842-1929
xButler,inf/Mary 10 aug 1914   /Butler,Jeanette Jenkins 1854-1912
/Butler,Maria E. 1844-1919   /Butler,Margaret 23 mar 1933 30y
xButler,Moses 2 aug 1917   xButler,Mary Hood 14 sep 1925
/Butler,Timothy S.1830-1912   /Butler,Dr.Wm.Earl 1880-1912
xButler,Ruby K.31 oct 1918   xByers,Billie J. 31 mar 1919
xByers,Ella 17 feb 1930   xByers,infs 1917,1917,1922,1927-/oAl 1918
xByers,Paul 8 mar 1921   xByers,Richard inf 4 dec 1936
xByrd,Sarah Ann 15 aug 1915   xByron,Bettie 3 oct 1916
/Byrd,Ora 1901-1924   xByron,Mollie 5 aug 1915
/Byrd,Oscar J.1899-1927   xCabell,inf 19 aug 1926
/Cain,Blackburn B.1884-1936   xCaivens,inf/o LV 13 sep 1920
/Cain,W.F.1869-1896   /Caldwell,Beulah 14 mar-12 sep 1879
xCaldwell,Estella May 3/28/21   /Caldwell,Foree Dabney 17 dec 1880-3 feb36
/Caldwell,Carrie F.1851-1921   /Caldwell,George Jackson 4/13/1883-11/17/27
xCaldwell,Foree D.3/30/71   /Caldwell,Judge George H.1844-1910
/Caldwell,Maggie 1871-1935   /Caldwell,James Lewis 20 may 1846-18 oct23
/Caldwell,James Lewis Jr.   /Caldwell,John Turner 1921-22
   1 sep 1888-2 nov 1933   /Caldwell,Mary Odamian Smith
/Caldwell,Nicholas Smith   22 Jan 1852-2 oct 1927
   21 aug 1890-31 dec 1928   /Caldwell,W.A. 1857-1927
/Calhoun,John C.1875-1907   /Calico,Edith 10 apr 1923
xCalicoat,Richard A.9/19/1931   xCallaghan,Frank C. 18 Jul 1938
xCall,Luther J. 21 Jul 1923   /Callahan,Margaret B.1864-1927
xCalkins,H.L.14 apr 1916   xCallahan,Dan 21 Jan 1911
xCallahan,J.H. 1 Jun 1916   xCallahan,John S.23 nov 1919
/Callahan,John S.1875-1907   /Callahan,Walter O. 1887-1909 s/o JH&FM
xCallahan.Shelby 10 Jan 1936   /Callicoat,Abigail S. 1866-1910 w/o SR
xCallaway,Guy 17 Jul 1927   xCallaway,Elbert Mayo 8 Jul 1937

xCallaway,Emily 15 apr 1912   xCallaway,John 11 oct 1914
xCallaway,Lillie 1895   xCallaway,William 1 Jun 1920
xCalloway,Chas.Mayo 11/20/26   xCalville,Josie 9 Jun 1920
xCamel,Katie 18 Jul 1925   /Cammack,Lucius H.1867-1925
/Cammack,John Henry 1843-1920 /Cammack,Bertha Louella 1867-1926
/Cammack,John Willie 1869-70   /Cammack,Mary Jane 1843-1925
xCamp,Mrs.Ella 4 dec 1917   xCamp,Harry M. 27 Jan 1922
xCamp,W.D. 15 nov 1921   xCampbell,Bessie E.22 Jul 1920
xCampbell,Albert 1 Jul 1924   /Campbell,Carlos B. 1876-1936
/Campbell,Audrey L.1917-18   xCampbell,Carrie E. 21 Jan 1928
/Campbell,Coral 1861-1881   xCampbell,Eugene 1870
xCampbell,Deborah J.1860-1907 /Campbell,Eugene M. 1856-1902
xCampbell,Ella V.29 may 1919   xCampbell,Emma 7 Jul 1924
xCampbell,George 29 Jul 1918   /Campbell,Ida Lola 19 dec 1878-8 aug 1912
/Campbell,H.L.--   xCampbell,Hugh 2 feb 1933
/Campbell,James T. 1825-1901   xCampbell,J.H. 28 Jul 1921
xCampbell,John A. 27 Jan 1937 xCampbell,Lula S.1855-1895
/Campbell,Leroy 1854-1937   /Campbell,Nancy 1828-1906
     Mary A. 1852-1918   xCampbell,Robert E.21 dec 1936
xCampbell,Nelson E.8 apr 1929 /Campbell,Rebecca V.1848-1934
/Campbell,Mary --   /Campbell,Virginia E. 1892-1919
/Campbell,Oral 1904-1924   /Canada,Hammond 17 Jul 1869-25 may 1908
                               xCanady,Willie B. 5 mar 1934
/Canning,George W.1868-1911   /Canterberry,Kenley 9 Jun 1933 54y
/Canning,Lulu B.1889-1917   xCanterbury,George W. 21 may 1910
xCanterbury,Orga 27 oct 1933   xCanterbury,Evid 165 Jul 1923 inf
xCantrell,Carl H.7/4/33 inf   xCantrow,Nancy 19 sep 1909
/Cantrell,Eva Frances 1922   /Capehart,Joseph Water 1894-1921
/Cantrell,A.J.--   /Capehart,Katherine Neal 1875-1926
/Caplan,Etta Angel 1907-1934   xCapehart,Catherine Hope 23 dec 1926
/Carder,George L. 1850-1910   xCapehart,inf/o HC 28 may 1915
/Carder,Martha 1850-1936   xCarey,Florence 13 apr 1932
xCarder,Dr.A.S. 1867-1893   xCarey,Jacob 14 feb 1936
     Agnes 1870-1892   /Cardwell,Noah 1878-1937
/Carico,E.C. 1885-1913   /Cardwell,Leonore 1850-1918
/Carico,E.D. 1909-2-1906   /Carico,E.W. 1889-1900
xCarley,Benjamin 12 mar 1915   xCarmine,Joseph 2 feb 1924
xCarnes,Ellen L.1930 inf   xCarney,Luther W. 13 apr 1932
/Carnohan,Carl C. 1901-1915   xCarney,inf/o R.C. 29 may 1920
/Carnohan,Fred A. 1891-1915   /Carnohan,Jeanette page 1870-1917
xCarpenter,Hamnal 28 Jun 1921 xCarpenter,Hattie 12 feb 1923
xCarpenter,Mary 18 nov 1914   /Carper,Chester B.1853-1903
/Carr,James C.10 feb 1935 60y /Carper,Mary V.1862-1921
xCarrans,Jane 31 aug 1921   xCarrigan,J.F.15 nov 1923
xCarroll,Annie 1865 inf   xCarroll,Annie 1883 inf
xCarroll,Catherine 1858-1903   xCarroll,Elizabeth Downey 1854-1891
xCarroll,Ellen C. 1888 inf   xCarroll,Emily 20 aug 1928
xCarroll,George 1865-1918   /Carrol,Florence M. 6 apr 1889 11m
/Carrol,Harry 13 Jul 1891inf   /Carrol,George F.26 Jul 1885 1y4m16d
/Carrol,James 1833-1894   xCarroll,James W. 27 mar 1910
xCarroll,Lawrence Leo 1890inf xCarroll,Margaret A. 1848-1907
xCarroll,Mary Fee 1835-1972   xCarroll,Michael Henry 1848-1927
xCarroll,Robt.L. 21 Jul 1914   xCarroll,Thomas 1812-1876
xCarroll,Cozzetta 30 mar 1925 /Carson,J.H.Jr. 1886-1918

/Carter,Dr.A.S.1867-1893 /Carter,Albert 22 oct 1937 WWI
    Agnes K. 1870-1892   /Carter,ALlce Hawkins 1852-1905
/Carter,Annie 1911-1928 xCarter,A.R. 8 Jan 1919
xCarter,Abe 21 mar 1939 xCarter,Alexander 29 dec 1921
xCarter,Alfred 5 mar 1915 xCarter,Angus 7 Jan 1922
xCarter,Annie M.14 dec 1927 xCarter,Angus 28 Jun 1915 inf
xCarter,Arthur W.15 may 1928 xCarter,Bessie H. 23 feb 1916
xCarter,Carl 21 oct 1920 xCarter,Florence 7 Jun 1918
xCarter,Carrie 12 mar 1913 /Carter,Ed. 27 apr 1935 41y
/Carter,Daisy 1875-1905 xCarter,Daisy 23 feb 1915
/Carter,Edna M. 1889-1912 xCarter,E.A. 1890
xCarter,Elbert W. 24 oct 1937xCarter,Ellen 29 nov 1910
/Carter,Donnie 1908-1909 /Carter,Frank M. 18 oct 1937 WWI
/Carter,Rev.H.B. -- /Carter,Henry 25 nov 1820-26 feb 1903
/Carter,John 1849-1910   Mary Elizabeth 22 Jul 1824-20 feb 1906
xCarter,James Ray 10/4/1931 xCarter,Irvin W. 3 mar 1917
xCarter,Jennie 1911 xCarter,John 10 eb 1916
xCarter,John A. 2 Jun 1910 /Carter,Joshua C.1867-29 nov 1936
xCarter,Joseph W. 21 sep 1920/Carter,Rebecca B.31 oct 1855 62y11m
/Carter,Lonnie&Lennie 1908-09   w/o Edward Standard
/Carter,Lillie J.1869-1913 /Carter,J.Auburn 1881-1909
/Carter,Lennie 1875-1934 xCarter,Lula 3 sep 1916
xCarter,Leevis 16 apr 1916 /Carter,Mary 1 apr 1838-28 dec 1913
/Carter,Mary Howard 1859-1919/Carter,Mary E. 1875-1930 w/o C.O.
/Carter,Mary E.1833-1910 xCarter,Myrtle 16 mar 1934
xCarter,Mary 1824-1906 /Carter,Myrtle Clara 1892-1915 w/o A.R.Jr.
xCarter,Nancy E. 26 mar 1930 xCarter,Pauline 6 oct 1913
/Carter,W.Basil 1898-1936 /Carter,Virgil H. 6 aug 1926 9m21d
/Carter,W.M.1870-1920 xCarter,inf/o V.B. 26 Jul 1912
xCarter,Willie A. 6 aug 1921 /Cartmill,John Gilbert 7 feb 1844-25 Jun27
xCartmill,Edsel F.19 Jun 1931xCartmill,Lewis Wade 13 may 1931
xCartmill,Mary A. 16 may 1931xCartmill,R.H. 27 mar 1918
/Cartwright,Ann 1853-1917 /Cartmill,Virginia Helen McGuire
/Cartwright,James 1849-1930   17 feb 1845-28 feb 1920
/Cartwright,Thomas 1825-1909 /Cartwright,Eliz.1827-1911
xCarver,Caroline 17 apr 1927 /Carver,James 1840-1917
xCarver,Emma 13 Jul 1916 xCarver,James E. 3 Jun 1912
/Cassady,Hazel V.1896-1924 /Caseley,Ruth Velma 1916-1925
/Cassell,J.W. 58y Civil War /Cassidy,Edna F. 8 feb 1935 78y2m21d
/Cassler,Ana B.1844-1927 /Cassidy,James T. 12 feb 1830(?) 60y6m21d
/Cassler,Inez L.1865-1929 xCastello,Phil 3 oct 1928
xCassler,John A.1843-1898 /Castle,Julia d28 sep 1870
/Cassler,Wm.P.1863-1925 #Castle,John W. CoI 37th VA Inf CSA
                          /Castle,W.Bruce 24 Jun 1899-9 dec 1918
xCaster,Boney 8 sep 1934 xCastner,Marcum 26 Jun 1920
/Casto,Paul 4 may 1933 /Cawthorne,Tennessee Marcum 1868-1912
xCastro,Virginia 25 mar 1919 xCavendish,Florence W. 17 Jul 1917
/Cavendish,Leslie 1884-1938 /Cavendish,Florence Wolcott 1869-1910
/Cavendish,Louie Christine /Cavendish,Fredrick 1910-1920
    1903-1904 d/o LF&Lucy /Cavendish,Margaret 1890-1918
/Caverlee,Frank Thomas /Caverlee,Robert J.4 sep 1846-5 Jun 1914
    11 Jun 1859-2 dec 1913 /Caverlee,Sarah E.26 mar 1854-10 Jan 1935
/Caverly,Walter H.1896-1935 xChadwick,Hanna 29 dec 1924
xChaffin,Clarence 25 mar 1921xChadwick,Nellie 21 sep 1909

xChaffin,S. 10 dec 1923   /Chalmers,Sallie 14 Jul 1935   33y1-m10d
/Chaffin,Bertha M. 1896-1925 xChain,inf/o Thos.29 nov 1908
xChaffin,William C. 1893   /Chambers,Cleo 1898-1901
xChambers,Annie Lee 7/16/1913xChambers,Brook 27 nov 1931
xChambers,inf/Frank W. 1919 xChambers,Brooks 1932
/Chambers,George 1901-1902   xChambers,Garland 26 nov 1919
xChambers,H.S. 29 apr 1931   /Chambers,Henry Holt 1912-1918
xChambers,Helen H.1840-1909 xChambers,Henry W. 1889-18909
/Chambers,Jennie C.   /Chambers,John 11 Jun 1838-24 sep 1921
    1869-1938   /Chambers,Luther Lybrook 1856-1906
/Chambers,John Weymar 1901-03/Chambers,Martha Carter 1851-1928
xChambers,Mathew V. 1880-1917xChambers,Martha Jane 29 nov 1930
/Chambers,Dixie A.Runyon   /Chambers,Russell M. 1897-1917
    1877-1905 w/o J.A.   xChambers,Russel T.1881-1891
xChambers,Rebecca 1852-1889 xChambers,Susan C.7 apr 1930
xChamp,Ruby E. 27 feb 1914   xChamp,Robert L. 5 Jun 1925
    & inf 27 feb 1914   xChamp,Ruby E. 1 may 1914
/Champion,Jefferson 1848-1920xChandler,Ira D.3 Jul 1937
xChandler,Laura M. 3 mar 1932xChandler,Milton L. 20 oct 1937
/Chandler,Mary A. 1861-1914   /Chandler,Grover C.24 feb 1893-14 feb 1914
/Chapell,Bertie 1890-1906   /Chapelle,Jean C.1926 inf
/Chapman,Archie H.1868-1910   /Chapman,Alexander H. 1835-1877
xChapman,Alfred 29 feb 1924 xChapman,Annie Louise 25 may 1921
xChapman,Buford 1911 inf/Art xChapman,C.B.18 Jun 1922
xChapman,C.E. 7 oct 1927   /Chapman,Clifton E.1 nov 1931 inf
/Chapman,Emily 1847-1929   /Chapman,Charles C. 7 Jan 1939 WWI
/Chapman,Floyd S.1871-1930(2)/Chapman,Charles Edger 1883-1923
xChapman,Elijah F.1 feb 1927 xChapman,Elizabeth
xChapman,Ella 11 Jul 1922   xChapman,Erva 6 aug 1915
xChapman,George 17 aug 1921 xChapman,George
xChapman,inf/Fred 1911   xChapman,inf/John O. 1936
xChapman,inf/W.C. 1916   xChapman,inf/R.C. 1921
xChapman,John W.8 may 1921   xChapman,Lou F. 5 oct 1911
/Chapman,Louise 1860-1920   xChapman,Milton Robert 1 apr 1936
/Chapman,Martin V.1842-1903   /Chapman,Julia E.1845-1915 w/o AG
/Chapman,Minta 1842-1926   /Chapman,Nellie Louise 22 Jul-14 nov 1931
xChapman,O.K. 23 sep 1924   xChapman,Sadie D.16 nov 1936
/Chapman,Oscar L.1895-1917   /Chapman,Tammy J. 9/3/1870-4/12/1898w/Lew F
xChapman,Susan 3 feb 1921   xChapman,tommy 16 oct 1911
/Chapman,Virginia 1912-1930 xChapman,William A. 1872-1890
/Chapman,Warner 1886-1933   /Chase,Paul B.
/Chase,Anna S. 1856-1923   /Chase,Lizzie 1824-1976
/Chase,Edward W.1846-1928   xChatfield,Jennie W. 3 mar 1924
xCherry,Lang 24 nov 1920   xChilders,John Boster 13 nov 1918
/Childers,A.J. 1868-1916   /Childers,Bertha L.1/20/1890-4/16/1903CM&ME
/Childers,Glenn 1898-1901   xChilders,Louise 23 mar 1917
xChilders,Sarah 29 mar 1925 xChilders,Sarah 10 oct 1923
xChildress,William 1881-82
/Childrey,Annie 1853-1932   /Childrey,Jesse B. 4 may 1901 29y3m15d
/Childrey,Vianna 1846-1918   /Childrey,William 27 feb 1867-3 aug 1891
/Chittum,Samuel 1910 RA&Ida xChittum,Ida 28 Jan 1924
xChittum,inf/Josphine 1917   xChristian,Mrs.B.F. 19 feb 1920
xChristian,Elizabeth 1905   xChristian,J.C. 21 nov 1923
xChristain,Walter inf 1892   /Christian,Richard A. 1872-1928

/Christian,Mary 1925-1933   /Christian,Rebecca 23 nov 1857-19 aug 1906
/Christian,Oscar M.1873-1914   w/o E.C.Christian
xChristodonlia,John 1/9/31   xChristy,Francis 23 FEB 1929
xChristodonlia,Gene 8/30/32 xChristy,John C.7 Jan 1925
xChristy,Susie B.30 may 1937xChristy,Mary Ellen 15 aug 1937
/Christy,Clarence A.1902- 36/Christy,Mattie E. 1848-1937
/Christy,John W.1838-1917   /Church,Charles A.9 aug 1933   58y6m13d
/Church,A.G. 1833-1909   /Church,Mabel 7 mar 1934
/Church,Mary C.1853-1926   xChurch,inf/Woodson W. 1915
xChurch,Mary J. 23 Jan 1928 xChurch,inf/Will 1912
xCircle,Charles E.22 apr1921 /Citron,Peter--VA Cav CSA
xCircle,Marion E. 11 oct 1921/Clagg,Lillie A. 7 dec 1931 68y1m29d
/Clagg,John W.18 dec 1926 6y /Clark,Anna M.Haberle 1880-1925
/Clark,Alice Laird 1854-1925 /Clark,Alma Louise 1924-25
/Clark,Charles E. 1870-1914 /Clark,Charles F. 1857-1925
xClark,Christa 1904 inf   /Clark,Fred D. 29 nov 1931
xClark,inf/o TC 15 Jun 1920   Tennessee 1855-1921
xClark,General 13 mar 1910   /Clark,Herman Kelsel 16 Jan 1916
/Clark,James WWI   /Clark,James 1850-1926
/Clark,James 5 oct 1932   xClark,inf/Fred 15 feb 1910
/Clark,inf/MH 28 Jan 1916   xClark,Jeanette 9 feb 1921
xClark,John W. 5 aug 1933   xClark,Julia Ann 1828-1903
xClark,Levisa R. 9 mar 1913 /Clark,Margaret 1862-1933
xClark,Mary K. 9 aug 1928   xClark,Otto 12 feb 1913
/Clark,Roland 1841-1884   /Clark,Martha Wadell 1854-1916
/Clark,Susie E. 1848-1931   xClark,Thomas Jefferson 24 may 1919
/Clark,William T. 36thVA Inf /Clark,Walter R. 29 Jan 1902-19 mar 1924
/Clark,W.J. 1859-1903   xClark,William Lyman 1811-1888
/Clark,W.R. 1852-1914   xClark,Williana 22 nov 1938
xClarke,Ama L. 29 Jul 1925   xClaston,inf/Eugena 27 dec 1913
xClaughton,Lucy T.2 nov 1919 xClay,Edward F. 12 apr 1933
xClay,inf/Jac 2 may 1911   xClay,John D. 26 mar 1924
/Clay,Earl R. 1894-1930   xClay,Roda 23 Jul 1919
/Clay,Susie 1870-1921   xClay,Stephen G. 7 aug 1934
xClaypool,Kenneth C.6/3/1926 /Clayborn,Curtis G.12 may 1887-29 Jul 1937I
/Claypool,Azel Z. 1892--1913 xCleaton,Harry C. 11 Jul 1926
xClelland,Irene Rose 3/11/1933/Clements,Ida H. 21 aug 1856-17 feb 1913
/Clements,Harlow T.1884-1931   W.H. 8 Jan 1856-20 feb 1904
/Clements,Bernard C.1882-1918xClements,Charles B. 15 mar 1926
xClemens,Josephine 3/14/1931 xClements,Martha 27 Jul 1931
xClemons,John 3 may 1911   /Clendenning,Robert 1 apr 1938 WWI
xCliff,George 5 apr 1929   xClifton,inf/Chas.W. 1922
xCliff,inf/Karl P.1915   xCline,John Weaver 13 Jan 1938
/Close,John H. 1848-1915   xCloninger,Elmer 1 Jan 1931
/Close,Mary V. 1853-1938   xClouson,Betty Jane 26 Jan 1927
xClose,John Alexander9/2/39 /Clouston,Elizabeth Branum 1866-1932
/Clouston,James McVey 1837-19/Clouston,Elmer Ward 1862-1926
/Clouston,Lizzie Holmes   /Clouston,Robert Milton 1865-1923
   1835-1921   xClouston,Charles H. 4 feb 1933
xClutter,Dorothy 25 mar 1937 xClutter,Eula 7 sep 1931
xClutter,inf/Robt 1914   xClutter,inf/Ruth 1918
xClutter,John R. 28 mar 1931 xClutter,John R. 15 may 1923
/Coates,Harriett 1853-1906   xCoaul,Blake Stein 3 dec 1919
xCobb,Charles 27 Jul 1919   xCobb,E. 5 oct 1919

xCobb,inf/Hubert 1918   xCobb,inf.RF&Florence 11 apr 1917
xCobb,Mary E. 22 may 1921   /Coburn,Alberta 1867-1918 Mrs.J.S.
/Cobb,Hester 1882-1929   /Coburn,Bert W. 1894-1917
/Cochran,Ina 1917-1921   /Cochran,Willie F. 29 nov 1919
/Cochran,Nina d 1921   /Cochran,Vina d1921
xCochran/J.C. 19 nov 1914   xCochran,inf/Chas.D. 15 sep 1934
/Cochran,Minnie 1875-1919   xCochrin,Robert 16 Jul 1931
/Cocke,Charmian B.1856-8/18/17 /Cocke,William J. 1844-1938
/Cocke,C.Irma 1878-1923   /Cocke,Clarence E. 1876-1907
/Cocke,Rebecca O.1880-1901   xCockrill,Laura Ball 23 apr 1934
/Coda,Albert 1911-1920   /Coe,inf 1915-d/o AS&LH
xCoda,S.C. 2 nov 1922   xCoe,Andrew 14 Jan 1915 inf
/Coe,Mary 1816-28 dec 1880   /Coe,Sarah Stephenson 19 oct 1933 74y6m21d
    Seldon S.1816- 1 aug 1874 xCoe,John 31 dec 1923
xCoe,Robert Henson 12/24/1919 xCoffey,Annie 7 Jun 1921
xCoffin,Caleb 12 aug 1925   xCoffman,Anna Rose Maxine 27 mar 1934
xCoffman,Alfred 27 Jul 1928   xCoffman,Howard 4 apr 1919
xCoffman,John 23 apr 1913   xCoffman,J.W. 5 mar 1924
xCoffman,Lucy 27 mar 1922   xCoffman,Pauline Josephine 1926-1939
xCoffman,Noah   xCoffman,Rose Alice 19 mar 1935
/Coffman,R.E.S. 1863-1911   /Coffman,Dixie L. 1902-05 s/o REL&ME
/Coffman,Paul Everett1901-37   /Coffman,Ralph Miller 1909-1911s/oCB&GM
xCohen,Forest Jr.15 mar 1920   /Coffren,Caleb F. 1842-1925
/Cohen,Charles 1855-1907   /Cogbill,John A. 1840-1898 CSA
/Cohen,Fannie 1841-1899   xColas,James 14 may 1934
xCohen,Moses 15 feb 1928   /Colburn,Otna B. 23 feb 1938 WWI
/Cole,Herbert 1879-1935   xColburne,Robert Hammond 23 nov 1915
xCole,James 29 apr 1940   xColeburn,Ofway 27 may 1939
/Cole,Charles W. SpAm   /Cole,Flora Catherine 8 Jul 1903 11m6d
xColeman,Annie Leona 7/14/34   /Cole,James W. 29 mar 1936 78y5m12d
/Coleman,Nellie 1890-1930   Mary Frances Greene 22 Jan 1918 47y10m
xColeman,Elizabeth 9/23/1924   /Coles,James 1851-1934
xColeman,George 28 mar 1917   /Coles,Sidy 17 Jul 1887-30 apr 1904
xColeman,Jimmie 29 may 1938   xColes,William 18 nov 1937
xColley,Barbara 4 oct 1919   /Colley,William D. 1895-1913
xColley,James M. 1876-1901   /Collier,Beulah 1892-1898
/Collier,Elizabeth 1858-1919   /Collier,Joseph-1861-Tr.E.8th VA Cav CSA
/Collier,James W. 1856-1933   /Collier,Margaret Gaw 1858-1917
/Collier,Sarah Ann 1886-1908   /Collier,Nellie 9 may 1869-28 Jun 1915
/Collins,Albert 1867-1935   /Collins,Bernie 30 mar 1926 18y18m
    Sallie K. 1854-1933   xCollins,Carol Louise 3 aug 1931
/Collins,Carrie 1882-1918   xCollins,R.F. 27 oct 1915
xCollins,Darlene 29 mar 1921   xCollins,Dennis Mervin 26 dec 1911
xCollins,E.W. 18 Jan 1918   xCollins,Eva 8 feb 1932
xCollins,Floyd 7 Jan 1929   xCollins,Eva 31 may 1909
/Collins,James W. 1884-1921   xCollins,inf/Minnie 1916-inf/Wm 1917
/Collins,Lulie 1882-1904   xCollins,Lillian C.19 may 1931
xCollins,Mary 15 sep 1926   xCollins,Mary Jane 13 feb 1936
xCollins,nancy 27 sep 1918   /Collins,Marion C. 5 Jan 1935 78y8m19d
/Collins,Oscar M. 1872-1919   /Collins,William A. 1874-1934
xCollins,William 21 sep 1923   /Collingsworth,Bethana 1868-1913
/Colston,Annie L. 1923-1926   xColston,Otis 4 mar 1932
xColston,William--   xColston,William 3 sep 1929
xComich,charles 4 may 1916   /Combs,Jessie Stepp 1911-1936 w/o Alex

/Comer,R.Harold 1913-1918   /Comer,Harriet Winston 1837-1925 w/oDr.J.A.
xCompton,C.M. 27 mar 1934   xCompton,G.K. 18 Jul 1916
xConeson,Theodore 15 sep 1923xConley,Carroll 17 apr 1934
/Conley,Cecil E. 1906-1910   /Conley,James L.16 oct 1922-8 sep 1923
/Conley,John 1884-1918   /Conley,Ora Evelin 1 Jul 1930   3y2m27d
/Conley,Willie D. 1908-1912   xConley,J.L. 9 sep 1923
xConn,Clarence D.8 may 1930   xConn,Inf/FD 25 feb 1913
xConn,Mary 19 may 1924   xConn,Orval 29 oct 1911
xConnell,Robt.Leroy 3/25/19   /Connell,Inf 1911 inf Inez d/o   EP&AB
/Connell,W.D. 1885-1919   /Connolly,D.E. 1885-1929
xConnelly,Alice 17 dec 1918   /Conrad,Wilfred 25 feb 1937 24y9m19d
xConnelly,John 7 apr 1918   xConner,Edna M.11 aug 1921
xConway,Sue 6 sep 1918   xConner,Pearl 4 sep 1921
xConway,John A. 1881-1932   /Cook,Fronie 3/13/1935 51y1m
/Cook,Katherine R.1866-1913   /Cooksey,William 1868-1927
   Joseph Lassiter 1852-1921   xCoon,Emma
/Coon,Elizabeth 1823-1909   xCoon,Ethel 24 Jul 1910
xCoon,George 6 feb 1909   /Coon,John V.Jr. 1897-1907
/Coon,Harry W. 1880-1913   /Coon,John W. 1860-1932
/Cooper,Cora L 23 Jun 1936 53yxCooper,Jennie 5 mar 1913
xCooper,Kenneth 10 feb 1911   xCooper,Leo 9 may 1923
xCooper,Margaret 10 apr 1923   /Copeland,Virginia 5 Jul 1935   21y9m25d
/Copen,C.Etxel 1900-1929   xCopeland,Willie 1892
/Copelin,J.M.1886s/o JM&C   xCopley,Charles 22 Jan 1924
/Copperstone,Raymond 1931-34   xCopley,T.S. 17 mar 1924
/Corbly,Branson L.1861-1926   /Corbly,Lawrence T. 1901-1914
/Corbly,H.Seymour 1863-1909   /Corbly,Elizabeth H.1860-1906
/Corbly,Martha J. 1857-1928   /Corbly,Lawrence J. 1858-1935
xCornell,Carrie Della 7/28/39/Cornell,Robert 19 Jul 1913-14 mar 1919
xCornell,Louie E.7 Jun 1922   xCornish,Mary 27 Jan 1922
/Cornett,George Washington   /Corns,Mabel B. 1902-1904
   13 Jun 1932   68y8m16d   xCorns,Myrtle Irene 3 mar 1918 inf
/Correll,Gorden 1909-1935   xCorns,Zella 10 sep 1929
xCorum,Hazel 9 may 1930   xCorwin,Corlis H.28 Jan 1931
/Corwin,Nora E.1880-1922   /Corwine,Louise 1865-1923w/o Corlis H.
xCorshine,Lavine 29 mar 1922   xCosby,Norris 5 may 1912
xCottle,Elsie 2 Jun 1915 inf xCosby,Winnie 2 oct 1910
/Cottle,Effie L. 1873-1909   /Cottle,Nellie Humphries 1865-1914
/Cottle,J.A. 1836-1924   /Cottle,Virginia B. 1865-1927
/Cottle,Lyle F.1895-1927   /Cottle,Olivia A. 1832-1914
xCottle,Roy 11 sep 1935   xCotton,Elie 12 aug 1924
/Cottrell,Curtis J.1894-1921 xCotton,Tennessee 18 oct 1923
/Cottrell,Ella 1875-1910 wAlonzaxCottrill,Clayton 23 may 1938
 xCoulter,Harrison 9 mar 1914 xCotrill,Henry 20 feb 1937
/Coulter,Carl R.1892-1931   /Coughenour,inf 1907 s/o EC&JMF
/Courtney,Margaret 1873-1926   /Coup,Laura R. 11 Oct 1881 15y6m23d
/Courtney,Frank L.1878-1930   xCovert,Loretta 31 oct 1938
/Covington,Elizabeth 1857-38 xCovert,Lorna Doon 25 nov 1934
xCovington,Elizabeth 2/27/38 xCovington,Ernest James 9 oct 1934
xCovington,Fannie I.11/9/31   xCovington,Grosie 1905
xCovington,Earl E.11 sep 1915xCovington,inf/E. 13 aug 1915
xCovington,inf/Inez 1919   xCovington,Katie 5 Jan 1925
/Covington,Howard L.   /Covington,James H. 1860-1919
   22 may 1927   18y10m   xCovington,Tincy Albert E.19 dec 1912

/Cowherd,Mary K. 1859-1930   xCox,Albert E.1860-1935
/Cox,Albert Chase 1896-1918   /Cox,John A.28 oct 1830-19 aug 1886
/Cox,Babe feb 1910 s/o Eli   Adela R.6 dec 1833-7 may 1903
/Cox,Delbert F. 1887-1912   /Cox,Earl L.10 may 1891 s/o AH&JE
/Cox,Della F. 1866-1939   xCox,Ely 7 Jun 1931
xCox,Frances 19 dec 1924   /Cox,Mary F.30 Jan 1911-11 mar 1922 d/oEli
/Cox,James C.1919 s/o Eli   xCox,inf/Eli 1911,12,13,17 & 18
xCox,Jack E. 17 mar 1927   xCox,John A. 1830-1896
xCox,Mary J.1888-1901   /Cox,Nannie J.28 may 1853-25 aug 1907wWm.T
/Cox,Nancy 16 sep 1866 78y7d xCox,Patsy Ruth 1 feb 1931
xCox,Pauline 13 aug 1924   /Cox,Sharon Lee 8-11 apr 1938
xCox,William 29 Jul 1921   xCox,William T. 9 Jul 1930
/Cradick,Jesse 25 mar 1919 WI/Cradick,Clyde 21 apr 1897-9 feb 1915
xCraddick,Annie 20 apr 1919   /Cradick,Pat 11 Jun 1882-17 may 1913
xCraddock,George 9 jan 1916   xCraft,Mabel 25 feb 1929
xCraft,Missouri 31 dec 1918   xCraft,W.H. 31 dec 1918
xCrafton,Francis 1857-1874   xCrafton,Francis A. 1 Jun 1874
xCrager,Samuel A. 1903   xCraig,Edward 28 nov 1923
/Craig,Mary E.1875-1938_A.W. xCraig,inf/JW 1911----inf/Morgan 1919
xCraig,James A. 26 feb 1920   xCraig,William 25 nov 1919
xCrank,Wiley G.17 mar 1932   /Crary,Herman lodwick 10 Jun 1936 58y9m4d
/Crary,Mary S. 1846-1918   /Crary,Dr.Archibald 1846-1907
xCraven,Harvey L.13 sep 1918 xCrawford,Ada M. 29 nov 1941
/Crawford,A.J. 1833-1905   /Crawford,Alice Mathews 1858-1914
/Crawford,A.W. 1848-1922   /Crawford,Arch B.6 may 1939 WWI
/Crawford,Calvin C.1844-1928 /Crawford,Fanny C.1846-1932
xCrawford,Mildred 9 feb 1915 xCrawford,Francis B.3 Jun 1934
/Crawford,Wilbur 1867-1907   /Crawford,Willie d/o GC&FC 15y
/Creamer,Edward J.1875-1929   /Creamer,Mary 27 oct 1935 5m
xCreamer,Norman 7 aug 1933   xCreasym,inf/Wm.16 apr 1918
/Creco,Frank J.1931-1932   xCremeans,inf/AA 1916-1916-1917
/Crenshaw,Dorrance Park 1926 xCrews,Richard E. 8 sep 1920
xCrider,Jacob C. 1876   xCrider,Levi 8 Jun 1917
xCrider,Lula C.1880-82   xCrider,Quendaro L.27 Jun 1928
xCrider,Owen,W.1894   xCrisen,inf/HG 12 oct 1920
/Criser,Nannie Lee 1872-1924 /Criser,A.B.7feb 1935 82y11m10d
xCriser,C.C. 1 aug 1935   xCriser,Jane 28 dec 1921
xCrist,Jackey Leroy 7/14/1939xCritt,Leunervia 17 Jul 1923
xCroger,Jane 12 apr 1914   xCrockett,D.D.P. 19 mar 1922
/Crocker,Roy L.1874-1914   /Crockett,Carroll Evans 1921-23
xCroker,Phylis 24 feb 1916   /Crockett,Lena Coda 1905-1933
/Cronin,inf 1 dec 1938   xCrockett,James 13 apr 1921
xCrook,Lucy E. 25 mar 1931   xCrockett,Luther 22 apr 1927
/Crook,William M.1843-1918   /Crooks,C.F. 14th Va Cav CSA
  Sgt Co H 13th Reg WV CI xCross,Isaac 29 sep 1918
xCrouse,Mary 3 Jun 1925   xCrowder,Edith May 17 Jan 1933
xCrowler,Ed 17 mar 1915   /Crowell,J,Henry 1884-1901 s/o JH&EH
/Crozer,margaret 1846-1930   /Crum,Mollie Greer 1864-1914
xCrumb,Francis J.21 Jan 1931 xCrumb,James 13 sep 1910
xCrumb,Theodore T.21 mar 1938xCrump,George E. 6 Jun 1927
/Crump,George H.1860-1929   /Crump,Catherine 1869-1912 w/o CH
  Ida 14 sep 1970-9 Jun 1892 xCrump,G.H. 1869-1912
xCrump,Isaac 1822-1903   xCrump,Nancy 1831-1904
xCullen,A.H. 2 sep 1930   /Cullen,Ernest B. 24 aug 1911

xCullen,Elizabeth
xCullen,Kate 29 Jan 1937
/Cullett,Harry 1900-1921
/Cullett,Oscar 1886-1921
/Culton,Grace A.1914-24JH&GS
/Cummings,Joseph H.WWI
  13 feb 1895-20 aug 1915
xCumpson,Scena Mathis 1944
xCumpston,Charles M.1901
xCumpston,Inf/CC 10 Jul 1916
xCumpston,James A. 1896
xCumpston,James D. 9/15/1939
xCumpston,Mary 13 oct 1916
xCumpston,William R. 1901
xCunningham,C.D. 19 dec 1928
xCunningham,Claude 6 dec 1936
xCunningham,Effie 14 may 1930
xCunningham,Lizzie--
xCunningham,Myrtle--
xCurnell,Paul 223 may 1923
xCurnell,Polly 31 may 1931
xCurrie,Mrs.H.D.21 may 1907
xCurry,Ada--
xCurry,Inf/Robt 21 feb 1918
xCurry,Martha Ellen 10/12/31
xCurry,Ralph 25 Jan 1932
xCurry,Walter 14 Jun 1916
xCurry,Wm.H.1 mar 1925
xCurtis,Inf/Ed 8 Jun 1916
/Curtis,Hayden Gail 10/7/1938
xCurtis,Ira S. 18 oct 1918
xCurtis,Mathew 4 dec 1934
xCurtis,Merrilita 6 Jul 1931
/Cutler,Harry 1878-1932
xCutler,James H. 25 aug 1931
xCyrus,Pearl 8 nov 1914
/Cyrus,Ora E. 1874-1935
/Cyrus,W.E. 1862-1919
xDabney,Kate 20 Jan 1918
/Daft,Emma 30 Jan 1935
/Daft,Charlotte J.3 oct 1908
/Daft,George W.--
/Daft,Henry C.25 nov 1925
/Dailey,Taylor G.1850-1927
xDailey,Anne--
/Dale,Isadora Myers 1856-32
/Damron,Belle 1869-1937
xDamron,Elizabeth 18 apr 1922
xDamron,inf/WM 1 apr 1919
xDamron,J.R. 9 apr 1934
/Damron,Maggie B. 1904-1922
xDamron,Rev.S.J. 17 aug 1918
xDaniel,Ella 6 Jul 1932
xDaniel,Thomas 29 oct 1923

xCullen,George Sr. 14 aug 1911
xCullen,George Jr.11 oct 1913
xCullen,Margaret 15 may 1923
xCumines,Jane 23 mar 1925
/Cummings,William Grant 4 oct 1938 47y9m5d
xCummings,Inf/Bessie B.10 nov 1915
xCummings,Elizabeth 6 dec 1920
xCummings,Jane 1925
xCummings,Lon 30 may 1930
/Cumpston,Sarah Bertha 5 may 1935 58y27d
/Cumpston,Stella May 23 Jun 1938 34y9m1d
xCumpston,Lucinda 25 mar 1929
xCumpston,Mary M. 1901
xCumpston,Winnie 1887
/Cunningham,Dorage Lee 1925-26
xCunningham,Bessie May 22 oct 1922
xCunningham,Frank J. 1850-1899
xCunningham,James R. 27 sep 1932
xCunningham,Louisa 26 dec 1918
xCurnell,Dolly Pinnell 28 oct 1918
xCurran,W.J. 22 sep 1923
xCurry,Emma 19 mar 1923
/Curry,Jane Ann 24 dec 1853-4 sep 1904
/Curry,Robert Jr.31 may 1875-5 sep 1905
/Curry,Robert Sr.1847-2 oct 1906
xCurry,Robert 15 Jul 1909
/Curry,Virginia 11 feb 1911-24 oct 1918
xCurtis,Clayborn G.21 Jul 1937
/Curtis,Robert Q.9/6/1929 5y
xCurtis,inf/Lester 1 mar 1938
xCurtis,Margarite 6 dec 1925
/Curtis,Vera T. 1891-1892 d/o WG&HB
xCustom,Robert 1 dec 1919
/Cutler,Ruth V.5 sep 1935 81y
xCutler,William 20 Jun 1921
/Cutright,inf 1906 s/oHL&RG Tolle
/Cyrus,Carl Emerson 1910-12
xDabney,Martha J.12 dec 1910
xDabney,Richard 11 apr 1921
/Dabney,Francis Wiatt 1847-1927
/Daft,Jane 9 nov 1926
/Daft,Mattie J.9 apr 1911
/Dagastino,Domenico 1894-1934
xDailey,inf/DW 5 mar 1909
xDailey,William S.--
xDales 3 may 1914
xDamron,Elizabeth 12 nov 1932
xDamron,inf/Moses 15 Jul 1917
/Damron,Lucy Davis Biggs 10 oct 1929
xDamron,Mabel 22 feb 1919
xDamron,Moses 7 apr 1924
/Danaher,Frances A. 1866-1927
/Danaher,William J.1865-1931
/Daniels,Andrew V.1862-1936

/Daniels,Goldie V. 1894-1918 /Daniels,Anthony C. 8 Jun 1824-8 dec 1897
     James O. 1890-1918   s/o Peter & Catherine
/Daniels,James O.Jr1914-1936   Ann Preston 1824-8 sep 1886
/Daniels,Virginia Louise1913 /Daniels,Emmett 2 nov 1934 WWI
/Danniels,Fred E.12/29/1934wIxDaniels,Fred 29 Jan 1924
xDaniels,Gladys E.17 apr 1921xDaniels,H/Inf 21 Jan 1927
xDaniels,Ida B.2 feb 1924   xDaniels,J.E. 20 Jul 1924
xDaniels,Minnie 8 Jun 1924   xDaniels,Theodore 31 dec 1931
/Darling,Sarah Clark 1863-1920
/Darette,Adelia 1859-1937   /Darnell,Martin Harold 1916-1917
/Darett,Pearly 1897-1936   /Darnell,Morton Carroll 18 sep 1916-6Jan1923
/Bausch,Babe 29 nov 1937   /Daugherty,Nancy 1806-1881 w/o Daniel
xDaughan,James 18 aug 1915   xDaugherty,Doctor Black 9 sep 1939
/Dauthit,Harry D. 1873-1910   xDavenport,Dorothy 22 aug 1910
/Davidson,George 1817-1906   xDavidson,Inf/LC 13 nov 1915
xDavidson,Mary Frances 12/12/30/Davidson,Rex C. 7 feb 1935   54y6m6d
/Davies,Ann L. 1849-1929   /Davies,Ben L. 1870-1934
/Davies,Cora Ansell 1879-1910/Davies,Evan J. 1844-1917
/Davies,John 1834-1907   /Davies,Tom E. 1874-1937
/Davies,Will A. 1872-1936   /Daves,Annie Laurie 1869-1914
/Davis,B.V. 1880-1933   /Davies,BeneJah Thomas 1842-1936
/Davis,Cary Nelson 1874-1930 xDavis,B.T.Jr. 1884-1938
/Davis,Charles H.6 nov 1915   /Davis,Blanche A.1894-1895 d/o EA&EAB
xDavis,Carl S. 1 feb 1919 infxDavis,Burwell Booth 17 dec 1933
xDavis,Charles 19 sep 1921   xDavis,Charles 7 dec 1916
xDavis,Charlie 3 dec 1921   /Davis,Claude Austin 13 Jun 1905-1 Jan 28
xDavis,Clinton 19 nov 1923   /Davis,Claude 9 nov 1872-12 oct 1935
xDavis,Crandall D.28 Jul 1928/Davis,Clesta Comer 1861-1918 w/o BT
xDavis,Cynthia A. 1848-1907 xDavis,Earl 1908
xDavis,Edward 17 Jun 1921   xDavis,Elizabeth 1 mar 1934
xDavis,Elmer 1904-05   xDavis,Elizabeth 3 mar 1912
/Davis,Elimra 1877-1893   /Davis,Eustace G.1883-1912
/Davis,E. 1831-1921   xDavis,Emma 10 nov 1916
     Mary Susan 1844-1914   /Davis,Rev.E.A.29 Jan 1866-22 Jan 1903
xDavis,Eva 14 apr 1931   xDavis,Francis P. 17 oct 1928
xDavis,George T. 10 sep 1935 xDavis,George W. 29 mar 1918
xDavis,Inf/GWJ 29 mar 1918   xDavis,Harry 17 Jul 1919 inf
xDavis,Harry M. 30 dec 1938   xDavis,Harvey A. 15 Jan 1937
xDavis,Hazel 1886-1892   xDavis,Hazel L.20 nov 1935
xDavis,Henderson 30 mar 1933 xDavis,Henry W. 1887-1918
xDavis,Hilda 13 mar 1916   xDavis,H.W. 7 aug 1921
xDavis,Inf/o Patricia 1928   xDavis,Imogene Fonatain 9 feb 1935
/Davis,Julia H.1870-1931   /Davis,Kathleen Fontaine 1910-1917
xDavis,Inf/John 29 oct 1911   xDavis,Capt.J.W. 22 feb 1916
xDavis,James G. 29 Jun 1937   xDavis,John S. 2 Jun 1933
xDaivs,Joseph S. 9 Jul 1930   xDavis,Lois 24 oct 1920
/Davis,John 1859-1932   xDavis,Lovina Jane 12 nov 1935
/Davis,Mary 1837-1901   /Davis,Lawrence J.1875-1921
xDavis,Mary 29 sep 1938   xDavis,Luncinda 9 apr 1923
xDavis,Mary 1907   xDavis,Mary S. 21 may 1934
xDavis,Mary S. 1831-1921   xDavis,Maude 29 apr 1911
xDavis,Myette 11 mar 1919   xDavis,Myrtle D. 23 apr 1934
xDavis,Nannie 6 mar 1906   /Davis,Paulina F.1844-1926
/Davis,Nannie 1869-1925   xDavis,Paul Allen 18 Jan 1916 inf

xDavis,Nellie 17 feb 1937   xDavis,R.C. 8 oct 1915
xDavis,Russell 1906 inf   /Davis,Robert Cary 1911 inf
/Davis,Samuel T.1847-1934 /Davis,Capt.Robt.C.Co A 52 VA Inf CSA10/14/20
   Sally B. 1880-1932   xDavis,S.F. 9 mar 1925
xDavis,Sam 24 nov 1930   xDavis,Sim 25 nov 1911
xDavis,Sarah Ann 23 Jul 1934 xDavis,Supealice 24 Jan 1920
xDavis,Susan 14 Jul 1914   /Davis,Thomas Boyd 1878-1935
xDavis,Thomas 20 mar 1924   xDavis,V.B. 23 sep 1934
xDavis,Wade H. 6 Jul 1938   xDavis,Victor 29 mar 1926
/Davis,Walter 1866-1909   /Davis,Vaught 20 dec 1876-1 feb 1907
/Davis,William B.1861-1937   /Davis,William M. 1839-1916
xDawkins,Grace E. 13 feb 1933/Dawson,Susie 8 nov 1860-20 Jan 1923
xDawkins,Wm.F.18 feb 1932   x T.H. b6 sep 1862
xDawson,Elizabeth 19 Jul 1915xDawson,George 22 mar 1939
xDawson,Hobart 16 nov 1930   xDawson,Jennie 19 sep 1909
xDawson,L.T. 12 mar 1913   xDawson,Melba 12 sep 1923 inf
xDay,Carol 10 aug 1935 inf   xDay,Elizabeth Ann 3 Jul 1959
/Day,Flossie 1y6m6d   /Day,Fannie 24 may 1923 36y1m29d
/Day,Mary J.1855-1936   xDay,Martha 28 Jun 1923
/Day,Robert L. 1853-1928   xDay,Nannie 27 may 1923
xDean,Ada leon 14 nov 1910   xDean,inf/L.J. 9 dec 1914
/Dean,George William 1924   /Dean,Carrie 12 Jul 1935 51y22d
/Dean,John W. 1858-1903   /Dean,Gerleaner oct-nov 1937
xDean,Jackson,19 Jun 1919   xDean,Lillie Phillips 20 Jul 1927
/Dean,Vaughn Deloss 1914   xDean,Lilliam M. 13 may 1929
xDean,William A.17 mar 1914   /Dean,Virgil L.10 oct 1923 36y
xDean,Wayland O.14 oct 1921   xDean,Wayland 1 sep 1926
xDean,Wayland O.13 apr 1927   xDeBolt,Philip Y,1872-1938
/DeBord,Catherine 1872-1938   /DeBolt,Gerturde A. 1878-1937
/DeBord,F.Leo 1896-1938
/DeBord,Marion J.1856-1918   /Decker,James I.12 mar 1885s/oJA&MA8y2m25d
/Decker,James A.1837-1902   /Decker,Martha A. 1847-1899
/DeFoor,Eugene 1866-1924   /Dekle,Martha Nunn 18 Jan 1934 83y
xDegermitte,Walter 2 dec 1919xDeLancy,Isabelle 22 Jul 1921
xDelono,Herbert 25 mar 1926   xDeLancy,Athalia 12 apr 1914
/Dempsey,George W.1851-1909   /Delancy,Joshua 7 Jan 1848-27 Jun 1899
/Dempsey,Mary J. 1849-1929   /Delancy,Isabella F.20 Jul 1821-8 aug 1843
xDempsey,Joe 2 may 1936   /Dempsey,Haidee Gerturde 1882-1939
xDempsey,Mary 27 Jan 1929   xDempsey,Edna Clay 12 may 1916 inf
xDempsey,Walter Lee 1875-1908xDenice,inf 23 mar 1916
xDennison,Audrey O.2 feb 1923/Dennson,Pauline May 3 Jun 1921-11 Jan 1923
xDennisonn,James 18 nov 1918 xDennison,Julia 13 Jan 1924
xDennison,Nancy C.6 feb 1916 xDent,margarett 19 oct 1934
/DeNoon,John Hoyt   /DeNore,Warren H. 11 nov 1932 74y9m19d
   19 aug 1895-27 Jan 1922   /Derbyshire,Henry J.1833-1902
/Deprie,Eleanor 1899-1923   /Derbyshire,Sabina Gibbins 1846-1931
xDeshow,William 16 may 1920   xDerbyshire,Thomas G.15 feb 1926
xDeskins,Bobby 27 Jul 1932   xDeuvenger,Eugene 28 dec 1918 inf
xDevore,Mrs.Eugene 12/20/24   xDeval,Wallace Dean 21 feb 1911 inf
xDevore,Otis Clyde 9/9/15inf   xDewees,Nettie 23 may 1926
/DeVillard,Mary V.1873-1915   /Dial,James Harold Jr.28 feb 1938 inf
xDick,Letha 10 Jan 1938   xDial,Marge Mildred 18 sep 1926
xDickey,Rachael Ann 9/7/27   xDickerson,T.M. 30 dec 1918
/Dickey,George W.1834-1916   /Dickerson,John Co G 151 NY Inf

```
       Rachel A. 1841-1927        /Dickerson,S.C.Cleveland 1885-1932
/Dickey,H.L. 1844-1904            /Dickey,Helen 1845-1899 w/o Hamilton L.
/Dickey,John L.1847-1927          /Dickey,Iva 28 apr 1850-2 feb 1923
/Dickey,Mary E.1853-1935          /Dickey,Mary O.16 Jul 1864-22 feb 1932
/Dickey,Helen 1845-1899           /Dickey,Wealthy M.1877-1892
/Diefenbach,Edward 1860-1914      /Dickinson,Charles H,Jr. 1904-1918
xDickinson,James 27 sep 1928      xDickinson,J.Hansford 14 sep 1918
xDickinson,Mary G.1 Jun 1929      xDickinson,Millie 21 mar 1910
xDickson,Byron P.20 mar 1920      xDickson,F.M. 23 Jul 1918
xDickson,John D. 10 oct 1915      xDickson,Mary 30 apr 1926
/Diehl,Albert L.1890-1891         /Diehl,Louis 22 feb 1819-14 nov 1893
/Diehl,Amey 1889 inf             /Diehl,Louisa 1 aug 1855-25 nov 1856
/Diehl,inf 1889                   /Diehl,Robert 1860-1934
/Diehl,Matilda M. 1890-1891       /Diehl,Rosa 27 dec 1821-18 nov 1906
/Diehl,Robert 1857-1858           xDillard,James 6 aug 1934
xDill,Mary Etta 30 dec 1925       /Dillard,Luther E.23 feb 1888-18 feb 1934
/Dillon,Annie A. 1859-1920        /Dillard,Eva 28 apr 1876-24 dec 1933
/Dillon,Etha O.1901               /Dillon,Della Marie 8 Jan 1933 34y1m14d
/Dillon,John M. 1865-1937         /Dillon,Frank Leslie 1891-1913
/Dillon,John R. 1861-1938         xDillon,Flossie 2 oct 1937
/Dillon,L.Clarebee 1887-1913      xDillon,Jessie E. 21 aug 1917
xDillon,Maggie 28 feb 1912        xDillon,Margaret 13 apr 1911
/Dillon,Mamie 1900-1901           /Dillon,Margaret Ella 1898-1910 d/o JE&CA
/Dillon,Mary 1889-1921            xDillon,Roy 31 oct 1918
/Dillon,Z.T. 1849-1900            xDimpkins,Ada 5 may 1926
/Dingess,John 1865-1911           xDinken,inf/WE 15 nov 1924
/Dixon,Cassius L. 1860-1920       xDinken,Jessie S.2 sep 1930
/Dixon,Clayton C. 1892-1914       xDixon,Emma 24 apr 1930
xDixon,Johnnie 10 Jun 1914        xDixon,Stephen G.5 Jun 1932
xDober,Martin 28 Jun 1934         xDobbins,Julia 14 Jan 1930
/Dober,Paul M.Jr.1892-1935        /Dobbins,Wesley Charles 1903-1922
/Dodd,Ira M. 1889-1931            /Dobey,Theodore 1 sep 1935 28y1m3d
xDodd,Arie 18 sep 1928            xDodd,Ellen E.7 Jan 1930
/Dodd,Lola M. 1885-1938           xDodd,Isaac 25 mar 1922
/Doddridge,Schulyer 1879-1915xDodson,Earnest 19 nov 1935
/Dodson,Peter C. 1873-1924        /Dodson,Margaret Ruth 1902-1928
/Dodson,Raymond E. 1913           /Dodson,Rebecca Va. 5 Jan 1937 55y5m21
/Dodson,Robert L 1911-1919        xDonahue,Alexander 4 oct 1929
xDonigan,J.J. 4 feb 1928          /Donnella,Coriolanus 1850-6/30/1873 23y7m3d
/Doolittle,Chloe A.1831-1901      /Donnilla,Lenn 1863-1 Jul 1874 s/oS&M
/Doolittle,Eliz.1863-1936         /Doolittle,Alice Murphy 1860-3 nov 1890
/Doolittle,Frank 1856-1921             Edward Sturdevant 1854-1914
/Doolittle,L.1829-1909            /Doolittle,Florence Bryan 1888-1890d/ES&A
/Doolittle,Lambert                xDoolittle,Anna Learney 31 dec 1931
   McChesney 1896-1930             /Dorn,Clara 1864-1936
/Dosey,Ruth Arnold 1894-1918      /Dorn,Jacob 1853-1930
/Dotson,Carlos L.1911-1927        /Dotson,Fleming C. 1846-1920
/Dotson,Mary E. 1848-1916         xDotson,Gladys 1 may 1927
/Dotson,Mary Marsh 9 Jul 1925xDotson,Hatton 18 nov 1918
xDotson,Rebecca V. 7 Jan 1937xDould,Ruth 14 Jan 1914
/Douglass,Edward J.1838-1922      /Douthit,Edith 1873-8 nov 1887 d/o WH&JA
   Emeline Stevens 1844-1905      /Douthit,Elizabeth 13 Jun 1855-3 nov 1916
xDouthit,Charlotte 9 mar 1917xDouthit,H.D. 5 sep 1910
xDouthit,E.T. 22 mar 1934         xDouthit,Richard H. 15 apr 1910
```

/Douthit,Gracie 1867-1888
/Douthit,Frank W.5 aug 1872 2y8m11d WH&JA
/Douthit,inf d/o EF&E
/Douthit,Jennie 7 nov 1850-28 may 1907w WH
/Douthit,John L.1842-1903
/Douthit,Mary C.1868-11 jun 1886wRH 18y4m6d
/Douthit,William H.9 jun 1917
/Douthit,Lawrence 13 aug 1885 s/o JL&LM
xDover,Grant 31 jan 1917
xDowis,Mrs.W.F. 24 mar 1921
/Dowler,Fred J. 1856-1933
xDowis,W.F. 10 jan 1924
/Dowler,Anna 1858-1931
xDowner,Carrie C.1827-1896
xDowney,Delie 3 dec 1923
/Downer,Willie S. 11 apr 1865-15 jan 1879
/Downey,Bridget 1862-1923
/Downer,,W.S.1 dec 1821-8 may 1877
xDowney,Alice 5 mar 1915
xDowdy,John B. 16 mar 1932
xDowney,inf/John T.7 apr 1916
xDowdy,inf/JB 13 aug 1910
xDowns,W.M.21 nov 1926
/Doyle,Lucy M. 1850-1921
/Doyle,James T. 1846-1916
/Doyle,James E. 3 dec 1938 55y2m21d
xDrake,William 1 nov 1926
/Drayne,John 1906-1927
/Dreehouse,Fred L.1879-1936
/Drayne,Sarah F.12 aug 1881-24 jun 1918
xDresbillis,S.O. 10 oct 1918
/Driggs,Benjamin P.9 mar 1829-5 jan 1917
/Drown,Ella M, 1860-1937
/Driggs,Sarah E.12 may 1819-26 feb 1894
/Drown,Garland s/o NF&E
xDrown,Edna S.7 jun 1920
    4 dec 1880-5 jul 1882
xDrown,Dickey E.& Hershel 1937 Tw inf
xDrown,Lindsey 11/16/1915 inf
/Drown,Maude Grace 1878-1882 NF&E
/Drown,Henrietta 1884 inf
/Drown,Rufas P.14 may 1826-7 apr 1910
/Drown,Newton F.
    Sarah E.Chadwick 18 apr 1838-25 may 1906
    8 may 1855-24 feb 1890
/Drumm,Lillian Johnson 1888-1920
xDrummonds,N.M. 12 jun 1919
xDrummon,Myrtle A. 10 feb 1928
/Drummond,D.Neal 1901-1910
/Dudding,F.F. 1903-1933
/Drummond,Wallace 1909-1911
xDuckworth,--6 feb 1929
xDuckworth,Clarence M. 5/14/34
xDuckworth,Alice V. 22 may 1932
xDuckworth,Jesse 24 mar 1937
xDuckworth,Josephine 2 jan 1926
/Dudding,Winnie B. 1900-1921
xDudding,inf/AO 9 jun 1913
xDudley,Margaret 24 nov 1929
xDuFour,Cora Jane 15 oct 1930 w/o LG
xDugan,A.J. 25 feb 1911
xDucker,Lucian 1 jan 1939
/Dugan,James S. 1850-1928
/Duncan,Jennie J.6 jan 1869 w/o HC ??
/Dugan,Lizzie W. 1853-1923
xDuncan,Alice 26 dec 1932 ??
/Duncan,Alice 1859-1937 ??
xDuncan,Elizabeth 17 nov 1915
/Duncan,John 28 jul 1937 WWI
xDuncan,J.W. 24 mar 1923
xDuncan,Mattie B.21 dec 1920
xDuncan,Jennie 8 jan 1933 ??
xDuncan,Robert 1906
xDuncan,Opal May 5 jan 1922 inf
/Dundas,Lucy 1840-1921
xDunfee,Caroline M. 1828-1906
xDunkle,Arden 1886
xDunfee,John 1822-1905
xDunkle,Eglantine 15 mar 1899
xDunn,E.S. 7 sep 1926
/Dunkle,J.D. Co G 1st WV Cav
/Dunn,Elizabeth 1860-1925
xDunkle,James David 3/3/20inf
/Dunn,William Ward 1851-1937
/Dunshie,Joseph S.1896 WR&S
/Dunshie,W.R.9 mar 1864-5 jan 1896
xDurea,Cora Provo--
/Dunshie,William 1892-1894 s/o WR&S
xDurea,Cyrena 14 oct 1908
/Durea,Charles J.14 jun 1883 46y10m25d
xDurea,Elzworth 20 mar 1922
/Durea,Barney W.8 sep 1883 8y2m8d s/CJ&CE
xDurea,Isaac--
/Durea,James W. 15 apr 1884 22y6m8d CJ&CE
xDurick,Mary Lou 7 jul 1927
/Durfee,John S.8 may 1822-9 jun 1905
/Durkin,Anna L.1850-1912
/Durfee,Caroline M.5 sep 1828-11 mar 1906
    James 1850-1930
xDurkin,J.W. 2 dec 1921
xDurkin,Peter L.20 feb 1937
xDurkin,Michel 2 dec 1921
xDurkin,Mrs.Peter 25 jun 1911
/Dusenberry,Burmak C.1893-1922
/Dusenberry,inf 1896
/Dusenberry,Annie F.1858-1915
xDusenberry,inf/Cole1892&1896
    Caleb C.1853-1929

xDusenberry,Cole B.C.1853-1929/Dusenberry,William C.1860-27 Jan 1935
/Dusenberry,Mary A.1849-1894 /Dusenberry,William.F.1826-1903
/Dusenberry,Little Cale   Cynthia 1. 1824-1886
   5 mar 1892-7 apr 1893   /Dusenbury,Chas O.23 aug 1828-15 aug 1891
xDushman,Benjamin 1861-1939 xDuty,Blanch 8 may 1923
/Dwyer,Malachy 1883-1918   xDuty,Inf/H.M. 1 dec 1919
/Dwyer,Mary Colbert 1839-1911/Dwyer,Mathew F. 1876-1928
xDwyer,Pauline 6 dec 1935   /Dwyer,Tim P.1878-1934
/Dwyer,Timothy Sr.1832-1888 /Dyke,Anna V.22 feb 1938 44y6m19d
xDyers,Rachel 30 nov 1923   xEagan,George 1909
/Eades,Rebecca A.1846-1931   /Eagan,John H.18 dec 1908-1 jan 1927
xEaglerton,--17 may 1923   xEagen,R.L. 20 mar 1912
xEagleston,N.B. 8 may 1924   xEams,James 8 feb 1939
xEagleston,Sarah 24 mar 1933 /Eans,Richard Lee 14 aug 1937 5y2m7d
xEarl,Bernard L.1927 inf   xEarl,Charles henry 13 aug 1939
/Earl,Celia 1830-1911   xEarl,David Lee 6 aug 1933
/Earl,David 1833-1916   xEarl,Dorothy Taylor 2 nov 1927
/Earl,inf 1938   xEarl,Fannie--
/Earl,Eva Porter 1876-1911   xEarl,inf/EF 11 sep 1911
/Earl,Lillian 1900 inf   xEarl,inf/James E. 29 Jan 1914
/Earl,Sarah Ellen 20 oct 1919xEarl,inf/Robt.8 feb 1916
/Earles,Alice M.1867-1915   /Earles,Charles A, 1898 inf
/Earles,Violet 1906-1917   xEarles,Darward Belmont 23 aug 1908
xEarls,Garnett L.3 Jul 1912 xEarls,James 29 jan 1914
xEarls,Larua--   xEarls,Lucian E.29 mar 1926
xEarley,Maria 17 feb 1916   /Earley,H.W.D. 7th WV Cav-Civil War-GAR
/East,Ida M.1881-1918   /Early,Ashley E.Jr.1916-1921
xEast,Myrtle 14 may 1930   xEarly,Maria 17 feb 1916
xEast,Wyatt C.15 may 1930   xEarly,M.A. 8 mar 1923
xEary,Fredrick 24 apr 1924   xEastham,Bobby 29 nov 1925
xEastman, 2 infs 1927   xEastham,Lola L. 10 apr 1920
xEaves,Jessie 9 Jan 1933   xEaston,Dan 7 jan 1913
xEaston,Minnie 23 mar 1910   xEaston,William 27 sep 1913
/Eba,Alice F. 1867-1892   /Easton,Mary Jane 16 feb 1933   66y
xEchols,Gordie M.29 Jan 1935 xEchols,inf/Chas.Wallace 6 dec 1915
xEchols,inf/Earl 21 Jul 1911 xEckhart,G.W. 18 apr 1921
xEddy,Ross M. 23 nov 1918inf /Eckhart,George 17 aug 1839-18 aug 1909
/Edelen,Adalai S.1890-1932   Co K 91th OVI Civil War
/Edelen,Emma 1857-1919   xEden,Doris Ruth 21 sep 1930
xEdelen,Robert 4 dec 1936   xEden,James C.8 apr 1925
xEdens,Amanda Jane 5/16/36   xEden, Julia 1930
/Edens,Addie 1883-1922wSilas /Edens,Alma M.25 nov 1895-7 sep 1906 S&L
xEdens,J.D.-   xEdens,Gladys maxine 30 Jul 1915
xEdens,Silas 6 aug 1931   xEdens,inf/S.8 oct 1911
/Edgell,Albert N. 1865-1918 /Edison,Isaac 1868-27 dec 1938   70y4m
xEdmondson,John 13 dec 1915 xEdwards,Annie 2 may 1938
/Edmunds,Joseph 1865-1908   /Edwards,Caroline E.1847-1932
xEdwards,Eva 2 oct 1918   xEdwards,Fannie 17 jun 1918
/Edwards,Richard A.1841-1902 /Edwards,Myrtle Rodgers 1881-1912
/Edwards,George B.1849-1917 xEdwards,inf/Clifford 22 feb 1929
/Effingham,A.E.1900-1918 WWI /Effingham,Bessie 1888-1895 d/o JH&RM
xEffingham,Creed A.2/22/1929 xEffingham,Eliza E.16 nov 1911
xEffingham,Garnet 25 Jul 1927xEffingham,Harry J.18 may 1918 inf
xEffingham,J.E. 10 feb 1924 xEffingham,Henry 26 Jul 1911 inf

xEffingham,Jasper 30 nov 1924xEffingham,John Henry 3 mar 1936
xEffingham,Mrs.R.M.11/21/1921/Eggleston,N.B.1880-1924
/Eifort,John E.W. 1849-1917 /Egri,Lena Klein 25 dec 1875-21 mar 1921
xEisenman,Philomena-- /Eiland,Irene V.1918-1921 d/o RR&G
xEiseman,Anton-- xEkins,Elsie 17 mar 1917 inf
/Eiseman,Birdie B.1898 inf /Elam,Mary Booker 1885-1936
/Eiseman,Israel L,1859-1902 xElam,2 infs 1917
xElder,Edna P.--
/Elder,Dr.B.D. 1831-1917 /Elder,James Basil 19 may 1938
/Elder,Dr.J.T. 1868-1920 /Elder,John Basil 1914 inf
/Elder,Marianna 1909-1910 /Elder,Mary V.J. 1909 inf
/Elegar,Adam 1880-1931 /Elderman,Annie 1848-1922 w/o I.
/Elegar,Charles W.1879-1927 /Elegar,Jacob 1851-1923
/Elegar,Mary 1850-1913 xElegar,Stanley 16 may 1915
xElhannon,--1865-1904 xElkins,Ernist 1894
/Elkins,Callie R. 1864-1939 /Elkins,Charles M. 1894-1895 s/o JD&Callie
/Elkins,J.D. 1849-1923 /Elkins,Ettie 5 Jun 1889-15 aug 1902
/Elkins,inf 15 may 1939 /Elkins,Patricia Joan 1938 inf
/Elkins,R.E. 1890-1928 xElkins,Herbert 26 Jul 1918
xElkins,Minnie 29 feb 1912infxEllette,J.C. 16 Jun 1937
/Ellington,Elizabeth 1887-23 xEllette,Maria C.19 feb 1915
/Ellington,Frank S.1912-13 xEllette,S.J.--
xElliott,Abigal 15 sep 1923 /Elliott,Sam G.1863-29 may 1937 64y1m13d
xElliott,Annie 1862-1906 /Elliott,Wanda 30 Jan 1918-18 dec 1923
xElliott,Harry 18 apr 1924 xElliott,Mabel Baker 22 mar 1927
xElliott,Wm.John 9 Jul 1913
xEllis,Anna E.1835-1904 xEllis,Dorothy Mae 18 oct 1937
xEllis,Charles 11/12/1914infxEllis,Erma virginia 5 Jul 1932 inf
/Ellis,J.L. 1876-1933 /Ellis,Bertie May 1901-1920 d/o JD&Vernie
xEllis,inf/Chas.2/18/1918 xEllis,inf/NA 27 nov 1911
/Ellis,Laura B.1875-1937 /Ellis,Eliza J, 1845-1888 w/o G.W.
    Merton 21 aug 1938 xEllis,Laura Alice 1870-1939
xEllis,Lillian 22 dec 1921 xEllis,Lucy 9 aug 1910
xEllis,Mary 4 dec 1911 xEllis,Napeleon B.22 may 1930
xEllis,Ola May 23 apr 1932 xEllis,Rhoda 22 may 1920 inf
xEllis,Sarah 7 may 1913 xEllis,Virginia 6 Jul 1932
xEllis,Virginia 9 nov 1927 /Ellison,Leta Maude 1898-1918
/Elliston,Theodore 1880-1920xEllison,Ray 20 Jun 1935
xElri,Nettie 1889-1909 xElmore,Cahterine 1896
xElwicher,F.W. 1916 inf xElmore,Rosa M.1896
xElwood,Marion 27 Jun 1925 xEmanuel,Beula 29 oct 1914
/Emerick,Maria J. 1850-1933 /Emerick,Walter 1885-1933
/Emerick,William O.1870-1930xEmmons,Arthur S.1852-1927
/Emerson,L.Edmund 1882-1922 /Emmons,Minnie 27 dec 1890 inf
/Emmons,Delos W.1828-1905 /Emmons,Collis 23 aug 1835-12 Jun 1886
    Mary J.1831-1916 /Emmons,Collis Huntington 1852-1927
/Emmons,Julius Alden   Sibyl Sherwood 1874-1903
    1863-1915 /Emmons,Charleton Delos 1858-1937
/Emmons,May Petrie 1860-1926   Minnie Gibson-19 apr 1939
    w/o A.S. Emmons /Emmons,Lillian Hooe 1892-1934 d/oJA&GH
/Engart,Emma 1886-1913 /Engbersen,Mary Eugenia 1897-1937
xEngell,Irene M.17 apr 1926 xEngbersen,Mary Ann 27 Jul 1925
xEnglish,James 2 Jun 1934 xEnsign,Mae L. 13 Jun 1940
/Ensign,Jenry M. 1861-1937 /Ensign,Ely 19 dec 1840-27 Jan 1902

/Ensign,John Fredrick 1912   Mary G.Walton 18 Jul 1848-7 feb 1915
/Ensley,Asa Newton   /Ensign,John Walton 1871-1932
    14 sep 1905-17 Jun 1907   Lena Lobban 22 Jan 1875-23 oct 1908
xEnsley,Lon 11 may 1919   xEnsign,sidney 26 aug 1940
/Ensley,Mary Prentice   /Ensley,Mary C. 16 dec 1864-23 dec 1928
    7 feb 1873-24 apr 1889   Charles E. 29 mar 1939
/Enslow,A.Blanche 1861-1917 /Enslow,Corydon R. 1853-1923
/Enslow,A.Mace 1863-1914   /Enslow,Edward Bliss 1859-1912
/Enslow,Florence 1860-1934 /Enslow,Garland 1892s/oFrank B.and Julia L.
/Enslow,Frank Bliss 1853-1917/Enslow,Howard 1884 s/o Frank B & Julia L.
/Enslow,Julia Lyell 1840-1899/Enslow,Juliette Buffington 1873-1936
/Enslow,George R. 1902 inf /Enslow,Mattie McClure 1872-1902
/Enslow,Nora L. 1871-1924   /Enslow,Nancy Maria Bliss 1828-1913
/Enslow,Revilo 1830-1918   /Enslow,Sophia 1829-1904
xEnyart,Emma 29 Jun 1913   xEplin,roy 12 Jan 1922 inf
xEpperly,Charles 25 Jun 1921/Epps,Abe 1854-1930
/Epperly,Mildred 19 Jun 1921/Epps,Levi 30 dec 1895-25 mar 1927
/Epps,Toney 1862-1932   xEpps,Gus 3 oct 1915
xEpps,Rachael 2 apr 1922   xErskine,Cline 8 dec 1919
xErskine,Eliza 26 Jul 1923   xErskine,Lessie J.19 nov 1909
xErskine,Paul R.9 nov 1918   /Erskine,William T. 21 Jan 1858-7 oct 1891
xErvin,Lillie Bell 12/8/1931xErwin,Harry A. 26 oct 1921
xErwin,Henry O.24 Jul 1913   xErwin,inf/CO 9 Jan 1925
xErwin,inf/WH 24 feb 1911   /Erwin,Pauline L. 1922--
xEsque,C.Everett 10 apr 1916xEsque,Deloria 10 nov 1912
xEsque,Dyke 10 may 1931   xEsque,Elmer 8 nov 1918 inf
xEsque,Elvira 1928   xEsque,Eula Maxine 17 Jul 1904
xEsque,French 1 Jul 1935   xEsque,Ira J.19 Jan 1922
xEsque,John 18 Jun 1916   xEsque,Media Ater 1898-4 aug 1919
xEsque,Mrs.John 13 apr 1915 xEsque,Orma 15 aug 1920
xEstep,Albert 19 apr 1920   /Esque,Robert L. 10 sep 1891-27 mar 1915
xEstep,Carter E.12 Jun 1913 xEstep.Charles W. 23 sep 1922
xEstep,Elizabeth 18 feb 1907xEstep,G.P. 27 nov 1924
xEstep,inf/GW 5 may 1911   xEstep,Geo. 27 nov 1924 ??
xEstep,Joseph 30 Jan 1927?? xEstep,James 18 Jul 1922
/Estep,J.S. 1875-1927   xEstep,Mrs.M.M. 7 nov 1916
xEstep,Waddle 3 dec 1917   /Estep,Sarah Knight 1875-1932
xEster,Lucinda 12 Jun 1923   xEvans,Amelia 14 oct 1918
xEvans,Dell 23 apr 1912   xEvans,David thomas 15 aug 1925
xEvans,inf/HL 12 Jul 1911   xEvans,inf/Marshall 24 oct 1911
/Evans,Herbert 1881-1919   /Evans,Louis 1927-1929
/Evans,Lucille M. 1901-1918 xEvans,Mollie 30 sep 1923
/Evans,Thomas L. 1850-1910   xEvans,inf.Wm.Franklin 10 sep 1915
xEvans,Wm.H. 1 nov 1940   /Evans,Virginia Dent 1858-1935
xEverett,George S.11/24/1932/Everett,Charles T. 6 may 1829-17 dec 1861
xEverette,Eliza J.4 apr 1912   Naomi Northcott 1846-1925
xEverette,Tempa A. 6 dec 1924/Eversole,George T. 1869-1898
xEwing,Eva 18 aug 1922   /Eversole,Earl B. 1893-1906
xEwing,Fred 1 aug 1929   /Eversole,George 1830-1912
xFahrlander,Emily 14 feb 1919/Eversole,Mary H. 1843-1922
/Faier,David 1883-1930   /Facklin,Annie B.Clark 1876-1933
xFair,Rachel 7 nov 1930   xFalley,Harry 22 mar 1935
/Falls,inf 3 apr 1933   xFarley,Marian 11 Jul 1921
xFarr,V.G. 30 may 1942   xFarley,George 13 may 1928

/Farr,Estella 1878-1907   xFarrar,George 10 oct 1925inf
xFarrell,Brooker Q.8/28/1929   /Farrell,John L.10 nov 1849-14 Jun 1919
xFarrell,Henry L.28 nov 1921   xFarrell,inf/Mabel 28 aug 1910
xFarrell,Maggie 1929   xFarrelly,Maria 6 Jan 1933 6y
xFarrington,Chas.R.5/20/1934   /Farris,William 27 feb 1939 72y2m
xFarrington,inf/CM 8/29/19   xFarris,Lythie 16 dec 1913
xFarrow,Louise 17 Jun 1936   xFarris,Roy 31 oct 1918
/Farrow,Preston 2/7/1927 40y   /Farrow,Clarence 11/22/1923 34y
xFaulkner,Mrs.Epres 5/2/1922   /Faulkner,Hugh McChestney 1899-1912
xFaulkner,Edward 12 Jan 1936   /Faulkner,Fielding Carlton 1896-1911
xFaulkner,inf/JC 25 Jul 1912   /Fazzare,Mary 1861-31 mar 1938 77y9m24d
xFaussett,John 28 aug 1912infxFawcett,H.J. 14 feb 1920
/Feazel,Amacette V.1834-1918   /Feazel,Alice J.20 nov 1854-7 sep 1878
xFeazel,William E.7/15/34   /Feazel,Harry Eugene 29 Jun 1873-11 apr75
/Feeley,Earl 1886-1922   /Feazel,William E.24 Jul 1825-23 mar 1882
/Feeley,Clifford 1888-1891   xFelix,inf/E.W. 5 apr 1916
/Feeley,Carrie 1890-1891   xFemorer/inf 15 oct 1925
xFerguson,Chas.F. 15 aug 1939/Ferguson,Annie Carr Ellis 1868-1903
xFerguson,Chas.18 feb 1940   Milton J.23 oct 1940
/Ferguson,Elizabeth J.1828-97/Ferguson,Ceda 14 feb 1939 40y
/Ferguson,Edward R. 1858-1900/Ferguson,Ethel Garnett 1901-1921
xFerguson,Ella M.9 Jul 1940   xFerguson,Elizabeth 12/15/1910
xFerguson,Estal 10 Jan 1919   xFerguson,Everet 11 sep 1917 inf
xFerguson,Faris 13 may 1913in/Ferguson,Etta Levenia 1921-1922
xFerguson,Floria B.9 feb 1939xFerguson,Fred 7 Jun 1923
/Ferguson,James M.1825-1894   /Ferguson,inf/Henry C. 10 mar 1917
/Ferguson,Howard 27 Jun 1925   /Ferguson,Harvey 17 apr 1878-17 nov 1910
xFerguson,Ida May 1 feb 1934   xFerguson,inf/AW 6 feb 1918
xFerguson,inf/Edward 10/31/10xFerguson,Jasper 11 mar 1910
xFerguson,John A. 9 nov 1925   xFerguson,John H. 9 mar 1925
xFerguson,Juanita 21 feb 1919/Ferguson,Josephine 1893-1918 w/oClyde
xFerguson,Mary A. 9 feb 1937   xFerguson,Mabel 10 nov 1918 inf
/Ferguson,Malinda 1851-1914   xFerguson,Marie B.12 mar 1937
/Ferguson,Mary J. 1858-1937   /Ferguson,Mary E.16 nov 1926
/Ferguson,Nannie D.1829-1911   /Ferguson,Lucy F.18 Jul 1932 82y4m4d
xFerguson,Pharoah 15 oct 1936/Ferguson,Lydia 23 dec 1861-21 sep 1890
xFerguson,Roscoe 1885-86 inf xFerguson,Nancy J.1847-1916 w/o A.P.
/Ferguson,Roxie R.1880-1917   /Ferguson,Sarah A.28 dec 1829-30 sep 1925
    Thomas Y. 1879-1917   xFerguson,Stella 18 feb 1917 inf
xFerguson,Samuel T.9/9/1918   xFerguson,Vamon 12 Jan 1917 inf
/Ferguson,William W.1855-1925xFerguson,Virgie 31 oct 1918
/Ferguson,Wayne P. 1843-1917 xFerguson,William H.2 feb 1922
/Ferguson,W.V.1850-1923   xFerguson,William W.1 feb 1925
xFertig,W.A. 8 oct 1914   /Ferris,Alice Rebecca 1863-1918
/Ferris,Mary Ann b3 aug 1933 /Ferris,Rufus W.1856-1932
/Fesenmeier,J.J.1863-1920   /Fesenmeier,Mary 31 may 1931
    Mary T.1876-1921   /Fesenmeier,Michael W. 1903-1938
xFetty,Ben L. 4 may 1933   xFetty,Earl Leon 11 feb 1928
xFetty,Martha M.3 oct 1924   /Fetty,E.H. 6 oct 1832-25 dec 1903
xFetty,Wm.Elsworth 7 mar 1930xFielder,Dora 6 Jul 1927
/Fielder,J.A. 1857-1903   /Fielder,Kathleen L.1915-1931
xFielder,May C. 28 may 1924   xFielder,Mildred 29 Jan 1922
/Fields,James E. 1893-1926   /Fife,Marie feb 1903-Oct 1907
/Fields,W.W. 1868-1929   xFife,Arnold 14 Jul 1919

xFigg,A.J. 8 Jun 1939   xFife,David A. 18 Jan 1935
xFigg,Drucila 25 Jul 1921   xFife,Elsie 11 dec 1916
xFigg,Olivia 26 oct 1917 Inf   xFife,Ruth Child 5 nov 1918
xFiggs,Dora 29 mar 1918Inf   xFiggin,Calvin 12 Jun 1917
xFiggs,V.E. 27 aug 1917   xFigley,Alice / Aline tws 7/5/22
xFillingman,Mrs.V.J.5/15/1918   xFigley,Frances L.1 Jun 1921
xFillinger,Maxwell 13 Jun 1913xFillinger,Ethel May 15 nov 1924
xFillinger,Willie 27 may 1921xFillinger,rosa Lee 27 dec 1934
xFilmore,Dorthea 19 may 1924   /Filwider,Roger M.3 may 1902-6 sep 1908
/Finch,Marjorie E.1912-1913   xFincher,Joe 8 apr 1923
xFindley,Thomas 31 oct 1919   xFinley,Helena 9 nov 1939
xFinley,Luhter E.24 feb 1920   xFinley,Infs Jamia 1934-Mable 1914
/Fink,John H. 1859-1916   /Finnell,Inf 1914 s/o JC&Eupha
xFischer,Chris 20 apr 1893   /Finnell,John C. 1861-1916
xFischer,Hannah 7 Jul 1926   /Fish,Barnet 1870-1930
xFischer,Homer 2 Jan 1913   /Fish,Fannie 1872-1935
xFisher,Carrie K.24 Jun 1929   /Fischback,Inf 1935 d/o Julius&Mildred
/Fisher,Alice 1862-1939   /Fischback,Julius 4 dec 1856-23 aug 1922
xFisher,Delbert 21 oct 1920   /Fisher,Ella 5 aug 1936 7y
xFisher,Helen H.2 dec 1915Inf/Fisher,Fred K.7 may 1938 42y5m21d
/Fisher,Levenia Dugan 1878-31xFisher,Mrs.James 4 mar 1912
/Fisher,Mattie Hite 1859-1919/Fisher,James T.9 Jan 1938 77y9m4d
xFisher,Nathaniel A.9/16/1933xFisher,Oscar Pack 16 feb 1919
/Fisher,Pembroke 1840-1919   xFisher,Sarah G. 18 dec 1916
xFisher,Thomas J.16 Jan 1914 xFitzgerald,Inf 1933
xFitzpatrick,M.L.12/31/1923   /Fitzgerald,Charlotte 1843-1907
xFitzwater,A.W. 28 apr 1920   /Fitzgerald,J.Vinton 10 Jan 1902-8 mar 1913
xFitzwater,Elizabeth 2/11/26   /Flaherty,John J. 1873-1926
xFlannagan,Blanche W.2/6/1936/Flanngan,Mary Ann 21 Jul 1828-2 Jun 1879
/Flannagan,Cora Lee 1888-1918/Flannagan,Willie Ann 1853-1906
xFlannagan,James C.1852-1901 /Flannagan,William S. 1917-8s/o SS&Cora
xFlannery,Mrs.Elviria 8/26/17/Fleckenstein,s/o F&V 1893
xFlannery,Felix 3 oct 1932   /Fleckenstein,Virgie May 1878-1913
xFlesher,Mary A. 1860-1920   /Flesher,Bessie B.w/o M.B.1884-1926
xFletcher,Ben Jackson 1/16/36/Flesher,Benjamin Taylor 1855-1928s/oAJ&S
/Fletcher,Carrie G.1883-1919   Mary Addie 1860-1920
xFletcher,Florence 5/10/1910 xFloding,Charlotte 1844-1889
xFlora,Gunnett 4 feb 1917 InfxFloding,Ed 2 feb 1935
xFlowers,Belva Irene 7/13/25 xFloding,George 1914
/Flowers,Arnold 1913 inf   /Floding,Estelle 1904-1919
/Flowers,Anna L. 1869-1925   /Floding,Robert Owen 29 dec 1938 61y7m27d
/Flowers,Earl M. 1873-1930   xFlowers,Emily Nilson 16 dec 1926
xFlowers,Martha 7 Jan 1924   /Flowers,H.H.2 oct 1906-24 apr 1913 s/oA&BM
/Flowers,Inf 1938   /Flowers,Llian 1889-1909
/Flowers,Mack 1850-1899   /Flowers,Mary Mack 1886-1886
/Flowers,Mary K. 1851-1937   xFlowers,Twylah Louise 6 Jun 1918 inf
xFlowers,Stanley 20 mar 1916 /Flowers,Virgie 1891-1914 w/o J.F.
/Flowers,Thadeus 1840-1918   /Flowers,William E. 1888-1900
xFloyd,Eliza 13 Jul 1923   /Foley,Hugh G. 1837-1909
xFloyd,Inf/WP 1 aug 1917   /Foley,Charles J. 1881-1882 s/o HC&N
xFloyd,Sallie B.2 mar 1920   /Foley,Ellen Gamble 1849-1914
xFodal,Infs 1919/1926   /Fontaine,Stella M. 1861-1929
xFolos,Janis 25 apr 1927 inf /Fontaine,John J.14 feb 1857-31 may 1889
/Forbes,Rena 30 Jan 1917   /Fountain,Lucille 1890-1915

/Forbin,Delia M. 1843-1912   xForbush,Carrie 1885 inf
xForbush,Edward 1885-1905   xForbush,Fern 27 dec 1912
xForbush,Fredrick 1 Jan 1914 xForbush,George 1883-1886
/Forbush,Iva Louise 1909-1911xForbush,inf/TE 14 may 1911
xForbush,John 28 dec 1912   xForbush,John 1906
xForbush,Mary 21 dec 1916   /Forbush,T.Elwood 1884-1928
xForce,Fred 8 sep 1921   /Force,Ida May 9 aug 1935   7m17d
xForce,Nina May 10 aug 1935 xForeman,inf/Alfred 9 Jul 1911
/Ford,Betty Jane 21 jan 1935 /Forgey,Clemath E. 1886-1939
/Ford,Charles B. 1872-1915   /Forgey,Ernelloue W. 1863-1928
xForgitt,inf 6 dec 1926   xForls,Lewis 8 mar 1911
xForte,Arthue 15 apr 1923   xForrest,Maria Smith 16 apr 1922
xFortune,Carrio 1890-1939   /Forster,Margaret 1839-1908 w/oJames W.
/Fosburg,Agnes 1879-1929   xFoster,Agnes Lucile 19 jan 1919
/Foster,Bettie 1865-1923   /Foster,Bradley W.2 dec 1834-22 mar 1922
xFoster,Carrie 23 mar 1910   xFoster,Mrs.C.P. 31 aug 1911
/Foster,Herbert D.1910-1923 /Foster,Rezin J.1844-1892 Co D 11th WV Inf
/Foster,Mary Frances 1903-30   Elizabeth A. 16 sep 1847-17 oct 1900
xFoster,James W. 5 Jan 1922 xFoster,Laura 23 oct 1918
xFoster,Mary 17 Jun 1919   xFoster,Okey 17 nov 1925
xFoster,Robert 13 may 1923   /Foster,M.Lenora H.7 aug 1841-10 feb 1920
xFout,Charles 24 dec 1930   xFoultz,Martha J.20 Jun 1910
xFout,Peter 23 may 1918   /Fowlkes,F.H. 1872-1932
xFox,Asa D. 26 aug 1936   /Fowler,Robert M.7 oct 1932 inf
/Fox,Catherine A.1821-1905   /Fowler,Dr.Charles A. 1880-1916
/Fox,Blanche Goodman, 1896-23/Fox,Edna Roach 1893-1920
xFox,Edwin A. 15 aug 1939   xFox,Fay 7 dec 1923
/Fox,Henrietta 1862-1911   /Fox,Henry B. 1854-1934
/Fox,Lillian 1898-1903   xFox,Irwin 1896-1939
/Fox,Nannie 1864-1930   xFox,Sam 14 aug 1911
/Fox,Sam 1863-1930   /Fox,Wilbur W. 1888-1914
xFrame,William 26 nov 1927   /Frampton,Albert G.27 Jul 1862-19 Jul 1890
/Frampton,Blanche M.1871-1920/Frampton,Bernard Gallatin 1889-1913
/Frampton,Ella 1863-1937   /Frampton,George W.18 dec 1860-5 feb 1905
/Frampton,Fae G. 1890-1914   /Frampton,Gracie Lee 1887-1888 d/o AG&E
/France,Cora 1881-1935   /Frampton,James Isaac 13 dec 1860-31 Jul1904
xFrance,Ana G.4 apr 1931   xFrance,Charles 11 oct 1931
/France,Jane 1850-1925   xFrance,John J. 6 sep 1941
/France,Ivan 1900-1904BF&CoraxFrance Lepie Lee 17 apr 1923
xFrance,Martha A. 17 nov 1930xFrance,Mattie 26 sep 1933
xFrance,Parris 30 sep 1920   /France,Seth 2 aug 1929
/France,Ruby 1919-1926   Civil War WVth 158 (GAR ?)
/Franklin,Florence 1849-1929 /Franden,Oscar 13 mar 1934-13th IL Cav GAR
/Franklin,Mary C. 1883-1930 /Franzell,A.J. 7 Jul 1863-13 oct 1937
/Frazier,Albert 1876-1918   xFrazier,Caroline Burchill 31 oct 1910
xFrazier,Cora 1 Jul 1910   xFrazier,Hallie ann 24 mar 1936
/Frazier,Mamie 1879-1921   xFreedman,Abraham 14 aug 1919
/Freeland,Clara S. 1864-1937 /Freeman,Alfred E.9 Jul 1911 inf
/Freeland,,Robt. A.5 Jan 1927/Freeman,Charles 19 nov 1910
/Freeman,D.W. 24 oct 1930   /Freeman,Maria L. 1862-1922
xFreema,Millard 5 apr 1931   /Freeman,Millie P. 29 may 1939
/Freeman,Moses A.1841-1906/ Freeman,Ricd Valery 25 apr 1858-27 nov 1889
    Sarah A. 1849-1910   /Freeman,W.H.--86y
xFreeman,Willie P.1873-1939 xFreeze,Neal & Ned 26 Jan 1927

xFren,inf/John Jr.18 apr 1918xFrench,J.B. 14 oct 1923
/Freutel,Alex H. 1860-1927   /Freutel,Julius 28 feb 1826-1900
/Freutel,C.T.W. 1852-1922   Sophia 16 oct 1823-x18 oct 1904
xFreutel,C.Henry 1 aug 1888   xFretuel,Margaret F. 1863-1865
xFreutel,William L.--   xFreutel,William, A. 2 mar 1917
xFrey,Alfred 9 sep 1910   xFricotot,Variobey 1 mar 1922
xFrey,Edgar 27 may 1916 inf   xFrizzell,W.S. 16 apr 1937
/Frizzell,Alfred M.1828-1907 /Frizzell,Kate B. Handley 1863-1913
/Frizzell,Catherine 1836-1919/Frost,Ellis Poeter Jr.1912-1913
/Frost,Haidee S. 1877-1899   /Frost,Jack P. 1903-1932
/Frost,Meshach 1854-1907   /Frost,Sidney H. 1856-1899
/Fry,Chapman,1855-1920   /Fry,Eleanor Ann 13 sep 1937   34y1m7d
/Fry,Ellen Napier 1856-1939   /Fry,James W.26 jun 1937 69y7m2d
/Fry,J.Fox 1884-1937   xFry,Edmond 23 Jul 1930
xFry,Pat H.16 Jan 1937   /Fry,Johnson 11 dec 1829-25 dec 1891
xFugitt,Clara 21 oct 1918   /Fugate,Charles H.1871-1930
xFugitt,W.M.--   /Fulkerson,Darline 12 oct 1929-20 aug 1930
/Fuller,Bundy 1906-1908   /Fuller,Frank Daw 7 may 1936 78y5m20d
/Fuller,Fred E. 1876-1929   /Fuller,Iven F.1916 inf s/o OC&A
/Fuller,James M. 1883-1938   xFuller,Ida J. 12 aug 1934
    Mrs.J.M. 24 Jun 1910   /Fuller,Jasper B.1842-1884
/Fuller,Jerome H. 1858-1917   /Fuller,J.M. 1846-1924
   Laura B.1870-1919   /Fuller,Kate M. 3 Jun 1863-6 nov 1889w/oFD
/Fuller,Lelia B. 1886-1935   /Fuller,Sara Davis 1842-1916
/Fuller,F.Fred 1907 inf   /Fuller,S.E. 1852-1910
xFullerton,E.C. 26 oct 1918   /Fulleron,Mabel Beckner 1887-1924
xFullerton,Elizabeth 5 aug 38/Fullerton,Mary Catherine 1840-1987
xFullerton,Ezekiel P.8 aug 28/Fullerton,Harrison Morton 17 aug 1889sEP&E
xFullerton,Father 1859-1928   xFullerton,Fannie 1884-x27 may 1918
xFullum,Alice J. 1 apr 1910   Earnest 1886-1918
xFullwood,Emmitt V.10/17/1933/Fulton,George R.10 mar 1928
xFultz,Andrew 3 aug 1937   xFulwider,Roger M.1902-08
/Funk,Ida D. 1856-1924   /Funk,Louisa M. 182601886
/Funk,James D. 1845-1909   /Funk,James 1821-1886
/Furr,G.G. 1872-1923   /Funk,William Emery 1859-1937
/Fyvie,Ruby 13 may 1935   41y
/Gadsby,George G. 1853-1905   /Gadsby,James M. 10 oct 1892   8y3m10d
xGagai,John Edwin 18 sep 1939 xGadsby,Sarah Madill 10 Jun 1941
/Gall,Lenora Letulle 1839-1903/Gallagher,James 25 nov 1873 89y
/Gallaher,James R. 1827-1895   Sarah L. 12 sep 1883 89y
    Mary E. 1837-1917   /Gallaher,Mary E.1 oct 1856 d/o Wm.&Mary
xGallery,John 7 feb 1910   /Gallaher,Obediah Co I 29th IL Inf
/Gallick,Joseph R. 1856-1926 xGalligher,May E. 5 sep 1920
xGallick,Harriet B.1870-1954 xGalliger,Martha C.1904
xGalloway,Tibatha 27 dec 1914xGalliger,Myrtle E.1900
xGambille,Mary 8 nov 1932   xGang,H.W. 29 Jan 1938
xGarden,thomas 19 dec 1920   xGang,inf/EH 1914--inf/HW 1916
xGarder,W.M. 2 dec 1923   /Gardner,Dr.C.K. 14 apr 1901   43y
xGaritson,Beatrice H.1/4/32   xGardner,Lola 26 dec 1923
/Garland,Dr.David 1890-1917   /Garland,Erskine R. 1875-1924
/Garland,James B. 1911-1916   xGarland,Eldar 7 Jan 1925
/Garland,Louise 1880-1881   /Garland,Richard Henry 1840-1893
/Garland,Thomas 1846-1918   xGarner,Della 23 may 1923
xGarrett,Bessie 24 oct 1923   /Garner,Arminta Bell 19 mar 1862-20apr1913

xGarrett,James Jr.8 mar 1925 /Garthee,Katie R.1873-1922 w/o Hiram
xGarrett,Thelma A.2 feb 1920 xGarrett,Bernard Hamilton 13 nov 1939
xGarten,Ewel 13 dec 1914   /Gasnay,Rose Victoria 16 dec 1889-25Jul1933
xGarwthrop,Ida 28 Jan 1922   xGaston,Mallard 1 dec 1923
xGates,Marie 7 Jun 1910   /Gassler,John A. 12 mar 1843-14 mar 1898
xGatewood,Henrietta 27 Jul 33xGatz,inf 25 feb 1916
xGau,Margaret 25 Jul 1917   /Gaule,Alice V. 1883-1937
xGaugot,Claud 27 mar 1926   /Gaule,Mary 18 apr 1938   65y1m22d
/Gawthrop,Ida 1866-1922   /Gayhart,Eliza 1857-1914
/Gebhardt,Joseph W.1877-1919 /Gayrich,Mike 1875-Oct 27 1920
xGee,Jack 15 Jul 1936   /Geer,Jane N. 1845-1929
xGee,Jack 6 Jun 1922   /Gentry,T.F. 1848-1920
xGee,Lizzie 20 oct 1928   /Gentry,Lyall C. 5 sep 1937
xGeorge,Jacob 19 may 1911   xGentry,J.F. 20 Jun 1918 inf
/George,Elmer E.1/27/1939 71y/Gerard,W.M. 1860-1922
xGeorge,Lillabel Close   T.Winona 1868-1926   /
xGerger,Lula 25 sep 1928   xGerlach,Henry 18 may 1930
xGernand,Catherine 27 aug 07 /Gerlach,Hannah M.28 dec 1850-19 Jan 1908
xGernand,Elizabeth 18 Jun 17 xGerrin,Clarence C.4 dec 1914
xGernand,Mr.1903   xGesley,James 17 nov 1924
xGhiz,William 11 oct 1929   /Gibblin,Bartley 1846-1910
xGibbs,Edward,18 aug 1926   xGibins,inf 30 Jun 1927
xGibbs,Sarah 14 oct 1918   xGibson,Beckie 4 Jan 1930
xGibbs,Zona 4 feb 1925   xGibson,Betty 18 sep 1926
/Gibson,Barbara 1884-1932   xGibson,Betty Jane 11 sep 1920
/Gibson,Charles F. 1885-1918 xGibson,Catherine 29 dec 1934
xGibson,C.H. 14 oct 1918   xGibson,Daisy 29 aug 1921
/Gibson,Donald M.1893-1920   xGibson,Emma 16 Jul 1916
xGibson,Francis 12 oct 1926   /Gibson,Emma 8 feb 1903-17 aug 1914
xGibson,Frank M.30 apr 1919   /Gibson,Eustace 10 dec 1900 Capt. CSA
/Gibson,Hannah E.1858-1935   /Gibson.Hattie Jane 29 mar 1922
/Gibson,J.M.1887-1913   /Gibson,H.Irene 2 oct 1902-3 may 1935
xGibson,inf/John 11 Jun 1917 xGibson,Howard Clay 24 Jan 1914inf
xGibson,Ira 7 Jun 1912   /Gibson,Irene 10 Jul 1933   23y3m11d
xGibson,Jake 1 nov 1910   /Gibson,Jane 22 apr 1937   72y3m26d
/Gibson,Lewis 1888-1913   xGibson,James 28 apr 1912
/Gibson,Lucinda 1834-1917   xGibson,Lacy 1 Jun 1928
xGibson,Martha 25 apr 1909   xGibson,Mrs.M.B. 28 aug 1918
/Gibson,Martha A.1853-1921   /Gibson,Marilla 25 sep 1888 38y w/o John
/Gibson,Mary G. 1883-1918   /Gibson,Okey Charles 1914-1937
xGibson,Mary 29 Jul 1931inf   xGibson,Mrs.Okey 3 nov 1914
xGibson,Nero 15 apr 1912   xGibson,Pearl 18 dec 1910
/Gibson,Omar 1886-1912   xGibson,Pierre 25 oct 1912
/Gibson,Opal F.1911-1918   xGibson,Proctor 10 Jun 1912
xGibson,Robt.L.1888-89   /Gibson,Roscoe 31 aug 1874-4 feb 1902
xGibson,Susan E.15 mar 1937   /Gibson,Ruth 20 may 1888-17 oct 1912
/Gibson,William Jr. 1917 inf /Gibson,William 29 dec 1859-16 Jun 1930
/Gibson,Zibia 1859-1935   /Gideon,Dora 14 mar 1846-20 feb 1923
xGilchrist,Robt.Allen 10/18/26/Gideon,Samuel 19 oct 1836-20 Jun 1923
/Gilbert,A.1856-1916   /Gilbert,Thomas R.1853-1937
   Lola Belle 1853-1927   /Gilbert,Hettie R. 1856-1919
xGiles,Lize 22 oct 1923   xGilkerson,Andrew 1905
/Gilkerson,E.Morris 1891-1934xGilkerson,Cleveland 1907
xGilkerson,Marie W.26 may 34 xGilkerson,Noble 20 may 1920

126

xGill,Benj.Lee 8/13/29inf   xGill,Jennie Rose 6 sep 1913
xGill,Leland 29 Jul 1925   xGillard,Eva 27 dec 1933
/Gillespie,Charles W.1864-10 /Gillard,John Jenkins 1907-1922
/Gillespie,Lewis J.1876-1929 /Gillard,Sara M.15 aug 1934 54y11m5y
xGillespie,Andrew W.2 nov 34 xGillespie,Annazenida 4 sep 1924
xGillespie,James B.7 mar 1910xGillespie Lewellyn 10 aug 1909
/Gillespie,Minnie S.1869-1934/Gillispie,Olive Reid 1876-1919
xGillespie,Sarah E. nov 1929 xGillespie Sarah C.19 Jun 1896
/Gillespy,Nellie Ruth 1928-1936/Gillispie,Thurman 21 nov 1934 WWI
xGillett,Wanda 22 may 1915   xGilliard,John 10 apr 1937
/Gillette,Elmer G.1888-1933 /Gilliland,George Law 11 aug 1886-25 nov06
/Gillette,Francis R.1918-1934xGillispie,Mrs.H.C.31 mar 1919
xGillispie,John 4 Jan 1919   xGillispie,Louis 10 aug 1909
xGilmore,A.M. 17 aug 1918   xGilmore,Eugene 12 sep 1913
xGilmore,Marion 11 nov 1925   /Gilmore,Jenkin Jones1 Jan 1888-9 nov 1929
/Gilmore,Mathew L.1847-1924   /Gilmore,Louisa J. 1845-1934
/Gilmore,Oscar H. 1892-1933   W.M.1845-sep 1916 Co H 45th KY Inf
/Gilmore,S.S. 1870-1927   /Gilmore,May 1886-188 d/o ML&M
/Gilmore,Ola E.Neal 1883-1913/Gilmore,Sura A.13 mar 1937 68y10d
/Gitt,Jennie Rece 1860-1913   xGladstone,Wm.Sheldon 1900
xGlaphios,Josephine 19 may 32xGlatfelter,Martha 20 oct 1951
xGlass,L.D. 2 apr 1928   /Glatfelter,C.R. 6 Jan 1930 64y
/Glasow,Fred 1882-1909   xGlendenning,Alwidda Jul 1904
xGlendenning,Earl 1893   xGlendenning,George K. 9 may 1911
xGlendenning,W.D.12/27/1918   xGlenn,Melva 10 Jan 1925
/Glick,David H. 1903-1929   xGodfrey,Auttus 24 dec 1917
/Glick,Samuel J. 1872-1925   /Goen,Lucy Ann 19 oct 1936
xGogbill,John A. 1884-1898   xGoheen,Billie 31 dec 1931
xGolden,Helen 31 dec 1923   xGoheen,Mary Ann 27 Jan 1938
xGolden,James I. 2 Jun 1921   xGoheen,Sarah E.16 Jan 1926
xGolden,Mrs.James 7/26/19   xGolembrewski,John 11 oct 1935
xGolden,Maggie 15 Jun 1924   /Golberg,Sol 1876-1935x
xGolden,Oscar J. 9 dec 1920   xGoodall,Betty Ann 27 aug 1934
xGoldstein,Fannie 1888-1931   /Goodall,Erskine 1898-1914
xGoodbar,Harry 16 Jan 1914   xGoodall,Josie M. 1 Jan 1934
/Goodbar,Mary L.28 mar 1922   /Goodfriend,David 3 Jun 1911-29 dec 1931
/Goodlois,W.O. 28 dec 1920   /Goodfriend,Max 1869-1933
xGoodlow,Florence 30 mar 1925xGoodson,Hester Ellen 3 nov 1926
/Goodwin,Frank 1887-1892   xGoodson,Mrs.J. 16 oct 1925
/Goodwin,Inf 1893   /Goodwin,Richard A. 1845-1919
/Goolsby,B.F. 1855-1912   xGoolsby,Harold Jeane 18 oct 1931
xGoolsby,H.M. 16 Jul 1928   /Goolsby,Rebecca Ann 1 Jan 1866-3 feb 1939
xGoolsby,J.W. 13 dec 1915   /Goolsby,Susie L. 1866-1930
/Goolsby,J.Hampton 1877-1903 xGoolsby,S.J. 24 dec 1910
xGoolsby,W.T. 15 dec 1917   /Gorden,Marabelle 1849-1939
/Gorden,Harry 1840-1910   xGordon,A.L. 4 aug 1931
   Angie 29 aug 1887 39y5m16dxGordon,Clopatra 16 Jul 1914
xGordon,Edward C.1899   xGordon,Elizabeth 1928
xGordon,Janette 9 sep 1918   xGordon,Margaret 6 sep 1925
xGore,Thelma 8 may 1914inf   /Gorham,Lucy Ann 14 Jun 1889 36y8m2dw/oHL
/Gorman,Katie Swain 1880-1906/Gorham,Willie H.30 Jul 1882 6y10m18 HL&LA
xGorman,C.A.8 Jun 1910   xGorvich,Mike 29 oct 1920
xGorman,Chas.A.7 feb 1937   xGosnay,Rose V.27 Jul 1933
xGorman,Jennie 24 oct 1936   xGotchal,Uriah R.7 nov 1914

xGothard, America R.8/15/1903 /Gothard, Agnes Viola 1864-1919
xGothard, Azel 6 Jun 1932 inf /Gothard, Otie L. 1885-1920
xGothard, Jerry 11 Jun 1933 xGothard, inf/OL 9 oct 1912
xGothard, John A. 15 feb 1928 xGothard, L.O. 22 sep 1911
    Mrs.J.A. 7 mar 1913 xGothard, Minnie 27 Jun 1932
xGothard, Nettie 25 Jan 1898 /Gotshall, James H. 1885-1911
/Gould, Amos B. 1854-1936 /Gotshall, Mary Allison 1853-1934
/Gould, Edward Jr.1923-1928 /Gotshall, Uriah Richard 1843-1914
xGould, Inez M. 14 apr 1915 xGould, Joseph B.13 sep 1833-21 may 1885
/Gould, John V. 1905-1910 /Gould, Stephen 9 may 1868-28 Jan 1927
/Gould, Telewanda 1904-1909 /Gould, William 1906 inf
xGoulding, James 3 Jun 1921 xGowdy, George 29 nov 1918
xGoulding, Oscar J.9 dec 1920 xGrabbit, Willie 2 apr 1926
xGraham, inf/J.L. 9 Jan 1919 /Grafton, Frances 1 Jun 1874 17y2m1d w/o A.
xGraham, Irene 26 aug 1926 inf/Graham, Clark 26 may 1852-15 feb 1935
xGraham, James 19 Jul 1925 /Graham, John S.18 may 1883-19 may 1886
xGraham, Lulie 4 may 1921 /Graham, Rev.Melville C.1868-1916
xGraham, Mrs.M.J. 13 dec 1916 xGraham, Thomas H.27 dec 1917
/Graley, William C.1880-1902SAxGraner, Milton E. 22 may 1926
/Grass, Charles E.1878-1908 /Grant, Charlie W. 22 feb 1859-3 nov 1917
/Grass, James F. 1840-1919 /Grant, Harriett M.24 mar 1858-29 apr 1922
xGrass, Marthe E. 13 nov 1934 xGrant, Alice 1 aug 1910
/Grass, Mary J. 1850-1936 xGravely, Lucy Agnes 21 dec 1933
/Gray, Catherine 1848-1903 xGravely, Nathamie P.19 Jun 1934
xGray, James L.8 dec 1917 /Graves, Florida 1903-1910
/Gray, Mary Ellen 2 nov 1920 /Graves, F.J. 1861-1913
/Gray, Margaret 1874-1915 /Graves, F.J.Sr.1834-1889
/Gray, Samuel B.1849-1923 xGraves, Robt.18 Jun 1930
xGray, Samuel B.Jr.1870-1915 xGraybill, Virginia 7 apr 1926
xGray, Wm.W. 9 feb 1928 /Grayson, Mary Joyce 1925-1932
xGrayhart, Eliza 6 may 1914 xGraco, Frannk J.nov 1932
xGreen, Ida E.13 may 1925 xGreene, Boregard H.20 aug 1934
xGreen, V.M. 30 sep 1900 xGreene, Irene 9 Jul 1918 inf
xGreen, Woodson 12 Jan 1915 /Greenvill, Ray 5 sep 1854-20 may 1888
/Greener, Mary J. 1856-1916 /Greenwell, Julia E.Ault 1856-1926
/Gregg, Cora K. 1857-1929   H.C.Sr.1845-1930
/Gregory, Milton L. 1886-1918 /Gregory, Nannie Lucille 1913 d/o ML&NB
xGregory, Etta 4 feb 1933 xGregory, W.L. 19 Jan 1919
xGreinor, Mrs.W.S. 23 mar 1920xGreiss, William A. 14 oct 1921
xGrendale, James 2 dec 1936 xGrengan, Albert 31 mar 1925
xGribbin, Sarah 5 Jan 1927 /Grider, Jacob Chase 1876inf
/Grider, Lula Chase 1880-1882 /Grider, Quindoro L.1857-1928
/Grider, Owen Chase 1894 inf /Grider, Levi 1862-1917
xGriffin, Alphonso 18 aug 1933xGriffin, James A. 24 may 1937
xGriffin, Louise 27 feb 1917 /Griffith, H.B.Sr. 1836-1920
xGriffith, Louisa 1837-1926 /Griffith, Jessie May 1903-1916
/Griffith, Nina A. 1892-1917 /Griffith, Oscar C. 1869-1934
/Griffiht, Ruth 1905-1921 /Griffith, Sewards G. 1866-1936
/Griffith, S.L. 7 dec 1902 58yxGrigsby, Glen R.25 may 1936
/Grippo, Gerturde Irene 1866-08/Grimm, Mary J. 1852-1919 w/o Elim
xGrippo, Joe 24 apr 1938 xGrizzell, Thomas 16 may 1921
xGrogan, Mrs.Ada 16 feb 1919 xGrobe, Elizabeth J.12 Jun 1910
xGrogan, Chas.W.15 apr 1915 /Grobe, George W. Co D 8th VA Cav CSA
/Grogan, George P.1872-1927 /Grobe, John T. 1869-1919

xGrogan,Luther 2 oct 1919   xGrooms,C.D. 2 mar 1916
xGross,August 11 dec 1917   xGross,Daisy Thelma 1903-1934
xGross,Emley 29 dec 1915   xGross,Flossie 20 dec 1900-10 may 1923
/Grothe,Edna W. 9 feb 1933   xGrover,John 27 apr 1921
xGroves,Alva Jennings 7/5/39 xGrubbs,Mary Louise 8 dec 1928
xGroves,Clifton P.29 Jul 1932xGruber,Daniel 15 apr 1910
/Gruner,Hugo Herman 1878-1938xGrune,Robert 17 Jan 1934
/Gue,Emma 1840-1929   /Guest,S.J. 5 oct 1879-20 nov 1902
   Samuel D. 1842-1919   xGuinn,George H.27 mar 1910
      Co D 9th Reg USA   xGuinn,George W.1902
xGullette,Earle 23 Jan 1926 xGuinn,Harry O.17 Jul 1921
xGullett,Edward 2 mar 1932   xGuinn,Martha 8 aug 1900
xGullett,H.W. 11 may 1921   /Gullett,Mary A.1862-1910 w/Tom
xGullett,Ruby 29 sep 1922 infxGullett,Oscar 20 apr 1921
xGunnoe,Wm.H. 13 Jan 1910   /Gunnoe,Shurman S. 1 Jan 1910 13y
xGussler,Hester 3 Jun 1911   xGuther,Phoeba 17 oct 1931
/Gussler,Annie H. 1865-1909 /Guthrie,John W. Co E 8th VA Cav CSA
   w/o John L.   xGuthrie,Eliza Alice 8 dec 1931
xGwin,Edith Boswell 18 aug 34/Guthrie,Lewis Van Glider
/Gwin,C.Eugene 1861-1928   8 Jan 1864-20 sep 1930
/Gwinn,Anne 1839-1901   xGuthrie,Stella M. 1870-1929
xGwinn,Alice 20 sep 1927   xGwinn,Elizabeth 6 may 1934
xGwinn,Eugene C. 16 feb 1928 /Gwinn,Lizzie A. 1863-1934
/Gwinn,C.H. 1871-1937   /Gwinn,Dr.Van Henry 11 nov 1867-8 Jul 1933
/Gwinn,Henry 1830-1909   xGwinn,Thelma O.31 may 1922
xGwinn,J.M. 15 oct 1929   /Gwinn,Susan 1860-1917 w/o R.L.
/Gwinn,Walter W. 1859-1915   /Gwinn,Weyman 1889-1905
    /Haberle,Jacob 5 Jul 1858-27 mar 1939
       Schmieheim,Baden,Germany
    /Haberle,Clara M. 13 may 1867-12 nov 1930
xHaan,A.E. 5 aug 1924   Saxony,Germany
xHackett,Hattie 22 Jun 1914 xHaberlie,John 6 nov 1935
xHackney,Julia M. 4 apr 1929 xHaberlie,John 9 may 1926
xHaddox,David D.10 Jan 1933 xHaeberle,Herman H.8 aug 1931
xHaddox,Edith 18 Jul 1934   /Hackworth,Charles 26 nov 1933 64y7m16d
/Haden,Tema 27 Jun 1923   /Hackworth,Jessie 23 apr 1935 30y22d
xHagaman,Agnes 1858-1911   /Haeberle,Jacob J.27 mar 1939 80y8m22d
/Hagan,Barbara 1857-1919   /Haeberle,John 3 nov 1935 81y4m29d
/Hagan,Dorothy 1860-1913   xHagan,G.Bernard 10 mar 1912
/Hagan,Joseph B.1852-1912   /Hagan,Fannie B.1852-1935
   Grace Dixon 1889-1938   /Hagan,Salome-1889-1906
/Hagan,Robert E.1849-1938   /Hagan,Mary C.13 aug 1856-2 oct 1886w/oBern
   Lucy T.10 Jan 1857-7/16/1890xHagatte,Ruby G.7 dec 1915
/Hagen,Ambrose 1902-03   xHage,Joseph 24 oct 1932
/Hagen,Hugh B.1866-1932   /Hagen.Mary J.8 Jun 1824-15 aug 1885
/Hagen,James Wm.1852-1928   William H.22 may 1823-4 feb 1898
xHagen,Baynard 27 dec 1918   xHagen,Ernest S.8 aug 1921
/Hager,David Earl 1905-1937 /Hagen Peter Buffington 13 sep 1868 9y2m20d
xHager,E.D. 25 aug 1922   /Hager,George D.1853-1925
xHager,Grant 11 nov 1917   xHager,George 2 may 1923 inf
/Hager,Hezekiah 1844-1921   xHager,Harold Gordon 25 feb 1939
/Hager,H.Ray 1906-1928   /Hager,Madgie 1912-1917 d/o Marion & Lizzie
xHager,Ina Gray 2 Jan 1937   xHager,James 21 nov 1919
xHager,Pauline 1 may 1913   /Hager,Thurman Lee 1888-1912

xHagley,James P. 30 Jan 1925 xHagley,James P. 13 Jun 1921
xHagley,J.V. 26 Jul 1924   /Hagley,Katherine 1863-1929
xHagley,Patrick 9 mar 1926   xHagley,Sarah 31 Jan 1913
xHague,C.W. 28 dec 1938   xHailey,Sallie 19 oct 1914
/Hague,Gerturde M. 1872-1936   /Halbert,Mary cole 1897-1917
xHague,Lourina 3 may 1920   /Hale,Gladys 25 Jun 1898-1 nov 1906
xHague,W.M. 31 oct 1923   Earnest 25 Jun 1898-19 sep 1989
xHale,Jacob, 28 may 1919   xHale,J.Albert 25 Jul 1932
xHale,Marie 20 oct 1926   /Hale,James Thomas 18 feb 1937
xHale,Matilda 13 dec 1915   /Hale,Mont 1869-1913
xHale,Mary Lu 7 Jan 1912   xHaley,Alice 4 dec 1934
/Haley,Janie P.1899-1926   /Haley,Charlie B.2 aug 1871-10 oct 1896
xHaley,Diana 22 feb 1923   /Haley,Lulu 1876 d/o T&DV
xHall,Alberta 1862-1905   xHall,Alice C. 10 Jan 1931
xHall,Arthur 13 feb 1934   xHall,Bennett R.16 Jan 1928
/Hall,Benj.M. 1861-1914   xHall,Bessie M.30Jul 1918
xHall,Charles 3 dec 1923   xHall,Clariss 27 Jan 1919
xHall,Elizabeth 12 aug 1910   /Hall,D.R.1851-17 Jul 1892   41y6m21d
/Hall,Elizabeth 1827-1895   xHall,Florence 9 nov 1939
xHall,Franklin M.10/24/1935   /Hall,George F. 1850-1914
/Hall,Frank 1889-1896   /Hall,Harry 1876-1878
xHall,Henry A.19 Jun 1932   /Hall,Howard P.1890-1937WWI
/Hall,Ida B.1858-1936   xHall,Edna Isabelle 14 may 1940
/Hall,James H.1886-1921   /Hall,Joseph B.6 Jun 1879-4 Jul 1897
/Hall,Karl T. 1883-1917   /Hall,Mary A. 1857-1920
/Hall,Mary Reed 189-1933   /Hall,Mattie Page 1862-1931
xHall,Mathew 24 Jun 1936   xHall,Ollie 26 Jan 1928
xHall,Paul Leslie 27 Jan 1924xHall,Truner 2 dec 1926
xHall,William 1893   xHall,William C. 6 feb 1927
xHall,William F. 30 Jun 1937   Mrs.Wm.C. 24 sep 1913
/Haller,John Jr. 7/11/1922   /Haller,Alexander Standard 1877-1880
/Haller,J.J. 1875-1929   /Haller,Margaret Hatfield 1858-1933
/Haller,Mary Louise   xHaller,May E. 20 apr 1926
/Haller,Wm. Jacob 1852-1912   /Haller,Wm.Pickney 1882-1928
xHalley,Ethel 24 aug 1919   xHalley,J.C. 23 oct 1922
xHalley,John 24 aug 1919   xHalley,Mary 15 oct 1936
xHalsey,Jesse 27 nov 1937   /Halstead,Emily 1853-1907
xHalstead,H.B.5 may 1915   /Halstead,Stacia Miller 1888-1917
xHambleton,Laura G.10/25/25   /Hambleton,Mary E.6 oct 1901 w/o A.C.
/Hambrick,James A.1851-1917   /Hamilton,Carrol Stephenson 1884-1906
/Hambrick,J.Walton 1878-1913   /Hamilton,Edward H. 1897-1908-s/o KL&SP
xHamilton,Addie 1865-1939   /Hamilton,Edward W.1860-1908
/Hamilton,Frances L.1892-1918Hamilton,Kendall L.1848-1919
/Hamilton,Lillie 1884-1909   xHamilton,Ralph Lee 5 may 1931
xHamilton,Rebecca 12/7/1915   xHamilton,Sallie Pruddence 22 Jun 1933
xHamilton,Stella May 7/13/1925xHamke,Robert Sherman 19 nov 1925
/Hamlin,Madora 1869-1912w/oAF/Hammaker,Susan May 1856-1928
xHamlin,A.F. 31 oct 1919   Winfield Scott 1849-1928
xHamlin,Emma G. 18 aug 1929   /Hamm,Mary Alice M.1853-1923
xHammdes,Robert Lee 6 Jun 21   /Hamm,William 1859-1921
xHamon,Alice M. 1853-1923   /Hamm,George 1910-1928
/Hammond,Lillian May   xHampton,Francis Terry 23 dec 1930
    31 mar 1932 30y11m6d   xHampton,John 31 oct 1927
xHancen,Luncelot 14 Jun 1926 xHancher,Zina Wiley 26 aug 1929

xHancock,Jessie G.20 feb 1920/Hancock,Arminta 13 nov 1938   79y8m
xHancock,Peter P.29 Jun 1912 xHancock,Robert 18 feb 1933
xHanders,Frank K.23 Jun 1930 /Handley,Alex C.1821-1887
/Handley,Ella 1872-1917   /Handley,Elizabeth Alexander 1849-1933
/Handley,Edward C.1861-1901 /Handley,Elizabeth Burns 1826-1894
/Handley,Harriet 1866-1932   /Handley,Mrs.John W. 19 aug 1918
/Handley,Howard 1858-1932   xHandley,Julia M. 31 dec 1937
/Handley,Isabelle 1853-1933 /Handley,Lycurgus 1843-1918
/Handley,Oliver W.1855-1929 xHandlin,Cassie 17 Jul 1928
xHaner,Joseph B.1852-1919   /Handlin,Mattie B.9 mar 1847-19 mar 1896
xHaner,Hollena Wall 1862-1933   xRobert J.31 Jan 1917
xHaner,Mary E.1817-1904   /Hanger,inf 1938--Ruth 1930
xHaner,Mary Letilla 1897-1902xHankocky,inf 28 may 1935
xHaner,Noah 1815-1855   xHanks,Christina 31 Jul 1925
/Hanley,A.A.1842-1918   /Hanley,Cecil H.1873-1910
/Hanley,Clarissa 1840-1928   /Hanley,Ernest C.1876-1914
xHanley,Harry Lee 27 Jun 1937/Hanley,Eliza A.7 sep 1820-17 Jul 1888
xHanley,Mrs.Ike 1 oct 1915   /Hanley,Levi M.1842-1928
    Ike 7 Jan 1958   /Hanley,Isaac E.25 dec 1814-28 may 1891
/Hanley,Naomi May 1884-1927 /Hanley,Thomas 1878-1912
xHansford,Monroe 1823-1908   /Hanna,Annie 1848-1937
/Hanshaw,John A.1846-1927   /Hanna,John M.1846-1922
    Betsy Ann 1851-1937   xHanna,James A.21 aug 1920
/Hanshaw,Ernest 1887-1936   /Hansher,Isabelle 1865-1919
/Hansucker,inf 28 apr 1935   xHarbour,Ellen L.14 feb 1922
/Harbour,Margaret 1864-1922 /Harbour,Luther F.1894-1935 s/o JR
/Harbour,Mary Harrold 1874-38xHarbours,2 inf/Wm. 1922---
xHardiman,Loveda 1919 inf   xHardin,inf/WP 21 mar 1918
xHardway,Mattie 5 feb 1935   /Hardin,Phebe W. 1813-20 aug 1865 52y1m16d
/Hardwick,Clarice May 1930inf/Hardy,Albert 27 Jan 1937 53y
/Hardwick,Richd Ed.1855-1916 /Hardy,Viola V.1878-1917 w/o Ernest
xHark,Patie 1 may 1923   xHarkness,Bessie 16 sep 1938
xHarler,Anthela 17 apr 1930 xHarless,Muriel 10 sep 1923
xHarler,William 1 Jul 1936   /Harless,Roy E.1897-1918
xHarlowe,C.E. 27 sep 1922   xHarmon,Clinton 8 aug 1928
/Harman,Gordon C.1849-1909   xHarmon,J.Gordon 18 feb 1920
/Harman,John Gordon 1895-1919xHarmon,Robert 18 Jun 1932
/Harman,J.G.Jr.1918-19   xHarmon,Sarah Jane 14 Jun 1939
/Harper,Charles A. 1886-1919 /Harmon,Florence 16 aug 1936 83y5m25d
/Harper,Essie Elder 1860-1892/Harper,Cyrus S.15 Jan 1864-6 Jan 1894
xHarper,Mrs.J.S.17 Jun 1922 /Harper,S.Jack 1883-1919
/Harper,Mina Martin 1884-1937xHarper,James G.3 may 1910
xHarper,Mary A. 5 sep 1913   xHarper,Pearl A. 1880-1896
/Harrington,J.M. 1861-1927   /Harris,Aimee F.Thornton w/o R.W.
/Harris,Flora M.1866-1921   24 dec 1869-20 apr 1892
xHarris,Cora 30 dec 1926   xHarris,Drucella F.Barnes 26 dec 1933
xHarris,Mary 5 aug 1910   /Harris,John P.1909-1911 s/oJP&Della
/Harris,Texana C.1847-1918   /Harris,Odell 15 nov 1923
    W.L. 1856-1921   /Harris,Robert F.4 aug 1911 60y11m21d
xHarris,Sarah 31 mar 1913   /Harris,Sallye C.Peck 1889-1917
xHarris,Virginia 10 Jan 1921 xHarris,Woodrow 26 may 1917
xHarrison,Allen 1892   xHarrison,Clyde Lee 25 mar 1937
xHarrison,Henry H.31 dec 1932/Harrison,Lucien E.16 oct 1937   82y11m8d
/Harrison,J.H. 1838-1918   xHarrison,John H.16 dec 1935

        Rachel Frances 1846-1920   xHarrison,Otis 6 Jun 1910
xHarrison,Ruth 10 aug 1918   xHarrison,Rachael M.16 feb 1921
/Harrold,Blanche 1893-95   /Harrold,C.B.1855-1929
xHarrold,George W.25 Jul 1918/Harrold,Bessie Florence 1890-92 d/CB&GL
/Harrold,Jane M.1836-1900   /Harrold,Georgia L.1861-1921
/Harrold,James M.1828-1901   /Harshbarger,Joseph 1850-1935
/Hart,Harryt D.10 sep 1935wwI/Harshbarger,Edna D.29 feb 1867-10 Jan 1938
xHart,Margaret J.23 mar 1930 /Harshbarger,Margaret 1850-1917
xHartigan,Joseph F.17 Jun 1925xHartley,Bertha M.1870-1909
    Mrs.Jos.F.14 apr 1919   xHartley,F.C. 3 feb 1936
/Hartley,Robert 1878-1932   /Hartley,Irene 30 Jan 1934 35y9m2d
xHartley,mabel 1903-06   /Hartley,William T.1864-1939
xHartsmith,Frank 11 feb 1910 xHartz,Leon H.1896-1938
xHarvey,Jennie 24 oct 1930   /Hartzell,Abbie Scott 1863-1903 w/o Enos
/Harvey,B.T. 1862-1931   /Harvey,Clayton 5 nov 1847-4 sep 1915
   Judith A. 1863-1918   /Harvey,Margaret Lynn 14 nov 1844-28 oct 16
/Harvey,Charlotte E.1829-1921/Harvey,Henry C.14 apr 1854-14 feb 1931
                              Imogene A.Haqgan 20 apr 1857-19 sep 45
/Harvey,John J.   /Harvey,Thomas Hope 24 may 1844-7 may 1929
    14 Jul 1840-14 oct 1921   Emma F.McCullough 12 apr 1852-11 may 27
xHarvey,John 26 apr 1932   xHarvey,Julia 14 mar 1918
/Harvey,James 16 mar 1929 25yxHarvey,Maymie 19 dec 1915
xHarvey,R.M. 22 apr 1926   xHarvey,Susie 29 Jan 1919
/Harvey,Dr.Robert S.   /Harvey,Robert T.24 Jun 1814-5 Jun 1896
    7 nov 1849-7 Jan 1894   Anna M.Hope 29 mar 1821-25 Jan 1889
xHarwood,Cynthia H.1835-1886 /Harwood,Katherine J.1859-1933
/Hassel,Max Alfred 1917-1933 /Harwood,Charles B.1854-1933
xHassion,Carrie 17 mar 1924 /Hasselman,Ethel 10 feb 1895-7 mar 1924
xHastings,Gerturde 18 dec 1923/Hastings,M.Josephine 1903-1939
/Hasting,Wm.A.2 oct 1932   /Hastings,Margaret 1916-19JM&RP
xHastings,Thelma 24 apr 1917 /Hatch,Charles 1861-1904
/Hatcher,Anna M.1856-1929   /Hatch,Charles Jr.1895-1919
xHatcher,Charles 15 Jan 1917 /Hatchett,J.B.1875-1919
xHatcher,Mrs.John 22 feb 1919/Hatcher,W.H.1854-1936
xHachett,Rev.Jousha 3/23/1919xHatfield,Blanche L.12 sep 1934
/Hatfield,Jim Joe 1928-1934 /Hatfield,Crystal F.1905-1923 w/o HO
xHatten,Anna R. 16 mar 1929 xHatten,Anna Catherine 4 may 1932
xHatten,Charles R.24 aug 1937/Hatten,Carrie B.1873-1937
/Hatten,Gerturde L.1897-1925 /Hatten,Charles R.6 feb 1882-25 feb 1913
xHatten,H.E. 16 aug 1916   xHatten,Howard 18 sep 1916
/Hatten,Lafe S.1865-1932   /Hatten,Meredith D.1845-1916
xHatton,Charles Jr.1895-1919 /Haucke,Conrad 26 dec 1909 CoH 70th OH
xHauche,William E.23 dec 1924xHaucke,Mary Anna 1 mar 1933
/Haverty,C.D. 1847-1901   xHaverty,Niza 11 may 1919
xHaverty,S.M. 31 Jul 1925   /Haverty,Vietta 1845-1906
xHaviston,Emma 21 dec 1918 /Hawkins,Fernie Stilwell 9 apr 1939 50y10m25
xHawkins,Thomas P.6 Jul 1914 /Hawkins,J.Marshall 11 may 1939 72y9m13d
xHawkins,W.W. 25 mar 1914   /Hawkins,Nora Beuhring 1868-1899
/Haworth,Clarence E.1860-1929xHawkworth,Hannah L.1837-1904
    Hattie Vinton 1862-1901   Samuel L. 1827-1886
xHay,Adaline 19 may 1915   /Hay,Franklin 1853-4 sep 1887
xHay,Strother 29 aug 1911   /Hayden,Inf 1936 ch/oS.B.
xHayes,Augusta 19 oct 1922   xHayden,Caroline 15 feb 1914
xHayes,Faye E. 27 Jan 1936   /Hayes,Authur L.23 mar 1886-26 aug 1938

xHayes,J. 27 Jan 1936   /Hayes,Henrietta B.1852-1925
xHayes,R. 27 Jan 1936   xHayes,Ora Orlona 8 Jun 1932
/Hayes,Preston M. 1852-1928   xHaynes,Harry 11 apr 1922
/Haywood,Ellen L. 1847-1939   xHaynes,Earnest S.8 sep 1916
xHaywood,John Wesley 6/11/40   xHazelett,Missouri E.13 aug 1932
/Hazlett,Anna May 1903-1931   /Hazlett,Missouri 1924-25
xHazlett,Nellie 16 nov 1910   /Hazlett,Robert 16 dec 1937
xHealy,John F. 4 nov 1924   /Healy,James E. dec 1850-apr 1919
xHealey,Katerine M.1901-29   /Healy,Kathleen Malone 1901-1929
/Healy,Philip B.1898-1921   xHealey,May Morgan 15 aug 1926
xHealey,Wanda E. 4 Jan 1937   /Hearholzer,John 1898 inf
/Hearholzer,Kathryn 1865-1902/Hearholzer,Elizabeth 1889-90
xHearholtzer,William 10/27/42/Hearholzer,Lawrence T. 1887-1934
/Hearthman,Pearl M.1888-1918 xHeathman,Myra 21 Jul 1917
xHeck,Anna H. 1878-1995   /Heck,Caroline 1848-19 Jan 1907 59y9m
/Hedrick,Fronia 1867-1932   xDavid 15 nov 1918
/Hedrick,Nora O. 1875-1937   /Hedinger,William Waldon 1915-18
xHedrick,James O. 20 Jun 1921xHedinger,Violet M.25 oct 1918 inf
xHeffey,George R.29 Jun 1899 xHeffner,Charles F. 8 Jan 1926
xHeffey,Coydon 3 Jul 1914 inf/Heffner,Clarence W. 1915 inf s/o R&J
/Heffner,Joseph K.1892-1929   /Heffner,Julia M.1884-1918 w/o R.F.
/Heffner,J,Frank 1859-1930   /Heffner,Mary I.1860-1921
xHeffner,Robert F.23 Jul 1939/Heffner,Ruby C.1904-1926 w/o Mark
xHeffner,Vesta M. 1881-1885   /Heffner,James Walter 1887-1918
xHeffner,Zadid 12 apr 1936   xHefflin,David 9 Jan 1913
xHelmick,Vida 6 may 1929   xHeinerman,Sallie F.30 Jan 1932
xHelms,Carrie 7 nay 1934   /Helton,George 1884-1911
xHelms,Chas.Franklin 3 aug 12/Helton,Nancy J.1854-1934
xHelwig,C.G. 11 nov 1923   xHelwig,Ruth 28 nov 1919
xHelwig,Mary Ann 1 oct 1924   xHemming,Viola 22 mar 1935
xHenderson,C.H. 28 Jun 1923   /Henderson,James 30 Jan 1934 55y
xHenderosn,Dan 16 aug 1914   /Henderson,Jane Gibbs 1843-1926
/Henderson,Elias A.1858-1928 xHenderson,James A. 18 Jun 1926
xHenderson,Nan 22 aug 1918   /Henderson,Thomas E.1837-1913
/Henderson,Stonie 1867-1923   /Hendricks,Lewis CoE 8th VA Cav CSA
/Henley,J.F.E. 1875-1923   /Henley,Charley 28 aug 1865-5 Jun 1893
/Henley,T.A. 1863-1923   /Henley,Chloe 11 Jun 1834-27 feb 1911
/Henley,W.T. 1867-1920   /Henley,Mary 25 oct 1856-5 Jan 1891
xHenney,Charles 3 mar 1889   /Hennion,John H.1831-1912
    Fannie Jun 1884   /Hennion,Maria 1840-1923
xHenning,Margurite E.1/6/1935/Henry,Polidore 1860-1926
xHenning,Margaret 21 may 1911/Henry,Rosence 1858-1925
xHensley,Addie 28 feb 1912   xHensley,Mrs.C.E. 24 oct 1915
xHensley,Georgia 14 may 1923 xHensley,Julian C.25 mar 1912 inf
xHensley,John W.17 dec 1934   xHensley,Lawrence 1 nov 1918
xHensley,Mary A.22 may 1924   /Hensley,Lyle 5 apr 1900-14 aug 1939
xHensley,Maud 29 aug 1932   xHensley,Mary Alice 22 may 1924
/Hensley,Susie 1884-1913w/oDJ/Hensley,Minnie 7 Jun 1884-2 sep 1937
xHensley,Ovina 2 sep 1910   /Hentrich,Carl 1900-1921
xHerchel,Gerturde 29 may 1919xHermanson,Ida P.1859-1934
/Hermanson,Max L. 1854-1933 xHermanson,Rachael 10 nov 1939
/Hermanson,Samuel L.1889-1937xHern,Frank E. 13 oct 1914
xHerdon,Effie M.1854-1909   xHerdon,Cynthia A. 19 feb 1933
xHerdon,Harry M.16 oct 1925   xHerdon,James Franklin 4 Jun 1926

xHerdon,John W.21 mar 1932   xHerren,Garland 1903-05
xHerring,Geo.M.19 Jan 1912   xHerring,Catherine LS 28 dec 1910
xHerring,May sep 30 1920   xHerron,John Henry 10 feb 1938
xHersey,Ella 3 feb 1915   xHess,Anna Elinor 6 apr 1932
xHersey,F.L. 10 mar 1923   xHess,Fannie Sanders 12 sep 1936
xHersey,Sarah Victoria8/27/28xHess,James L.Col 4th VA Inf CSA
xHeuser,Lucille 1 may 1921   xHewlett,Donald L.16 mar 1929
xHichel,J.P.2 mar 1927   xHickel,Margaret C.26 Jun 1931
xHickel,S.Sheldon 9 oct 1928 xHickel,Viola 18 mar 1939
xHickman,A.W. 15 Jul 1930   xHickman,Edith 15 nov 1930
xHickman,James 12 feb 1937   xHickman,John 11 Jan 1927
xHickman,Virginia 23 nov 1915xHicks,Albert F.16 apr 1932
xHicks,Edward B.10 nov 1937   xHicks,Ethel A. 24 dec 1931
xHicks,G.W. 18 nov 1927   xHicks,Inf/JO 3 oct 1912
xHiggason,Margaret 10 oct 939xHiggson,Martha V.1898-1921 d/o M. Gibson
xHiggason,Martha 12 sep 1921 xHiggins,Alfred T.1862-1902
xHiggins,Bernice 26 Jul 1920 xHiggins,Elizabeth 6 dec 1916
xHiggins,James L. 11 feb 1928xHiggins,Mercedes 30 aug 1927
xHiggins,Rolland 1902 inf   xHiggins,Phillip Josiah 14 mar 1927
/Hill,Alfred B.1848-1933   xHill,A.B. 31 mar 1933
   Martha E.1851-1933   xHill,Arthur 23 mar 1925
xHill,Carrie E. 14 oct 1918   xHill,Charles C.1 sep 1938
xHill,Clifford 5 Jul 1911   xHill,Dan 3 Jul 1925
xHill,George 16 oct 1931   xHill,Hargis 19 Jun 1913
xHill,Harvey E. 12 aug 1925   xHill,Kate 13 mar 1929
xHill,Leander 26 mar 1934   xHill,Linwood J.Jr. 3 feb 1936
xHill,Leroy S.1871-1921   xHill,Linwood,J.Sr. 16 oct 1936
xHill,Mabel 6 Jun 1918   xHill,Martha 30 mar 1919
xHill,Martha E. 26 nov 1933   xHill,Mary E. 26 apr 1931
xHill,Nancy 27 Jun 1932   xHill,Octavo 4 Jun
xHill,Ray S.16 dec 1921   xHill,Robt.T.1859-1902
xHill,Sarah 10 mar 1923   xHill,Ruth Elizabeth 17 aug 1937
xHill,W.T. 7 apr 1919   xHillary,Mrs.Kate 16 Jul 1930
xHilton,Clara 19 mar 1915   xHilton,George 22 nov 1911
xHilton,Robert 3 sep 1916   xHilton,Nancy 22 mar 1934
/Hilton,Glenn D.1861-1895   /Hiltbruner,E.A. 6 Jan 1891 33y11m14d
/Hilton,Mary Louise 1865-1923 /Hiltbruner,Perry 20 Jan 1849 s/oJ&M 3y3m
xHilterbrand,Clow 17 Jul 1927 /Hiltbruner,Jacob 28 sep 1849 s/oJ&M 2y21
/Himes,Charles Edwin 1924-25 /Hiltbruner,Mary 27 sep 1877 w/o Jacob
/Himes,George Earnest 1915-18 xHinds,E.W. 27 mar 1911
xHinckle Eva 21 mar 1921   /Hinerman,David 1830-1905
xHinkle,inf/WL 7 aug 1914   /Hinerman,Sallie F.1879-1932 w/ DO
/Hines,Betty 1910-1930   xHinerman,Josephine 4 nov 1946
/Hines,Carey R. 1895-1913   xHinerman,W.G. 15 may 1923
/Hines,Edna L. 1880-1915   /Hines,Elizabeth 1858-1924
/Hines,Frank P. 1858-1926   xHindledier,G.G. 5 dec 1923
/Hite,A.J. 25 nov 1925   /Hite,Ella d1 Jun 1925
/Hite,Effie 1879-1914 w/o AJ xHite,Daisy Viola 5 mar 1926
xHite,Elive N. 16 dec 1910   xHite,James F. 29 Jul 1925
xHite,Lafayette 9 oct 1931   xHite,Olive Nancy 1983-1911
/Hite,John B.1855-1916   /Hite,Jacob 8 apr 1776-24 sep 1857********
   Elizabeth 1818-1897   Sarah Scales 5 Jan 1782-29 nov 1869
/Hite,Wm.1901 inf/oWF&Anna   /Hite,John W.8 Jun 1903-28 mar 1879
/Hite,Nancy E. 1852-1912   Malinda McMahon 19 Jan 1807-28 feb 1877

James E. 1850-1919 /Hite,Kate 3 sep 1844-2 Jan 1884
/Hitner,REv.John K.1839-1927 CW/Hively,Julia 10 dec 1896-29 Jul 1933
  xHively,Levisa W.J.27 Jul 18 xHively,William 13 Jan 1929
  /Hoard,Arma S.1860-1932   /Hoard,C.B. 1805-1886
  /Hoard,Charles P.1859-1916   /Hoard,Floyd 1842-1925
  /Hoard,George E.1865-1887   /Hoard,Julia T.1837-1894
  /Hoback,Jacob 1886 79y   /Hoard,Pitt 1832-1921
     Martha C.9 apr 1884 75y   /Hoback,J.T. 20 Jun 1889 39y3m
  /Hoback,J.W. 1873-1904   /Hoback,James T.12 Jan 1835-16 dec 1890
  xHoback,Edward M.20 Jul 1939 xHoback,Eliza Jane 14 feb 1929
  xHoback,Martha 1809-1875   xHoback,Staley 26 Jan 1938
  /Hoban,Rilla B.1881-1908   /Hobbs,Jasper G.1891-1938
  xHobson,John 4 may 1931   /Hobbs,Mary E. 24 Jul 1939 74y8m18d
  xHobson,Shelton 18 sep 1918 xHock,Pauline 4 may 1926
  /Hodges,Ross F.1875-1918   xHodges,Marinda 9 Jan 1931
  xHodgesm,Grace 13 Jan 1920   xHodges,Mattie 22 Jul 1930
  /Hoffman,Julia 1883-1936   /Hoff,Minnie Wilson 1872-1921 w/oSM
  xHoffman,Annietta 12 oct1923 xHoff,Silas Marner 28 dec 1944
  xHoffman,Henry H,15 nov 1910 xHoffman,May 1908
  xHoffman,Myrtle 2 Jul 1910   xHoffman,Willie 18--
  /Hoffman,J.S. CoD 95th OH Inf/Hoffman,Mary M. 1883-1939
                               /Holbroook,T.R. 1932-33
  xHogsett,Fredrick 10 oct 1918xHolbrook,Benny Lee 27 aug 1926
  xHogsett,Paul 23 Jun 1926   xHolden,James L.21 sep 1930
  xHogestt,Roberta S.1 sep 1932xHolden,Samuel Jr.17 Jul 1937
  /Holderby,Clarence W. 1873-76/Holderby,Adelaide C.1841-1903
  xHolderby,Eliza P.1840   /Holderby,George W. CoE 8th VA Cav CSA Lt.
  /Holderby,Edward S.1844-1890 /Holderby,inf 1871 d/o ES&CA
  /Holderby,Edward S.Jr.1880-83xHolderby,E.T. 10 may 1925
  xHolderby,Mrs.E.S. 1 sep 1931/Holderby,James 17 aug 1855 73y7m9d
  /Holderby,Hallie V.1852-1927   Lucy P.8 may 1857 52y8m9d
  /Holderby,James A. 1832-1904 /Holderby,Robert 8 Jun 1852 64y
  /Holderby,W.P. d5 sep 1880   Susan A. 1806-1868
  xHolland,May 3 sep 1926   xHolderby,Susie 15 feb 1928
  /Holland,Capt,C.N.1865-1937 /Holland,Anna 23 Jun 1933 48y3m3m
     Mabel F. 1877-1928   /Holland,Annie Robertson 1877-1903 w/o BO
  xHolley,Alem H.1 feb 1932   xHolley,Charles 10 may 1927
  xHolley,Ella 9 apr 1920   xHolley,James T. 22 Jun 1921
  /Holley,John A. 1856-1922   /Holley,Mildred Anita 1927-28
  /Holley,Sarah C. 1859-1927   /Holley,Russell C.1901-1938
  /Holley,Allen H.1873-1932   xHollingsworth,Frank 28 sep 1926
  xHolmes,Eliza 2 feb 1915   /Holloway,Gerard 1879-1922
  /Holston,Paul E. 1900-1920   /Holloway,Wm.Delaney 7 may 1934 70y8m28d
  /Holt,Effie Ewing 1861-1917 /Holswade,Georgella 1856-1905
  /Holt,Homer E. 1887-1936   /Holswade,Quindora Martha 1876 inf
  /Holt,John H. 1859-1933   /Holswade,Wm.Henry Harrison 1847-1908
  xHolt,Victoria 21 apr 1913   /Holton,Ernest 1891-1930
  /Holtzworth,Mary Eliz.1892-22xHolton,Nettie 14 Jul 1932
  xHomer,Virginia 3 nov 1939   /Honaker,Margarite 1924 inf
  /Honaker,H.A. 1843-1927   /Honaker,Ina D. 1908-1930
  /Honaker,W.B.1841-1921   /Honaker,Lillian R.1896-1912
  /Hooser,Virginia May 1915-18 xHoorn,inf 12 sep 1924
  xHoover,Robt.G. 12 Jun 1922inxHoose,inf 10 may 1923
  /Hoover,Dixie 29 dec 1928 18y/Hopkins,Dr.C.L. 1863-1918

xHopking, Howard 1 dec 1932   xHopkins, alford 2 feb 1927
xHopkins, Belle 30 nov 1913   xHopkins, Charles C.26 aug 1933
xHopkins, Edna 2 apr 1932   xHopkins, James Edgar 23 nov 1911
xHopkins, Jane 16 apr 1922   xHopkins, J.Sarah 27 sep 1935
/Hopkins, Jones d1918   /Hopkins, Nina M. 1894-1910 d/o CL&E
xHorne, B.F. 14 mar 1924   xHorne, Benjamin 13 nov 1914
xHorne, Bessie 10 mar 1911   /Horchler, Gottfried 1868-1913
xHorne, Francis 5 sep 1923   /Horr, Rosie 15 oct 1863-28 Jun 1931
xHorne, B.F. 14 mar 1924   xHorne, Benjamin 13 nov 1914
xHorne, Bessie 10 mar 1911   xHorne, Francis 5 sep 1923
xHorton, Minnie 1 nov 1925   xHorton, Robert 1860-1902
xHorton, Reginal 24 oct 1930   xHorton, William 23 oct 1936
xHosey, Paul 21 may 1925   /Houchins, Granville 1835-1918
xHouck, J.E. 7 nov 1921   /Houck, Willia E. 1904 inf
/Houch, Carrie L.20 dec 1910   /Houck, Emma L.1872-1904 w/o JE
xHouredy, John 2 sep 1913   /Housen, Herman 1906-1918 s/o CF&Mary
xHousen, Dorca Ann 19 sep 1913   /Housen, Launcelot 1902-1926 s/o CF&Mary
xHousen, Florence 9 Jun 1920   xHousen, Mary 13 aug 1914
/Hovey, inf 1934   xHowaldy, John 2 sep 1913
xHoward, Aaron 18 apr 1934   /Howard, A.A. 1857-1910
xHoward, Albert 27 feb 1913   xHoward, Charles 11 sep 1921
xHoward, Elbert 7 sep 1915   /Howard, H.B. 1898-1937
/Howard, Mary 29 Jun 1935   xHoward, Louise Johnson 12 Jan 1935
xHoward, Mary 16 feb 1919   xHoward, Nannie 17 sep 1917
xHoward, Susie 18 mar 1913   xHoward, William Jr.9 Jan 1914
xHoward, William M. 7 apr 1931 xHowell, Earl Raymond 1901-1912
xHowell, Harold   xHowell, Georgia Irene 1 Jan 1919
xHowes, H.E. 27 sep 1924   xHowell, Margaret 16 may 1923
/Howell, Irene 1902-1918   /Howell, maymie L. 1879-1936
xHowland, Nancy B. 14 feb 1917 xHowell, Molly 26 oct 1926
xHowland, W.T. 8 mar 1933   xHowland, Walter B.14 nov 1917
xHubbard, Charles W.23 oct 1922 xHubbard, Gerald W.30 sep 1931
xHuddleston, John 1861 CW   xHudson, Annie 2 Jul 1912
/Huddleston, Charles C.1876-17 /Hudson, Davis G. 13 Jun 1893 s/o JF&LH
/Huddleston, Mary A.1871-1931   /Hudson, Gerturde 16 apr 1890 3y6m3d
/Huddleston, Russell F.1891-20 /Hudson, Mary B. 1836-1906
/Huddleston, Thomas   /Hudson, Morris E. 5 Jan 1936   77y10m10d
     CSA Kanawha Rangers   xHudson, H.H. 18 dec 1937
xHuff, J.M. 20 may 1920   xHudson, Henry 1 sep 1930
/Huff, Eliza J.Stephson   xHudson, J.N. 4 nov 1921
     1857-1912 w/o JA   xHudson, James 4 Jun 1913
/Huff, Fleetwood 1 aug 1932WWI xHudson, Mrs.L.2 aug 1922
/Huff, Frank P.5 mar 1932 CW   xHudson, Elizabeth Crawford 1 Jan 1942
xHuff, J.M.20 may 1920   xHuffman, John E.28 dec 1918
xHuff, Mapheney 17 dec 1922   /Huffman, Hattie 1896-1919
xHuff, Myrtle 16 Jul 1918   /Huffman, inf 1919
xHughes, Daniel A. 1933   xHughes, Daniel 20 Jun 1923
xHughes, Emma 21 mar 1925   xHughes, James 19 feb 1937
/Hughes, G.W.1865-1923   /Hughes, Charles Morris 18 dec 1937 15y
/Hughes, James A. 1861-1930   /Hughes, Nancy Jane 2 apr 1938   53y15d
xHughes, May 19 dec 1915   xHughes, Minnie 8 feb 1928
xHughes, Sam 7 nov 1912   xHughes, Thomas C.2 aug 1938
/Hulbert, Lydia 1836-1916   xHumphries, Robert 25 Jan 1911
/Hulbert, Alonzo 1832-1906   /Humphreys, Ann 1829-1987

/Humphreys,Edward 1826-1912   xHumphreys,J.H. 25 oct 1937
/Humphreys,James H.1876-1937   /Humphreys,J.Harry 1867-1926
/Humphreys,John N.1853-1938   /Humphreys,John David 1909 s/o Harry & Marie
/Humphreys,Mabel L.1885-1918   /Humphreys,Oletha Rice 1860-1935
/Humphreys,Roger E.1904-08   /Humphries,Thomas W.27 oct 1853-20 oct 1884
/Hungerford,Laura A. 1830-1922   s/o John O.& W.A.
    Maurice C.1853-1906   /Hunley,Golden 26 mar 1937 36y5m5d
    CoH 185th NY Inf   /Hunley,Oscar 27 Jan 1877-26 sep 1913
xHunt,A.R.7 Jan 1939   xHunt,Charles Robert 2 may 1926
xHunt,LaVance 27 aug 1921   xHunter,C.H. 14 apr 1921
/Hunter,Avaline C. 1845-1916   /Hunter,Charles W.8 aug 1848-20 Jun 1909
    G.W. 1844-1915   /Hunter,John SpAm 13th WV Inf-Corpl.
/Hunter,Ruba E.   Julia A. 6 oct 1874 42y1m24d
    30 sep 1888-19 nov 1906   xHunter,Myrtle Mae hall 27 sep 1920
xHunter,Mary 23 aug 1917   xHuntington,Edith 22 dec 1953
/Huntington,Charles P.1861-35 xHuntington,Emily W.7 Jun 1943
xHuntington,H,E.13 Jan 1915   /Huntington,Frances mary 1830-1908
/Hurd,Florence E. d/o C&MA   /Huntington,Farnham Parmelee 1825-1906
  4 feb 1869-8 dec 1915   /Hurley,Homer 1903-1937
xHurd,Emma 17 nov 1925   xHurt,Catherine 13 Jul 1921
xHurt,Kat 11 Jan 1923   xHurt,Mumford 14 dec 1939
xHurts,Emma M.17 mar 1930   xHurst,Eveline 15 may 1923
xHusks,Everett W.26 Jul 1937   /Huss,Kathryn Schoyer 1909-1934
/Hutcheson,Pansy L.Graham   /Hutchinson,George 1841-1916 CoH 14th
    1888-1908 w/o Rev.S.E.   Ky Inf CSA -Com Sgt
/Hutchison,Charley 1884-1916   /Hutchinson,James E. 1913-1936
/Hutchison,Lon H. 1857-1928   /Hutchison,George W.1841-1916
/Hutchison,Luna E.1857-1938   SpAm CoH KY Inf -Com Sgt
/Hutchison,Sidney 1821-1916   xHutchinson,Martha 11 aug 1912
/Hutchison,Tenna 1844-1918   /Hutchison,William L.1874-1913
xHyder,Hugh 1904   /Hyden,Frank M.1 nov 1936 74y5m27d
/Hyder,Clifford H.6/11/1935WI xHylton,Alfred 24 Jan 1939
xHyder,James 16 nov 1924   /Hyman,Eddie
/Hyman,Sanford Barnett 1932-35 /Hysell,Bettie F.1843-1901
/Hymus,Nannie 11 sep 1932   /Hysell,Joseph T.1840-1918
/Ingham,Bettie F.1843-1901   xIngham,G.W.27 apr 1925
/Ingham,Jesse-1865-1878   /Ingham,Sarah J.1832-1914
/Ingham,Joseph T. 1840-1918   /Ingham,Capt.Smith W.1833-1925
xInnaan,Raymond 5 apr 1931   /Ingram,Fredrick Eldon dec 1883s/oMH&CP
xInnman,Harley A.19 mar 1922   /Ingram.George P.1852-1912
xInsco,Ellen 1 may 1931   Helen M.Goeway 14 dec 1891 32y7m4d
xInsco,Emza 1909   /Insco,James 25 feb 1900 65y
/Insco,John W.29 Jul 1891 22y /Insco,Ida 1906
xInsco,Mary Jane 1906   xInsco,Richard 9 apr 1931
/Irion,J.Bert 1860-1938   xIrby,John C.17 mar 1916 inf
xIrion,Lilly Dickie 1/11/1929 /Irving,Lena Belle 8 aug 1931 43y
/Irvin,Walter L.1861-1898   xIrving,Lill 14 may 1090
xirvin,Mrs.J.T.10 Jun 1912   /Irwin,Anna 1867-1925
/Irwin,Ella C.1841-1918   /Irwin,Fredrick B.1870-1937
/Irwin,Harry 1899-1918   xIrwin,Myra 12 dec 1936
xIrwin,Mrs.R.W.11 Jul 1918   xIsaacs,Mrs.Thomas 23 oct 1918
/Izzo,Eva Lena 1891-1918   137

/Jack,Beatrice V. 1855-1911   /Jack,Earl Raymond 18 may 1904-30 oct12
/Jack,Robert Andra 1851-1901   /Jack,Robert A.29 dec 1892-25 nov 1911
/Jackson,Adella 1870-1925   /Jackson,Bertie 25 feb 1934
xJackson,Anna 13 feb 1932   xJackson,Charles A.24 oct 1922
xJackson,Cora L.27 dec 1916   xJackson,Charlotte Rebecca 7 oct 1918
/Jackson,Etta A.1882-1902   /Jackson,Claude L.30 nov 1904-1 oct1922
xJackson,Cransford 11 aug 1923   xJackson,Elizabeth M.29 mar 1920
xJackson,General A.8 Jun 1935   xJackson,Eunia 8 mar 1939
/Jackson,inf 8 feb 1913   /Jackson,James F.18 Jan 1868-17 apr 1936
/Jackson,inf 1915   /Jackson,Joseph 11 oct 1910-25 Jun 1911
/Jackson,Irene Jarrell 1904-1923   /Jackson,Josephine H. 1910-1912
xJackson,Irvin 13 Jan 1920   /Jackson,J.Miller 1890-1934
xJackson,Louise 23 mar 1925   xJackson,Morris 7 may 1926
xJackson,Relevina 17 Jun 1922   /Jackson,Roy 2 mar 1877-31 aug 1906
/Jackson,Rosie B.1886-1906   xJackson,Solomon
xJackson,W.J. 3 dec 1922   xJackson,W.W.17 apr 1915
xJackson,Wiliam 11 Jan 1920   /Jacobs,Charles 30 apr 1939   79y4m
/Jacob,Anna 15 feb 1938 77y   xJacobs,Charles S.26 apr 1928
xJacobs,Robert 2 sep 1920   xJacobson,Jerry 15 apr 1918
xJaeger,Ida F.1863-1939   xJacobson,Mollie 27 Jul 1926
xJaeger,Otto 11 Jun 1941   /James,Alfred CoE 56th OH Inf
xJames,Beatrice 9 Jul 1916 inf   xJames,Bertha L.3 Jun 1921
/James,Bessie 22 Jul 1885   xJames,Charles H.17 may 1927
/James,Edna 1898-1913   xJames,Ellen 10 nov 1924
xJames,George 20 feb 1922   xJames,Gerturde 19 dec 1914
xJames,Harless,30 aug 1926   /James,Jessie O.16 Jun 1886 9y5m28d1d
xJames,Martha Ellen 30 Jun 1931   xJames,Leota Ray 15 sep 1926
xJames,Nelson 28 aug 1922   /James,Sarah B.1879 inf
xJames,William 16 aug 1923   xJames,W.O.2 may 1915
xJamison,Edna 20 nov 1923   /Jameson,James Virgil 1936-38
xJardu,Thomas 5 nov 1921   /Jameson,Vancel Josephine 1905-1938
xJarrell,Annie 26 apr 1915   xJarrell,Clara Ann 6 aug 1924
xJarrell,Ellen 24 feb 1926   xJarrell,George 20 Jan 1914
/Jarrell,Lola V.1900-1919   xJarrell,Mary E.9 dec 1912
xJarvis.Mrs.A.L.2 feb 1924   /Jarvis,Belle M.2 may 1934   67y2m24d
/Jarvis,Alice M.1854-1934   /Jarvis,Floyd W.30 may 1890-22 nov 1892
/Jarvis,Eliza 1823-1892   xJarvis,George 29 Jan 1914
/Jarvis,Ida Beatrice 1869-1913   /Jarvis,George 1816-1900
/Jarvis,James C. 1848-1925   xJarvis,Mrs.J.16 nov 1923
/Jarvis,John W.1865-1937   xJarvis,John 1880-1928
xJarvis,John H.8 Jan 1928   xJarvis,Joshua 9 mar 1918
xJasper,Martha M.1 nov 1931   /Jarvis,Sarah Elizabeth 1851-1922
/Jaswick,James   WWI   xJauch,Bernard 30 oct 1939
/Jaswicz,Joe 5 dec 1920 vet   xJauch,Edith--
xJavins,Alice 30 dec 1925   /Jeandell,Joseph D.1890-1917
xJeffers,Edna 5 nov 1918   xJeffers,Frank 20 dec 1923
xJeffers,Garnette 5 Jul 1924   xJeffers,Grant 28 aug 1924
/Jeffers,Homer 19 sep 1931 WWI   xJeffers,Wiliam 5 may 1922
xJeffery,Theresa 12 aug 1916   xJenkins,Bernard 5 aug 1921
/Jenkins,Clyde,C.14 apr 1935 WWI   /Jenkins,Emma 13 nov 1893-19 Jun 1938H&I
xJenkins,Donald R.25 Jan 1923   xJenkins,Geaolda 19 sep 1922
xJenkins,Harry W.22 aug 1938   xJenkins,Herman 1826-1913
/Jenkins,Julia Holderby 1857-1903/Jenkins,Gen.Albert Gallatin 21 may 1864
xJenkins,Kate 29 Jul 1921   d.Dublin Station,Pulaski Co.VA 33y-CSA
/Jenkins,Kenrick A. 1861-1868   /Jenkins,Julia M.1829-1894

xJenkins,Norma 23 Jan 1923
xJenkins,Mrs.Robt.C.16 nov 1911
/Jenkins,Susan Holderby 1836-1927
xJenkins,Rome Gerturde 31 Jan 34
/Jenkins,Sue C. 1863-1935
xJenkins,William E.29 Jun 1925
/Jenkinson,Donald R.1923 inf
/Jenkinson,Norman L. 1923 inf
/Jennings,J.C.1851-1904
xJennings,Imogene 1 sep 1925
/Jesse,James M.1844-1909
/Jesse,James M.1882-1909
/Jesse,Joshua E.2 may 1938   vet
xJobe,Bessie 17 mar 1932
xJobe,Carlos 22 mar 1920,
xJobe,Otis 20 aug 1932
/Johns,Viola M. 1886-1937
xJohnson,Anna 17 sep 1935
xJohnson,Anna Cara 19 oct 1939
xJohnson,Arthur 12 apr 1938
/Johnson,Benjamin F.1893-1936
xJohnson,Beulah 28 mar 1934
/Johnson,Clarence E.1868-1933
/Johnson,Claude C.1883-1905
xJohnson,Charles 19 nov 1915
xJohnson,Edward S.7 may 1932
/Johnson,Edith Drown 1854-1906
/Johnson,Emma Payne 1858-1927
xJohnson,Ella 3 feb 1931
xJohnson,Elmer E.15 aug 1936
xJohnson,Ester 24 may 1911
/Johnson,Eurania 1870-1934
/Johnson,inf 29 nov 1927
xJohnson,Halley 24 Jun 1909
xJohnson,Harry 29 apr 1917
/Johnson,Huldah S.1826-1904
/Johnson,Ira Eugene 1895-1920
xJohnson,Ira Burl 25 oct 1935
/Johnson,Rev.J.W.1877-1914
       May 25 sep 1917
xJohnson,Katie apr 1896
/Johnson,Lillie M.1890-1911
xJohnson,Lettie 8 mar 1910
xJohnson,Lula T.17 feb 1932
xJohnson,Mammie 23 oct 1913
xJohnson,Margie 23 Jul 1923
xJohnson,Mary 23 aug 1928
xJohnson,Mary 15 Jan 1911
xJohnson,Maxwell 1885-1891
xJohnson,R.M.22 may 1925
/Johnson,Rebecca A. 1850-1913
xJohnson,Rebecca 20 dec 1917
xJohnson,Sadie 11 Jun 1920
/Johnson,S.A. 1900-1911
xJohnson,Wanda 20 Jun 1911

/Jenkins,Laura P.25 aug 1859-11 may 1879
xJenkins,M.J.--
/Jenkins,M.J.28 mar 1823-9 oct 1904w/oBW
xJenkins,Trent R. 2 dec 1934
/Jenkins,Thomas J. 1827-1 aug 1872 45y
/Jenkins,Virginia L.23 nov 1933 57y7m17d
/Jenkins,Dr,Wm.A.1828-18 apr 1877 48y4m
xJenkins,L.W. 11 may 1927
/Jimison,Julia 18 mar 1879-14 nov 1879
xJimison,Tillethia 9 dec 1910
/Jimison,Charlotte E.2 Jun 1872-1873
/Jimison,Harriett 17 Jan 1871-29 may1886
/Jimison,Isaac B.9 may 1880-2 sep 1900
/Jobe,Charley 1 sep 1881 22y s/o SP&RL
xJobe,Charlie 13 Jan 1927
xJobe,Rachel S.7 mar 1934
xJohnson,Albert Moore 26 may 1934
xJohnson,Anna 22 may 1925
xJohnson,Annie V. 1855-1890
xJohnson,Arthur 2 Jul 1927
/Johnson,Audrey 18 sep 1878-28 aug 1930
xJohnson,Buck 1 sep 1912
/Johnson,Belle Critt 29 nov 1936   70y
/Johnson,Calvin C. 1881-1931
xJohnson,Charlotte 2 Jul 1925
xJohnson,Debrathe 17 dec 1928
/Johnson,Dahl G.4 sep 1891   24y7m14d
/Johnson,Della 13 Jul 1939 60y8m10d
xJohnson,Fannie 1905
xJohnson,Frank 3 nov 1919
xJohnson,Frank Jr.16 nov 1915
/Johnson,George W. 9 mar 1886   63y7m15d
xJohnson,George W.1863-1886
xJohnson,Harlen 24 sep 1926
xJohnson,Hattie B.17 apr 1923
xJohnson,inf/Andrew 6 Jun 1910
/Johnson,James Richard 1934 inf
xJohnson,Johanna 2 sep 1928
xJohnson,John W.24 nov 1914
xJohnson,Julius L.8 aug 1917
/Johnson,Lena 1888-1915   w/o S.A.
xJohnson,Lennie M.18 apr 1922
xJohnson,Lennie May 17 oct 1930
xJohnson,Mabel 21 feb 1924
xJohnson,Margie 23 Jul 1923
xJohnson,Martha B.31 may 1930
xJohnson,Mary 25 nov 1918
xJohnson,Mary C.mar 1886
/Johnson,Myrtle 1885-1924
/Johnson,Roy 1898-1917
xJohnson,Richard J.30 oct 1913
xJohnson,Ruth E.Wyont 1929
/Johnson,Thomas P. 1846-1933
/Johnson,Virginia L.1894-1920 w/oD.C.
xJohnson,William 4 feb 1937

/Johnson,William F.1892-1937   /Johnson,William 30 nov 1916
xJohnson,William K.10 Jul 1921   xJohnson,William 4 feb 1937
/Johnson,Wm.14 apr 1936   /Johnson,Wm.L.13 Jul 1891-20 Jul1907WR&CM
/Johnston,Abner T.1850-1926   /Johnston,Annie V.10/6/1855-2/12/1891wJE
/Johnston,Ada P.1861-1931   /Johnston,Ada Sikes 1868-1933
/Johnston,Albert M.Sr.1852-1934   /Johnston,Alice Everett 1902 inf
/Johnston,Anna L.1865-1925   /Johnston,Arthur 1909-1927
/Johnston,B.F.1854-1932   /Johnston,Daniel Webster 26 feb 1938 77y
/Johnston,Emma L,1865-1911   xJohnston,Earnest 27 may 1924
xJohnston,Eliza Jane 16 Jun 1913   xJohnston,Elmore 24 mar 1926
xJohnston,Eugenia D.20 feb 1904   xJohnston,Fanny 11 nov 1926
/Johnston,Kennon 1888-1907   /Johnston,Frank E.11 oct 1934   69y9m9d
xJohnston,Gloria 29 Jun 1925   /Johnston,Lorena E.1886-1924
xJohnston,Harvey 30 aug 1908   /Johnston,John L.11 Jul 1828-22 nov 1906
xJohnston,Ida S.28 Jun 1933   Mary J.6 Jul 1834-5 may 1906
/Johnston,Lucy 1866-1933   xJohnston,Levi 28 Jan 1926
xJohnston,Louise 12 Jan 1935   /Johnston,Maggie 2 feb 1872-30 Jan 1888
/Johnston,Mary J.1856-1932   xJohnston,Martha H.1833-1908
/Johnston,Malinda K. 1843-1923   /Johnston,Maxwell 18 feb 1885-29 oct1891
/Johnston,Mildred 1889-1918   xJohnston,Robert M.22 mar 1922
/Johnston,N.B. 1841-1909   /Johnston,Rebecca 39 mar 1817-8 mar 1843
xJohnston,Rosie 14 sep 1927   xJohnston,Ruth 3 aug 1926
xJohnston,Roy 18 may 1917   /Johnston,S.W.8 mar 1812-16 dec 1883
/Johnston,Sarah E. 1845-1922   /Johnston,Susan L.Gould 1828-1905 w/WmL.
/Johnston,Sarah J.1824-1906   xJohnston,Stephen G.29 Jan 1927
/Johnston,Wm.Paul 1892-1908   xJones,Annie B. 8 oct 1939
/Jones,Anna E.1866-1932   /Jones,Addie Cottle 1893-1933w/o Paul C.
/Jones,Arthur 1872-1936   xJones,Arvine 17 Jan 1912
xJones,C.M.1860-1882   /Jones,Clyde B.1893-94 s/o Col.&Melissa
/Jones,Dora 1867-1906   xJones,David 10 oct 1921
xJones,Edward 7 Jan 1911
xJones,Ethel 13 aug 1925   xJones,Frances A. 6 nov 1932
/Jones,Frank J.1905-1923   /Jones,E.Macon 2 dec 1850-18 feb 1904
    xMrs.Frank 5 mar 1911   /Jones,G.N. 22 Jan 1882 32y
/Jones,Helen M. 1919-1935   xJones,G.H.19 may 1933
xJones,James 30 Jul 1924   xJones,James Joseph 6 mar 1921
/Jones,Jean d14 Jan 1933   /Jones,John A. 1854-1911
/Jones,John S. 1833-1864   /Jones,John P. 31 Jan 1884 42y
   Elizabeth Wurts 1835-1907   xJones,Joseph 7 feb 1914
xJones,Kate 3 oct 1917   xJones,Lottie 6 dec 1937
xJones,Louisa 2 nov 1917   xJones,Lula L, 1896
/Jones,Levi 1854-1937   /Jones,Margaret Barnette 1876-1936
   Emma Blake 1860-1929   xJones,Mrs. 20 may 1917
xJones,Orma Eleanoer 21 nov 1930   /Jones,Mollie 23 feb 1876-19 dec 1922
/Jones,Oscar A.1856-1920   /Jones,Mary Hite 12 Jun 1902-19 Jul 1930
/Jones,Pearl Alice 1884-1904   /Jones,Melissa Miller 1863-1907w/o Col.J
/Jones,Richard S.18869-1906   xJones,Mattie E. 13 aug 1933
/Jones,Robert W.1858-1904   /Jones,Samuel C.12 mar 1873-1 Jun 1904
/Jones,Sallye Mae 1884-1934   /Jones,T.B.10 Jun 1849-2 nov 1904
/Jones,Sarah E.1865-1 may 1935   /Jones,Walter E. 1896-1918
xJones,Walter D.1907   /Jones,William Gordon d 18 dec 1931
/Jopling,Laura 1873-1918   /Jordan,Henry C.23 nov 1879-20 may 1896
/Jordan,Annie A. 1857-1913   /Jordan,Ervin L. 12 Jun 1885 s// SR&AA
/Jordan,Charles R.1853-1945
/Jordan,Dora 1869-1916   /Jordan,Eliza F.24 aug 1820-28 aug 1856

/Jordan, Edward 1864-1914
xJordan, Earl 24 oct 1918
xJordan, Elizabeth 3 apr 1925
xJordan, Harvey 22 Jul 1927
xJorden, John C.28 Jul 1925
xJordan, Mary 31 aug 1928
/Jordan, Roy Jr.24 apr 1917
/Joy, James 1865-1925
/Joy, Homer H.1898-1937
/Joy, Lina 1875-1924
xJulian, Hattie 29 apr 1916
xJustice, James paul 10 Jan 1935
xJustice, Lillian 20 apr 1920
/Kahliel, Helen 2 feb 1936 68y
/Kahn, Berthrand 14 sep 1892   38y
xKaneff, Lillian M.28 oct 1913
/Kanode, Fredrick Stanley 1911-14
/Kanode, Marshall 1845-1923
/Kanode, Mary E. 1854-1928
/Kazee, Sarah 21 apr 1938 69y11m20
xKaygorn, Mike 7 dec 1925
/Kearney, Andrew 1908-1938
/Kearney, John J. 1866-1915
/Kearney, Sarah d 1934
xKeeler, Catherine 21 may 1934
xKeeler, Fred 17 sep 1917
xKeeling, George 12 sep 1908
xkeeling, J.H.18 Jan 1912
xKeeling, Lula 1 mar 1939
/Keenan, Cornelia 1889-1910
xKeenan, Edna Irene 6 mar 1929
/Keenan, Louis C. 1884-1927
/Keenan, Rose, F.1855-1925
/Keenan, Sanford C.1853-1893
/Keener, Francis Annie 1924
xKeeney, L.M. 6 apr 1911
xKeeney, Leah Amm 5 aug 1925
xKeeney, William A.29 Jun 1920
xKees, Myrtle 31 dec 1903
/Keister, Samuel H.1854-1916
/Keller, Adam 1805-1889
    Nancy 1810-1894
xKeller, John T.23 oct 1921
/Kelley, Edward 1878-1920
/Kelley, Henry 1852-1920
xKelley, Henry 1862-1889
/Kelley, Ira I.1884-1913
/Kelley, John 1866-1917
/Kelley, John Sr. 1828-1910
    Nancy 1831-1902
/Kelley, William A, 1868-1910
/Kelling, J.H.1860-1912
    Lula W. 27 feb 1939 74y7m6d
xKemiss, Emma E.26 oct 1927
xKemiss, George 1931

        w/o thomas J.L.
xJordan, Edna 1820-1856********
xJordan, Elizabeth 23 aug 1910
xJordan, Henry C.1879-1896
xJordan, Margaret A.12 Jun 1918
xJordan, Nancy Louise 6 Jul 1925
xJordan, Walter 1 jan 1919
/Joseph, Charles 28 feb 1835-9 aug 1895
/Joseph, Joe 1907-1936
/Joseph, John 1875-1937
xJullah, Mary Elizabeth 30 aug 1926
/Justice, Benjamin H. 1841-1912
    Levise 1841-1923
xKain, Anna 1847-1926
/Kane, Ed.Stuart 17 nov 1859-10 Jul 1938
xKasee, Louise 23 mar 1924
/Kastner, Anna 11 nov 1863-30 dec 1886wH
/Kastner, Paul 1886 inf s/o HA
/Katool, Astanas 1854-1928
xKatool, Joe N.1 dec 1942
xKaylor, Evelyn 26 sep 1923
xkearney, J.J. 1 mar 1932
/Kearney, Michael E. 1897-1931
/Kearney, Dr.W.S.1866-1902
xKeeler, F.S. 22 dec 1922
xKeeley, Robert A.1 sep 1931
xKeen, Elizabeth 3 Jul 1911
xKeene, Daisy 12 Jul 1923
/Keenan, Andrew J.1819-1907
/Keenan, Clay N. d 24 mar 1912 vet
xKeenan, Fannie 1 Jun 1922
/Keenan, Rebecca A.E.1824-1904
xKeenan, Samuel N.7 sep 1907
xKeenan, Sanford 28 feb 1914
xKeeney, Charles--
xKeeney, Mary--
xKeeney, Stella
xKeeney, Walter A. 17 may 1916
xKeller, Albert F.19 Jun 1922
/Kellar, Katherine 19 may 1934 41y4d
/Keller, Frank S. 1859-1922
/Keller, Katheine E. 1901-1912
xKelley, Anna 13 apr 1939
/Kelley, David O. 1829-1891
        Mary Constance 1839-1871
/Kelley, Heath Holman 1863-1891 s/DO
/Kelley, James 1860-1900
/Kelle, Mary E.Kilgore 10 nov 1928
/Kelley, Ruth 1900-1906 d/o FM&Laura
xKelly, Rebecca D.1853-1898
xKelley, Richard 1839-1871
xKelley, Richard 23 may 1938
xKendall, James B.20 Jun 1934 52y3m9d
xKendall, Ruby 29 dec 1915
xKenedy, Amebia 16 Jul 1914

/Kenidy, Inf/RM 1930   /Kennedy, Bent 30 nov 1934 46y9m1d
xKennedy, Emma D.30 Jan 1928   xKennedy, Pat 22 dec 1913
xKennedy, William 19 Jun 1926   xKenner, Eugenia Davie 24 feb 1938
/Kennet, Francis A.6 feb 1883 46y   /Kennet, John C.C.4 dec 1884-29 Jan 1904
/Kennet, Latitia F. 1843-1915   /Kennet, Levi L. 8 nov 1818-4 Jun 1895
/Kennett, Ben Franklin 1861-1930   /Kennet, John H.5 Jul 1845-6 aug 1905
/Kennett, William L.1859-1911   /Kennett, Eliz.10 apr 1886 50y11m25dwPeter
xKennett, Andrew Clay 21 Jan 1933   xKenney, Kate 1 may 1915
/Kenney, Winifred 1861-1932   /Kennon, -- 1888-1907
/Kenney, Maria Gaffney 1859-1932   /Kent, Roderic C.1906-1926
/Kerr, James L.1883-1919   xKent, Flora S.27 feb 1934
/Kerr, Francis W. 1858-1923   xKent, Joy Louise 28 apr 1920
/Kerr, Jean Isabel 1888-1914   xKessee, Earl 3 aug 1921
/Kessler, Etta 1872-1922   /Kessenger, Mamie Ruth 22 may 1937
/Kessler, George Wm.14 Jun 1936   /Kessinger, Almilda M. 1871-1916
xkessler, Dr.Joseph C.30 oct 1941   xKessinger, Jack E.2 Jul 1921
/Ketos, Leora 17 feb 1925 37y   xKessinger, Mona 27 may 1937
xKeyser, Molly S.13 oct 1939   xKessinger, Okay 18 may 1920
/Keyser, Frank 1892-1913   /Keyser, F.M. 3 dec 1849-9 dec 1920
/Keyser, Stephen C.1854-1922   Jennie 22 may 1856-22 Jan 1918
xKidd, Elizabeth M.15 aug 1926   /Kidd, Mollie 1882-1916 w/o Thomas
xKidd, Samuel 10 feb 1919   /Kidd, Samuel P. 1861-1918
xKiefer, Grace E.7 nov 1910   xKies, J.H. 2 mar 1926
xKilcargen, Andrew 8 oct 1924   xKilcoyne, Thomas 5 Jul 1920
xKilcargen, Ann 8 oct 1924   xKilgore, Buddy 1922
xKilgore, Dewitt Jr.9 oct 1917   xKilgore, Elizabeth Ellen 14 Jan 1939
xKilgore, Ida M.24 oct 1928   xKilgore, Jimmy 1937
/Killgore, Joseph 1847-1921   xKilltosston, Joe 4 dec 1926
xKimler, Lucian C.5 may 1925   /Kim, Woo 28 aug 1864-16 dec 1912
/Kincade, Mariah 4 apr 1912   43y   xKincaid, Allen J.9 Jan 1931
/Kincade, Mary Sheets 1889-1915   xKincaid, Mary M. 5 Jul 1914
xKincaid, Robert 9 Jul 1925   /Kincaid, Thos Addison Bell 2 apr 1939 65y
/Kincaid, Inf/oTA&MM   xKincaid, Thomas 1889-1958
xKing, Alford 18 sep 1924   xKing, Alma E. 9 sep 1926
/King, Cora L. 1875-1921   /King, Albert St.C.6 apr 1881 9y10s/oJ&SB
/King, C.N. 1860-1934   /King, Bessie J.15 may 1887 12yd/oJ&SB
xKing, Charles M.29 oct 1934   /King, Catherine M.29 Jan 1879 66y
/King, George A.1866-1921   /King, Carrie Kincaid 1842-1896 w/o SW
xKing, Harriet 1 mar 1925   /King, Esta May 12 may 1935 39y3m12d
xKing, Jane 23 dec 1915   xKing, Lizzie 17 Jan 1916
xKing, Lyda Mason 16 nov 1931   /King, James 20 nov 1830-21 sep 1910
xKing, Mary C.11 feb 1924   Sarah B.30 Jun 1883-18 Jan 1914
/King, M.W.1858-1883   /King, Marion C.12 may 1883 20y d/o J&SB
/King, Lida McClung 1870-1931   /King, Mae 1873-1917
/King, Margaret V.1819-1896   /King, Thomas A.1847-1913
    Moses A. 1819-1899   xKingery, Goldie 29 oct 1918
/Kingley, Lulu F.1 sep 1921   xKingery, John A.25 feb 1922
xKingret, George 8 sep 1931   xKingrey, H.E. 25 mar 1920
/Kinnaird, W.A.1833-1901   /Kinkead, Louise Frances 1882-1917
xKinnard, M.T.16 Jul 1922   /Kinkead, John P.1839-1896
xKinnard, W.T.26 Jun 1934   Martha 1846-1896
/Kinney, Ralph 1909-1911   /Kins, Ralph H.1901-02 s/oBC&EM
/Kinnison, Alexander 11 oct 1931WIxKirby, Fannie 2 oct 1936
/Kinzer, Mamie M.17 Jun 1934   xKirby, John W.11 apr 1925
/Kirk, Charles Z.1874-1925   xKirby, Nancy 15 feb 1931

/Kirk,Charles Jr.1898-1902
xKirk,Douglas 24 dec 1932
xKirk,Paris 26 apr 1925
xKirkley,Annie 23 Jun 1918
xKirksey,Robert 25 Jan 1935
/Kiser,Blanche P.1879-1938
/Klein,Mani 1848-1934
xKlingel,Lucy 2 aug 1917
/Klingel,George F.1847-1928
    Flora Elvena 1853-1900
/Klosterman,Carrie 1879-1918
xKnight,Jane Ann 17 feb 1925
/Knight,Harry C.1907-08s/o JT&ES
/Knight,L.S.25 feb 1903 36y
/Knoll,Elvera 1909-1920
xKoletka,Frank M.21 oct 1939
xKoletka,Jemima Perry 22 aug 1939
/Koontz,Ary M.1872-1921
xKoontz,Arthur 14 nov 1934
xKnootz,Harry E.1905
xKnootz,Mattie 8 sep 1912
xKnootz,Rorah 4 nov 1918
/Krantz,Josephine M.1922-29
xKroger,James 21 nov 1922
xKroger,Sarah 22 dec 1938
/Kraus,Coustav d19 Jan 1892
/Kyle,Mollie 7 apr 1935 70y8m11d
xLackey,Mrs.George 23 nov 1917
xLackey,H.C.11 apr 1926
xLackland,W.E. 22 may 1918
/Lacock,Benjamin 1826-1903
/Lacock,Sarah J.1835-1926
/Lacock,Daniel P.1867-1924
/Lacock,Ralph H.1897-1936
xLafon,Helen 8 may 1934
xLafon,Marie 17 apr 1934
/Laidley,Albert 7 dec 1876 52y6m
/Laidley,A.Ulysses 1828-1895
    Vesta 1823-1907
/Laidley,John B.1849-1898
/Laidley,Marion P.1836-1919
xLaidley,Eliza M.1835-1868
xLair,John A.15 dec 1926
/Lair,David 1883-1930
/Lair,Hallie May 1893-94
/Lakin,Catherine 1843-1910
    Rev.C.H. 1838-1918
/Lallance,John B.1845-1917
    Charlotte C.1850-1938
/Lallance,Edgar 1873 inf
/Lallance,Florence M.1855-1925
/Lallance,Fred 1880-1906
/Lallance,Gerturde 1875-1916
/Lallance,Guss M.1888-1916
xLallance,J.B. 18 may 1917

/Kirk,Ellen 1850-1892 w/o Jerry
/Kirk,Ernest 1883-1903
/Kirk,Zella 1875-1902
/Kirkland,E.Lyle 28 may 1938 34y10m23d
xKittle,J.R.--
xKittle,Mrs.T.B. 1884
xKlein,Bernice E.8 mar 1925
/Kitchen,Mildred 15 Jan 1820-2 dec 1920
    William 1 may 1822-13 nov 1900
/Kneff,Katherine A. d28 sep 1824******
/Kneff,Lyman P. d 13 dec 1823*******
xKnight,Lafeyette 20 jun 1917
/Knight,Lucy 15 oct 1847-23 aug 1896wLafe
xKnight,William 9 jul 1933
/Knowlton,Clement 1893-1897 s/o H&J
/Knowlton,Harry M.1857-1920
/Kohler,Lena Bess 26 may 1938   45y8m
xKonatstine,Konstantive 10 aug 1925
xKoontz,Charles H.3 Jan 1914
xKnootz,I.C.28 Jun 1922
/Koontz,Robert Lester 4 Jun 1939 42y
xKraft,--1923
xKraushopf,T.P. 9 aug 1935
/Kristian,Joseph 18 dec 1938 52y4m4d
/Kromer,Michael A.1881-1926
xKyle,Nola 11 feb 1918
xKyle,Violet 4 Jan 1932
xLackey,Maggie May 28 nov 1926
xLackey,Columbia Douthat 5 nov 1936
/Lackey,Julia Rutherford 1873 3ySR&JC
xLacock,John A.11 apr 1933
/Lacock,James S. 1853-1922
/Lacock,Cassius P.1872-1929
xLacy,Eustacia Jenkins 1873
/Lahey,Dennis E.11 sep 1869-25 nov 1937
xLafon,Patricia 31 mar 1924
/Laidley,Benjamin 1850 2y s/oAl.&Vesta
xLaidley,John B.1823-1907
/Laidley,Thomas 1/1/1756-3/17/1838******
/Laidley,John 14 apr 1863   71y11m16d
    Mary Scales Hite 6 sep 1801-14 nov1876

xLake,John 27 jun 1915
/Lake,Amelia 1849-1908
/Lake,Dorgas 1914-21
/Lake,James P. 1907 CoB 19th VA Cav CSA
/Lake,William 1874-1928
/Lallance,Carmel 1886 inf
xLallance,Charles N.4 oct 1917
xLallance,Emma H.1 aug 1923
/Lallance,Harry M. 1864-1870
/Lallance,Henrietta 1867-1871
/Lallance,Herman Parker 16sep1882-1Jul06
/Lallance,Katie A.1871-72
xLallance,Mary Jessie 12 Jun 1922

/Lallance,Millard F.1851-1916 /Lallance,Martha Ellan 15may1842-25sep06
/Lallance,M.A.1815-1914 /Lallance,Sarah 1836-1915
/Lallance,R.S.1835-1907 xLamb,Charles 16 feb 1920
xLamb,Mrs.Eyle A.22 feb 1922 /Lamb,Eliz.18 aug 1871-21 aug 1905wW.W.
xLamb,Reuben 21 Jan 1932 xLambert,Betty Jane 10 sep 1931
xLambert,Elizabeth 1846-1930 /Lambert,Eliza,A.Swain 1876-1907 w/o RF
/Lambert,Joyce A.8 aug 1933 /Lambert,Minnie 23 may 1938 45y12d
xLambert,L.John 9 mar 1929 xLambert,Nowell 11 Jul 1920
/Lambert,Va.Lee 29 Jul 1938 inf /Lambert,Ralph 1895-1919
xLane,Charles L.25 feb 1920 /Landers,Edwin 1906-1931
/Lane,Fred 1920-1934 /Landers,Frank R.1909-1930
xLane,Mary C.20 Jun 1929 /Lane,Sherdian C.1884-1934
/Lane,Kathleen 1915-18SG&Anna xLane,Nick 26 apr 1914
xLane,Okley 12 may 1932 xLane,W.M.H.28 feb 1923
xLaney,Laura B.13 mar 1930 xLang,Charles 1876-1939
xLang,Florence E.1939 /Lang,Henry 4 mar 1934 590y3m2d
xLang,Max V.8 Jun 1933 /Lang,Jette 7 nov 1812-25 may 1896
/Langdon,Mattie J.1877-1925 /Langhorst,Adaline 1891-1933
xLangdon,Francis 23 dec 1923 /Langford,James K.24 feb 1934 76y
/Langley,Marylee Collins 1918-34 xLanty,J.E. 16 sep 1922
/Lapelle,Joseph 1937 inf /Larrow,Preston 7 feb 1927
xLatham,Dr.C.A. 21 Jan 1930 xLason,Walter 17 apr 1924
/Latham,Mary Rebecca 1898-1929 /Lattin,Nannie R.1871-1912 w/o George M.
/Latham,Melvin Holmes 1859-1937 xLavalley,Ella J.15 apr 1928
xLaub,Isadore 1880-1930 /Lavalley,Benjamin F. 1848-1915
/Lavalley,Charles R. 1844-1917 /Lavelley,Helen Sullings 1849-1931
  CoB 1st Maine HA xLaventhall,Hoda Shons 20 nov 1939
xLavlis,Christina 3 may 1936 /Law,Ernest D.5 mar 1887-9 oct 1914
xLawrence,Betty 27 nov 1923 xLawson,Ada 10 mar 1927
xLawrence,Charles 20 may 1925 xLawson,Alice 21 sep 1926
xLawrence,Herculice 16 feb 1923 xLawson,Isaac 10 mar 1920
xLayman,John 11 Jun 1911 xLawson,Joseph L.4 dec 1929
xLayne,George 13 nov 1937 xLawson,Tommy 6 Jul 1925
/Layne,Hattie Bland 1883-1935 xLawson,William 5 Jul 1934
/Layne,inf 1917 s/oCM&AM /Layne,Cleopratra 19may1890-19mar1910G&E
/Layne,J.M.7/12/1847-7/23/1890 xLayne,Hugh 11 feb 1930
xLayne,Jessie 1890 xLayne,Sarah E.1890
xLayne,Shields 1932 /Lazarus,Sarah S.1886-1933
/Lear,Annie Parks 1837-1927 /Leake,Willie Ona 6Jul1881-5Jul1898JC&EF
xLeap,Margaret 12 mar 1924 xLeake,Elvina F.1861-1899
/Leason,Norval 1890-1925 xLeake,James C.22 sep 1923
#Leckey,Lottie Gunoe 1881-1917
/Lee,Anna L.1 Jan 1873-9 nov 1925xLee,Cander 23 nov 1915
xLee,George W.24 Jun 1930 /Lee,John Jr.1881-1886
/Lee,John 1841-1926 xLee,Howard D.1 sep 1938
  Ella 13 Jul 1889 29yw/oJ.W. /Lee,Lillian 1889-1902
/Lee,Lillie May 1866-1937 xLee,Lizzie 31 dec 1912
/Lee,Mary Joe 1883-84 xLee,Margaret S.29 Jul 1939
/Lee,Verna 1864-1928 xLee,Ruth 28 sep 1921
xLee,W.N.15 aug 1923 /Leece,Charles 1872-1935
xLeedig,inf/oH 13 apr 1909 xLeedom,Mary Louise Thompson 27 apr 1934
xLeete,Ada A. 1877-1889 xLeete,Emma 1864-1911
xLeete,L.W.30 mar 1937 /Lefkowitch,L.1841-1919
xLegg,Henry H.28 Jan 1915 xLegge,Dolly May 23 dec 1927
xLegge,Fred 1 apr 1915 xlegge,Henry H.15 mar 1931

/Legg,Violet 1923-1933
xLeGrand,George 4 Jan 1935
xLegrand,Joseph 22 may 1923
xLeGrand,Maurine 22 Jun 1937
xLegrand,Wanda Lee 17 Jun 1930
xLeighton,Alva Clyde 4 Jun 1930
/Leist,Bertie 1864-1928
/Leist,Sumner E.1887-1929
/LeMaster,Charles A.1891-1912
/LeMaster,Lizzie 1888-1906
/LeMaster,Russell 25 feb 1938 27y
xLenard,J.C. 4 feb 1924
/Leonard,Adam 1834-1925
       Mary 21 apr 1838-26 apr 1905
/Lesage,Mary C.E.8/21/1917 77y
/Lesage,Joseph A.28 Jan 1892 53y
/Lesher,Emma 4/4/1883-18 oct 1934
/Lester,C.A.1844-1919
/Lester,Margaret C.1840-1909
xLester,Norma Eugenia 8/12/1928
xLetulle,Fannie V.1847-1900
/Letulle,James L.1849-1899
       Margaret A. 1853-1864
/Letulle,Josephine 1847-1920
/Letulle,Sarah J.1843-1927
/Levine,Jacob 1871-1936
/Levine,Leibchen 1841-1917
xLevine,Moses--
/Leviskis,Bessie 12/30/1913-9/2/31
/Leviskis,Vitautas 1924-1928
xLevinski,Wete 7 Jun 1928
/Lewis,America 1844-1932
/Lewis,Beahiah 1870-1923
xLewis,C.Q. 20 dec 1937
/Lewis,D.W.
/Lewis,Elizabeth Joy 1932-1938
/Lewis,Eva Marcella 1888-1929wLJ
xLewis,Elsie F.15 sep 1920
xLewis,Emamuel 31 may 1923
xLewis,E.F. Jr.8 apr 1921
xLewis,Hannah 24 Jul 1913
xLewis,Katie 25 mar 1923
/Lewis,Lizzie B.1865-1922
xLewis,Mary 2 aug 1918
/Lewis,Rosa 1851-1933
xLewis,Sarah 21 Jan 1919
xLewis,Spencer J.13 Jun 1932
/Lewis,Van Clark 17 Jul 1924 41y
xLiddy,Mary Ellen 24 oct 1934
xLiggins,Audrey 24 sep 1920 inf
xLiggins,Mrs.J.L.4 Jul 1919
xLigins,Bertha Lee 29 may 1920
/Lilly,Caroline Hall 1903-1930
/Lilly,Joyce 12 may 1901
/Lindemood,Laura 5 Jan 1936 55y

/Legg,Minnie Jo 7 mar 1932 inf
xLegrand,Harvert Jr.23 oct 1924
xLeGrand,Laura 10 feb 1928
xLeGrand,Thomas 1 aug 1924
/Leigh,Lora 1886-87
/Leitner,Jacob 11 Jan 1860-14 mar 1930
/Leitner,Elizabeth 22 nov 1859-24 Jul 23
xLemax,Peter Balson 31 mar 1936
/Lemley,Clorah Catherine 1858-1916
/Lemon,J.W.1868-1921
xLennis,John 23 aug 1924
/Leny,Leon M.27 Jun 1871-6 oct 1892
/Leroy,James N.1910 inf s/oHC&BM
xLeronk,Betty 28 aug 1924
/Lerry,Fannie Broh 1848-1929
/Lerry,Marx 1840-1928
xLeslie,Sarah D.11 mar 1914
/Leslie,John 18 oct 1934 68y
xLeslie,Kenneth 30 may 1919
/Lette,Ada A.3 may 1889 42y11m3d
xLette,Betty May 13 feb 1926
/Lette,Lewis W.9 Jul 1860-28 mar 1937
/Letulle,Victor 11 Jul 1783-21 Jan 1853
       Nancy Forgery 1810-1892(2nd)
       (1st-buried Guyandotte)
xLevy,Marx--
xLevel,Silas 23 Jul 1926
/Levine,Simon 18 may 1861-30 sep 1909
/Levine,David 15 may 1846-25 apr 1909
/Lewis,Alice C.--
xLewis,Rev.A.D.24 mar 1922
xLewis,Alvin 15 mar 1923
xLewis,Chester R.28 Jun 1918
xLewis,Charlie 10 sep 1930
/Lewis,Charles O. 1861-1937
       Hattie I.1865-1921
/Lewis,Ethel L.1898 inf
xLewis,Elizabeth J.16 Jul 1928
xLewis,Ethel 10 mar 1924
xLewis,Fallid 6 Jul 1927
xLewis,Harry 12 sep 1918 inf/o BF
xLewis,Mrs.Harry W. 9 oct 1918
xLewis,Margaret 21 sep 1918
xLewis,Melissa 1929
/Lewis,Mary Steel 24 Jun 1924   34y
xLewis,Sanfirscoo 20 Jun 1921
xLewis,Walter 25 oct 1936
xLewis,William 31 mar 1910
/Light,Rosa L.1878-1937
xLiggins,Bernice 11 dec 1920
xLiggins,Nathaniel G. 1907
xLikins,Ida May 17 apr 19297
xLikins,John 20 feb 1924
xLilly,J.S. 7 nov 1919
xLind,Dr.George D.7 Jul 1929

xLindenmood,A.L. 14 oct 1918   /Lind,Betty Humphries 8 may 1937 76y7m
xLindenmood,Katrine 23 apr 1916 xLindmood,R.L. 10 oct 1937
xLindsey,John 31 Jul 1927   /Lindsey,Fannie R.1855-1937
/Lindsey,James W. 1848-1928   xLindsey,L.Loyd 1 Jun 1918
/Lindsey,Harry R.1882-1920   xLingan,Mrs,H.B.13 oct 1917
xLinkous,Mary N. 7 Jul 1924   xLinville,George 28 Jan 1921
xList,Douglas S.Jr.29 mar 1920   xLittleton,Angelicca 31 Jan 1915
/Littleton,John S. 1875-1918   xLittleton,Henry 19 mar 1912
xLitton,James 11 aug 1921   /Lively,Mary Eliz.25 apr 1925
xLivington,William H. 18 oct 1917/Livingston,Archie 28mar1863-25apr1892
/Loar,Andrew J.1848-1921   xLivington,Lloyd Samuel 31 oct 1919
xLoar,Burke 19 apr 1926   /Lloyd,Bertha Cottle 1884-1902 w/oJW
/Loar,Eliz,Spencer 1863-1937   /Loar,Chester Andrew 1894-1937
xLoar,Helen 1 Jul 1909   xLoar,Lettie 30 Jan 1925
/Loar,Peter H.1852-1905   xLobaldo,Theresa 7 feb 1929
/Lock,Eugene 1912-1918   /Locke,Lola M.1894-1928
xLocke,Ruth Steves 19 dec 1931   /Locke,Thomas P.1 may 1858-25 Jun 1939
xLocke,Zora 19 may 1927   /Locke,Vincent 1914-16
/Lockhart,Abah Evelyn 1917-24AE&AxLockett,Charles 26 sep 1925
xLockhart,Arnold E.28 mar 1933   /Lockhart,Inf 1933
/Lockhart,Charles L. 1867-1926   /Lockhart,Minnie L.1874-1932
xLockridge,Edwin 9 aug 1928   /Logan,Vivian Vesta 12 oct 1935 11y
xLombard,James B.1882-1899   /Long,Allen 1861 CSA Border Ranger
xLombard,Roy Z.6 nov 1926   /Long,Anna Louise 4 mar 1891-13 Jan 34
xLong,Bertha 18 Jul 1927   xLong,Clarence G.18 mar 1911
xLong,Cora E.8 aug 1924   /Long,Florence E. 1846-1939
xLong,J.P.2 Jun 1924   xLong,John 7 Jul 1911
xLong,Lena Thompson 8/18/1913   /Long,John L.16 may 1918-12 Jun 1935
xLong,Ruby 1 Jun 1918   /Lookbill,Alvit L.1856-1918
xLongo,Anthony 11 may 1936   xLookabill,Lulu M.3 aug 1921
/Louderback,Dr.W.H.1845-1906   /Losey,Clarence 6 mar 1888-21 nov 1907
/Louise,Kate 1853-1928   /Louisa,Hannah 15 may 1837-4 apr 1904
/Love,Kate 1853-1928   /Love,Albert C.10 oct 1936 53y7m3d
    Lon 1864 CoE 8th VA Cav CSA /Love,Ann A.19 sep 1833-18 dec 1910
/Love,James S.   /Love,Mildred 25 aug 1904-3 sep 1925
    19 oct 1861-11 Jan 1900   /Love,Minnie F.18 mar 1936 62y
/Lovett,Harvey T.1869-1923   /Love,Peter E.13 Jun 1833-28 oct 1912
xLow,Lucy C.1832-1876   /Love,Thomas L.9 Jan 1864-10 may 1897
xLowe,Addie 4 may 1935   /Lovins,Josephine 7 may 1856-30 Jan 1935
/Lowe,Demaras 1842-1936   James Harvey 10/15/1848-3/21/1935
    xMrs.Demora 11 may 1936   /Lowe,Garfield 1883-1908
/Lowe,Georgia L.1887-1928   /Lowe,Harry 1874-1917
xLowe,Samuel 4 nov 1915   /Lowe,William W. 1871-1911
/Lowenstein,Samuel 1848-1892   /Lowery,Bertie J.1871-1929
xLowery,Chester 24 apr 1926   xLowery,T.C. 13 apr 1919
/Lowther,Julia Drain 1875-1935   /Lowery,Hannibal H.1867-1917
xLowther,Inda 30 Jun 1933   xLucas,Willie Roy 24 sep 1936
/Lucas,Ida W. 1912-1914   /Lucile,Lena 1914-1920
/Lucitt,1835-1859***********   /Lukes,Lucious 28 dec 1938 25y
xLumpy,Margurite 23 may 1918   xLunford,Mrs.G. 16 may 1911
xLunford,Gordon 31 oct 1922   xLunford,James k.26 feb 1934
xLunford,Katie 23 dec 1921   xLunford,Ruby 30 mar 1909
xLupine,Toney 14 Jul 1921   xLusher,E.M. 6 Jul 1926
xLusher,Mathew 23 nov 1910   xLusher,Roxy 1906
/Lusher,Maria Louise 1842-1918   /Lusk,Anna Clark 2 apr 1910 71y

/Lutes,Ernest W.1858-1925
xLutz,E.W. 6 Jul 1925
xLybrook,ch/o O. 13 oct 1915
xLykins,Annie 17 Jul 122
/Lykins,David J.1855-1928
/Lynch inf 1927 s/o CE&LJ
xLynch,Flora 18 oct 1931
/Lyons,Harry J.1877-1916
xLyons,Mary C.7 dec 1933
/Lyons,William A.1825-1887
/Lyons,W.F.5 mar 1865-7 Jul 1893
xMacatie,inf/CA 10 Jul 1915
/MacDonald,James 1857-1934
xMackey,Catherine 1889-
xMaddox,Amelia 1853-1939
xMaddox,James 21 nov 1925
     CoK 16th VA Cav CSA
xMaddy,Edward F.1 Jul 1910
xMaddy,Willie L. 1868-1869
xMadison,Will 14 apr 1935
xMagarillo,Anna 23 Jan 1928
xMaghee,Ruby L.12 dec 1934
/Mahan,Lyle Franklin 1892-1918
/Mahoney,Abbie Courtney 1877-1937
xMahoney,Mrs.Loma P.25 apr 1915
xMaize,inf 11 oct 1920
xMaize,James C.28 apr 1892
/Malick,Frank W. 1889-1890
/Mallon,HUgh J.1887-1932
/Malcolm,Alice Pritchard1860-1935
/Malone,John L.1904-1930
/Malone,Rosa Lee 1884-1927
xMangrum,James A. 12 Jun 1912
/Mann,alfred T.1859-1938
xManning,Clayburn C.7 apr 1931
/Mannon,Ellen 1861-1937
/Mannon,Thomas 1853-1928
xManns,Wallace 27 may 1925
/Mansford,Monroe 1823-1906
/Mantle,Joseph 1870-1937
xMantle,Lowell Joseph 1 oct 1939
/Marcella,Sis.Mary 27 feb 1938
xMarchetti,Frank 16 oct 1939
/Marcum,James H.1842-1926
/Marcum,Eunice V.1841-1885
/Marcum,Herbert M.27 Jul 1935
xMarcum.Lacy 5 Jun 1932
/Marcum,Mary A. 1874-1899
/Marcum,Dr.M.D.1871-1931
/Marcum,Pearlie M.1880-1898
/Marcum,William H.1844-1912
xMarett,E.Lemuel 30 Jan 1938
/Marks,John M.8 Jun 1892 42y6m
xMarks,Lusetia 1923

/Lusk,Susan 6 feb 1850-18 nov 1918
xLusk,Chessie 8 feb 1917
xLycains,Mrs.Polly 1 dec 1924
xLykins,Margaret E.6 nov 1912
xLykins,William P.6 aug 1911
xLyma,inf 8 aug 1921
xLyne,Eugine M.18 feb 1921
/Lyons,Charles J.25 Jan 1935 71y
xLyons,Child Lawrence O.5 dec 1918
/Lyons,Robert M.24 mar 1935 40y8m22d
xLyons,Virginia B.7 dec 1933
/MacDonald,Fredrick A.1873-1913
/Macdonald,Willie B.1876-1938
xMackey,Samuel 1885
/Maddy,Anna 25 apr 1936 69y8m29d
/Maddy,Maria S.9 dec 1833-17 apr 1899
    W.L. 4 dec 1825-15 aug 1890
/Maddy,Mattie B. d/o WL&MS
    17 aug 1869-8 nov 1888
/Magnalio,R.16 may 1883
/Magoriello,Hattie 1898-1919
/Maguet,Mary E.1878-1927
xMaguet,Pauline W. 30 Jul 1936
xMahood,Thomas A. 25 may 1916
/Maier,Fred 1880-1918
/Maine,Howard P.23 Jan 1858-24 dec 1933
/Maize,Ida 30 apr 1924 64y1m17d
/Malick,Samuel 1862-1926
/Malafarina,Joe 16 aug 1895-11 Jun 1923
xMaloney,Claud D. 18 feb 1933
/Malone,Patrick H.1868-1938
/Malone,Sallie M.1863-1932
/Manilla,Angeline F.1928-1929
/Manilla,Evangeline 1928-1929
/Manning,Globe 1881-1931
/Manning,Lizzie 1851-1929
xMansfield,E.W. 20 oct 1926
/Mansfield,Clara Eliz. 5 feb 1934 57y
/Mansfield,Isabel 1861-1911
/Mansfield,Katherine 1896 inf
/Mansfield,W.L. 1854-1922
xMarcell,Flora 28 feb 1923
xMarcum,Elizabeth 30 dec 1922
/Marcum,Emma Wellman 30Jul1854-27dec27
xMarcu,Fred D. 1872-1931
/Marcum,L.Frank 1877-1936
/Marcum,John S.17 Jul 1851-12 mar 1932
/Marcum,Mary E. 1858-1925
/Marcum,Pearl G.1894-1923
/Marcum,Taylor V.1880-1908
xMarcum,William 1916
/Markin,Florence 1905-1917 d/oJL*&Sarah
/Markin,Viola 24 aug 1893-27 aug 1917
xMarksham,Betty J.16 oct 1916

xMarks,Mary 20 feb 1924
/Maroney,A.J.1856-1929
xMaroney,Stephen S. 12 aug 1927
/Maroney,Verena 1866-1915
xMars--2 feb 1899
xMarshall,F.Thomas 30 oct 1911
/Marshall,Jesse 1837-1907
xMarshall,J.W. 29 mar 1914
/Marshall,Mary C.1845-1929
xMartin,A.W. 10 aug 1919
xMartin,Alvina 9 jan 1920
/Martin,C.E. 1871-1924
xMartin,Clarence 5 dec 1918
xMartin,Elizabeth 24 jun 1911
xMartin,Freddie S.29 apr 1938
/Martin,Fay W. 1831-1890
/Martin,George A. 1850-1912
        Sarah C.25 may 1859-1 jan 1903
/Martin,Joseph 1882-1936
/Martin,J.E. 1856-1914
xMartin,J.D.17 mar 1912
/Martin,Lizzie 1883-1916w/oRA
xMartin,L.M. 4 mar 1919
xMartin,Mary 22 jul 1922
xMartin,Melissa 1853-1892
/Martin,Olive A.1849-1888
xMartin,Oliver C.12 apr 1931
xMartin,Richard 1 nov 1927
/Martin,Thomas 1843-1933
        Susan 1845-1923
xMartin,Silvester 2 mar 1918
xMartin,Thomas feb 1930
xMartin,Travillian E. 13 jan 1915
/Martin,Victoria C. 9 apr 1930
xMartin,William Jr.1 apr 1917
/Martt,E.L. 1857-1938
xMarvel,Harvey L.30 oct 1916
/Masinter,Selig Joe 1885-1934
/Mason,John Hite 1855-1907
/Masser,Henry 10 feb 1939 58y6m6d
xMassie,Adam 26 nov 1921
xMassie,Charles M.4 jan 1930
xMassie,Eugenia 26 feb 1934
xMassie,Ida 22 dec 1933
xMassie,Frank 27 jun 1920
/Massie,Henry F.1890-1918
xMassie,Henry 26 jan 1918
xMassie,Henry 21 oct 1918
/Massie,Maggie 13 jan 1935 57y2m
/Massie,Rosy M. 1899-1919
xMathens,Anna 1 nov 1923
/Mather,Bessie A. 1882-1884

xMather,Summer 7 aug 1914
/Mather,Elizabeth 1838-1912

xMarple,A.E.26 may 1919
xMarple,Herbert 29 oct 1925
/Marple,Nora Kessler 1895-1918
xMarple,Margarette 22 Jan 1938
/Marsh,Richard B.sep 1847-aug 1911
xMarshall,Haskell 14 nov 1924
xMarshall,James 22 aug 1938
xMarshall,Mary 8 sep 1923
/Martin,Anthony 1824-1909
xMartin,Abbie 11 mar 1922
xMartin,Anthony 29 sep 1920
xMartin,Chancey 26 jan 1918
xMartin,Clarinda 7 oct 1918
xMartin,Ella 10 feb 1921
/Martin,Freddie S.27 apr 1939 77y1m5d
/Martin,George O.1869-1914
/Martin,George E.27 sep 1891 22y5m2d
xMartin,Harriet 23 dec 1915
xMartin,Inez M.18 may 1919
/Martin,J.F.1855-1926
xMartin,James Henry 11 mar 1931
/Martin,Lucia 1888-1920
/Martin,Lucile Fountain 1890-1915w/ThosW
xMartin,Minnie 16 jun 1927
xMartin,Margaret L.1894-1931w/oThosW
/Martin,Ora 16 sep 1873-6 nov 1936
/Martin,Nora 1858-1918
/Martin,Ruby 8 jul 1911-25 jun 1935
xMartin,Sarah 1859-1903
xMartin,Sarah Jane 7 jun 1928
xMartin,Susan 25 feb 1913
xMartin,Tennessee 13 jan 1924
xMartin,Virginia C.27 mar 1920
xMartin,W.H.1 apr 1917
xMartino,Joseph 1936
/Martindale,Hugh 1848-1934
        Lucinda M. 3 oct 1849-21 nov 1916
xMason,Mrs.C.G.9 jun 1911
/Mason,John Weston 1934-1937
xMassey,America J.30 dec 1910
xMassey,Alex 14 jan 1933
xMassey,Dora 19 feb 1919
xMassey,Ewing 6 dec 1935
/Massey,Irving 4 dec 1937 55y8m16d
xMassey,Sarah E. 25 sep 1930
/Massey,Sylvester 1886-1937
xMasterson,Charles 28 aug 1923
xMasterson,J.E. 13 jan 1922
xMasterson,Mattie 30 jun 1914
xMatheny,David 24 oct 1938
/Matheny,Mary Louise 10 nov 1933 21y
/Mather,Augusta G.25 dec 1827-26 aug 191

/Mather,Emma A.21 may 1848-22 may 1923
/Mather,John H.21 nov 1842-19 may 1899

0

/Mathers,Maud B. d12 apr 1907   /Mather,Oscar W.22 feb 1823-2 mar 1905
xMatherson,Maria 13 jan 1918   xMathews,Altha G.31 mar 1928
/Mathews,Alice 1862-1863   xMathews,Alice E.1 jan 1933
xMathews,Anna 2 jun 1913   xMathews,Daisy 1909-1936
/Mathews,John T. 25 jan 1933 WWI   xMathews,Joseph E. 1869-1925
/Mathews,Letitia 1852-1929   xMathews,Robert P.1898-1939
/Matthews,Delia 1842-1929   xMathews,Samuel V.6 mar 1860-26 nov 1914
/Matthews,Alice Haworth 1857-1932/Matthews,Mary J.3 oct 1836-9 mar 1907
/Matthews,John W.1837-1919   /Matthews,Miles Clifton 1/1/1882-1/25/94
/Matthews,Beryl 1900-1935   /Matthews,Norris 1844-1914 CoK 1st WV Cav

/Matthews,May 1885-1907   /Matthews,R.A.25 oct 1829-24 jul 1894
/Matthews,Mary alice 1900-07 SV&E/Mathews,Robert P.1898-1939
/Matthews,Walter C. 1879-1918   /Mathewson,Delimore 1852-1915
/Mathia,C.M.P.Sister 22 oct 1931   xMathewson,Loretta 4 may 1936
/Matier,Mary 1842-1924   xMathewson,W.P. 23 feb 1915
/Matier,William 1836-1914   xMatthewson,Harriet 1 jun 1916
/Mattox,Franklin 15 may 1936   xMaupin,Henry K.13 dec 1933
/Maupin,A.B.1852-1936   /Maupin,Chapman,W.5 may 1811-5 oct 1900
xMaupin,James H.1864-1897   Matilda F.Hope 23 oct 1824-1 jan 1905
/Maupin,James H.25 oct 1867 inf   /Maupin,America McGinnis   w/o Dr.Wm.L.
xMaupin,Keaton, 8 jan 1931   9 aug 1925-16 may 1885
xMaupin,Nancy C. 2 sep 1930   xMaupin,Maggie Elizabeth 31 may 1910
/Maupin,S.W.1857-1910   /Maupin,Socrates A. 1857-1933
xMaxwell,Belle 15 aug 1939   xMaxwell,Charles Leonard 8 may 1921
xMaxwell,Earnest 22 may 1918   xMaxwell,Ira 2 jun 1925
xMaxwell,Irene--   xMaxwell,J.S. 9 jan 1915 inf
xMaxwell,Mary F. 23 jan 1933   /Maxwell,Robert H.1843-1922 CoK 11th WV Vol
/Mayes,Virginia H.19 jul 1936   /May,Adrain B.Jr. 1937 inf
/May,Belle 1898-1913 d/o VG&Lou   /May,Lillian Rose 6 sep 1933 14y3m19d
xMayhew,Lilly 12 jul 1923   /May,V.G. 1867-1923
/Maynard,Lutie I.1879-1906   /Mayo,Dr.M.L.--
xMaynard,J.M. 26 dec 1925   Susan 14 jul 1828-31 dec 1897
xMays,Amos 17 aug 1825   xMayo,Ruth 13 jan 1924
xMays,Charles W.10 jun 1925   xMays,Henry 1 mar 1929
xMays,Merlin 2 mar 1920   xMays,Nobil 23 jun 1937
xMays,Strother 25 jun 1922   xMcAboy,Lucy 11 jul 1919
xMcAboy,Mary W. 11 dec 1926   /McAboy,Oscar B.22 oct 1860-12 feb 1896
xMcAboy,Melissa 17 jun 1918   /McAboy,W.P. 1858-1921
/McAlhatten,Mary C.1833-1918   xMcAlhatten,william A. 6 may 1939
/McAllister,Ruth 13 aug 1938 67y   /McAlhatten,Rosie B.1870-1917
xMcAllister,Marian H.6 apr 1935   xMcBrayer,Marian 2 dec 1932
/McBride,Martha A.1831-1915   xMcCaffrey,A.S. 15 dec 1921
xMcCaffrey,Agnes 4 jul 1921   /McCaffery,Kelly 26 aug 1935 64y3m28d
/McCaffery,Dr.C.C.1874-1910   /McCaffery,Elmer 1879-1913
xMcCaffery,Mabel 31 oct 1918   xMcCaffery,Wilma 1899-1907
/McCaffery,William D. 1880-1937   /McCaffery,Russell Henry 1912-1934
xMcCain,Laura 11 jul 1925   xMcCall,Alfred 6 feb 1925
/McCallen,William M. 1835-1904   /McCallister,Harlen 1915-1916
    Martha A. 1845-1937   xMcCallister,James 1930
xMcCallister,Lafayette 24 aug 28 /McCallister,Marion H.4 apr 1935   31y
xMcCallister,Maggie A.24 feb 1930/McCallister,Monie Louise 5 apr 1936 10y
/McCan,Thomas J. CoK 56th OH Inf xMcCallister,Virginia E.23 oct 1927
xMcCanha,Ann 1903   /McCallister,Walter L.1894-1929
xMcCann,Alga L.20 mar 1918 inf   xMcCann,Anna 18 dec 1930

xMcCann,C.A. 20 Jan 1919   xMcCann,Garnett 3 nov 1912
xMcCann,Maud 3 Jun 1914   xMcCarter,Ed 1 nov 1918
/McCarty,John CoK 11 VA Inf   /McCarthy,Fannie 29 Jan 1936 55y
xMcCaw,Beauregard 11 may 1913   /McCaw,Mathew H.1865-1917
xMcCaw,Dora 3 Jul 1934   /McClain,Delores Jean 1933-34
xMcClain,F.E. 29 dec 1919   xMcClain,Fred 17 feb 1932
/McClain,Leota 1890-1922   /McClain,Lillian E.1912-1917
xMcClain,Milton 1908   xMcClain,Minnie Merton 20 apr 1936
/McClain,Tempa E. 1902-1919   xMcClane,Carl 4 apr 1919
xMcClane,John C. 15 mar 1921   xMcClane,John M.1896
xMcClane,Julia 1910   xMcClanty,Edith 24 sep 1925
xMcClary,Mary Va.1906   xMcClean,Belle 28 sep 1926
xMcClary,Mamie 1904   xMcClean,Christine I.--
xMcClean,James C.--   xMcClean,Margaret--
xMcClean,William A.6 aug 1939   xMcClintic,Grace C.30 Jan 1921
/McClintock,Chas.Alden 1846-1914 xMcClintock,Grace 2 mar 1911
/McClintock,John Thos.1874-1939 xMcClintock,James P.12 aug 1936
xMcClintock,John T. 1 feb 1939 /McClintock,Jershua Tenant 1807-1904
xMcClintock,Mary 18 feb 1911   /McClintock,Laura Starr 1899-1907
xMcClintock,Mary A,Richey1847-1914/McClung,James Crawford 1839-1908
/McClung,Mary Rosson 1849-1932 /McClung,Martha Atkins 1893-1922
xMcClure,Charles W.28 dec 1930 xMcClure,Mrs.Etta 8 sep 1915
/McClure,Margaret d9 Jan 1934   /McClure,Nancy E. 1886-1934
/McClure,S.Morris 1872-4 dec 1919xMcComas--1891
/McComas,Armetta 1877 inf   xMcComas,Agnes 8 apr 1927
/McComas,C.H.6 may 1868-8 Jan 1891/McComas,America 29 dec 1936 79y1m12d
xMcComas,Elizabeth 21 apr 1922 /McComas George W.Dewey 1898-1927
/McComas,Elizabeth 1887 inf   /McComas,Eliz.A.13 nov 1844-23 Jul 1914
xMcComas,.Everett 1 oct 1936   w/o D.D.McComas 19 dec 1932
/McComas,George J.1863-1921   /McComas,James Orville 1904-1927
xMcComas,Liza 1901   xMcComas,M.F. 11 oct 1922
xMcComas,T.J. 1891   /McComas,Minnie L.17 Jul 1878-25 Jul 03
/McComas,Samuel C. 1875-1877   xMcComas,Walter 1891
xMcComb,Nadine 24 apr 1942   /McComb,R.Lee 1868-1920
xMcComb,Robert Lee 8 Jan 1933   xMcConnell,Blanch 13 oct 1910
xMcConnell,Henry 22 aug 1919   xMcConnell,Lola Mary 3 aug 1928
/McConaughy,Hugh 1852-1936   /McConnell,James K 16 may 1860-1880sW&M
    Sophia 1852-1928   /McConnell,Mary A31 dec 1830-24 may 94wW
/McCormick,Alexander C.1847-1926 /McCormick,Bettie A.1855-1928
/McCormick,Dickie 1883-1887   xMcCormick,Mrs.Guy 1 mar 1910
/McCormick,Phebe 1792-1874   xMcCormick,Virgie 24 mar 1912
    Levi 14 nov 1868 82y5m   xMcCowen,Omanta 28 oct 1916
/McCow,Dora Ramsey 1874-1934   /McCowan,Beulah M. 1898-1937
xMcCoy,Georgia 28 nov 1936   /McCowen,Myrtle M. 1876-1908
/McCoy,Anna Wiatt 1853-1928   /McCoy,Samuel Edwin 1845-1930
/McCready,Maude H.1874-1928   /McCreery,James C.1856-20 apr 1893 37y
/McCready,Thomas 1863-1928   xMcCrosky,Mrs.Robert 5 feb 1915
xMcCullough,Frank F.19 may 1924 /McCullough,Howard 1867-10 Jul 1888GW&SJ
/McCullough,Fannie M.1833-1910 /McCullough,Flora 18 aug 1897-18 aug1906
/McCullough,George W.1833-1917 xMcCullough,George W.15 Jun 1916
/McCullough,J.W. 1843-1883   /McCullough,P.H. 1872-1919
/McCullough,Mary 1853-1933   /McCullough,P.H.12 Jul 1816-30 may 1892
/McCullough,Sarah J. 1834-1921 /McCurry,Dallas R. 1887-1937
/McCurdy,B.F. 1860-1902   xMcDade,Paul 12 apr 1935

151

/McCurdy,Clara 1858-1938
/McCurdy,Lillian 1898-1918
xMcDaniel,Annie L.30 nov 1920
/McDaniel,Anna 1832-1919
xMcDaniels,Maurine B.30 nov 1936
xMcDaniels,Phyllis 6 dec 1919
xMcDelda,Katherine Elma 18 Jun 14
/McDonald,John F.20 Jan 1936 58y
/McDonald,John W. 1907-1936
/McDonald,Fredrick L.1873-1913
/McDonald,James 1857-1934
/McDonald,Willie B.1876-1938
xMcDonie,Charles B.23 dec 1924
/McDonie,Madeline Fae 1913-1920
xMcDougal,Thomas T.8 Jan 1929
xMcDowell,J.E. 18 feb 1915
xMcDowell,Minera 23 oct 1927
/McElroy,Catherine 1866-1928
xMcElroy,John F. 2 may 1925
xMcEwen,James F. 23 Jun 1926
xMcFadden,George 16 dec 1925
xMeGenety,C.C.17 Jun 1922
/McGhee,Laura C.1863-1927
xMcGhee,Charles E.10 may 1937
xMcGhee,Shriffie A. 7 dec 1914
/McGhee,Major 1871-1923
/McGinnis,A.T. 1861-1924
/McGinnis,Eva 1866-1874 BD&SE
/McGinnis,Daniel J.1853-1928

xMcGinnis,Flavin J.21 Jun 1933
/McGinnis,Ira James 1912-15
/McGonigal,Sue 1860-1928
        J.J.1855-1912
/McGowney,Ralph C.1910-1926
xMcGraw,John P.7 oct 1936
xMcGraw,Wanita 28 sep 1926
xMcGuire,Abigal 13 may 1923
xMcGuire,Harrison 22 dec 1929
xMcGuire,Harrison,26 Jul 1912
xMcGuire,William 12 Jun 1935
xMcIntosh,Annie 1877-1887
/McIntosh,Charles W.1863-1920
/McIntosh,Edith E. 1873-1938
/McIntyre,Kathrien 1827-1911
/McIntyre,Thomas 1823-1916
xMcKellar,Eliza C.2 dec 1918
/McKellar,Clyde Cary 1891-1918
/McKeller,Jennie 1863-1938
xMcKendree,Louise 24 nov 1921
xMcKendree,Samuel 1 apr 1919
xMcKenzie,Mary 29 dec 1922
xMcKenzie,Sarah E. 25 may 1922
/McLaughlin,Caroline 1840-1919
/McLaughlin,James S.1839-1915

/McDanial,Margaret Grove 1917-1937
    James Lee s/o Margaret
/McDaniel,Solom J.CoB 31th VA Inf CSA
xMcDaniels,Ed 4 Jan 1918
/McDaniels,Fletcher C.1853-1917
/McDermott,Patrick J. 1892-1939
/McDermott,Patrick J.1928 inf
        Michael F. 1928 inf
xMcDonald,F.A.7 Jan 1913
xMcDonald,Frank 15 dec 1937
xMcDonald,Rebecca 19 mar 1917
/McDonie,Bonella d1926
xMcDonie,Lelia M.9feb 1935
xMcDorman,Elizabeth 16 feb 1918
/McDowell,Frank 16 sep 1875-1 mar 1926
/McDowell,Frank 12 dec 1932 49y1m24d
/McDowell,Robert 3 Jul 1935 42y
xMcElroy,Francis 21 Jan 1938
xMcElroy,Sarah K.29 Jan 1928
xMcFadden,Charles 25 Jan 1927
xMcFadden,Rosa 3 dec 1936
/McGaffrey,A.S. 1848-1921
/McGaffery,Agnes Harless 1853-1921
xMcGinety,C.C. 2 nov 1913
xMcGinety,Elizabeth--
/McGinnis,Arminda 1867-1920
/McGinnis,B.D.1822-1908
    Sarah E. 1842-1900
/McGinnis,Emma Beuhring 8/22/1858-6/21/1890

xMcGinnis,Julia M.6 aug 1918
xMcGinnis,Kate H.1844-1884
/McGlathery,Kate 1854-1911
/McGlathery,Louis S.1854-1933
/McGlathery,Will C.2 Jun 1878-28 may 1904
/McGue,Lora Ellen d29 mar 1936
/McGue,Oscar James 14 Jul 1934 inf
xMcGue,Samuel L.14 Jan 1934
xMcGuire,Harrison, 30 Jan 1916
xMcGuire,L.25 sep 1920
/McGuire,William H 22 dec 1929 44y9m21d
/McHenry,J.W.28 apr 1891 50y
xMcIntosh,Cornelia 10 Jan 1936
xMcIntosh,George R.--
xMcIntosh,Robert E.12 apr 1917
xMcKee,Calvin 10 Jul 1925
xMcKee,Clifford C.20 oct 1921
/McKendree,George 1834-1908
xMcKendree,George 1890-1909
/McKendree,Irene McComas 1843-1913
/McKendree,Lucy Garland 3 may 1935 62y
/McKinley,Sarah Evans 1849-1922
/McKinney,Maud M. 1888-1937
/McLaughlin,Harry A. 1808-1902
/McLaughlin,Mary E. 1877-1885

151

/McLellon,Joseph L.1858-1897   /McLaughlin,William J.1867-1929
xMcLellon,Joseph L. 1858-1897   xMcLonyklem,--18 sep 1924
xMcLellon,J.G.Jr.30 oct 1914   /McLeod,James Wm.11 apr 1938 51y
/McMahon,George W.31 dec 1884 31/McMahon,Jessie Dusenberg 4 aug 1935 76y
xMcNally,Lucy 28 nov 1939   /McMillen,America E.17 Jun 1841-6 may1904
xMcNeely,Madeline 1 nov 1925   /McMillen,Archibald J.29 apr 1827-2 apr78
/McNeer,Marvin R.1882-1935   /McMillen,Egede C.10 nov 1864-21 mar 1904
xMcNeer,Kathryn 27 feb 1951   /McMillen,E.M. 1858-1921
/McNervey,William R. 1882-1923   /McMillon,Margaret Champion 1854-1935
/McNulty,Alice E. 1907-1920   xMcNichols,Henry 8 nov 1939
/McNulty,Charles W. 1860-1933   xMcVickers,J.A. 8 oct 1912
xMcVay,--15 Jan 1918   /McVickers,Dorothy Theresa 1917-1932
/McWorther,Louis P. 1854-1936   /McVickers,Martha 1867-1939
xMcWhorter,Missouri E.5 Jun 1938   /McWilliams,Elva Va.1854-1934
xMcWhorter,Sarah 21 nov 1931   /McWilliams,Robert L. 1880-1932
xMead,Bessie 27 Jan 1933   /McWilliams,Robert W.1854-1913
/Meador,John Henry 1850-1930   xMeadows,Betty Lee 6 Jun 1917
xMeadows,Doris V.1910-1929   xMeadows,Dorothy 6 nov 1918
xMeadows,Ethel 21 may 1925   /Meadows,George Lyell 1898-1924
/Meadows,Emily A.1831-1906   xMeadows,Francis 7 nov 1923
xMeadows,Henry 7 nov 1923   /Meadows,Guy D.14 oct 1934 WWI
/Meadows,H.W. 1858-1932   /Meadows,James Goebel 1900-1927
/Meadows,Isabelle 1856-1931   /Meadows,John L.7 oct 1863-6 aug 1901
xMeadows,Ireland 22 mar 1916   xMeadows,James 27 Jun 1919
xMeadows,Leslie 27 nov 1919   xMeadows,Luville 18 feb 1924
xMeadows,Mary 10 nov 1920   xMeadows,Mary M-3 Jul 1932
xMeadows,Nancy J,19 nov 1920   xMeadows,Thomas E.15 Jan 1932
xMeadows,Virginia 2 apr 1926   xMeadows,W.E.7 sep 1926
/Mearns,Maude Greenwell 1884-1911   /Medby,Bessie 25 Jan 1933   39y11m24d
xMears-Ed.29 dec 1917   /Medley,Fredrick H.1872-1926
/Meddings,Edna W.1908-1924 d/oJW&A/Medows,G.W. d1917
/Meek,Charlie Burgess 7/13/1938 54yxMefford,Elizabeth 11 Jan 1930
xMefford,Charles J.Jr.22 Jun 1920 /Mefford,Kenneth 6 Jan 1938 inf
xMefford,Thomas 9 feb 1935   /Mehale,Charles J.Jr, d1918
/Meisel,Clara d1920   /Mehrle,Clara E. 1 may 1933 75y10m13d
xMeisel,Joseph 1920   /Mellert,George 1861-1930
xMeredith,Melvin 18 dec 1912   /Mellert,Missouri E.McWhorter 1859-1934
xMerick,James N.27 aug 1925   xMers,Charles E.17 Jun 193
xMerrell,Va.Lee 27 aug 1930   /Mers,O.E. 17 Jun 1938
/Messenger,Hiro O.1846-18 apr 1891 xMers,Christian 7 feb 1922
        CoG 45thWV Vol Inf   /Messersmith,Elsworth 1903-1917s/oGL&H
xMessinger,Frona Waugh 20 nov 1931xMessersmith,Ellen 8 oct 1932
/Messenger,Sarah L.2 may 1881HA&M /Messersmith,G.L. 1878-1923
xMessinger,Joseph 13 apr 1924   /Messersmith,Harry E.1883-1918
xMessinger,Margarite 1 Jul 1935   /Messer,Virgie
xMestel,Frederick J.6 Jan 1934   /Metheny,David 21 oct 1938   45y3m23d
xMetcalf,Bertha 10 aug 1935   /Metheny,James Virgil 17 Jul 1932 65y
xMetaski,Paul 23 feb 1930   xMetheny,Mary Louise 12 nov 1933
xMyers,Agnes 1889-1897   xMyers,Charles R. 23 Jan 1939
xMyers,Esker 1900-1920   xMyers,Fred 1886-1921
xMyers,Mattie 1883-1918   xMichaels,Daniels 14 dec 1939
/Mickens,John 1844-1914   xMickens,Daniels 19 dec 1917
xMickens,Mollie--   xMiddlebrook,Viola 17 Jan 1912
xMidish,Mich 10 sep 1923   xMidkiff,Ann 15 sep 1920

/Midkiff,Allie Fair 1890-94
xMidkiff,Gordon 8 Jul 1910
/Midkiff,Solomon, 1854-1921
/Midkiff,Susan H.1857-1921
/Miles,Bert E.J. 1903 inf
/Miles,Henry Edgar 1877-1914
/Miles,Lee S. b1861
xMiles,Jennie 20 aug 1926
/Miles,Nannie M. 1864-1921
xMiller,A.A. 24 oct 1939
/Miller,Anne M. 1826-1913
xMiller,Blanche 3 aug 1915
xMiller,Catherine 15 Jul 1924
/Miller,C.I. 1887-1920
/Miller,Donald E. 1915-1919
xMiller,Eugenia 23 aug 1932
xMiller,Eva C.6 Jan 1933 50y4m6d
xMiller,Fanny 1905
/Miller,Florence I.1848-1909
/Miller,Joseph S.1848-1921
xMiller,Isaac 26 mar 1916
/Miller,Leo 1842-1929
xMiller,Mrs.James P. 21 Jan 1918
xMiller,J.R. 11 aug 1910
xMiller,Kent 25 dec 1904
xMiller,Mary E. 1850-1924
/Miller,Mary E. 12 apr 1852
xMiller,Mary E. 19 feb 1942
/Miller,Morgan 1846-1917
xMiller,Peter A.23 oct 1921
xMiller,Robert 2 dec 1913
/Miller,Rosa Belle 1868-1881
/Miller,Salome 1850-1913
xMiller,Teresa 8 Jan 1923
xMiller,W.C. 1855-1897
xMiller,Wm.C. 23 feb 1928
/Miller,A.D. 1856-1921
/Mills,Carl A. 1896-1918 WWI
xMills,Harry C.13 may 1928
/Mills,James 1838-1894
/Mills,James P.Sr.1824-1903
/Mills,James P.Jr.1850-1928
xMills,Laura 8 sep 1920
/Mills,Lucinda F. 1846-1915
/Mills,Lucy 1856-1933
/Mills,Maria E. 1840-1910
/Mills,William L.1882-1918
/Mills,Willie 1884-87
/Milstead,Clarence 1934-38
xMilton,Nannie 28 may 1917
xMinor,Isaacs 31 dec 1937
/Miser,A.J. CoE 6th OH Inf GAR
/Miser,Eano 1879-1926

/Midkiff,Archie 1896 inf
/Midkiff,Lillie M. 1870-1896
xMidkiff,Robert M. 30 mar 1934
/Midkiff,William 1866-1896
/Miles,Anna M. 1 nov 1831-17 may 1898
    M.E. 2 apr 1829-25 mar 1902
xMiles,Ettie 28 aug 1938
/Miles,Sarah Maupin 1857-1909
xMiller,Bathrim 13 aug 1927
/Miller,Barbara Ann 24 Jan 1933 4y
xMiller,Belle H.5 Jul 1892
xMiller,Bettie G. 17 feb 1925
/Miller,Cecelia A.24 dec 1855-16 may 94
/Miller,Eliza A.5 aug 1817-24 Jul 1898
xMiller,E,Homer 16 Jan 1922
xMiller,Emily 28 sep 1919
/Miller,George F.13 mar 1884-6 sep 1910
xMiller,Harry 16 aug 1915
xMiller,H.L. 1817
/Miller,H.H.2 dec 1813-6 Jun 1904
xMiller,James I.10 Jan 1935
/Miller,Dr.James 5 dec 1880-6 Jan 1935
xMiller,James T. 18 oct 1918
xMiller,Katherine 13 aug 1927
xMiller,Lucile 11 Jul 1921
xMiller,Lucy 14 dec 1923
/Miller,Lucie B.9 may 1856-8 Jan 1888
xMiller,Margaretta 16 oct 1911
/Miller,Paul 24 mar 1925 WWI
xMiller,Paul R. 27 mar 1921
xMiller,Russell 26 Jul 1917
/Miller,Rebecca M.1831-1880 w/o HL
/Miller,Sarah A.Chapman w/John G.
       31 Jun 1810-4 aug 1855
/Miller,W.J.Jr.3 Jan 1850-4 dec 1917
/Millirows,Mary B.1860-1913
/Mills,Charles 20 feb 1880   36y6m23d
     /Mills,Daniel 3 Jan 1937 71y29d
/Mills,Dora 7 sep 1887 inf d/oJL&J
/Mills,Jennie 1871-1926
/Mills,Juan L.1861-1936
xMills,John 1861-1936
/Mills,Lizzie N.12 apr 1871 w/o SO
/Mills,Lola Eva 1892-1893 d/o SO&LN
/Mills,Ray H. 1893-1939
/Mills,Mariah G.1825-1920
xMills,Nevada 28 sep 1919
xMilstead,James W. 8 apr 1926
xMilstead,Ben 26 nov 1925
/Milton,Samuel 17 Jun 1827-14 feb 1886
xMinor,Ruth P.20 nov 1930
xMiser,James G.23 Jun 1921
/Miser,Matthew 1879-1929

/Miser,Sarah 1850-1937
/Mitchell,Arthur P.1840-1912
xMitchell,Catherine 3 Jul 1910
xMithcell,Claud P.1874-1876
/Mitchell,Emelia B.9 oct 1920 5y
/Mitchell,E.Spencer 17Jan1887 13y
/Mitchell,GL&EJ 1888-1901

xMitchell,Harold 30 apr 1937
xMithcelll,Hugh 3 Jan 1933
/Mitchell,Lona calhoun 1875-1928
xMitchell,Lula 11 apr 1922
/Mitchell,Marshall C. 1893-1894
xMitchell,Rowena 5 Jun 1930
/Mitchell,Robert 9 mar 1938 42y2m
xMitchell,Thomas 1893-1910
/Mitchell,Thomas 1889-1900s/oGL&FJ
/Mize,Stella 1897-1908 d/oFB&JB
xMize,John D. 2 Jun 1911
/Moatz,Norman 1908-1911
/Moesser,Donald F.11 dec 1933
/Mollar,Maddalena 1855-1925
/Molter,Conrad 1839-1926
xMolter,Edward 17 Jan 1920
/Molter,Elizabeth 1844-1912
/Molter,Louis 1834-1907
/Molter,Mary 1836-1903
xMoltar,Minnie 22 aug 1925
/Monk,Dale Carter Jr.1922 inf
xMoody,Pauline 4 Jan 1938
xMoore,Alfred S.23 sep 1934
/Moore,Cathleen
/Moore,Dabney J.1848-1911
/Moore,Dorothy Jean 1922-27
xMoore,Harvey 2 may 1938
/Moore,inf 1913-14 s/o JF&Belle
/Moore,Isaac H.1842-1926
/Moore,Kate P. 1847-19115
/Moore,Mary A. 1841-1930
/Moore,Mary M. 1889-1929
xMoore,Mahala 12 feb 1939
xMoore,Mosie 24 sep 1912
xMoore,Rosie 8 nov 1924
xMoore,Sarah E.1841--
/Moore,Wesley 1831-1941
xMoore,Wesley 25 mar 1924
/Morean,Curtis 18 oct 1933 44y7m17
xMorelland,Alfred H.16 Jan 1914
/Moreland,Charles W.1871-1915
    Anna M. 1867-1933
/Moreland,Fred L. d1895 s/oCW&AM
xMoreland,Joseph H.13 apr 1934
xMoreland,Millie 26 dec 1903
/Moreland,Susie 1868-1917
xMoreland,Susan 9 nov 1916

/Miser,Virginia 1883-1914 w/o AC
/Mitchell,Annie 8 aug 1884-13 Jun 1927
/Mitchell,Cesko 4 mar 1894-22 sep 1911
/Mitchell,Charles M.7 oct 1878-15 Jun92
xMitchell,Edward 29 dec 1937
/Mitchell,Eliza T.24 sep 1814-12 sep 86
/Mitchell,Elizabeth M.10/24/1820-1/21/09
/Mitchell,George H.11/10/1899-9/10/1908
/Mithcell,I.H.27 Jun 1876 28y8m8d
/Mitchell,Leah H.1899-1903
xMitchell,May E. 30 may 1927
/Mitchell,Minnie 28 dec 1891-13 oct1908
xMitchell,Sam 21 mar 1922
xMitchell,Samuel 31 may 1915
/Mitchell,William 1865-1917
    M.Olive Wells 1870-1912
/Mobayed,Albert 1873-1935
xMobayed,Ralph 20 dec 1936
/Mobus,Frederick 1899 inf
/Mobus,Leslie 1889-1893
/Mobus,S.Edith Wells 1868-1937 w/o Geo.
xMolter,Fredrick 13 aug 1918
/Molter,Katie 2 feb 1873-25 mar 1900
/Molter,Linnie 1877-1902 w/o C
/Molter,William 1835-1915
xMolter,William C.1867-1940
xMondania,Lurge 16 mar 1926
xMontgomery--12 Jan 1917
xMooney,Wm.H. 6 oct 1909
xMoore,Columbia 1 apr 1933
/Moore,Charles T. 1874-1912
/Moore,Elias 1838-1907 CoC 4th Reg USA
/Moore,Estella 1888 inf
xMoore,Estella 4 oct 1936
/Moore,Isabella Hite 1821-1907
/Moore,Laquince M. 1847-1935
xMoore,Lariunie 2 sep 1925
xMoore,Lenora 27 nov 1930
xMoore,Mabel Everett 30 dec 1924
xMoore,Minnie 22 apr 1933
xMoore,Myrtle 10 sep 1924
xMoore,Sarah E.1 feb 1928
/Moore,Samuel T. 27 may 1843-24may1889
/Moore,Wm. Wm.D.6 feb 1873-15 may 1906
/Moore,William 5 may 1938 12y
xMoorman,Elizabeth L.22 oct 1919
xMoreland,Anna L. 28 dec 1930
/Moreland,Harry G.1897-1918
/Moreland,Wm.H. 1857-1928
    Lora A. 1859-1927
xMoreland,mary G. 15 nov 1918
xMoreland,Robert L. 14 aug 1920
xMoreland,Tennie 17 Jun 1925
/Morgan,Arnold E. d1918

xMorgan,Alice 30 Jun 1934   xMorgan,Curtis 21 oct 1933
/Morgan,Charles Henry 1875-1938   /Morgan,Chloe Gardner 1855-1917
/Morgan,Charles L. 1887-1932   xMorgan,Isaac S.16 nov 1931
xMorgan,Mrs.M.E, 5 mar 1916   /Morgan,Orphia E.1856-1928
/Morgan,Maggie 1877-1935   xMorgan,Natalie J.21 aug 1930
xMorgan,Wiliam 20 feb 1920   /Morin,Letha 11 mar 1938   42y1m13d
/Morison,Thos.W. d18 Jul 1937   /Morris,Alfred E. 1877-1934
/Morris,Anna Bell 1870-1920   /Morris,inf 7 apr 1928
/Morris,Catherine 1910-12   /Morris,C.D. Col 8th VA Cav CSA
/Morris,C.H.30 Jan 1891 46y9m18d   /Morris,Daisy A. 1880-1929
     Mary E. d19 Jan 1874   xMorris,Daniel C.2#Jan 1932
xMorris,Effie 18 may 1925   xMorris,Daniel M. 2 Jul 1932
/Morris,Elihu 1872-1896   /Morris,Elijz L.1845-1937
/Morris,Emma 1879-1921   /Morris,Eva 1 apr 1872 d/o CH&ME
/Morris,Frances A. 1850-1938   /Morris,George W. 1848-1924
xMorris,G.H. 1845-1891   xMorris,Herman 24 Jul 1930
/Morris,Harry B.   /Morris Johnny 13 apr 1938 CSA 24th AL
/Morris,John O. 1845-1913   xMorris,James Arthur 25 sep 1925
xMorris,Maria 4 dec 1919   /Morris,Linsdey Sheldon 1901-1918RL&L
/Morris,Maggie 11 Jan 1886 CH&E   xMorris,Maud A. 9 nov 1933
xMorris,Mollie 13 sep 1911   xMorris,Moses 13 dec 1937
/Morris,Sudie S. 1868-1905   xMorris,Robert L. 24 nov 1931
xMorris,Sarah E.18 Jan 1931   /Morris,Stewart 15 mar 1886 CH&Einf
xMorris,William B.22 apr 1919   xMorrison,Billie Joe 13 may 1921
/Morrison,Cleo A. 1899-1930   /Morrison,Sarah C.1871-1936
/Morrison,S.N. 1867-1930   /Morrsion,Thomas W. WWI
xMorrow,Alice B.1932   /Morrow,Charles H.
/Morrow,D.L. 1847-1928   1839-1916 CoF 173D Reg OVI
/Morrow,Betty 24 feb 1928   Henrietta M. 1836-1912
/Morrow,Ruth V.1891-1928   /Morse,David M.1889-1913
xMorton,--- 3 aug 1918   xMorton,James 16 mar 1935
xMorton,Charles 20 feb 1922   /Morton,Cora A.9 oct 1873-5 dec 1902
xMoses,Manda B.21 oct 1939   xMosby,Samuel 29 may 1913
/Moses,John H.1845-1899   /Mossgrove,Marian M.4 mar 1830-7Jun1898
xMosis,Latchie 12 sep 1923   xMosgrove,George 21 Jul 1926
/Mossman,Dan A. 1860-1928   /Mostel,Freaerich 4 Jan 1934 74y
/Mossman,John W. 1857-1919   xMotier,Frank J. 9 dec 1931
/Mossman,Zalissa 1897-1929   xMotier,Mary 7 dec 1924
xMoton,Elizabeth 4 feb 1925   xMotier,William 1836-1914
/Mount,Will 1872-1938   xMowery,Maude 21 nov 1919
xMoyer,Alie 30 Jul 1924   xMoyle,Laura 7 dec 1910
xMoyer,J.J. 23 mar 1916   /Moyle,Maggie 1879-1897 d/oWF&G
xMueller,A.L.19 dec 1921   xMullen,Isabell D.1888
/Mullen,G.Cecil 1900-1938   xMullen,Joseph 11 apr 1917
xMullen,Margaret--   xMullen,Nettie 17 sep 1923
/Mullen,inf 1911 s/o JC&M   /Mullens,Paul Carol 1 nov 1930 inf
/Mullen,Mary Eliz.1870-1938 w/oJC xMullen,Richard D.28 sep 1926
/Mumford,Minnie L. 1880-1918   xMumms,Mattie 20 mar 1933
xMurell,Evaline 22 may 1923   /Murdock,Ralph Atlee 1914 inf s/oIN&ML
xMurphy,Betty Joe 23 dec 1927   xMurphy,Bewey 1924
/Murphy,James 28 Jan 1939 75y6m24d xMurphy,Mabel 8 oct 1919
/Murphy,Mae Evans d14 oct 1925   /Murray,Bertha Isabell 1879-1928
/Murrell,Mary C. 1844-1923   /Murray,James Harry 1874-1928
/Murrell,Bennett DP 1845-1910   /Murray,Mary Alice 1906-1910

/Murrell,James WL 1870-1895   /Murray,Sallie A.29 sep 1836-5 aug 1910
xMurrell,Walter H.22 feb 1937   xMurry,Sadie 6 mar 1922
/Murrill,C.S. 1811-1903   xMurth,Miss M.L. 31 jul 1935
    Elizabeth 1816-1897   xMuth,Lucy 14 dec 1935
/Myer,Agnes 1889-1897   xMuth,Mary 14 dec 1935
/Myer,Charles H.1864-1897   /Myer,Esker 1900-1920
/Myer,Charles R. 1856-1939   /Myer,Fred G.1886-1921
/Myers,Alice 1845-1913 w/oJ   /Myer,Mattie 1883-1918
/Myers,Annie M. 1884-1910   xMyers,Benjamin 9 sep 1914
    Pearl E.1884-1910   xMyers,C.A. 7 jul 1924
xMyers,C.C. 19 sep 1923   xMyers,Cordelia 20 oct 1936
/Myers,Charles Edward 1854-1883   /Myers,Cynthia J. 1854-1928 w/o Thos.J.
/Myers,Clarence Lee 1881-1936   xMyers,Ed.26 sep 1914
xMyers,Chester 16 oct 1918   xMyers,Ed.26 sep 1916
xMyers,Ed.1904   /Myers,Harry 9 apr 1877 9y s/oJ&ME
xMyers,J.Orville 16 aug 1919   /Myers,John 1824-1879 CoF 10th KY Cav
xMyers,James D. 15 dec 1926   xMyers,Jonnie 29 nov 1920
/Myers,Joseph 1853-1935   xMyers,Linsley I.23 apr 1918
/Myers,Katherine Banks 1883-1907   /Myers,Leslie A. 1915-16
xMyers,Mary 2 dec 1912   /Myers,Mary
/Myers,Maude   xMyers,Oakey K,1876-1904
/Myers,Pearl E. 1884-1910   /Myers,Roxie 13 mar 1892 w/o Grayton H.
xMyers,Thomas J.18 jun 1936   /Myers,Virgie 27 jan 1927 2y
/Myers,William Perry 1883-1936   /Mylar,inf twins 1936
/Myrtle,Clarence Albert 6 mar 1936/Mylar,James Albert 1937 inf
/Myska,Effie 31 mar 1926 23y1m8d
xNance,Albert 1900   xNagle,Alvin H.15 jan 1929
/Nance,Alva 1899-1927   /Nance,Edward B.1908 inf
/Nance,Edward W. 1875-1909   xNance,Garnett 1907
xNance,Gilbert 9 mar 1927   /Nance,Hadie 23 may 1905-28 oct 1928
xNance,Henry 18 nov 1928   xNance,Jesse 3 aug 1923
/Nance,Renie 1877-1938   /Nance,Thomas 1936-38
/Narcise,Aldo,1925-1930   xNash,Helen C.5 apr 1932
/Nash,John J. 1865-1917   xNash,Josephine 4 apr 1932
xNash,Nancy R.26 mar 1919   xNash,Shelby 27 may 1926
/Naylor,John M. 1856-1930   xNasser,George 12 feb 1939
/Naylor,Russell A. 1889-1919   xNawak,Frank 2 oct 1922
/Neal,Alice Ruth 1922   xNeal,Ann Collins 29 feb 1936
xNeal,Artie C. 27 oct 1918   xNeal,Dillon 22 sep 1923
/Neal,John A. 1847-1917   xNeal,Ina 14 apr 1930
/Neal,John Clarke 1917-18   xNeal,Irene 1902-1935
xNeal,Lillie 12 nov 1920   /Neal,Kathleen Burns 1877-1905
xNeal,Robert 16 sep 1916   /Neal,Virginia 1915-1927 d/oGI&E
/Neale,Anna E. 1846-1913   /Neale,George N.1842-1914
/Neale,Grace E.Willis 1892-1922wGJ/Neale,Sophia E. 1833-1893
xNebber,Toney 22 sep 1922   /Nease,James V. 1904-1937
xNeicamp,Conard 2 jul 1913 inf   xNeel,Mary 11 feb 1926
/Neiuman,Mattie O. 1888-19111   xNeff,Cora E.25 mar 1919
xNeighbert,William 9 may 1915   xNellons,Arthur 2 jul 1928
/Nellons,William 1858-1923   xNellons,C.J. 14 jul 1932
/Nelson,Clarence Lee 1903-1911   xNelson,Clarence 15 may 1917
xNelson,Eli 12 jan 1920   xNelson,H.W. 11 may 1909
xNelson,Josephine,13 jul 1923   xNelson,Thelma 24 feb 1923
/Nepper,Herman J.1886-1922   xNetedon,Audy 6 jul 1922

NEEL, ANN COLLINS 1928-31   NEEL, MARY NANNETTE 1926-nd

/Nesperly,Lida 28 Jan 1935 75y3m xNethercutt,J.O. 27 feb
/New,F.A. CoF 5th VA Inf CSA   /Neulman,Anna H. 1860-1921
/Newberne,Thomas B.1920-21   /Newberry,Frazier 1900-1919
/Newberry,Inf 1911   /Newberry,Jeff 1861-1938
/Newberry,Jeff Jr.1915-1917   /Newcomb,James F. 27 aug 1936 WWI
/Newcomb,Labon B. 1869-1918   xNewcomb,Margaret E.31 dec 1930
xNewcomb,Mary E. 10 Jun 1927   xNewcomb,Quincey 16 aug 1936
xNewell,A.W. 27 aug 1920   /Newhouse,Elizabeth 1860-1914
xNewell,J.F.17 mar 1911   /Newhouse,George 17 Jul 1893 16y10m
xNewlon,A.C. 25 mar 1916   xNewlon,Edna Olive 12 Jul 1913
xNewman,America 1907   xNewman,Armour 29 dec 1927
/Newman,Anna H.   /Newman,Blanche 1887-1911 d/oJW&Emma
xNewman,Bette Louise 1 sep 1924   xNewman,Burrell 1896
/Newman,Carrie 1847-1889 w/o H   /Newman,C.C. 17 Jul 1938
xNewman,Clarence 5 Jan 1927   xNewman,Clayton M.10 Jan 1921
/Newman, Emma 1864-1911   xNewman,Elmer 30 may 1923
    J.W. 1860-1928   xNewman,Emma 1896
/Newman,Ford S.1894-1916   xNewman,Floyd 11 Jun 1922
/Newman,Frances 1841-1929   xNewman,H.C. 10 feb 1924
/Newman,Hattie B. 1868-1907   /Newman,Helen B. 1867-1932
/Newman,Henrietta 1859-1937   /Newman,James B.1853-1936
/Newman,John E. 1847-1933   /Newman,James E. 1909-11 s/o LM&CE
    Nancy J. 1850-1910   /Newman,Joseph 1867-1923
xNewman,Isabelle 22 apr 1933   xNewman,Jessie 14 mar 1923
xNewman,John W.24 mar 1928   xNewman,John M. 17 dec 1919 GAR
xNewman,Leroy 1905   xNewman,Lyda 28 Jan 1926
/Newman,Lossen M. 1882-1919   /Newman,L.H. 1867-1931
xNewman,Manuet 1912 Inf   xNewman,Mattie C.1888-1911
xNewman,Mayne 7 apr 1917   xNewman,Myrtle 1892/3
xNewman,Norman Fredrick 15 Jul 1925xNewman,Pearl--
/Newman,Roberta Lee 29 aug 1938   /Newman,Samuel 4 apr 1880-26 Jul 1915
/Newman,Sadie Weil 1876-1924   xNewman,Shelva Jean 6 Jun 1937
xNewman,Samuel M. 9 aug 1940   xNewsom,Charles 3 Jun 1925
xNewton,A.H. 4 dec 1921   /Newton,Eliza 1836-8 mar 1925
xNewton,Nannie 14 Jun 1926   /Newton,Laura 1878-1933
/Newton,Ottis C.1866-1937   /Newton,Lois 1904-07
xNewton,W.J. 13 sep 1923   xNewton,Sylvester 1832(3)-1907
xNeylon,Joseph 16 Jun 1924   xNibert,Charles W. 3 Jun 1927
xNibert,Mary Anne 2 dec 1933   xNibert,Mary Jane 13 Jun 1930
xNibert,Sarah E. 21 nov 1912   /Nibert,Roscoe 12 Jul 1935
xNibert,Sunshine 5 oct 1925   /Nicely,Beauford B.27 sep 1937 32y3m22d
xNicholas,Eliza C.26 Jan 1926   xNicholas,James R. 14 mar 1928
xNicholas,Ella W 26 may 1925   xNicholas,Mary A. 1 nov 1923
/Nicholes,Anna Lee 1938 Inf   /Nichols,Maybell 1877Inf
/Nichols,Abbie 1887-1934   /Nichols,M.C.3 dec 1828-22 Jan 1899
/Nichols,Edward G. 1879 inf   /Nichols,Eliza C. 1843-1926
/Nicholson,Rosa 1858-1930   /Nichols,Owena D.27 sep 1874-15 mar1890
xNichols,Frances 26 feb 1923   /Nicholson,Daniel E. 1904-12 sep 1932
xNickells,George 25 aug 1913   xNickels,James 27 sep 1924
xNiebert,Sarah E.21 nov 1912   xNihbert,Richard 12 apr 1914
xNoel,Edwin 1908   /Nobel,Amanda D. 1841-1900
xNoel,Forest 25 nov 1938   /Nobel,Grace Crawford 1871-1926
xNoel,George 1905   /Nobel,James M 1831-1888
/Nolan,Fred C.17 aug 1930 33y7m   xNorris,Bette Irene 8 oct 1925

xNorris,Claude 15 may 1926   xNorris,Edward 4 nov 1920
/Norris,Ellen Mae 9 dec 1937 81y6m/Norris,Ellsworth 1866-1907
xNorris,Mrs.George 23 dec 1930   xNorris,Giles 9 Jan 1937
xNorris,Harriet 11 nov 1917   xNorris,Lewa 15 nov 1912
xNorth,Lizzie E. 19 feb 1920   xNorthcott,Gus A. 10 dec 1938
/Northcott,John W. 14 oct 1935 77y/Northcott,inf 1891 d/GA&MS
xNorton,Frank G.6 Jan 1916   /Norwood,Roger G.5 oct 1866-6 Jun 1888
xNotter,Albert R. 20 apr 1920   /Notter,Clyde E. 1890-1929
/Notter,Effie B.1874-1931   /Notter,Elizabeth A.1855-1925
/Notter,Hasley C.1900-1918   xNoter,Lewis 22 dec 1917 inf
/Notter,.Jesse A.1852-1938   /Notter,Mary Elizabeth 1909-1928 d/L&E
/Nuckols,Nora Lee 1897-1919   xNull,Mary D.C. 30 apr 1913
xNunl(la)ey,Golden 28 mar 1937   /Nunn,Jam.A>10/16/1876-2/4/1899s/AJ&MA
xNunn,A.J. 11 may 1922   /Nunn,Nora Ida 11/13/1879-11/20/1898 "
xOakes,George W.11 dec 1917   /Nunn,Samuel G.10/9/1883-6/27/1904AJ&MA
xOborn,Mrs.H.A. 23 mar 1910   /O'Briant Sol 1877-1937
xO'dell,Ernest Chester 1897-1901   /Odilia,C.M. P.Sr. 19 dec 1932
xO'Dell,Viola 9 mar 1913   xO'Halloran,Anna Louise 23 mar 1931
/Offutt,Mathew Neely Jr.1901-04   xOhrwell,Augusta 12 sep 1921
/Offutt,Mathew Neely 1870-1924   /Ohlinger,Paul Wm.18 Jun 1933 40y5m1d
    Sara B.Habeson 1878-1915   /O'Laughlin,Anna K.1876-1931
xOLaughlin,J.T. 27 feb 1939   /Oley,Brig.Gen.John Hunt   Union
xOlder,Waldo 13 feb 1912 inf   24 sep 1830-11 mar 1888 Civil War
xOliver,Alma 29 nov 1910   /Oliver,James M. 1835-1917
xOliver,Fannie 1 Jun 1918   /Oliver,Margaret A. 1846-1923
xOliver,FJ.M.Sr. 7 feb 1917   /Oliver,Thomas W. 1889-1912
/Oliver,Zephaniah CoE 5th WV Inf   /O'Neal,Richard Lee 1869-1930
xO'Neill,Earl Patrick 12 oct 1936   /Oney,Charles L. d 1896
/Oney,James K. 1856-1928   /Oney,Robert T. d1888
/Oney,Willie G.1860-1934   /Oppenheim,L.1813-1898
/Orme,Charles SpAm 25 feb 1934   xOrcutt,C.C. 20 nov 1917
/Orwig,Ethel L. d1920   /Orcutt,Elizabeth 9 sep 1852-4 Jun 1935
/Orwig,James 9 may 1931 58y10m16d   /Orcutt,Frank C. 27 Jan 1938 60y7m17d
/Orwig,Mary Louise d1926   xOrwig,Raymond 23 mar 1909
xOrwig,Rebecca 23 feb 1928   /Orwig,Russell 1924-1930
/Osborn,Harry Lee 16 dec 1938 ****/Osborne,Sarah 12 oct 1760-25 mar 1844
xOsborne,H.B.12 nov 1920   xOsborne,H.F.19 feb 1925
/Osgood,Catherine 1823-1919   /Osburn,Roland Ed. 25 feb 1929 inf
/Osgood,George K. 1850-1910   xOsgood,Harvey S. 1905
/Osgood,John H, 1822-1971   xOsgood,Mary E. 30 Jan 1927
xOskey,Ellison B. 8 dec 1932   xOskey,Mary 20 oct 1918
xOskey,Sarah 24 dec 1918   xOsky,Tom 2 mar 1922
/Oskey,Jake 6 dec 1932 vet   /Osolky,Carl d3 may 1924
xOverall,Alice 6 may 1939   /Otterstatter,John 3 Jan 1892 55y8m18d
xOverall,John 28 Jan 1920   xOverby,Warren Jr.1904-05
/Overbey,Warren Jr.1904-05   /Overby,Mirge Betts 1880-1884 d/oW&EL
/Overbey,Joseph L.1906-1936   /Overby,Eudora Leigh 7nov1861-18oct1891
/Overby,Nannie Estell 1883-1891W&E/Overby,Virgie 1880-1887 d/oW&EL
/Overstreet,Walter s/oJH&MA   /Overby,Warren Sr.19 oct 1822-28Jun1893
/Overstreet,J.H.   xOverstreet--1903
    27 sep 1845-23 dec 1937   xOverstreet,Charles W. 3 may 1921
xOverstreet Julia 26 dec 1937w/JH xOverstreet,Walter H.--
xOverton,-- 19 oct 1936   /Overton,Charles D.15 oct 1856-31 Jul 1899
xOverton,James --   xOverton,Olso 5 Jun 1916

xOverton,Lina --   xOverton,Clifford Lewis 2 Jun 1921
xOverton,Lillian May 11 nov 1926   xOverton,May 18 aug 1926
xOverton,Thomas 10 dec 1914   xOverturf,Elenor 6 dec 1918 inf
xOwens,Clara 9 feb 1919   xOwens,Cora 6 mar 1933
xOwens,John A. 28 dec 1913   xOwens,Mildred 25 feb 1912
/Owens,Robert D. 1895-1896   xOwens,Sam 15 feb 1921
/Oxley,Annie E. 1867-1924   /Pace,Clarence Willard 1925-12 oct 1933
/Pabody,Effie Afton 1854-1923   /Pace,Claude-1907-1911
/Pabody,Rodolphus G.1849-1909   /Pace,Bettie Lee 22 apr 1934
/Pace,Erastus S.1882-1926   /Pace-Oscar-1902-1919
xPack,Lillian 16 oct 1937   /Paden,inf 1918
xPack,Mary J.1 dec 1916   /Pafford,John Francis
xPage,A.G. 21 apr 1914   /Page,Della Smith 1857-1932
/Page,George Sheldon 1843-1912   /Page,Harry James 1872-1931
xPage,J.W. 11 feb 1919   xPage,Mary 31 oct 1923
/Page,Pearl 1878-79   /Page,R.Perry 1833-1899
/Page,W.H. 1871-1911   Sarah A. 1840-1910
/Page,Wayne W.30 Jun 1903   inf   /Paine,Arma Ellen 22 dec 1934 52y
xPaine,Charles W. 19 feb 1916   xPaine,Rebecca Lewis 29 sep 1939
/Paine-Sid B. 1869-1920   /Paine,Sarah Malinda 15 sep 1932 80y3m6
xPainter,Euttia A. 5 Jan 1921   xPaisley,George 17 dec 1918
xPaleen,H.W. 9 sep 1917   xPalmer,Alonzo--
xPalmer,D.E. 7 aug 1924   xPalmer,Mrs.Dallas C. 20 oct 1918
/Palmer,Edward 1876-1937   xPalmer,Howard E. 10 aug 1937
xPalmer,Mary 30 oct 1911   xPalmer,Mary H. 15 oct 1912
xPalmer,Nancy J.15 oct 1912   xPalmer,Neoma 15 sep 1925
/Pancake,Elizabeth 1890-1920 w/oGHxPancake,Elmer D. 4 dec 1909
xPancake,Ivan 1 Jun 1932   xPancake,Josephine 3 may 1932
xPannell,Alice V. 27 mar 1913   xPannell,Charles 1906
xPannell,Clyde 23 may 1916   xPannell,Mabel 29 mar 1915
xPannell,Mary Jane 1901   xPannell,Norman H. 5 feb 1921
xParcell,Clara 28 oct 1931   /Parcell,Orkey H.1887-1918
/Parker,Annie Y. d29 aug 1935   xParker,Calvin D.14 feb 1933
xParker,George 30 apr 1915   xParker,Herman 24 sep 1935
xParker,Mary Catherine 10 mar 1919xParker,Rev.S.L. 3 oct 1921
/Parker,Percy C.1847-1921   /Parr,Va.Pauline 12 Jan 1937 26y
/Parsley,Eliza   84y9m11d   /Parrish,Frank S.23 aug 1872-1 aug 1933
xParr,Frank Lesley 28 mar 1925   xParrish,Ed.Arthur 30 apr 1933
xParrish,Flemming 30 mar 1914   xParrish,Jack D. 29 apr 1926
xParsen,Elizabeth 12 aug 1923   /Parrish,Ruby Shrewsbury d 1Jun 1928
/Parsons,Dr,Alex M.1865-1915   xParsons,A.G. 12 nov 1921
xParsons,Amelia 26 dec 1914   xParsons,Billie E. 29 Jun 1925
xParsons,Cleopatra 4 dec 1923   /Parson,Charles Cristo 1925-1933
/Parson,Chester F. 1822-1897   /Parson,Deloss Emmons 28 Jan 1933 50y
/Parson,Etta E. 1848-1924   /Parsons,Henriette Stoddard 1846-1926
xParsons,Letha 4 mar 1935   /Parsons,Jethro Ray 1881-84
/Parsons,Dr,John W.1873-1918   /Parsons,J.M. 1858-1921
xParsons,Maxine--   /Parsons,Katherine Yarwood 1871-1918
/Parsons,Mandana S. 1830-1912   /Parsons,M.Ella 1890-1917
/Parsons,Mary Louise 1832-38   /Parsons,Warren J.1846-1925
/Parsons,Willis E. 1851-1918   /Pasquali,Joseph 1879-1939
/Patchell,Ida B. 1875-1899   xPasquali,Mary 10 mar 1941
/Pate,John A. 1884-1924   xPatten,Erastus 7 may 1917
/Patten,Samuel --   /Patterson,Adele 7 Jan 1939 37y2m6d

xPatterson,B.F. 11 feb 1937   xPatterson,Charles 11 sep 1913
xPatterson,Edward 7 mar 1919   /Patterson,Elizabeth 1866-1931
xPatterson,Emily 14 sep 1922   /Patterson,Gerald D. 1896-1903
xPatterson,John 22 apr 1919   /Patterson,Henry Franklin 1935inf
xPatterson,Minnie 20 oct 1914   xPatton,Ruby 28 Jul 1921
xPatton,Sam 7 Jul 1913   xPatton,Seril 9 sep 1925
xPattsy,Joe 27 sep 1920   /Paul,Beulah M. 1887-1901d/oJA&LB
/Paul,Jacob B.1859-1923   /Paul,John A. 1858-1933
xPaul,Lewis R. 21 Jun 1934   /Paul,Mertie Gallaher 1870-1923 w WE
xPaul Wm.,Edward 13 mar 1946   /Paul,Wm.Allen 1858-1933
/Pauley,Helen 1918-1919   /Payne,James B.6 Jul 1857-31 aug 1894
/Payne,John C.12 sep 1867-6 mar 28xPayne,Lizzie J. 14 Jan 1913
xPayne,Lucy 15 oct 1932   /Payne,Lyvenia 4 aug 1900 43y w/o RF
/Payton,Nella 1908-1911   /Payne,Mary J. 1840-1928
/Peaco,Erskine G.1886-1915   /Payne,Thomas C. 1875-1919
/Peaco,Florence J.1861-1930   /Pease,Susan 17 feb 1901 55y
/Peaco,John F. 1847-1907   /Pease,Effie 18 oct 1896-17 feb 1917
/Peaso,Mattie 21 sep 1887 d/o J&F xPearce,Alfred 26 Jun 1921
/Peaco,Walter D. 1883-1924   /Peck,Cecil 25 aug 1938 47y9m3d
/Peck,Charles M. 1854-1875   /Peck,Joel Edward 24 may 1931 56y4m2d
/Peck,Joseph A. 1849-1915   /Peck,Julia E. 1887-1918
/Peck,Rev.Marcellus 1861-1925   /Peck,Julia Y. 1850-1903
/Peck,Mallie M. 1885-1907   /Peeples,Sarah Ella 4 apr 1937 83y7m20d
xPegues,William J. 2 sep 1936   xPeeples,George W. 30 aug 1939
xPelle,Regina 28 oct 1920   xPelot,J.W. 29 aug 1913
xPelfrey,H.M. 4 dec 1934   /Pelot,Frances Riley 1861-1920
xPemberton,Mary Alice 12 apr 1912 /Pendleton,Langdon A.2Jul1883-1Jan1923
/Pence,Harry Cecil 1918-1937   /Pennington,B.L. 1921-22
/Pennybacker,Fanie E. 1859-1918   /Pennington,J.K. 1925-1927
/Pennybacker,Cline 1880-1924w/Clin/Pennington,Mary E.1870-1916 w/A.M.
xPennypacker,Fannie 6 mar 1914   xPennypacker,Fannie M 20 sep 1917
/Pennybacker,J.M.5 Jul 1881 45y   /Pepper,Ella M. 1861-1938
/Pennybacker,Wm.H.   /Pepper,Dr.R.H.1862-1922
     30 Jan 1840-10 apr 1910   /Pepper,Sally Barr 12 oct 1938
                                           /Pepper,William E.1863-1950
xPerdue,David 25 feb 1918   xPerdue,Edward J. 30 apr 1928
xPerdue,Homer Lee 19 mar 1929   /Perdue,James E.3 Jun 1897-26 may 1909
xPerdue,Moss--   xPerego,Ethel--
xPerego,Isaac W.13 may 1928   xPerego,L.H. 9 sep 1926
xPerkins,Abraham 1915   xPerkins,Hattie 17 mar 1917
/Perkins,H.Nicholas 1845-1901   xPerkins,Kazzey 29 Jul 1924
/Perkins,Molly B.1855-1929   /Perkins,Noah 7 feb 1924 inf
/Perkins,Robert H. 1849-1887   /Perkins,Robt.James 5/15/1854-4/20/1906
xPerkins,Sarah Estep 29 feb 1932   xPerkins,Sue Shelton 2 dec 1924
xPerrer,Richard 13 Jun 1929   xPerry,Mary B. 11 Jul 1911
xPersinger,Delores 19 may 1932   xPerson,Peter 8 feb 1938
/Perrsinger,Edgar A.1898-1923   /Peters,Elva M.1907-1911
xPeters,Charles 1 Jan 1923   xPeters,Emily 30 may 1927
xPeters,Irene Houck 8 Jun 1926   xPeters,Isreal 13 may 1920
xPeters,James M. 6 mar 1924   xPeters,Josephine 7 sep 1934
/Peters,Lawrence 1899-1926   /Peters,Margaret 1844-1915
/Peters,Paul F. 1855-1904   /Peters,Nellie Lee 1892-1912 w/oClyde
xPeters,Mamuel Norvel·12 dec 1925 /Peters,Wm.M. 7 Jan 1880-5 apr 1914
xPeters,Willie 4 may 1922   xPeterson,John H.2 Jun 1922

/Petit,Marietta C.1849-1915
/Petit,Mary J.1867-1904
/Petit,Noah 1843-1923
/Petit,Wm.M.1866-1935
xPeyton,Arnold 17 nov 1926
/Peyton,Bernard 1867-1919
xPeyton,Frances 5 mar 1923
xPeyton,Inf/Pansy 19 mar 1919
xPeyton,J.B. 19 Jan 1919
/Peyton,Sarah 1834-1893
/Peyton,William 11 sep 1924
xPeyton,W.W.14 sep 1927
/Pheiffer,Eva V. 1878-1917
xPfeifer,Louis 24 dec 1925
xPfouts,Helen M 1853-1884
/Pfouts,Eugene C.1882-1884
/Phillips,Aubrey
        14 feb 1899-8 mar 1915
xPhillips,David 27 jun 1934
xPhillips,Francine 12 Jan 1928
/Phillips,Grace Joyce 1885-1919
xPhillips,Lou Vinson 1918 inf
xPhillips,Jacqueline 22 Jan 1923
xPhillips,Jasper 10 mar 1915
xPhillips,M.L. 9 aug 1933
xPhillips,Sallie 15 nov 1930
xPhillips,Sallie W. 1846-1930
xPhillips,Willard V. 7 mar 1919
xPhipps,W.M.123 nov 1926
xPickett,Isabella 5 Jun 1912
xPierce,Henry 1 may 1912
xPierce,Malena 18 oct 1916
/Pierson,Isabella 5 Jun 1912
/Pigg,O.J.8 Jun 1939 68y3m15d
/Pigman,J.R.1830-1909
/Pigman,Mary 1835-1919
/Pine,Samuel Edward 1867-1930
xPine,Carl 6 Jul 1936
xPine,Talbert 21 dec 1929
xPinkerton,Lillian 14 nov 1916inf
/Pinkerton,Hannah 3/6/1857-2/8/1928
/Pinnell,B.M. 1883-1922
xPinnell,Mary Ellen 30 dec 1910
xPinnell,W.W. 29 nov 1912
/Pinnick,Mary E. 1853-1918
xPipins,Garfield 6 dec 1924
/Plymale,Ada
/Plymale,Belle Cora
/Plymale,John Harvey
/Plymale,Octavian 1842-1920
        Marietta 1851-1938
/Poage,Ada W.12 Jun 1909
/Poage,John Bayless 1856-1933
/Poage,Louise 27 feb 1915

/Petit,Charles H.23 mar 1867-3 mar 1934
/Petit,Simpson Burk 30 dec 1855 infN&M
/Petit,Sarah 10 Jun 1867-23 feb 1936
xPetway,Grace dec 1932
xPetway,John 13 Jun 1930
xPeyton,Elizabeth 1907
xPeyton,Gerturde 20 dec 1921
xPeyton,Inf/Loyd W. 1 mar 1914
/Peyton,Mary T.1867-1902
/Peyton,Sarah M. 1858-1923
/Peyton,Thomas West 1860-1912
/Peyton,Thomas West IV 1891-1949
xPfeifer,Irene--
xPfeifer,Viola 10 Jun 1910

/Phelps,Emily O.1885-1892
        Mina 25 Jan 1845-8 Jan 1887wOliver
xPhillips,Catherine 4 may 1925 w/oJA
xPhillips,David S. 25 feb 1922inf
/Phillips,Eunice Hinds 1900-1934
xPhillips,Hannah 27 apr 1939
xPhillips,J.M. 24 dec 1908
xPhillips,John A. 8 oct 1923
xPhillips,Mary 28 aug 1918
xPhillips,Otho P. 5 Jul 1913
/Phillips,Oliver Justice 1822-23
xPhillips,W.J. 22 apr 1915
/Phillips,Wendell O.1886-1922
/Picinni,John 17 Jul 1933 56y7m5d
xPierce,Charles Woodrow 12 mar 1929
xPierce,James R. 4 apr 1920
xPierce,Fanny 1849 inf
/Pierson,Fanny Florence 4 apr 1842
/Pilcher,Charles S.12 mar 1852-2 may 11
        Florence Jane 1857-1919
/Pilcher,Hiram E. 1882-1938
        Claudia Lee 1883-1918
xPilcher,Walter T.1885-1892
/Pinkerman,Rebecca J. 1856-1891
xPinkerty,Mabel L. 8 may 1932
/Pinnell,Perry Green 9 dec 1933 64y8m
xPinnell,Harry B. 15 apr 1917
xPinnell,Thomas 4 oct 1925
/Pluckette,Florence 1871-1913
/Pinnick,William T. 1848-1920
xPlyborn,Eliza 17 feb 1921
xPlymale,Drucilla 11 mar 1927
xPlymale,Hughey 15 apr 1925
xPlymale,Sylvester 1876-1939
/Plymale,Ves Billey
/Plymale,Vernie Casey 20aug1879-28Jan24
xPoage,Gallick 1862-1879
/Poage,James Harvey 25 feb 1888 71y
xPoage,Robert C.11 Jan 1932

/Poage,Mary Miller 1858-1930   /Poage,Sallie Kemper 4 may 1879 17yJ&S
/Poage,Sarah A.1830-28 apr 1895 65yxPoage,Sallie 1883
xPoe,Hugh Donald 28 Jul 1927   xPofford,John 1939 inf
xPoindexter,Emerline 7 oct 1926   /Poffenbarger,Helen 1852-1931
xPoindexter,Moses 4 dec 1910   /Pogue,Alberta 1858-1913
/Poindexter,Frank E.22 oct 1891 5y   Marcell A. 1830-1875
/Poindexter,W.W. 1858-1920   xPoints,W.W. 21 Jan 1920
xPoints,Mrs.W.W. 24 aug 1913   /Polan,Bertha M. 1887-1924
xPolk,Vistoria 25 apr 1917   /Pollard,Edith Kyle 1880-1899
/Pollard,Fannie C. 1844-1926   /Pollard,John C. 1839-1902
/Polloock,Ernest F.18 oct 1938 WWI/Pollock,Anna 29 oct 1900-17 Jan 1917
xPollock,Hamilton 16 aug 1926   /Pollock,Lavina 22 Jan 1867-28 feb 1933
xPollock,Love 17 dec 1938   /Pollock,Margaret J.1860-1930
xPollock,Phoebe L. 1903-1904   /Pollock,Phoeba Jane 21 Jan 1923 71y18d
/Pollock,Stephen 1885-1937   xPollock,Thomas 5 nov 1933
xPollock,Una 1895-1905   xPolsley,George 27 apr 1923
xPoole,Ollie 3 Jul 1937   /Poore,Addie M.1839-1917
/Poore,Lillian C.1867-68   /Poore,Mark 1835-1926
xPorter,Charles L. 9 oct 1930   /Porter,Edgar W. 1874-1907
xPorter,Edwin H. 23 Jan 1928   xPorter,Elizabeth 19 mar 1922
/Porter,Ethel Lee 1894-1928   /Porter,Mary B.27 Jan 1841-9 apr 1880
/Porter,inf 1939   w/o James W.S.
xPorter,William 26 dec 1935   xPorterfield,Mollie 29 may 1917
/Poteet,Fannie B.1856-1905   xPoteet,Lizzie 12 may 1922
/Poteet,H.C. 1830-1906   xPoter,inf/Effie 1918
/Potts,Eugenia 1850-1919   xPoter,John W. 26 Jan 1912
xPotts,J.N. 12 Jan 1931   xPotts,James O. 20 nov 1939
xPotts,Margaret A. 12 aug 1925   /Potts,James Newton 1838-1931
/Potts,Virgina W.1868-1876   /Potts,Virginia 19 oct 1878 8y d/C&M
xPoulos,Joe 10 aug 1918   xPoundertes,Emma S. 7 oct 1926
/Poulton,Frances 1864-1896wChas.   /Powell,Amelia B.1850-1936
xPowell,Alberta J. 29 Jan 1921   /Powell,Henreitta 1882-1923
/Powell,Justina M.1861-1917   /Powell,Perry A. 1848-1913
xPowell,W.R. 10 apr 1917   xPowell,W.R. Jr. 20 mar 1917
/Powers,Harvey S.1853-1917   xPowers,inf/J.O. 1911
xPowers,Mabel 20 feb 1925   xPowers,Mabel N. --
xPowers,Mollie A. 15 oct 1915   xPowers,William R. 20 nov 1934
/Poynter,Glen Howard 1924-25   /Pratt,Jesse T.1865-1914
xPrater,Anna 29 apr 1910 w/oGW   xPresgraves,Carl 3 aug 1924
xPrater,G.W. 16 mar 1922   xPresley,C.E. 22 nov 1923
/Price,Anna 1882-1939   /Price,Alice 10 Jul 1932 72y9m13d
xPrice,Evelyn 24 Jan 1924   /Price,Earl E. 3 Jul 1936 26y1m24d
/Price, inf/HE 3 nov 1912   /Price,Howard E.1879-1933
/Price,John R. d21 apr 1933   /Price,John L.1880-1936
/Price,Joseph 1814-1903   xPrice,Luruise 29 sep 1927
/Price,Mona M. 1899-1912   /Price,Manderville 4 aug 1936 79y
xPrice,Pansy 10 Jan 1937   xPrice,S.B.2 Jun 1933
xPrice,Texana 15 Jun 1923   /Price,William D.14 sep 1932 inf
xPrichard,Aline L. 11 Jun 1912   /Prichard,A.W.(E) 1850-1898
xPrichard,Celia J.11 apr 1911   Margaret C. 1851-1926
xPrichard Frances D. 26 dec 1926   /Prichard,C.N.5 Jun 1839-12 sep 1904
/Prichard,Oscar B.1885-1909   Sarah A.18 Jul 1839-6 Jan 1905
/Prichard,George F.1907-09   /Prichard,Hallie 30 oct 1869-6 may 1893
/Prichard,Hattie 1885-1914   /Prichard,Henreitta 20mar1875-14nov1892

/Prichard,Mabel 1911-1915   /Prichard,James 16 oct 1841-3 dec 1910
/Prichard,Va.Lee 1918-1921   /Prichard,Walter R.1850-1898
xPrichard,Walter 3 dec 1915   /Prichard,Clyde C.(L)1878-1908
    /Prit---,Oella 13 Jul 1868-10 apr 1911w/CL

xPugh,Mary Ferguson 1879-1939   xPuckette,Florence 17 may 1913
/Pugh,Della Mae 1890-1937   /Pruden,James Russell 1900-1903
/Pugh,James B.1856-1920   /Pruden,W.J.16 Jan 1857-3 dec 1904
/Pugh,Va.Belle 1864-1937   Jessie May 1 oct 1882-5 Jun 1905
/Pugh,Mary Ferguson d2 aug 1937   /Pruden,Mathew Talmage 1902-1903
xPullah,Edward 12 may 1924   /Pulley,Alice 1854-16 mar 1932
/Pulley,David 1862-17 dec 1912   /Pulley,Gordia 1888-1924
/Pulley,John CoK 5th WV Inf GAR   /Pulley,H.C. 1923 42y
xPulley,Lena 5 mar 1920   /Pulskamp,Winifred 1904-1919
/Pulverman,Blema 1862-1925w M.   /Pulskamp,James L.1869-1930
/Punko,John 9 feb 1934 43y11m25m   xPunko,Margaret 9 aug 1945
/Purcell,Charles W.1885-1927   /Purdue,E.J. 1862-1968
/Purcell,inf 1920s/oCW&M   /Puthuff,Elizabeth A. 1834-1889 w/JM
xPuthuff,James M.--   xPuthuff,Margaret J.26 mar 1937
xPuthuff,Mary 1 aug 1933   xPuthuff,Maude 11 Jan 1911
xPuthuff,Thomas 23 Jul 1910   xPuthuff,Wm.H. 26 oct 1917
/Pyles,Homer V.1913-23 s/oF&G   xPyles,William 24 Jun 1924
/Pyles,Mary A.1841-1927   xQualls--17 Jun 1922
xQueen,Henry M. 14 Jan 1932   /Queen,Laura 25 Jun 1939 59y4m1d
/Queensberry,Thelma 1901-1918   xQuest,S.J. 1874-1902
/Quinlan,Adelia 1901-1904   /Quillan,Wm.A.4 Jun 1876-26 dec 1935
/Quinlan,Catherine C.1874-1920   /Quinn,Osa 1891-1897
/Quinn,CHarles S. 1884-1931   xQuinn,inf/Paul 9 mar 1920
xQuinn,Joseph 7 Jul 1920   /Quinn,William 1846-1924
xRackes,Elizabeth J. 9 mar 1931   xRadcliff,Margaret 15 may 1913
xRadcliff,Rachael 4 Jan 1913   /Radcliff,Robert E.1895-1910
xRader,Betty Gay 2 Jan 1935   /Rader,Florence V.1867-1937
/Rader,Dr.Joseph E.1872-1932   xRader,Samuel T. 25 Jan 1931
xRadford,Elizabeth 5 Jul 1938   /Radford,Anderson 4 Jun 1847-11aug1917
xRaffel,Anna 1888-1937   /Radford,Henry 4 dec 1886-20 apr 1929
/Raffel,Elias D.1880-1934   /Raffel,Nachman D.1856-1926
xRagland,Grace 7 oct 1933   xRagland,Susie 19 aug 1920
xRagland,William 31 Jul 1931   xRaines,inf/Chas.1917
/Raines,Eliza Jane 1845-1930   xRaines,J.W. 1866-1902
/Raines,John 17 dec 1935 WWI   xRaines,Perry 5 sep 1922
/Raines,Margaret E. 1865-1935   /Raines,Susie J.1876-18 Jul 1891 W&E
xRaines,William 24 dec 1934   /Raines,Walter L.1866-1931
/Raines,Will D.1881-17 Jan 1908   /Raines,Wm.L.1843-1929
/Rains,J.W. 1866-1902   Cynthia A. 1845-1899
xRambo,Albert D. 19 sep 1920   /Ramey,Clara 22 aug 1939 30y11m
/Ramey,Fredrick 1886-1912   xRamey,Frank 6 oct 1928
xRamey,Martha 1847-1920   xRamey,Mary 26 aug 1939
xRamey,Mary 23 apr 1918   xRamey,Stonewall Jackson 14 may 1915
/Ramey,Walter Lyle 28 apr 1935 22yxRamsdell,Rosa Ruth 13 may 1915
xRamsey,Elizabeth 2 dec 1925   xRamsey,Emma R. 15 apr 1928
xRamsey,Halip Louise 1 dec 1925   xRamsey,inf/JM 28 may 1912
xRamsey,inf/Cecil 24 mar 1912   /Ramsey,Margaretta 1860-1923
/Ramsey,Dr.Robt Y.1841-1892   William 1859-1931
xRamsey,Taratha 20 feb 1933   xRandal,Clarence M.24 sep 1920
/Randall,Dorat 18 Jul 1873 inf   xRandall,Sarah E. 13 aug 1919

/Randall,Sarah E.25 may 1873 32y
xRandolph,Millicent 25 sep 1918
xRandolph,Wilton 30 dec 1917
/Ransbottom,Bertha 1905-1935wCllf
/Ransbottom,Cart 3 nov 1931 3y
xRansbottom,Virginia 15 feb 1922
xRapp,Charles,E. 8 nov 1924
xRarden,Iva May 1900-1938
xRarden,Worthy 1889-1913
xRaso,Frank
xRatcliff,Ada 9 sep 1920
/Ratcliff,Charles V.1882-1932
xRatcliff,Garland 5 Jun 1924
/Rau,John 1856-1923
/Rau,Katherine 1860-1931
xRay,Cole--
xRay,Elizabeth 12 Jan 1917
xRay,Earl T. 22 feb 1916 inf
xRay,Gladys I.23 nov 1910
xRay,H.T. 1 nov 1918 inf
xRay,Lawrence Raymond 7 nov 1927
/Ray,Laura 1911 d/VC&Emma
xRay,N.B. 21 apr 1936
xRay,Ruth 2 Jan 1924
xRay,William 9 apr 1926
/Ray,Will 28 sep 1938 WWI
/Raybould,Harry C.15 oct 1918
/Raybould,Rev.Wm.10 aug 1915
xRaynois ,W.M. 25 mar 1924
xReared,Robert 8 aug 1927
xReavesly,Eddie 13 dec 1930
xReavesly,George W. 23 dec 1930
xRece,Ashley S. 21 Jun 1932
/Rece,Alice L. 1845-1924
/Rece,Clyde 1883-1888
/Rece,James A. 1843-1913
/Rece,James T. 1842-1924
/Rece,Sue 1878-1922
xRector,Rose 14 aug 1911
xReece,Katherine Mae 6 Jan 1921
/Reed,Arlyn 1892-1893
xReed,Anderson dec 1930
xReed,Berta
xReed,Edwin Edward 8 Jun 1910
/Reed,Eliza Ann 23 oct 1914
xReed,J.M. 5 dec 1916 GAR
xReed,John Henry 27 nov 1939
xReed,Maggie 1906
xReed,Mary M. 1904
xReed,Vincent 3 apr 1934
xReeder,Edna L. 3 dec 1912
xReese,George 1851-1934
xReese,Olina Vornia 26 oct 1934
/Reese,Royal V.1886-1889s/HV&OV

xRandolph,Charlotte 11 apr 1919
xRandolph,Thomas E. 12 mar 1925
/Ransbottom,Infs 1935Willard&Willie
/Ransbottom,Hiram 10 oct 1832-4 may 06
   Harrietta 20 nov 1947-29 Jan 1919
xRansom,Mary Bell 12 aug 1918
xRappold,Margaret 29 oct 1918
xRardin,Ira W. 28 mar 1938
xRardin,James M.1842-1928
   Sarah Elizabeth 1846-1912
/Ratcliff,Anna M. 1882-1932
xRatcliff,Louisa J.7 aug 1919
/Ratcliff,John F. 1867-1924
/Ray,Anna 1902-1924
xRay,Boone 2 Jan 1924
xRay,Charlotte 2 apr 1918 inf
xRay,Frances 2 Jan 1916
xRay,Greenville 1854-1888
/Ray,Guy 1876-1938
xRay, inf/JH 15 sep 1924
/Ray,Leonara Lucretia 1846-1927
xRay,Melvine 20 may 1936
xRay,Rufus 24 aug 1928
xRay,Seldoh T.17 sep 1913
/Ray,Sadie 1894-1923
xRayle,2 infs 14 Jul 1926
/Raymond,William 1880-1934
/Raynes,Patricia Ann 24 may 1934 18y
xReagan,Gloria 10 dec 1938
/Reardon,Anna B.8 nov 1938 68y4m15d
/Reardon,James A. 9 nov 1938 84y11m
xRece,Alice 14 sep 1927
xRece,T.Heber 21 nov 1911
/Rece,Charles A. 1837-1929
/Rece,Edna Eugenia 12 mar 1933   83y6m5d
/Rece,Martha E.1841-1911
/Rece,Mary J. 1841-1910
/Rece,T.Herber 1847-1887
xRedmond,Wm.W.7 aug 1934
/Redd,Lizzie C.11 apr 1846-11 feb 1886
xRedmond,J.D. 25 sep 1922
xReed,Ben H. 9 may 1923
/Reed,Charles L.1865-1928
xReed,George 31 Jul 1939
/Reed,Fredrick E. Sr.1852-1931
xReed,John--
/Reed,Mary E.10 Jan 1931
xReed,Mary 20 oct 1914
xReed,Norman, G. 9 aug 1939
xReede,Laura E. 31 oct 1932
/Reese,Catherine May 1920-21
xReese,Dr.Hiram Vank 20 nov 1928
xReese,Olive H.1857-1933
/Reeves,Anna Royal 1872-1927

/Reffitt,George A.25 oct 1935   xReeves,Peter 16 Jun 1924
/Reffitt,JKelly 11 sep 1935 WWI   xReffeitt,D.B. 29 apr 1922
xReid,Joseph S. 20 aug 1914   /Reid,James A.G.28 dec 1880-3 oct 1898
xReid,Mary Jane 23 apr 1927   xReid,Willie B. 20 Jun 1923
xReich,Rosa Oppenheimer 1872-1935   xReif,Emma 22 Jun 1926
xReiley,Gerutrde L. 11 apr 1925   xReinwald,August 14 mar 1913
xReinwald,Nannie 12 mar 1913   xReinwald,W.F. 21 Jun 1927
/Reitz,Andrew 27 feb 1935 63y7m1d xReitz,Jesie 24 oct 1936
/Remke,Augusta G.28 Jun 1934 59y   /Reitz,John 1846-1907
/Renfro,Arthur Ralph 1896-1928   xRenison,Myrtle 25 Jan 1919
xRexrode,Charles Edward 6 oct 1924 /Reushlein,Francis Chase 1905-07
xReynolds,Amelia 23 sep 1924   xReynolds,Cary M. 23 Jun 1926
xReynolds,David P. 1932-1935   /Reynolds,C.O. 1883-1919
/Reynolds,Elizabeth C.1849-1925   xReynolds,Fredrick 1892
xReynolds,George 7 feb 1921   xReynolds,Marie 15 sep 1911
xReynolds,Mary A. 20 oct 1913   /Reynolds,W.I.CoB 115th OH Inf GAR
xRhodes,Bessie Mae 11 oct 1921   /Rhodes,Charles B.1892-1914
xRhodes,Jack 1919-1927   /Rhodes,Nellie Garnett 13 dec 1937 62y
xRhodes,Marshall 18 oct 1930   xRice,Annie E. 22 sep 1911
xRice,Dorothea 6 mar 1922   xRice,Harley Lee 15 dec 1913
xRice,John H. 5 sep 1934   /Rice,Mary Jane 29 apr 1933 inf
/Rich,Alexander R.1863-1922   xRichard,Oscar 4 mar 1918
/Rich,Mary 1904-1925   xRichards,John 18 dec 1917
xRichardson,Annie 17 aug 1928   /Richardson,Alice Henderson 1848-1927
xRichardson,Chainnice 21 Jul 1919   xRichardson,Charles 5 nov 1918
xRichardson,Earl 30 nov 1916   /Richardson,Emma 1861-1920
/Richardson,Ernest E. 2 Jun 1921   Frank H. 1859-1926
/Richardson,George W.1884-1917   xRichardson,Fred 23 may 1938
xRichardson,George 30 Jun 1924   xRichardson,Jas.C. 29 Jul 1922
xRichardson,Joe 18 Jan 1936   /Richardson,John Smythe 1887-1920
xRichardson,Lawrence 31 dec 1934   xRichardson,Lenie 14 dec 1924
xRichardson,Louise E.20 Jan 1939   /Richardson,Male Fannie 1903-1913
xRichardson,Mariah 6 sep 1916   xRichardson,Morris 3 Jul 1923
/Richard,Oppolls M. 1922-1923   xRichardson,Ray 3 dec 1923
/Richardson,Reginald O. 1901-1907   xRichardson,Wash 9 mar 1914
/Richardson,Wm.S. 1848-1910   xRichley,Arters 25 oct 1916
xRichie,Mary 4 NoV 1918   xRichmond,Charles 14 oct 1910
xRichamond,James Leslie 9 nov 1939 /Ricketts,Dr.G.C.27 nov 1821-6 mar 1859
/Ricketts,A.G. 1845-1863   /Ricketts,Charles H. 1856-1937
/Ricketts,G.C.1855-1924   Virginia Peyton 1855-1912
/Ricketts,G.H.1849-1925   xRicketts,Lucian C.1846-1906
/Ricketts,J.E. 1851-1889   /Ricketts,Virginia 1826-1923
xRicketts,Mrs.Fannie 2 feb 1915   xRickman,Ella 18 mar 1927
xRiddle,Susan Jan 1903   xRickman,Rosalie 23 nov 1933
xRiddle,Susan Jan 1903   /Rider,Isadora H.1842-1912
/Rider,John Wesley 1844-1903   xRiese,Henry 2 mar 1926
xRiffle,Mona Marie 12 nov 1934   /Riffle,Daniel I.1846-1918
/Riggs,Amanda 1858-1924   /Riggs,Basil J.1849-1922
/Riggs,Myrtle R.1885-1916d/oBJ&CE   /Riggs,Virginia 24 sep 1931 53y11m18d
xRiley,Henry 31 dec 1909   xRiley,India 6 Jul 1918
/Riley,Elizabeth R.1852-1932   /Rincer,Mildred V. 1919-1925
xRindwall,Augusta Nannie 14 mar 1913/Ring,Jennie S. 1867-1872
/Ring,John A. 1871-1876   /Ring,Mary 1815-1878
/Ring,Willie C.1875-76   xRinger,Mary Mildred 30 may 1925

xRishee,W.H. 12 feb 1920   /Ristell,Nancy Pearl29 Jan 1939
xRitchie,Cora 19 Jan 1932   xRitner,Louella 27 nov 1935
xRittenour,Dorothy 15 may 1923   /Ritner,Luella 25 nov 1935 63y2m23d
xRitenour,Inf/Orie 17 oct 1911   xRitter,Jeannie 23 Jan 1934
xRivercomb,Inf/JC 27 Jul 1915   xRizzto,Maggie 15 apr 1907
/Ritz,Eugene 1884-1889   /Ritz,Frankie 1895-1897
/Ritz,James M. 1846-1925   /Ritz,John Eldon 1882-1908
/Ritz,Kathryn M. 1850-1909   /Ritz,Paul 1879-1889
/Rivercomb,Julius E.1913-1915   /Roach,Dora 1880-1907
xRoach,Effie Florence 13 Jun 1931 /Roach,Edna 1895-1920
xRoach,Florence 2 may 1926
xRoach,Jacob 15 Jul 1907   xRoach,John E. 23--1896
xRoach,Mary E. 29 Jan 1921   xRoach,May H.4 mar 1926
xRoach,M.C. 23 feb 1910   /Roach,McCllelan 1863-1910
xRoach,Olin O. aug 1935   xRoach,Rosalie 12 apr 1935
xRoach,W.W. 6 Jan 1918   /Roadcap,Annie 1886-1917
/Robaugh,Inf 26 dec 1912   /Roadcap,A.G. 1850-1923
/Roberson,Marie K.1909-1922   xRoberson,Margaret K. 1909-1922
xRoberson,Mary J. 28 feb 1924   xRoberson,Ruah --
xRoberson,Sarah 10 Jan 1931   xRoberson,William M. 23 Jul 1930
xRoberts,Allen 13 Jun 1919   xRoberts,Charles R. 22 Jun 1931
/Roberts,Carlton V. 1912-1914   xRoberts,David 5 apr 1893
/Roberts,Emily Jane 1861-1912   xRoberts,Galliher 26 oct 1919
/Roberts,Frank N. 1831-1922   xRoberts,Hugh 22 dec 1918
xRoberts,Mrs Hugh 19 dec 1908   /Roberts,Rev.James 7aug1852-24nov1908
xRoberts,Inf/Frances 20 Jul 1916 xRoberts,Inf/CT 8 mar 1916
xRoberts,John L. 17 sep 1912   /Roberts,John Chas.9 mar 1932 72y2m14d
xRoberts,Julia 4 apr 1911   /Roberts,J.D. 18 dec 1861-5 apr 1893
xRoberts,Letha 15 apr 1924   xRoberts,Lula 8 nov 1925
/Roberts,Martha T.1878-1928   /Roberts,Mary H.1838-1920
xRoberts,Mary 13 Jul 1916   xRoberts,Mary Jane 22 sep 1935
xRoberts,Mary M/ 24 oct 1920   xRoberts,Mary V. 1868-1906
xRoberts,Oakey 20 may 1914   xRoberts,Oliver P. 19 Jun 1912
xRoberts,Mars S.J. 17 dec 1918   xRoberts,Silas F.28 oct 1916
xRoberts,Susan--   xRoberts,William 25 Jun 1924
xRobertson,Alonzo 23 dec 1932   xRobertson,Etta 27 Jun 1937
/Robertson,Chloe Ann 1866-1882   /Robertson,George L. 1879-1906
/Robertson,John Edwin Sr.1830-1898   Clara Edith 21 aug 1878-29 Jul 1902
/Robertson,John Edwin Jr.1868-1886/Robertson,Sidney B.3aug1864-19Jun1928
xRobertson,Inez 17 nov 1931   /Robertson,Leslie 25 Jun 1933 Inf
/Robertson,Wm.Edwin d14 Jun 1902 xRolinford,Annie 18 mar 1927
xRobison,B.F. 26 oct 1924   xRobinson,Aaron 21 may 1926
xRobinson,Alanzo 23 dec 1932   xRobinson,Andy 6 apr 1937
/Robinson,Charles L.1851-1899   xRobinson,Henry 21 feb 1936
xRobinson,Inf/AM 26 Jun 1911   xRobinson,Jack 5 Jul 1924
/Robinson,John M. 18 Jun 1939 WWI xRobinson,Lawrence 11 dec 1926
/Robinson,Luella 1868-1938   /Robinson,Mary F.Cook 12 mar 1938 48y9m
/Robinson,Richard 1836-1915   /Robinson,Matilda 27 nov 1937 71y7m23d
xRobinson,Ralph 25 aug 1917   /Robson,Mary J.1857-1924
xRoby,Mary Fannie 30 oct 1910   xRock,James 16 Jun 1891
/Roby,Walter A. Col 25th VA CavCSAxRock,Mary 30 oct 1930
xRodwick,Sophia 30 aug 1930   xRodgers,Emma D. 1864-1916
xRoffe,Nary E. 30 dec 1912   xRodgers,James H.1859-1917
xRoffe,T.I. 12 dec 1915   /Roe,Annie M.4 aug 1928 84y1m21d

/Rodgers,Dr.W.F. 1883-1916

/Roe,Joel 2 mar 1888 46y1m

xRogers,A.B. 13 apr 1914

xRogers,Adeen Bascum 21 sep 1912

xRogers,Amanada 25 apr 1926

xRogers,Ardester 3 dec 1924

xRogers,Charles 1863-1904

xRogers,Fenton 9 Jan 1915

xRogers,Francis 3 Jun 1909

xRogers,Rebecca 4 apr 1918

xRogers,Robert S. 23 oct 1939

xRogers,Thomas C. 26 Jul 1925

xRogers,Wilburn 17 Jan 1919

/Roland,Mae V.1886-1919

/Rohrbaugh,Madeline Sharp 1909-12

/Rolph,Lewis K. 1866-1919

xRollins,Letha 18 Jun 1918

/Rollyson,Dimmie M.1871-25w/oBurman L

xRollisons,Mrs.W. 25 nov 1918

xRollyson,Paul 22 feb 1937

xRolph,William V. 2 Jun 1939

xRomer,Sadie Ethel 13 sep 1939

/Romer,Samuel 1877-1932

/Romaine,Victoria Hite w/o W.H.

/Rood,Alford Wallace 1928-29

      7 Jul 1838-12 nov 1862

xRood,Alemta 21 Jan 1911

xRood,Annie 12 may 1921

/Rood,Delores Gale 1935-37

xRood,Edith 18 sep 1920

xRood,Edward 20 feb 1912

xRood,John 23 aug 1928

xRood,Olivia Oleta 24 apr 1920

xRood,Orie 11 feb 1915

xRood,Paul Wade 3 mar 1931

xRood,Sterling 1906

xRood,Sarah 1 aug 1924

/Rooker,Lucy 10 oct 1937

xRooney,Pat J. 3 feb 1922

/Roos,Louise 1872-1936

xRorrer,Donald E. 17 aug 1932

/Roos,Vincent 1856-1920

xRorrer,Eddie A. 11 feb 1931

/Rose,Anna 1872-1937

xRose--3 sep 1890

xRose,Althie 19 dec 1926

/Rose,C.E. 1837-1910

/Rose,Hettie 26 dec 1891-22 dec 1932

/Rose,Cyntha 1836-1911

xRose,Harriet 24 may 1925

/Rose,F.Co.E 17th VA Inf CSA

/Rose,Jimmie 4 nov 1918 inf

xRose,George 2 dec 1926

/Rose,James Thurman 1892-1934

xRose,James E. 9 may 1927

xRose,Lee 14 dec 1923

/Rose,Leora 1875-1921

/Rose,Lonnie 11 feb 1931 40y4m14d

xRose,Lizzie 31 nov 1939

xRose,Mary 21 Jul 1917

xRose,Mary 11 Jan 1910

xRose,Mary Ellen 11 may 1938

/Rose,Susan J. 1839-1921

xRose,William H. 30 apr 1939

xRose,William R. 1 Jul 1921

/Roseberry,Andrew 1829-1895

/Rosen,Marion 1861-1927

/Roseberry,Violet Dils 1836-1906

/Rosensteel,Henry F.1849-1919

/Rosenfeld,Ruth Sylvia 2mar1912-17mar1931

/Rosensteel,James Albert 15 Jan 1939

/Rosensteel,Lill I 1873-1893

xRosensteel,Annie E. 9 nov 1929

/Ross,Ceres Smith 1876-1939

xRoss,Enoch 15 feb 1921

/Ross,Delia Margarite 1909-1910 S&CM

xRoss,Floyd, 22 oct 1918

/Ross,Donald Lee 10 feb 1932 inf

xRoss,Hall 25 nov 1919

/Ross,Inez Barrett-1902-1931w/Whitfield

/Ross,James M.Sr.1847-1926

/Ross,James H.13 oct 1912 62y2m14d

xRoss,Margaret 15 may 1913

      Roxa A. 1857-1914

xRoss,Martha 5 may 1914

/Ross,Norma Eloise 1911-12 d/S&CM

xRoss,Prucillie 2 nov 1922

/Ross,Ora May 1873-1926

/Ross,Sarah Jane 1849-1936

/Ross,Owen 14 aug 1901 25y5m2ds/JM&JJ

/Ross,Stephen 30 nov 1936 54y5m3d

/Ross,Sarah Jane 1849-1936

xRoss,Tennesse D.8 mar 1937

xRossella,Jenny 3 dec 1937

/Rosson,Pamelia H.1827-1902

/Rossalla,Joseph 19 mar 1860-17 nov 14

/Roth,Hazel M.5 feb 1921

/Roswald,Axel Wm.1 Jun 1934 67y4m24d

xRoth,Margaret 10 nov 1912

xRoth,Mary M. 10 nov 1912

/Roth,William J.7 sep 1935 84y1m

/Rothgeb Z.1812-4 may 1898 86y

/Rothchild,Joseph H.1895-96s/oA&B

/Rothgeb,Alonzo H.1858-1930

/Rothchild,Rena May 1897-98d/oA&B

/Rothgeb,Olive J.1833-1920

xRottman,Rose 1903

/Row,Joseph J. 1886-1887 s/Dr.WD&B

/Rowsey,Allie Fair 1881-1890   /Row,Lawrence H. 1866-1910
xRowher,John 1851-1879   xRowsey,Alice 1881-1890
xRowsey,Enice 1929   xRowsey,Bertha 17 nov 1918
xRowsey,Henry L. 7 aug 1918   /Rowsey,John J. 1847-1906
xRowsey,Ivan T. 26 Jul 1931   xRowsey,Letha Ann 4 sep 1925
xRowsey,Marie 18 feb 1920   xRowsey,Nevil L. 2 may 1920
/Rowsey,Sarah E. 1852-1906   /Rowsey,Sarah Agnes 5 dec 1934 54y
xRucker,Emma Bell 15 mar 1935   xRucker,Goldie 8 feb 1918
xRucker,James T. 2 mar 1934   xRucker,John M.13 Jan 1931
xRucker,Margaret C.1904   xRucker,Smith 2 dec 1928
xRudd,Harless A.12 Jan 1931   /Rubin,Morris 1875-1929
/Rudd,Chas.Victor 1906-1931   /Rudolph,David Jennings 15 nov 1935 22y
/Rudd,Lewis L.1 may 1937 WWI   /Rudolph,Irene 1854-1927
xRudsill,Maggie 2 dec 1939   xRunion,James 28 sep 1927
/Runnels,Margaret Burns 1879-1924   /Runyon,James A.21 nov 1860-18 Jun 1914
/Runyan,Ada 18 Jul 1922   Sarah W. 12 may 1855-10 apr 1935
/Runyon,Harriet 1851-1907   xRunyon,J.A.29 Jun 1914
/Runyon,James 4 dec 1933 inf   xRunyon,Sarah 12 apr 1928
/Rush,Cynthia 29 Jul 1935 51y10m8   /Russell,Albert Gallatin 1825-1908
xRussell,Charles C.1904   /Russell,Fred 10aug1890-20apr1904AG&OM
xRussell,Daisy 28 sep 1927   xRussell,Hiram C. 11 may 1939
/Russell,John -War 1812   /Russell,James C. 1865-nov 1898 35y
/Russell,M.E. 1835-1919   /Russell,John T.17 Jan 1878 13yWH&SA
xRussell,Ida May--   xRussell,Ivan Stewart 29 oct 1931
xRussell,Mary Alice 9 mar 1935   xRussell,May 25 nov 1924
xRussell,Sarah M. 1935   xRussell,W.A. 6 mar 1919
/Russell,Sarah W. 1834-1918   /Russell,Olivia Mortimer 1847-1927
/Russell,Susan A. mar 1911   77y   /Russell,W.Henry 1831-dec 1901 70y
/Rutherford,George C.   /Rutherland,Nora Turley
     30 aug 1870-16 Jan 1922   18 nov 1871-24 oct 1926 w/oGeo.C.
xRuthlee,---7 may 1927   xRutherford,Golden 13 mar 1924
xRutledge,John W. 14 oct 1921   xRylesworth,D.J. 4 Jun 1923
xRymer,Claudius 1904 inf   xRyson,S.L. 28 dec 1918

xSaddler, Samuel 27 apr 1928
/Salman, A.E.1857-1931
xSammons, Herbert W.7 nov 1920
xSamples, Sarah Ellen 1 dec 1937
/Sampson, Alice R.1849-1919
/Sampson, Annett Zuck 1861-1921
/Sampson, George E. 1844-1930
   Mary Alice 1854-1913
/Sampson, Harry T. 1875-1920
/Sampson, John M. 1848-1922
xSanborn, C.P. 12 feb 1932
xSanborn, John H. 26 oct 1934
xSanders, G.W. 1 apr 1923
xSanders, James N. 10 Jan 1912

xSanders, John Mack 6 Jun 1933
/Sanders, F.J. 1864-1918
   Mary Stephenson 1866-1912
/Sanders, James Finley
   1866-30 may 1934 68y6m28d
xSanders, William C.7 Jan 1911
/Sands, William 1819-1905
/Sands, Margaret 1829-1916
xSanford, L.Maxine 28 apr 1935
xSanford, V.E. 4 Jul 1922
/Sandman, Harry s/oGeo,&Anna
/Sandman, Mamie d/o Geo.&Anna
/Sapienza, Maria M.
   20 nov 1879-30 dec 1925
/Sarah, Harry J.1842-1917
xSarras, Raymon 8 sep 1923
/Sarver, Columbia 1869-1916
xSarver, Bertha 10 may 1936
/Sarver, G.H.1860-1901
xSarver, Martha 4 feb 1911
xSarver, Samuel --
xSaunders, Elbert 4 dec 1922
xSaunders, F.J.24 Jan 1918
/Saunders, George W.1850-1923
/Saunders, James N.1877-1912
xSaunders, James F.31 may 1934
/Saunders, John P.1889-1930
xSaunders, John V. 9 Jun 1923
/Saunders, Missouri 1854-1908
xSaunders, Samilda 9 Jan 1935
/Saunders, Taylor Ashby 1904-05
xSaunders, William F. 1868-1927
xSavage, Martha 30 dec 1937
xSawyers, Owen G. 4 Jan 1935
xSayers, inf 7 aug 1924
xSayre, Gordon 1935
xSayre, John 11 may 1928
xSayre, Samuel Ben. 29 Jun 1930
xScales, Lillian 4 nov 1897
xScales, Mary R. 29 aug 1905 inf

xSagraves, Lela 1907
/Saleh, Mabel G.30 apr 1889-5 nov 1918
xSaleh, Ahmed 16 nov 1937
xSamples, Alice 3 Jun 1913
/Sample, Elizabeth 22 feb 1820-23 Jun 1899
/Sample, M.A. 9sep 1890 79y2m29d
/Sample, James T.7 Jul 1879 24ys/oMA&E
/Samson, inf 1922
/Samuels, A.H.1stLt CoE 8th VA Cav 1864CSA
xSamuel, Henry 3 may 1924
/Sanborn, Philomelia 6/21/1890-6/11/1934
/Sanborn, Wm.Edgar 1861-1912
/Sanders, Chas.Harrison 16 dec 1928 61y
/Sanders, Harry E.23 Jul 1885-8 aug 1907J&M
xSanders, John P. 3 Jan 1930
/Sanders, Mabel 1896-1911 d/CH&NM
/Sanders, Mary V.1862-1911   /
/Sanders, William F.1868-1927
/Sandman, Alberta A. 3 feb 1933
/Sandman, Anna 1844-1916
/Sandman, George 1844-1922
/Sandford, Alma Alberta 9/6/1880-1/13/1903
xSanford, Nathan 6 apr 1921
xSanford, W.T. 1845-- w-Mar.
/Sanford, John M. 1872-1920
/Sanford, Lizzie Douthit 1849-1931
/Sanford, Louisa Caroline 1882-1915
/Sanford, Margaret 15dec1849-16Jun1903wWT
/Sanford, Sarah 1884-85 d/oN&B
xSarrie, Marie 2 Jun 1923
/Sartin, Lucille 6 oct 1905-14 aug 1935
/Sarver, Geo.W.1891 s/o CH&Margie
xSarver, Maggie 9 aug 1919
xSarver, Raymond 1921-23
/Savage, Chris 19 oct 1911
xSaunders, Eliza 30 may 1925
xSaunders, Homer 4 mar 1930
/Saunders, Dr.E.T.15 dec 1839-14 may 1892
   Sarah K.22 may 1846-21 dec 1891
xSaunders, John A. 13 dec 1927
xSaunders, John H. 11 aug 1831
xSaunders, Mary S. 27 apr 1912
xSaunders, Moble 3 mar 1929
xSaunders, Silas Eugene 25 apr 1939
xSaunders, Virgil Charles 15 dec 1939
xSaurlock, Huckon 21 oct 1927
xSawyers, Ambrose 25 Jan 1922
xSaxton, Shirley 20 oct 1912
xSayles, L.C. 29 Jan 1918
/Sayles, Maude Bishop 1888-1931
xSayre, Maud K. 3 apr 1917
/Scales, Abigail S.Jewell 1838-1922
xScales, Lysle 4 nov 1897
/Scales, Lysle 1889-1890

xScales,Myrtle 28 aug 1905 xScales,Myrtle G. 11 aug 1905
/Scales,Otis J.1848-10 may 1917 xScales,Peter B. 11 feb 1928
xScales,Ruth 20 oct 1900 xScales,Thomas 17 mar 1885
xScanlon,Anna 23 dec 1925 /Scanlon,Drusilla 1891-93d/oTS&V
/Scanlon,Jennie V.1860-1925 /Scanlon,Patrick J. 1839-1916
/Scanlon,Timothy S.1858-1926 xScarberry,Clayton 31 dec 1936
/Scarberry,Earnestine 1931-1934 xScarff,Nellie Cain 13 feb 1928
/Scarff,Nell Carr 1852-1924 /Sceercy,Mary Evelyn 1919 inf
/Scarff,Theodore R.1848-1910 xSchaffer,Milton 9 feb 1928
xSchaber,inf 24 Jun 1921 /Schaffer,George 1874-1917
/Schaber,William 1873-1938   Margaret Every 8/30/1881-11/30/1902
/Schaub,Elizabeth S.1877-1908 xSchaub,Henry A. 6 mar 1917
/Schaub,Henry 1852-1933 /Schaub,Louise 1851-1931
xSchlabig,inf 18 mar 1921 /Schenker,Saul Isaac 1860-1931
/Schmidt,Sophie E. xSchenker,Sarah 1890-1932
xSchneider,Bernard-- xSchneider,Catherine 2 oct 1931
/Schneider,Christiana 1837-1900 /Schoenfeld,Antionette 1863-1929
/Schneider,Kasper 1830-1910 /Schoenfeld,Max 1860-1919
/Schneider,Katie B.1877-1931 /Schoenfeld,Moses 1884-1924
/Schossler,John 18 Jan 1892 /Schofield,Lane McNair
xSchools,inf 9 nov 1914 xSchofield,Laura 20 feb 1915
xSchossler,John 19 Jan 1892 xSchoulton,Alice Jul 1907
xSchramm,inf 22 apr 1912 xSchroyer,Robert L. 9 oct 1916
/Schreiber,Albert T. 1875-1936 /Schoonover,James S. 16 nov 1897 13y
/Schreiber,George F.1886-1890 /Schwarz,Adolph 1861-1933
/Schreiber,Louis 1846-1918 /Schwarz,Dora goodman 1862-1924
/Schreiber,Margaret 1848-1927 /Schweitzer,Donna Gay 1898-1938
xSchweitzer,Dornie G.13 mar 1928/Schweitzer,Nicholas C.1917-1926
/Scott,Annie 1865-1938 /Scott,Boston F.d1935
/Scott,Charles 18 Jan 1892 21y4m/Scott,Elizabeth 1841-1910-
xScott,Dorothy Lee 21 nov 1915 xScott,F.C. 28 apr 1918
xScott,Hazel 1900-1930 xScott,Isham 7 dec 1930
/Scott,Isabel Holmes 1865-1932 xScott,J.W.6 dec 1938
  Hezekiah 1842-1913 /Scott,James Edward 1873-1935
/Scott,James E.1906-1926 /Scott,John W. 1876-1936
/Scott,Leonard I.1879-1905 /Scott,Joseph Wm.Anderson 1863-1938
xScott,Liza 19 Jul 1924 /Scott,Lillie Gentry 1855-1936
xScott,Marie 31 oct 1918 xScott,Martha B.17 Jan 1931
xScott,Matilda 27 apr 1925 xScott,Stella 20 may 1926
/Scott,Sarah R. 1858-1916 /Scott,S.W.17 may 1838-22 apr 1895
/Scott,W.N. 29 may 1933 /Scott,Virginia L. 1855-1917
/Scott,Winfield 1853-1920 /Seale,Virginia 1900-10d/oRoss&Brook
xSeals,Mary 29 mar 1921 /Seamonds,Cora L 1881-1921
/Seamonds,Geneva C.1851-1916 /Seamonds,William H.1840-1920
/Seamonds,Peyton H. 1844-1923   Sarah H.1843-1923
xSearls,Wm.Alton 22 Jul 1939 /Seastrunk,Ellen Keenan 1878-1906
/Seay,Maurice Lewis 1915-1924 /Secic,Pete d25 may 1926
/Seay,Stanley Arthur 1925-1928 /Sedgwick,Frank 13 nov 1863-20 dec 1936
xSeiber,Peter 8 dec 1920 /Seiber,William 1869-1914
xSeimoer,inf 3 Jul 1936 /Sehon,Edmund 1843-1925
/Self,Gwendolyn E. 1914-1923 /Sehon,Eliza.J.Stuart 1845-1929
/Senseney,Jacob M.1848-1905 /Sellers,Clara 5 Jul 1874-10 feb 1893wDW
/Senseney,Sara M. 1851-1932 /Sentz,Zella H.1879-1896
/Senseney,mary 1887-1904 /Seward,Glenn A.Joseph 1938 inf

xSexton,Ada--
xSexton,Beaula 18 aug 1923
xSexton,Hattie 4 oct 1921
xSexton,Henry 1 Jun 1919
xSexton,Mildred 21 feb 1915
xSexton,Suda Jane 15 oct 1930
/Shackleford,John Jr.1894-96
/Shafer,Clyde Lee 1934-37
/Shafer,Evelyn L. 1920 inf
/Shafer,Libby Ann 1933-38
/Shafer,Martha V.1921 inf
xShafer,Texanna 31 oct 1918
xShaffer,Margaret 1881-1902
xShaffer,Roy 6 feb 1915
xShanan,Ellenor 8 feb 1917
xShamlin,George 1896
/Shank,Hugh P.1890-1932
/Shank,Vera Fay 1894-1918
xShannon,J.A. 3 oct 1917
xShannon,Pearl 18 may 1923
xSharah,Harry 1842-1917 GAR
/Sharah,Ruth Forbes 1845-1937
/Sharkey,Annie Marie 1925-1930
/Sharkey,inf 1933
/Sharp,Clyde,L. 1893-1931
xSharp,Helen L. 14 dec 1927
xSharp,Madaline 1909-1912
xShaver,Emma 9 dec 1932
xShaver,G.B. 10 Jan 1912
xShaver,Hobert 9 swp 1912
/Shaver,Nola D. 1892-1896
/Shaver,Sylvia 1896-1903
/Shaul,Elizabeth Ann 1911-12
/Shaw,Eliza 1877-1918
/Shaw,Lutitia 1825-1905
xShay,Cornelius 1830-1902
/Sheets,Jacob H.1858-1914
/Sheets,Samuel Lakin 1907--08
xShefferd,Stathy 20 Jan 1923
xSheffie,Sam 19 oct 1930
xShefield,John 4 dec 1925
xSheline,Bella B. 15 dec 1924
xSheline,John 24 mar 1926
xSheltoh--1889
/Shelton,Frank H.1858-1886
/Shelton,Inez Noel 1870-1938
xShelton,Mary 1 Jan 1924
xShelton,Mary 27 nov 1938
/Shelton,Mary J.1850-1929
/Shelton,Thomas A.1828-1909
/Shelton,V.Rosa 1870-1925
/Shelton,W.E.1866-1913
/Shepard,Charles T. 1854-1934
/Shepard,May E. 1857-1925

xSexton,Annie-14 Jun 1910
xSexton,Ella 21 Jan 1912
/Sexton,James Harry 5 apr 1934 45y2m5d
xSexton,Mrs.K.C. --
xSexton,Olet 31 dec 1929
/Shackleford,John 12 dec 1859-29 mar 1921
/Shafer,Brosia 1897-1913d/oSM&M
xShafer,Elizabeth Ann 20 Jan 1938
/Shafer,Lydia Dingess 16 Jan 1935 78y7d
xShafer,Mary P. 23 Jun 1919
xShafer,S.M. 4 may 1916
/Shaffer,Lizzie 24 aug 1894   43y8m10d
xShaffer,Milton 9 feb 1928
xShaffer,Mrs.S.J.31 aug 1915
/Shain,George A. 1861-1924
xShannon,Jesse A. 7 oct 1913
/Shannon,John B.30 nov 1846-17 sep 1912
/Shannon,Winnie d18 feb 1923
xShannon,Mary L. 5 Jun 1920
xShannon,Rose 5 apr 1922
xSharkey,James 18 feb 1933
xSharkey,Mary Josephine 24 mar 1932
/Sharky,Helen V.1911-1939
/Sharkey,Winifred 1917-1939
/Sharp,Dora 18601928
xSharp,Hugh H. 23 Jul 1921
xShaver,Ellen 4 apr 1911
/Shaver,Elmer Eugene 1903
xShaver,Harry 12 dec 1924
/Shaver,James H. 1865-1935
xShaver,Virginia Bell 8 apr 1940
xShavers,M.B. 8 Jan 1919
/Shaul,inf 1908
/Shaw,James C. 1825/6-1894
/Shaw,Mary A. 1844-1928
xShay,Mollie 1825-1893
xSheafer,Lydia Dingess 18 Jan 1935
/Sheets,Charles F.4 Jan 1923 inf
xSheffy,Mary 10 aug 1912
xSheffield,Statby 20 Jan 1923
xShein,Simon 1872-1936
xSheline,Harden 19 Jul 1910
/Shelton,Ann Eliza 1834-1911
xShelton,C.K. 18 Jul 1921
xShelton,Joseph R. 19 sep 1929
xShelton,Josephene 7 Jan 1917
/Shelton,J.H. 16 Jun 1874-5 Jul 1905
xShelton,Sopheouo 21 Jun 1920

/Shelton,Sallie Poage 24 apr 1883d/JR&MA
/Shelton,Walter Theo.1 Jun 1936 85y8m23d
/Shelton,Wm.T.1866-1922
/Shepherd,Charley 1876-1918
/Shepherd,Lula L.1 apr 1889-12Jun1926wRG

/Shepard,Marguarite 1903-1934
/Sheridan,Ida Bell 11 Jul 1936
    48y9m12d
/Sheridan,Maurice W.26 oct 1936
    18y8m14d
xShenrer,Sarah 1890-1932
xShepard,Myrtle 8 Jan 1923
/Shifflette,Carter S.1869-1905
/Shifflette,Jane C.1832-1910
/Shifflette,J.A.1861-1929(A.J.)
    Nannie H.1864-1918
/Shirley,Charles E. 1856-1926
/Short,Joan 1931-1932
/Short,Roy Omar d6 apr 1928 15y
xShort,Alice 25 oct 1919
xShort,Clement L. 1890-1927
xShort,Katherine 3 sep 1912
xShort,Rose 9 may 1933
/Shultz,Mary R.1836-1919
/Shultz,Jennie P.1847-1890wWA
/Shultz,Joseph 1843-1910
xShultz,William 8 aug 1933
/Shute,Frederic N.1886-1919
/Shy,Alberta 1886-1892
xShy,E.Dudley 25 Jan 1916
xShy,Frank 24 sep 1915
/Shy,H.W.1833-1918
/Shy,Josephine 1838-1916
xShy,Sara Olivia 1908
/Shy,W.E. 1864-1937
/Siers,Lon Jr.
xSiers,Leonidas 19 Jan 1935
xSiers,Lan 19 dec 1923
/Sikes,Colonel T.1836-1907
/Sikes,Minervia I.1843-1919
/Sikes,C.R. 1881-1896
/Sikes,Clara Frazier 1884-1905
    w/o Austin M.
/Sikes,Lee W.
/Sikes,Mamie 1869-1933
/Sikes,Clara Frazier 1884-1905
    w/o Austin M.
xSimmons,Fannie 19 sep 1912
xSimmons,Ollie V. 25 Jun 1930
xSimmons,Wanda J. 23 sep 1939
xSimons,Robert 6 aug 1910
/Simon,Anna 1855-1923
/Simon,Anna 1855-1923
xSimons,Charen A. 10 feb 1924
xSimons,John 7/19/1842-7/22/1890
/Simons,Katie May d4 oct 1878
/Simons,Katie May d26 Jun 1882
xSimpson,Della 21 mar 1939
xSimpson,John 31 may 1913

/Shepherd,Lurman 1908 inf/CM&B
/Shepherd,Nannie M.1852-1915
/Shiel,Francis W. 1894-1937
/Shiles,Edward 1839-1918
/Shiels,Sophia 1848-1926
/Shiels,George C. 1875-1911
xSheppard,Betty L.13 nov 1928
xShin,Leo A. 23 sep 1924
/Shipp,Burton J.1888-1915
/Shirer,Josephine 1855-1916
/Shirer,Milton 1855-1923
/Shockey,A.L.10 Jun 1865-25 may 1920
/Shoemaker,Carrie Adline 15 may 1939 63y
/Shore,Fannie G.1878-1892 d/o WE&ME
xShort,Carl 17 apr 1923
xShort,Edith 8 dec 1934
xShort,Robert 27 feb 1927
xShowen,Charlotte 9 nov 1925
xShrewsbury,Robert L. 19 feb 1918
/Shumaker,William CoC 36thBn VA Cav CSA
/Shumate,Frank A.1868-1928
/Shumate,Laura J.1872-1917
/Shumate,Lewis W. 1900-1918
/Shy,Christine E. 1911-1921
xShy,Elizabeth 1908
xShy,Lizzie 27 dec 1908
/Shy,Lawrence 1891 inf
/Shy,Mattie 1887-1897
 xShy,M.B. Jan 1907
/Sidebottom,Mont 1881-1915
 xSiders,J.L. 5 nov 1922
 xSiegrill,W.H.21 nov 1921
 xSifford,Julia 10 Jan 1937
/Sigler,Thomas Hope
/Siler,Julia 1860-1932
xSilman,Virginia 24 sep 1916
/Silvers,James E. 1865-1924
xSilvey -- 18 Jan 1919
xSimins,Mary 29 nov 1923
xSimmonds,Mattie 17 oct 1910
/Simmons,John Roy 1927 inf
xSimmons,Della 2 Jul 1923
xSimmons,Kate M. 1882
xSimons,Robert 6 aug 1910
xSimmons,Wm.20 Jun 1921
/Simms,Florence 22 may 1897   33y
/Simms,Henry Clay 1847-1906
/Simms,Katherine L.1860-1934
xSimms,John 23 dec 1910
/Simms,Robert Marshall 1892-1917
xSimplins,Helen 8 oct 1926
/Simpson,Edna M.1852-1913
xSimpson,Jacob--
/Simpson,Ola A.6 apr 1876-8 Jan 1903

/Simpson,Frank 1879-1925   /Simpson,L.L.1 oct 1860-19 aug 1890
/Simpson,Wm.T. 18501-1911   /Sims,John P. 1876-1910
xSimson,John M.3 apr 1923   xSims,L.W. 14 Jan 1918
/Singer,Gladys 1903-1919   /Margurite 19 may 1925 w/LD
xSinger,Nettie 21 Jan 1913   /Sinsel,Jessie G.1878-1920
/Singer,Henrietta 7 oct 1935 78y   /Skeene,James 1845-1916
xSister,Odrlia 19 dec 1932   xSkeens,Agnes 13 oct 1922
/Slagle,Carroll 1897-1919   xSkene,Mrs.James 1846-1922
xSlagle,Wilmer 26 sep 1926   xSloppen,Josephine 19 may 1932
/Sliger,Bessie R. 1880-1896   /Slayton,Lehanis 3 aug 1935 inf
/Sliger,George Alva 1875-1933   /Slayton,Ralph E.19 nov 1933 inf
/Sliger,inf 1889   /Sliger,J.Walter 1876-1935
/Sliger,J.Ernest 1886-89   /Sliger,Oscar M.1881-1908
/Sliger,Sarah A. 1851-1919   /Sliger,Thomas A. 1908 inf
/Sliger,Thomas J. 1847-1902   /Sloan,Chas.Wortham 8 Jan 1936 69y3m21d
xSloan,C.J. 17 sep 1928   xSloan,Margaret 19 Jun 1928
xSmallwood,Walter Sr.15 feb 1934   /Sloan,Morton Wortham 1843-1931
xSmallwood,Sarah 9 mar 1923   xSmallwood,Walter S.Jr. 8 oct 1920
xSmith,A.E 17 apr 1933   xSmith,Amanda 3 oct 1926
xSmith,Ambrose 22 may 1915   xSmith,Anna A. 2 mar 1922
xSmith Ann Henkle 1 Jan 1937   /Smith,Addie 21 apr 1934 80y
/Smith,Addie V.1864 inf   /Smith,Albert Emmett 1852-1929
/Smith,Alice S.1862-1905   /Smith,Amanda J.1846-1912
/Smith,Ben E. 1858-1916   /Smith,Anorille Grant 23apr1864-11oct33
/Smith,Bertha 1869-1904   /Smith,Bernard 1 Jul 1899-24 aug 1914
/Smith,Billy Carrol d 1926   /Smith,B.B. SpAm
xSmith,Ben.F. 31 dec 1934   xSmith,Belah 12 oct 1918
xSmith,C.E.30 Jan 1912   xSmith,Carlie 2 1aug 1930
xSmith,Cloutta 27 dec 1926   xSmith,Clara 2 apr 1927
xSmith,Mrs.Cora 5 mar 1922   /Smith,Cora Bell 1881-1938
/Smith,Carl M. 1900-1935   /Smith,Carl H.14 dec 1934 WWI
/Smith,Claude 1909 inf   /Smith,Cora Belle 11/5/1884-10/3/1914wJT
xSmith,David B.20 Jan 1913   xSmith,Earl 23 apr 1926
/Smith,Don D. 1906-1913   /Smith,Earnest Hale 1901-1905
/Smith,D.I. 1841-1921   /Smith,Edward A. 1831-1896
/Smith,Effie Mae 1866-1924   /Smith,Edward G. 1887-1910
/Smith,Elba M. 1879-1933   /Smith,Edward S. 1860-1870 s/o EA
/Smith,Eliza P. 1830-1912   /Smith,Eliz.Woody 25 dec 1863-15 nov 1935
/Smith,Emmett 1882-1908   /Smith,Emiline Burton 4 Jul 1834-20 dec15
xSmith,Edna H. 14 oct 1915   xSmith,Edward C. 21 mar 1915
xSmith,Effie 23 feb 1920   xSmith,Elizabeth 17 oct 1922
xSmith,Erie R. 18 mar 1912
/Smith,Eugenia P. 1870-1915   /Smith,Eva L. 2 apr 1931 42y3m1d
xSmith,Eugenia E. 9 oct 1912   xSmith.Ernest 1901-1905
/Smith,Frank G.1897-1926   /Smith,F.K.Bud 1898-1931
/Smith,Frank L.16 Jun 1926   /Smith,Frank S.WWI
xSmith,Frances M. 7 may 1928   xSmith,Mrs.Frank 12 feb 1911
xSmith,Garnet 21 aug 1930   /Smith,Geo.Edward 1886 inf/DB&E
/Smith,George Collard 1875-1939   /Smith,George W.1833-1919
xSmith,George W.16 mar 1937   /Smith,George Ann 1866-1947
xSmith,Mrs.Georgia 16 mar 1919   xSmith,Gladys 6 Jul 1928
/Smith,Hannah C. 1846-1933   /Smith,Harry H.2 feb 1938 pvt 22BN WV CW
xSmith,Hattie Mae 10 Jan 1922   xSmith,Harry E. 6 may 1931
xSmith,henry C. 30 aug 1928   xSmith,Harrsion 10 mar 1917 inf

/Smith,Howard G.1824-1926
/Smith,Hull 1896-1923
xSmith,J.B. 8 feb 1919
/Smith,Jennie B. 1835-1907
xSmith,Janie 1937
/Smith,John 1848-1924
/Smith,John B.1852-1914
/Smith,John T. 1849-1918
xSmith,Josephine H.1835-1906
xSmith,Laura Owens 19 mar 1931
xSmith,Lucy 7 may 1937
xSmith,Mae 11 oct 1921
xSmith,Mary 1 aug 1921
/Smith,Mary d1934
/Smith,Mary A.1826-1905
xSmith,Mary B. 1857-1914
/Smith,May 1894-1921
xSmith,Minnie 2 oct 1918
xSmith,Nannie B. 1 nov 1925
/Smith,Nicholas 1822-1900
xSmith,Nellie 6 jan 1937
/Smith,Obey Jr.5 oct 1918 WWI
xSmiith,Pearlie 10 jul 1929
/Smith,Percival 1796-1873
    Mary Chapman 1809-1934
/Smith,Percival Jr.1835-1904
  Josephine G.Hite 1835-1906
/Smith,Sarah P.1848-1918
/Smith,Sallie Wiatt 1855-1915
/Smith,Sidney R.1879-1931
/Smith,Snell M. 1834-1884
/Smith,Stacy E. 1904-1924
xSmith,T.B. 17 feb 1918
xSmith,Virginia May 11 nov 1925
xSmith,W.G.W. 7 jun 1921
/Smith,W.H. 1830-27 oct 1885
xSmith,William 1817-1881
xSmith,Wm.Edward 29 jan 1925
/Smith,Col.William 71y Civ War
/Smith,Willie 1874-1934
/Smith,Winifred A. 1899-1932
xSmith,Willie L.R. 14 mar 1921
xSmolosky,Andy 31 aug 1920
/Smoot,Frank 1880-1914
/Smoot,J.W. 1850-1916
/Smoot,Ruby 1883-1906
xSnead,Jos.A.24 feb 1913
xSnedegar,Annie 3 dec 1920
/Snedegar,Rachel 1884-1918
/Snedegar,Rachel A.1884-85
/Snedegar,Wm.J.4 oct 1917(bur)
    CoD 36th OH Inf
/Snider,Charles H.1849-1922
/Snider,Fernia 1860-1937

/Smith,Hoy 29 aug 1889-9 may 1913s/o J&P
/Smith,Ivan Jay 1882-1916
xSmith,Ira 21 jun 1915
/Smith,I.M. 19 jul 1875-19 sep 1910
xSmith,Jane 3 apr 1925
/Smith,John Nortington 9/17/1845-2/17/02
/Smith,John B.1849-1919
xSmith,John 15 jan 1910
xSmith,Kenneth B.6 sep 1924
/Smith,Lawrence Otto 1888-1911
xSmith,Lydia Ann 21 jun 1920
/Smith,Mabel Keren 29 jul 1884-16 feb 29
/Smith,Marguerite V.1913-14
/Smith,Mary E. d30 jul 1938 65y5m11d
/Smith,Mary J.25 jan 1857-30 jul 1903RJ&M
/Smith,Maude Burgess 1876-1915 w/o Wm.
/Smith,Mary Chapman 1804-1894 w/Percival
xSmith,Minnie 30 apr 1925
/Smith,Nathan 17 jan 1919 72yCSA
/Smith,Nannie M. 5 feb 1936 65y6m5d
/Smith,Obadiah 1861-1937
/Smith,Ora 1885-1927 w/oDouglas
/Smith,Ora E.3 sep 1895-10 sep 1921
/Smith,Robert 1891-92
/Smith,Roy 1897-1921
/Smith,Rush 1 aug 1924
xSmith,Samuel A. 19 mar 1924
/Smith,Sarah Ella 28 oct 1934 54y
/Smith,Sarah 1820-3 aug 1886 66y1m8d
xSmith,Signam C. 14 dec 1939
/Smith,Walter E. 1866-1892
xSmith,Talmage 20 may 1915
xSmith,Virgil B. 19 sep 1924
xSmith,W.F. 8 sep 1913
xSmith,Watles 19 oct 1925
/Smith,Wm.Henry 1848-1884
xSmith,William E. 2 oct 1934
xSmiht,William P. 28 oct 1921
/Smith,W.H.C.5 nov 1860-8 jan 1902
/Smith,Willie Wilson 1874-1903 w/o EL
/Smith,Wm.S.CoK 8th VA Cav 11 apr 1903CSA
/Smithson,Alice Blaker 1882-1930
xSmoot.Mrs.W.E. 5 oct 1910
/Smoot,Catherine Louise inf/o FW&ME
/Smoot,Luticia 1846-1920
/Snair,Shirley R.1920-1934
xSnead,inf/Joe 2 jun 1912
xSnedegar,inf/CH 18 feb 1915
/Snedegar,C.Bernard 1904-1908 s/oCH/MA
/Snedegar,Robert J.1843-1917 CoD 36th OH
    Mary C.1857-1918
/Snell,Bettie T.1856-1921
/Snuffer,Mary F.1857-1934
xSnider,Fred 18 dec 1934

xSnider,George W. 20 Jul 1930   xSnider,John E. 17 aug 1925
/Snider,Stella A1880-1905w/CW   /Snider,Joseph O.1853-1926
xSnow,Amanda 10 feb 1920   xSnow,Clementine 10 feb 1920
xSnow,Judy 6 dec 1926   xSnow,Ruby 9 sep 1926
xSnyder,George R.2 apr 1935   xSnyder,Helen L.7 nov 1921
/Snyder,Kate R.1851-1924   xSnyder,Lillian 22 Jan 1916
/Snyder,Kittie C.1884-1936   /Snyder,Samuel A.1874-1920
/Snyder,Vivian C.1890-1916   xSohnsor,Richard feb 1930
xSolomon,Mary H. 8 mar 1921   xSomers,Patric J. 14 oct 1938
xSonger,Lyle--   xSomer,Aileen G. 7 Jun 1926
/Songer,Nettie F.1878-1913   xSorter,Elizabeth M. 8 aug 1932
xSouthall,J.F. 11 sep 1915   xSortet,Arthur J.12 dec 1934 56y3m4d
xSouthall,Rosa 20 apr 1925   /Southworth,A.F.1846-1912
/Southworth,Chas.J.1870-1927   /Southworth,Elviry V.1850-1921
/Southworth,James P. 1903-1916   /Southworth,Fleming Over.30 oct 1937 35y
/Southworth,Stella M.1872-1953   xSouthworth,Susan 3 nov 1910
/Southworth,Wade H.1882-1924   xSouthworth,Walter B. 8 aug 1910
xSouthworth,W.B. 23 sep 1918   xSowards,Agnes 10 oct 1910
/Sowards,Burgess 1891-1918   xSowards,Edith 8 mar 1919
/Sowards,(3)inf 1922   /Sowards,Leondias W. 1906-1928
xSowards,Luvina 6 Jan 1935   xSowards,Maud 20 dec 1920
xSowards,Pearl 10 Jun 1927   xSpalding,Marie 15 apr 1927
xSpaulding,Betty Jane 9 Jun 1930/Spangenberg,Henry F.4/27/1837-2/2/1903
xSpaulding,Wm.13 apr 1931   /Spangenberg,Sarah A.3/1/1854-5/2/1930
xSparks,B.F. 22 oct 1918   /Sparks,Cecil B.1907-1915
xSparks,C.W. 21 nov 1910   xSparks,Charolette 8 dec 1923
xSparks,Everett F. 30 oct 1929   xSpears,inf 11 Jun 1923
/Spears,Estella S.1876-1921   /Spears,Everett I.1904-1912
/Spears,Gladys M.1900-1902   /Spears,Henry CoD 91 OH Inf Civil WarGAR
/Spears,Pearl 1892-1939   /Spears,Susan A.16 mar 1855-23 dec 1914
xSpears,Stella S.1876-1921   xSpears,U.G. 25 feb 1917
xSpears,Wiley 13 apr 1925   /Speisel,Joseph 1903-1927
xSpencer,Charles 25 Jan 1926   xSpicer,Grace 11 Jul 1915
/Spencer,Charlie 21 oct 1862 CW /Spicer,James 28 nov 1935 61y4m15d vet
/Spencer,Frances W.1829-1913   /Spicer,Nicholas 27 oct 1888 20y4mHT&L
xSpencer,Leli 6 oct 1923   /Spicer,Henry T.25 oct 1876 38y7m
/Spencer,Capt.T.W. 1821-1874 CW xSpicer,Lee 11 Jul 1915
xSpier,inf/AW 20 mar 1915   xSpicer,Lucetly 30 dec 1908
/Spilman,Henry E.1859-1920   /Spilman,H.Erskine 1892-1934
/Spilman,Marjorie 1895-1934   xSpinner,Minnie 9 feb 1939
xSpissel,Joseph 8 feb 1927   xSpradling,James 13 mar 1919
xSpradling,Mary Louise 9/25/1934xSpradling,Tennesse 24 nov 1915
xSpradling,Winfield 28 apr 1919 /Sprague,John P. 1860-1912
xSpraw,Charles 29 oct 1925   /Sprandenbert,Sarah A.1 mar 1854-2 may 19

xSprencher,Susie 20 aug 1917   /Sprecher,C.M.30 Jul 1897-3 Jan 1911
/Sprinkle,George CoD 91st OH Inf /Springston,Jefferson Davis   75y11m7d
xSprinkle,Ernest 13 aug 1914   26 Jun 1938
xSprow,Catherine 22 mar 1914   xSpringston,Mrs.J.D. 23 Jun 1917
/Sprow,Sallie 9 apr 1888 15yC&S xSpurlock,Ethel E. 14 nov 1926
/Spurlock,Kate M. 1886-1919   /Spurlock,Kenneth 25 mar 1939 28y8m8d
/Spurlock,Mary E. d1926   xSpurlock,Lucy Margaret 31 may 1932
xSpurlock,Magaline 29 mar 1910   /Spurlock,Mathew 1853-1924
xSpurlock,May E. 6 apr 1926   /Stachon,Alice 1840-1902
/Staf,Thomas 8 feb 1935 42y3m4d xStacey,Alice 15 Jan 1930

xStackhouse,B.F. 27 Jan 1923   xStacy,James B.12 dec 1927
/Stafford,Edna May 1931-34   xStafford,Susie Steward 19 nov 1931
/Stafford,W.H. 1897-1931   /Staley,Charles R.1904-1920
xStaley,Frank E. 23 Jan 1920   xStaley,Marg Bess mar 1908
/Staley,Opal May 1913-1919   /Staley,S.T. 1861-1892
/Staley,Wm.M. 1845-1919   /Stalnaker,inf 1916
     Nancy J.1850-1931   /Stamper,Margret Pollock 1877-1910wCarlis
/Stanard,Rebecca B.Carter   xStanford,Emmet A. 14 dec 1934
     1793-31 oct 1855 w/o Edward   xStanley,C.F. 18 nov 1916
xStanley,Cecil L. 3 Jun 1935   xStanley,Fred 14 oct 1918
xStanley,Isaac marian 3 Jan 1931   /Stanley,H.J.6 Jul 1865-10 sep 1899
/Stanley,James 1841-1900   /Stanley,Kate D.7 Jun 1889 inf/oBK&ME
/Stanley,Margaret E.1850-1933   xStanley,W.H. 28 mar 1919
/Stanley,Mary E.1852-1919   /Stanley,Phoebe A.1849-1932 w/oCecil E.
xStanley,William D. 31 oct 1918   xStapelton,Helen Hope 4 feb 1929
xStapleton,James 3 nov 1914   /Stapleton,Josephine 13 Jul 1934 18y7m29d
/Stapleton,Mary 3 oct 1926 45y   /Stapleton,Lawrence 1911-1916
xStapleton,Martha E. 21 oct 1931   xStapleton,Marian Abraham 6 nov 1924
xStapleton,Mary Etta 10/10/1927   xStapleton,Mary Bendes 15 aug 1918
xStapleton,William 9 mar 1914   /Starkey,D.W. 1869-1910
xStarkey,Hansdord 10 may 1925   /Starkey,Jennie Tharp
xStarkey,Tharp 13 Jul 1914 ??   2 may 1862-2 sep 1915 w/oFE
/Starkey,Tharp J.   /Starks,Emily J. 1831-1923
     17 aug 1895-24 Jun 1900   /Starks,James E. 1856-1930
/Starr,Harry D.1895-1912 sB&EJ   /Starks,Mattie 1856-1923
/Starski,Dorothy 1920-1928   /Staton,Blanche F>1874-1918
/Staton,Valeria M. 1851-1928   /Steele,Iva Wealthy 13 dec 1934 27y1m23d
xSteele,Grace 14 feb 1920   /Steele,Joe mack 7 mar 1922
xSteele,Mary A. 30 oct 1919   xSteen,inf/E 11 Jul 1917
xSteinbricker,F.M. 17 mar 1920   xSteinbricker,Fred M. 23 sep 1912
xSteinbrecker,Herman 22 apr 1927   xSteinbrecker,Wilma B. 9 Jan 1917
/Steir,Chris 11 oct 1933 58y1m28   xStemmler,Jean 19 Jun 1929
xStender,Gary Wm. 11 nov 1939   xStender,Gloria Ann 9 sep 1939
/Stender,John 1847-1925   xStender,Martha Isabelle 23 may 1936
/Stender,Joseph 1858-1934   /Stender,Mary M. 1847-1938
/Stender,Martha I.1887-1930   /Stender,Wendall 1854-1919
/Stender,Walter W.1884-1930   /Stender,William J. 1877-1932
xStephens,Eausetice 3 feb 1921   xStephens,George W.1907
xStephens,Richard 10 Jan 1923   /Stephens,James Virgil 27aug1896-3oct1915
xStephens,Roxie 10 Jan 1924   xStephenson,Allen B. 5 nov 1924
/Stephenson,Ashley 1916-17   xStephenson,Ann T. 1827-1895
/Stephenson,Conley 1909-1931   /Stephenson,C.R.1869-1912
/Stephenson,Constance 1907-08   /Stephenson,Era Ann 1847-1919
/Stephenson,Eddie b1912   /Stephenson,Etna C.18 sep 1889 32y
/Stephenson,Frances d 1918   /Stephenson,H.C. 1830-1898
/Stephenson,James M.1836-1920   Jane 1827-1897
xStephenson,inf/Eddie 14 aug 12   /Stephenson,Hanson 25 aug 1824-25 feb 1895
xStephenson,J.M. 30 Jan 1920   Ann Taylor 3 mar 1827-28 Jan 1895
xStephenson,Jeff B. 14 oct 1919   xStephenson,John M. 10 mar 1924
xStephenson,Robert L.13 dec 1913   /Stephenson,M.A. CoB 5th WV Inf GAR
/Stephenson,Newton E. 1876-1929   /Stephenson,Russell R.1911-1934
/Stephenson,S.J.1862-1926   /Stephenson,Vincent Witcher 1864-1924
xStephenson,W.J. 5 oct 1929   xStepp,Woodrow 28 apr 1935
/Sterling,Anna M. 1863-1935   /Sterling,Elizabeth E. 1862-1891

/Sterling,Richard W.1840-1909   /Sternberg,Robt.Allen 16 Jan 1938
xStevens,Mrs.H.M.4 feb 1910   /Steuers,Lenna J. 1865-1922
xStevens,H.M. 12 oct 1951   /Steuers,W.M. 1858-1934
/Stevens,Inf 1934   /Stevens,John Bernard 1891-1918
xStevens,Ivan F. 10 dec 1924   /Stevens,Wilson V. 1870-1937
xStevens,Nancy E. 24 feb 1915   Mamie E. Kilgore 24 dec 1875-8 mar 1903
xStevens,Rosie 19 sep 1931   xStevens,William C. 25 mar 1915
xStevens,Wilson W. 28 sep 1937   /Stevenson,Jesse C. 1881-1934
/Stevenson,John B.1868-1925   /Stevenson,Robert Lovett 29 apr 1932
xStephenson,Paul 5 Jul 1923   xStevers,Inf 9 nov 1934
/Stever,Laura B. 1872-1911   /Stevers,Lenna J. 1865-1922
    Noah A. 9 nov 1938 69y9m12d /Stevers,W.M. 1858-1934
/Stewart,Alice L, 1841-1922   /Stewart,Anna 1883-1935
/Stewart,Blanche 1880-1888   /Stewart,B.F.5 sep 1847-8 Jul 1934
xStewart,Bessie E. 19 Jul 1932   Matilda 29 Jan 1851-11 dec 1931
xStewart,Charlie 1910   /Stewart,Dora A. 1874-1928
xStewart,Edward 1 oct 1926   xStewart,Elizabeth J.1845-1929
xStewart,Ella 15 feb 1939   xStewart,Foster 6 oct 1930
/Stewart,Hansford 1843-1863   xStewart,Howard Lester 31 oct 1915
xStewart,Harry H.1863-1898   /Stewart,Herbert Francis 8 apr 1935 77y
/Stewart,H.W.1832-1912   /Stewart,James 1818-3 mar 1876 58y
/Stewart,Joseph S.1845-1911   /Stewart,James B. 1858-1908
xStewart,Lawrence S. 25 may 1926xStewart,Mack 26 nov 1927
/Stewart,Mary J. 1849-1921   /Stewart,Mary W. 1862-1924
xStewart,Matilda 13 dec 1931   /Stewart,Sarah Lakin 1822-1909
/Stickleman,Flora J. 1859-1927 /Stiens,Edward F.1872-1929
/Stickleman,John W. 1861-1930   xStiens,Marie H. 1931
xStier,Chris 13 oct 1933   xStiff,Arthur 20 Jul 1927
/Stinson,Jane 1833-12 mar 1893 /Stockhan,Walter Crawford 1891-1909
/Stock,Jacob S.11 may 1891 5y   /Stockhan,Hattie 1870-1930
/Stof,Thomas 8 feb 1935 42y3m4d xStokes,Helen 14 Jul 1919
xStombock,David 14 apr 1918   xStokes,Lizzie 18 Jan 1916
xStone,A.M.5 sep 1923   /Stone,Elizabeth A.1833-1904
/Stone,Andrew 1889-31 Jan 1923WIxStone,Eliza 1804-1887
/Stone,Grace A.1794-1880   xStone,Harry G. 24 nov 1939
/Stone,Lewis E. 1897-1931   xStone,Hattie Alma(Nadine) 24 sep 1930
xStone,James 16 aug 1923   xStone,Louis E. 3 Jan 1932
/Stone,Moss L.1894-1918   /Stone,Maggie L.3 oct 1879 w/o JB
/Stormezand,Helen M.1876-1920 xStrait,Archie 6 sep 1931
xStrait,Alice 22 sep 1920   xStrait,Howard 4 oct 1912
xStrand,John 3 apr 1924   /Straghan,Alice 1840-1902
/Strange,James R. 1849-1912   /Straghan,George O. 1819-1899
/Strange,Lucy Va.1858-1934   /Straghan,Samuel 1870-1931
/Strank,George 1923 CoM5th PA /Straghans,Lillie V. 1875-1891
xStrank,Anna 19 apr 1923   xStrank,Inf 10 Jul 1918
/Strohmeyer,Walter J.1901-1914 xStrother,A.S. 4 Jun 1935
xStrow,Earnest 27 mar 1935   /Stroud,Annie,E.4 aug 1877-2 dec 1936
/Strow,Annie 1873-1926   xStrow,Ella E.Wallace 9 Jul 1903
xStrow,Hannah 23 Jan 1938   xStrow,Isabella W.9 Jul 1903
xStrupe,Sarah 2 apr 1919   /Stuart,Blanche 1880-1888
/Stuck,James M.CoB 5th WV InfGAR/Stuart,Ella McConihay 1855-1939
/Stukins,Charles 1872-1920   /Stuart,Thomas F. 1856-1918
xStumbock,Mary F. 4 Jun 1925   xStumbock,Oma Jones 22 aug 1922
xStump,John S. 20 mar 1934   /Sturgeon,Minnie 1872-1903

/Strums,Margery Helen 1925-1934 xSudderth,Paul 6 dec 1923
/Suiter,Capt.A.T.1848-1922   /Suiter,Eva 1 apr 1939 64y4m2d
xSuiter,J.K. 8 apr 1925   xSuiter,Levina A. 23 dec 1914
/Suiter,Loving Moore B.1834-1914/Suiter,Kelley 20 mar 1866-22 aug 1894
/Sullivan,Alfred E.1889-1914   /Sullivan,D.C. 8 may 1850-1 Jan 1906
xSullivan,Clarence 16 feb 1919 xSullivan,David C. 8 oct 1914
/Sullivan,inf 1910   /Sullivan,Emma 7 sep 1853-17 Jul 1906
/Sullivan,inf 1913   /Sullivan,inf 1934
xSullivan,Hilda 24 may 1919   /Sullivan,John 23 dec 1850-15 mar 1919
/Sullivan,Mary Taylor 1849-1931 /Sullivan,John H.1885-1935
xSullivan,Malinda 24 feb 1918   /Sullivan,Lillie M.1879-1930
xSullivan,Nellie C.10 nov 1914 xSullivan,Nellie May 26 Jun 1923
xSullivan,Sarah 13 mar 1919   xSummerfield,Albert 23 Jan 1933
xSummers,John 14 may 1927   /Summerson,George M.8 Jan 1888 20y4m25d
/Summers,Leona Miller 1869-1913 /Summerson,Charles H. 5 feb 1829-8 dec14
/Supcoe,M.Ed.26 Jan 1937   /Summerson,Emma V.1 oct 1835-11 feb 1917
    39y7m17d WWI   xSurface,Barbara L. aug 1924 ??
/Sutherland,Natalie 1917-21 JS&NxSutton,Annie 22 oct 1911
xSutherland,Floyd 5 feb 1918   xSutton,Charlie 1902
xSwaddy,Loretta 12 dec 1921   /Swain,James C.1849-1921
/Swann,BenJ.F.2 mar 1938   /Swain,Jeanette Creigh 1838-1911
    VA 3rd US Cav sgt   /Swann,Francis J. 1902-1932
/Swann,inf 1909 s/o E&V   /Swann,Jefferson Bowen 17 Jan 1935 57y
xSwann,Joseph 28 nov 1927   xSwann,Martha -- w/o Joseph
xSwann,Oliver 18 dec 1927   /Swann,Virgie 1897-1923
xSwanson,Anna 22 Jan 1915   xSwartzel,Allen L.1 sep 1929
xSwanson,Bert 18 Jul 1922   /Sweeney,Arthur M. 1894-1922
xSweeney,Ivie Ethel 4 mar 1932 xSwing,Lena Bell 10 aug 1931
/Swink,Charles T. 1869-1935   /Swisher,Sibyl Staley 1873-1905
xSwink,Lucy 10 aug 1943   xSwisher,Wm.Lyle 21 Jun 1927
xSydenstricker,Helen 27 may 1924/Switzer,Edmund Clyde 1858-24 apr 1939
xSydenstricker,inf/JS 1928   Edna B. 1867-1949
xSydnor,Charles 14 Jan 1925   /Switzer,Ellen 26 may 1827-11 sep 1914
xSyers,Mary E. 3 may 1921   /Switzer,Jonathan 13 apr 1830-19 sep 1865
xSympson,Emma Irene 15 feb 1930 /Switzer,Thos.H. 19 sep 1862-13 nov 1911
xSympson,John Irwin 11 aug 1917 /Switzer,Va.S.27 oct 1863-1 may 1932
xSympson,Mary 7 dec 1917   xSympson,W.C. 31 Jan 1927

xTackett,Charles 13 apr 1913
/Tackett,Howard
/Taliaferro,Hannah C.1857-1927
/Taliaferro.Louis Q. 1857-1930
xTalley,Edward B.--
/Tanner,John W. 1906-08
/Tanner,Willie 1883-1908
xTanner,Jesse 16 nov 1939
xTapp,James T. 13 oct 1911
xTapp,Mary 25 dec 1911
/Tate,James Ernest 1879-1899
/Tate,Lee A.D. 1867-1937
xTate,Leusey L.Moore 4 sep 1913
/Tate,Lavina Wash 1843-1932
xTate,Lige 9 aug 1921
xTaylor,Alice 29 apr 1938
xTaylor,Anna 19 sep 1923
xTaylor,Anna D. 26 mar 1915
/Taylor,Bess E.1885-1917
xTaylor,Blanche 1911-1928
/Taylor,C.H.K. 1817-1902
/Taylor,C.Lee 1858-1938
xTaylor,Darrell G.2 nov 1925
xTaylor,George W. 18 nov 1923
xTaylor,Helen E. 9 aug 1916
xTaylor,J.A. 2 aug 1914
xTaylor,Jake 26 jan 1926
xTaylor,John 15 feb 1910
xTaylor,June 9 apr 1923
/Taylor,Lawrence 1883-1938
/Taylor,Lennie 1886-1921
/Taylor,Mary E.E. 1850-1915wMD
xTaylor,Milton 19 nov 1925
xTaylor,Mrs.N.F. 1 mar 1933
/Taylor,Owen Dilo 1886-1929
xTaylor,Paul 16 oct 1926
/Taylor,Quincy E. 1875-1915
xTaylro,Richard 31 dec 1924
/Taylor,Sarah Francis 1856-1935
/Taylor,Sarah R. 1861-1939
/Taylor,Thora June 1922-23
/Taylor,Virginia C.1848-1933
/Taylor,William C. 1875-1880
xTeel,Phillips 1849-1903
/Temple,Jerry Taylor 1835-1917
/Temple,,O.G. 1862-1934
xTerrell,Lewis C.3 Jul 1927
xTerrill,Ed 5 may 1907
xTerry,Mrs.Billie 17 Jun 1924
xTerry,Joseph 16 feb 1920
xTerry,Lallance 4 feb 1923
xTerry,Lillian 23 Jan 1917
xTestamueb,Margaret 6 Jul 1911
/Teubert,Alice V. 1856-1938

/Tackett,Wm.H.19 dec 1933 31y11m
/Taliaferro,Charles B.1857-1927
/Taliaferro,Martha S.1832-1902
xTalley,Catherine Mary 10 dec 1937
xTalley,Pearl--
xTanner,H.G. 18 apr 1917
    Helen 17 Jun 1915
xTanner,Thomas 15 sep 1926
xTarrer,Anna 16 mar 1934
xTassen,inf 10 dec 1927
xTate,James P. 1833-1908
xTate,John 2 Jun 1925
/Tauber,Anna Rosetta 10 mar 1933 60y10m
/Tauber,Bernhart 16 Jul 1930 84y5m8d
xTauber,Mary E. 27 mar 1924
/Taylor,Agnes S.1868-29 Jan 1897 39y
    James A. 31 Jul 1914 72y5m24d
xTaylor,Armstead 6 Jan 1917
xTaylor,Berni9ce S. 15 apr 1919
xTaylor,Charles B.24 may 1913
/Taylor,Emma 28 dec 1856-18 mar 1935
    John A. 18 nov 1840-13 Jan 1910
xTaylor,Francis 25 may 1935
xTaylor,Helen 3 dec 1924
xTaylor,J.A. 2 aug 1912
xTaylor,Dr. J.A. --
xTaylor,Jeremiah 1 nov 1913
xTaylor,John 2 dec 1935
xTaylor,Lydie 27 mar 12924
/Taylor,Maria Trueheart 1842-1923
/Taylor,Marie 1906-1922
xTaylor,M.D. 11 aug 1936
/Taylor,Norman 28 feb 1901 23y9m17d
xTaylor,Nellie May 20 oct 1931
/Taylor,Powhatan 1879-1897
xTaylor,R. 3 Jun 1924
xTaylor,Rex 10 oct 1913
xTaylor,Capt.Robert 19 Jun 1938
xTaylor,Sidney P. 26 Jan 1937
/Taylor,Tenna Ida 1895-97
/Taylor,Tho.W.6 dec 1930 CoB12thNCInf CSA
/Taylor,T.Wallace Jr. 1877-1896
xTeasdale,Beatrice 19 sep 1917 inf
/Teitelbaum,Rachel 1829-1895
/Temple,Mary Ann 1862-1932
xTenderson,J.G. 27 feb 1934
/Terrill,Caroline Cope 1862-1907 w/o C.L.
    C.L. 1860-19--

/Terry,Jabus L. 16 nov 1934 82y6m22d
xTerry,Mary 27 dec 1921
xTerry,W.C. 3 apr 1913
xTesteman,inf 31 Jul 1917
/Teubert,James H. 1850-1930

/Teubert,Edith A. 1878-1935   /Teubert,Grace E. 1890-96
xTeubert,Flora 1878-1897   xTeubert,John H. 26 may 1944
/Thacker,Sarah E. 1869-1934   /Thabit,Louis 20 apr 1885-18 oct 1918
/Thacker,Nancy 3 aug 1932 inf   /Thackett,Howard 21 jun 1906-25 feb 1925
/Thackston,Benj.Hudsen 1835-1918/Thackston,Bernice Smith 1870-1934
/Thackston,Chas.Cole 1870-1899   /Thackston,Eugenia Miller 1837-1924
/Thackston,Chas.Hampton 1893-94 /Thackston,James Alexander 1874-1934
/Thackston,Patricia Leigh 1927-9/Thackston,Sallie Coleman 1876-1937
/Tarf,Barney 1885-1909   /Thackston,Tillie Elegar 1874-1916
/Tharp,Harriet A. 1 Jan 1839--   /Tharp,Alfred 11 Jan 1835-19 dec 1895
xTharp,Riley 30 apr 1933   CoA 31st OH Inf GAR
xTheobald,Kate 1 mar 1931   xThomas,Archie 14 nov 1921
/Thomas,Agnes 1878-1931   /Thomas,Albert E. 1872-1914
/Thomas,Archa L. 1888-1919   /Thomas,Clara 7 may 1939 44y
xThomas,Dean 1 Jan 1890   xThomas,Emmett 11 sep 1911
/Thomas,George W. 1852-1915   xThomas Florence M.27 apr 1933
xThomas Glendore 23 oct 1919   xThomas,Franklin 1 jun 1926
xThomas,inf 18 oct 1921   /Thomas,Harry L.29 aug 1875-24 jul 1915
/Thomas,Ida J.H. 1865-1924   Mrs.Harry --
xThomas John 9 jun 1921   /Thomas,John L.1854-1912
xThomas Kate 2 sep 1920   /Thomas,Marion J.20 mar 1936 80y8m20d
xThomas,Mary 1908   /Thomas,Mary T. 5 apr 1845-13 feb 1922
/Thomas,Minnie 1884-1907   xThomas,Maude Talley 28 jul 1910
xThomas Mildred C.2 sep 1920   xThomas Phyllis Louise 21 sep 1920
xThomas,W.F. 20 jun 1927   /Thomason,Anna Bell Davis 1867-1927
/Thompson,Agnes 1873-1913   xThomason,Anna Gosbell 19 dec 1936
xThomason,George W. 23 aug 1922 /Thomason,Chas.Walter 6 dec 1919 WWI
xThomason,Helen K.19 oct 1931   /Thomason,Mamie V.1884-21 jun 1933
xThomason,Minerva 7 mar 1914   xThomason,Wm.R.16 nov 1932 53y5m14d
xThomason,Wm.F. 11 may 1930   /Thompson,Amos 13 feb 1842-25 apr 1902
xThompson,Alonzo 15 jun 1911   xThompson,Augustine 19 aug 1917
/Thompson,Clifford 1914-1938   /Thompson,Benj.S.26 mar 1818-29 dec 1907
/Thompson,C.A.1866-1918   xThompson,Birdie L. 13 nov 1924
xThompson,C.I.20 dec 1923   /Thompson,Cameron L.4/22/1844-9/14/1920
/Thompson,Chas.A.   xThompson,Clifford 11 jun 1938
     CoC 19th VA Inf CSA   xThompson,Cyrus N.7 mar 1930
/Thompson,Dessie 1890-92 d/JM&AE/Thompson,Eliz.L.25 oct 1819-22 jul 1907
xThompson,Edward 1 feb 1916   xThompson,Effie 1876-1895
xThompson,Elizabeth 29 jun 1912 xThompson,Elizabeth L.26 jul 1907
xThompson,Ernest L. 21 dec 1916 xThompson,Floyd 8 feb 1902
/Thompson,Frances 1920-24   xThompson,Frances 23 may 1923
/Thompson,Francis A.1848-1890   xThompson,George 6 apr 1926
/Thompson,Georgia A.1892-1918   /Thompson,Gus M. 11 aug 1933WWI
/Thompson,,inf 9 mar 1932   xThompson,Helen I. 1900-1905
/Thompson,Harry L.1886-1921   /Thompson,Josephine 30 jun 1890 26y10m24d
/Thompson,Harry J. 1903-1929   /Thompson,J.Speed 28 oct 1846-16 jan 1904
xThompsn,Isaac P.Jul 1892   /Thompson,Joseph E.1871-1926
/Thompson,Isabelle 1861-1920   xThompson,James 25 nov 1931
xThompson,John 30 aug 1916   xThompson,John W. 29 dec 1927
xThompson,James E. 1868-1894   xThompson,Kate 17 nov 1925
xThompson,Kattie 5 mar 1913   xThompson,Letha Ann 3 jan 1918
xThompson,Louise 1855-1935   /Thompson,Lola Biggs 1854-1882 28y
xThompson,Luther 9 apr 1915   /Thompsn,Margaret Eloise d1915
/Thompson,Lucille 1928-31   /Thompson,Mary 9 mar 1874-4 jul 1918

/Thompson,Mary A. 1894-1914
/Thompson,Mary E. 1809-1913
xThompson,Nannie S. 1850-1935
xThompson,Nevt 23 feb 1937
xThompson,Otho F. 28 dec 1920
/Thompson,Rachel 1842-1923
/Thompson,Roy 1891-1939
/Thompson,Sarah A. 1897-1915
xThompson,Sarah 18 dec 1921
xThompson,Silas 7 aug 1923
xThompson,Silas P.--
/Thompson,Thomas J. 1838-1918
xThompson,William 11 may 1918
/Thornburg,Barbara A. 1831-1897
/Thornburg,Collis V. 1835-1899
/Thornburg,Edgar 3 apr 1939 66y
xThornburg,Francis 19 mar 1931
/Thornburg,Georgie E.1865-1924
/Thornburg,inf/Ruth 1914
/Thonrburg,Hezekiah 1831-1908
/Thornburg,Jennie M. 1868-1911
/Thornburg,Mabel 1865-1931
/Thornburg,Moses M. 1862-1934
/Thornburg,Ruth Hawkins 1914 inf
/Thornburg,Sarah P. 1838-1918
xThornton,Aimee F. 1869-1892
xThornton,Anna 22 feb 1927
xThornton,George P.28 nov 1930
xThorosonCatherine 6 sep 1910
/Thuma Leonard 1872-1901
/Thuma,Thomas J. 1838-1913
/Thuma,Thomas J. 1913-1938
/Thuma,Mary Gerturde 31 mar 1934
     72y8m21d
xThuma,Mrs.M.J.17 sep 1918
xThuma,W.H. 29 may 1919
xTipton,James 18 aug 1924
/Tipton,Clarence 1886-1914
/Tipton,James A. 1856-1923
/Tipton,Jennie 4/10/1936 65y8m21
/Toberman,inf 1890 s/oET&EJ
/Todd,Julia Fagan
     5 Jan 1868-2 sep 1937
xTohey,Kate 3 sep 1925
/Tolle,Thelma 1904 inf
/Tompkins,,Francis B.1872-1938
/Tompson,Carlos V.1939 inf
xToney,Alonzo 1 oct 1914
xToney,Charity M./1846-1897
/Toney,Clara B.1873-1907
/Toney,Fannie 1856--1914
/Toney,Jesse 1853-1917
/Toney,Mary Belle 1923 inf
xToney,Mildred 23 aug 1932

/Thompson,Mary Louise 1894-1934
xThompson,McGinnis 24 sep 1926
xThompson,Neva 9 feb 1919
xThompson,Ona Belle 11 Jun 1934
xThompson,Pearl 2 nov 1918
xThompson,Ruthie M. 1894-95
/Thompson,Sarah 1874-1925
xThopmson,Sadie 3 Jan 1915
/Thompson,W.T. 1843-1895 52y
   Nancy Scales Hagen 8/15/1850-7/12/1935
/Thompson,Thelma 1923-1931
xThompson,Thomas 3 Jul 1921
xThompson,Wylie 16 feb 1919
/Thorn,Roy O.24 oct 1894-9 nov 1937
/Thornburg,Annie Bell 30 may 1891-1904
/Thornburg,Bertha M. 1876-1924 w/CH
xThornburg,G.W. 1854-1923
/Thornburg,Georgia Mae 13 aug 1934 19y
/Thornburg,John William 1826-1903
/Thornburg,Lenora Chapman 11/14/1932 92y
xThornburg,Josephine Lee 27 oct 1936
/Thornburg,Mildred Naomi 25 oct 1937 45y
xThornburg,Patricia 29 jun 1921
xThornburg,Ruthie 26 sep 1931
xThornhill,S.B>1 oct 1939
/Thornton,George P. 1867-1930
/Thornton,Annie Kitchen 1850-1917
   M.L. 184-1913 LT CoH 53rd PA Reg
/Throckmorton,Ella 1857-1894
xThrossell,Wm.T.4 mar 1931
/Throssell,John 20 sep 1886 inf s/o WT&MA
/Throssell,Mary Ann 19 nov 1886wWT 30y15d
/Throssell,Wm. 3 Jun 1884-27 apr 1937
xTingley,Howard 20 aug 1917
xTinsley,Joseph Co K 59th VA Inf CSA
/Tinsley,John R.1 Jan 1938 WWI
xTinsley,Nancy A.E. 14 Jul 1918
/Tisdale,Wm.S. 23 Jan 1936 WWI
/Titus,George L. 1861-1924
/Titus,Geo.Robt.1908-1913
/Titus,inf 1924 s/o WR&KF
/Titus,Ivor R. 1844-1919
/Titus,Katie 3 oct 1883-20 apr 1800
/Titus,Maggie 1857-1928
/Titus,Oney 27 aug 1881-12 Jun 1890
xTompkins,Frances E. 1873-1938
/Toney,Albert G.16 Jul 1936 65y6m1d
xToney,Catherine 1907
xToney,Emily J.11 oct 1936
/Toney,Emily Jane 1862-1938
xToney,Fred N. 29 oct 1918
/Toney,Mary J. 1866-1928
/Toney,Marcellus N. 1842-1914
/Toney,Nancy A. 1840-1921

/Toney,Sterling L. 1897-1932   xToney,Stella 1906
xToney,Ralph 13 sep 1923   /Toney,Theo 1847-1925
/Toney,Theodore 1868-1914   /Tong,Woo 2 feb 1880-28 oct 1917
/Toothman,R.L.1874-1918   xTormia,Michael 8 Jan 1931
xTowbridge,Jefferson 15 sep 1926/Townsend,Beulah B.1902-1915
xTrainer,Goldie 25 Jun 1911   xTrainer,Mary Lou 14 dec 1911
/Treanor,Mary Helen 1910-1913   /Trakaliot,Vasileke 25 aug 1921 inf
xTrent,Hazel May 1 nov 1925   /Trent,Dessie 23 Jan 1868-6 aug 1892
xTrent,J.H. 15 feb 1923   /Trent,Mary 1888-1935
/Trevillian,A.J.1856-1925   /Trevillian,Celia 1900-1912
/Trevillian,Harold A. 1896-1918 /Trevillian,John C. 1884-1934
/Trice,Andrew J. 1829-1894   /Trice,Harry L.1907
/Trice,Cora L 1899-1907   xTrice,Virginia S.13 Jan 1916
xTricohette,inf 27 nov 1922   xTrimble,alice Peyton 26 mar 1927
xTrimmer,Charley 1882   xTrimmer,Mary Bell 7 feb 1934
xTrimmer,Peggy 1882   xTrimmer,T.L. 3 may 1921
xTimmer,Tommy 1882   xTrosper,James Stockton 10 Jul 1930
xTrout,Grace 22 Jul 1934   /Trosper,John Paul 1899 inf
xTrowbridge,Mary 24 feb 1915   /Trowbridge,Clyde A.1900-1920
/Trowbridge,Indiana F.1876-1919 /Trowbridge,J.D.1860-1926
xTrue,Anna 29 dec 1924   xTrumbo,Mary J.10 Jan 1919
xTrue,J.M. 31 mar 1912   xTucker,C.C. 16 apr 1916
/Tucker,George W.25 feb 1858-1924/Tucker,Wm.J.16 Jan 1841-26 mar 1932
xTucker,Edward 10 dec 1936   Mildred M. 22 mar 18851-29 Jan 1924/
xTucker,Emma 12 nov 1911   xTucker,Margaret--
/Tufts,Albert T.1856-1918   xTufts,Mrs.Hattie 10 dec 1925
      Emma E.Kirk 1857-1933   /Tufts,Rachel B.1845-1929
/Turina,Fred Jr.7 Jun 1934   /Turley,Edwin 1865-1924
/Turley,Fred 1869-1934   /Turley,Lillian 26 dec 1912
/Turner,Adaline,1849-1934   xTurner,Annie M. 1884 inf
/Turner,Charles W.1859-1932   xTurner,Augusta --
xTurner,C.C. 28 nov 1934   xTurner,Daisy 7 may 1911
/Turner,Elmer,1886-1906   /Turner,Elizabeth 1 Jan 1933   62y9m9d
xTurner,Ernest Lee 6 Jan 1926   xTurner,G.W. 20 mar 1933
/Turner,George W. 1850-1929   /Turner,F.W.24 feb 1868-22 apr 1901
xTurner,George 14 mar 1913   xTurner,George 23 mar 1925
xTurner,Gerturde 9 dec 1919   xTurner,Ida May 20 Jan 1932
/Turner,Hannah J.1881-1886   /Turner,inf 1883
xTurner,James--   xTurner,Joseph--
/Turner,Lydia 1886-1937   /Turner,Mason 1879-1906
xTurner,Mary--   xTurner,May Ada 6 Jun 1925
/Turner,Minnie J.1859-1932   xTurner,Mrs.J. 1901
xTurner,Nathaniel--   xTurner,Robert E. 29 Jan 1926
xTurner,Zurelda--   /Turney,Anna McBride 1858-1915
/Turney,Emma L. 1853-1936   /Turney,Ellen Wilde 1916-1921
/Turney,Robert W.1853-1927   /Turney,Louderback 1884 inf s/o RW&Anna
/Tweel,James Joseph 2 mar 1933 /Twell,Eesper 1861-1926
/Tweel,Mary 1850-1931   xTwell,Michael 20 Jul 1939
/Tyree,Eugene M. 16 feb 1921 WWI/Tweel,Simon 1870-1924
xTwohig,Lee V. 6 Jun 1927   xTwyman,Cleopatra 21 mar 1920
xTwohig,Margaret G.4 apr 1933   xTynes,Anne 18 nov 1938
xUnderwood,A.L.29 Jul 1917   /Underwood,Winfield S.22 may 1923 WWI
xUpton,John --   xUpton,Lula--
xValdey,Julia Ann 19 nov 1931   xValentine,Mabel Alice 28 may 1935

/Valentine,Darling A.1863-1926 /Valentino,Emmett 16 oct 1933 8y
    John H. 1860-1926   /Valentine,Richard 1823-1908
xVallance,John 18 dec 1915   Sallie W. 1828-1902
/VanBibber,Cyrus Dewar 1859-1915xVandenbugh,George 1865-1936
/Vandiver,James H. 1820-1896   /Vandiver,Martha T. 1830-1854
xVandy,Annie 25 apr 1913   /Vandiver,R.B.13 oct 1897 42y
/VanFleet,Echelberry d1890   xVanhorn,Francis C.7 Jan 1936
/VanFleet,Mary Ella 1863-1923   /VanHorn,Samuel R. CoB 1st WV LA
xVanhorn,Melvin 30 dec 1917   10 nov 1910
/VanKirk,Charles P. 1851-1913   /VanMeter,Electa 1847-1915
/VanMeter,Gwinn 1838-1919   /VanMeter,Otho W. 1870-1934
xVannoy,robert 26 dec 1934   xVan Rompary,John 15 sep 1919
xVantard,Jules 12 Jan 1917   xVantrise,Pearl louise 11 aug 1928
/VanWay,Jesse 18 aug 1937 49y3m xVare,Burrill 11 nov 1930
/Vass,Robert L. 1863-1938   xVaughn,David 3 sep 1911
/Vaughn,Hershel 1907-1910   /Vaughn,Arthur 27 Jul 1887-13 feb 1910
xVaughan,Harry C. 1897   xVaughn,Henry B.6 sep 1930
xVaughn,James 18 aug 1925   xVaughn,Lucy 14 sep 1927
xVaughan,Margaret 21 nov 1929   xVaughn,Mattie 8 Jan 1939
xVaughn,Merion 17 aug 1925   xVaughn,William E. 1911-12
/Vaughn,Rosa M. 1909-1910   /Vendenbugh,George 6 Jul 1936 71y8m9d vet
/Vaughn,William E.1911-1914   /Verlander,Julia C.1881-1930
/Vernatter,A.J.CoI 7th WV CAV USxVernatt,Mary 1930
xVernatt,Bernice 1912   xVerney,Lucy 22 apr 1927
xVest,Virginia P.24 Jun 1931   /Vest,Earl Ray 1916-1918
/Vestal,Minnie D. 1858-1935   /Vest,Stacy(Bob) 1886-1931
xVickers,Fred C.24 may 1926   /Via,Henry O. 23 feb 1851-31 Jan 1938
/Vickers,Robt.Evans MD 1858-1929/Via,Peter W.1886-1922
/Vickers,Rose Franks 1849-1925 /Via,Virgil K. 7 mar 1913-25 mar 1920
/Vickers,Ruth Lois 1896-1898   xVillars,James M.23 nov 1916
xVincent,James F. 4 dec 1915 GAR/Vindiver,James H.1820-1896
/Vines,James W. 1861-1907   /Vinson,Arthur C.23 oct 1915 inf
/Vinson,Blair 1907-1915   /Vinson,Dr.B.C.7 Jun 1839-2 aug 1888
/Vinson,Lindsey T.Dr.1875-1934 /Vinson,Charles C.7 dec 1865-28 Jul 1900
/Vinson,Lyn Boyd 1871-1909   /Vinson,James A. 10 oct 1870-6 dec 1893
xVinson,inf 1916   xVinson,Josephine B.1862-1885
/Vinson,Mary 1836-1921   /Vinson,Mary F. 16 nov 1840-14 mar 1936
    Samuel S. 1833-1904   /Vinson,Maud 16 Jan 1873-8 Jul 1905
/Vinson,Z.Taylor 1857-1929   /Vinson,Willie Mae Holderby 1 aug 1916
xViol,Mary C. 14 may 1938   xViol,Victor,S.12 Jun 1929
/Viol,Victor J.1876-11 nov 1911 xVire,Susan 28 dec 1928
/Vittito,Mary A. 1841-1920   /Voct,Minnie 1880-1915
/Vrbanczyk,Barbara 1883-1919   xVreedenburg,G.W. 31 may 1925
xWade,Della 27 Jan 1937   xWaddy,James 2 nov 1939
/Wade,G.W. 1857-1920   /Waddell,Ethel 1891-1910 d/o FJ&EW
/Wade,Helen M.1921-27   /Waddell,Fred Joseph 1860-1914
xWade,Mrs.Harry 27 dec 1918   xWadlington,Emma 24 aug 1922
xWade,Preston 20 oct 1936   xWadlington,Ezra 26 apr 1911
xWagers,Minnie 5 nov 1932   xWadlington,John R. 16 oct 1926
/Wagner,Maggie 7 may 1922   /Waggoner,Amanda 9 apr 1935 91y4m21d
xWagoner,Jake 7 apr 1921   /Waggoner,James 2 sep 1919
xWagoner,L.30 Jan 1918   CoI 18th OH Inf GAR
xWagoner,Mrs.Maggie 13 may 1915 xWaid,Willie J. 10 feb 1925
xWainesley,Jas L.Jr,23 Jun 1919 xWake,Curtis 7 apr 1939

184

/Wakefield,Alice 1861-1931   /Walburn,Mabel Elizabeth 1910-1916
    Newton 1854-1904   xWalden,William 25 Jun 1925
/Walden,Estella 1859-1925   /Waldron,John 12 sep 1805-23 dec 1887
/Walden,Victoria 8 oct 1938 79y   Naomi 2 feb 1811-25 Jan 1895
xWaldon,Jerry 12 Jan 1929   xWaldron,Blake 24 oct 1921
xWaldon,Walle D.31 dec 1932   xWaldron,Elizabeth 28 dec 1919
/Walk,Claud C. 1881-1918   /Walker,Alderson 2 mar 1853-14 feb 1905
/Walk,Kimball M.21 dec 1934 8y   /Walker,Alexander 21 nov 1936 SpAm
xWalker,Clarence E. 19 nov 1916   /Walker,Carlton A. 13 aug 1905 inf
xWalker,Dora--   /Walker,Daniel W.1864-1916
xWalker,Ellen K.13 Jan 1931   /Walker,Mary Jane 1835-1920
xWalker,Garnett 30 apr 1923   Wm.Parkinson 1834-1905
xWalker,Gen S.25 Jul 1930   xWalker,George 14 may 1922
xWalker,Jennie 11 may 1915   xWalker,John 4 sep 1931
xWalker,Katherine 15 oct 1931   xWalker,Katherine Barnes 13 oct 1932
xWalker,Lawrence 3 Jul 1918inf   xWalker,Lewis 23 feb 1936
xxWalker,Lottie 1 mar 1918   xWalker,Lucy 14 Jun 1920
xWalker,Mary 4 Jun 1923   xWalker,Mary Jane 1835-1920
xWalker,Matilda J.13 Jan 1931   xWalker,Natalie 25 Jul 1921
xWalker,Pearl--   xWalker,Natalie Southerland 6 nov 1937
xWalker,R.E. 31 oct 1913   xWalker,Ruth G. 26 dec 1920
xWalker,Sophia 1891   xWalker,William P.1834-1905
/Wall,Dr.J.O.1847-2 oct 1885 36y   /Wallace,Aron Gene 1939 inf
/Wallace,Charles M.1864-1924   /Wallace,Clyde, 1896-1899
/Wallace,Charles 2 feb 1934 2y   /Wallace,Charlie A. 1874-1875s/oWF&MA
/Wallace,Ellen 1835-1913   xWallace,Em F. 1837-1907
/Wallace,George E.1869-1907   xWallace,Ella 1893-1896
/Wallace,Maggie 1838-1922   /Wallace,Macie 11 Jun 1902-5 aug 1911
/Wallace,William F. 1837-1907   /Wallace,Stph.R.1 nov 1933 83y9m21d vet
/Wallace,Willie W.1871-72sWF&MA   xWaller,Ada 15 Jul 1922
/Waller,George D. 1915-1922   xWaller,Homer F. 29 apr 1920
/Waller,Nannie B.1868-1918   /Waller,Rev.James B. 1858-1925
xWallis,John 3 aug 1926   /Walters,Charles G. 1827-1906
/Walters,Elhannan 1865-1904   /Walters,James P. 1884-1914
/Walters,Nora J.1868-1907   /Walters,John Sr. 12 Jun 1938 80y9m5d
/Walters,Margaret A. 1840-1923   /Walters,Wm.Addison 1854-1935
/Walton,Bennett W. 1889-1938   /Ward,Annie E. 4 oct 1873-18 dec 1908
xWalton,Billy Vinson 22 dec 1933   George A.29 mar 1864-15 dec 1915
xWalton,Mrs.Lorena 36 mar 1912   /Ward,Bernard E.10 dec 1930 WWI
xWamshey,Robert 26 dec 1923   /Ward,Catherine 5 aug 1824-14 Jun 1895
xWann,Sarah J.14 dec 1919   /Ward,Cecil G. 1871-1910
/Ward,Alice S.1868-1932   /Ward,Clara 1866-1913
xWard,Anna 12 apr 1916   xWard.C.A. 11 feb 1923
xWard,Arthur H.27 apr 1936   xWard,Carl B. 1933
/Ward,Bernard 1930-33   xWard,Clarence C.17 aug 1931
xWard,Columbia 20 dec 1918   xWard,Columbia 1806-1891
/Ward,Eliza M. 1853-1924   xWard,Estella 25 aug 1933
/Ward,Ernest 1911-1917 s/oE&E   xWard,Evelyn 17 aug 1934
xWard,Fannie 1867-1893   /Ward,George A. 1868-1906 s/o OW&CJ
xWard,George A. 19 dec 1915   xWard,J.A.15 sep 1926
/Ward,James 5 oct 1933 70y   /Ward,James Marshall 19 oct 1936 17y
xWard,James W.7 oct 1933   xWard,Joanna 26 dec 1912
/Ward,Jane 1844-1882   xWard,John S. 28 sep 1914
/Ward,Leda Vivian 1894-1902   xWard,Lenora 22 dec 1929

187

xWard,Leroy B.22 aug 1929	xWard,Monrow 27 nov 1926
/Ward,Lannie 1867-1893	/Ward,Mabel F. 1889-1923
/Ward,Mac 1872-1900	/Ward,Mary E. 1867-1901
xWard,Myrtle 2 feb 1925	/Ward,Mrs.O.W. 1846-1891
/Ward,Oren E. 1866-1907	/Ward,Oscar 1896-97
xWard,Phillip E.19 aug 1939	xWard,Rebecca Jane 1 Jan 1939
/Ward,Robert C. 1844-1907	xWard,Robert O.22 feb 1914
/Ward,Stephen D. 1832-1896	/Ward,William E. 1892-93
/Ward,William N.1862-1930	xWarden,S.24 Jun 1919 CSA
xWare,inf 1888	/Ware,Edwin Lee 14 Jul 1939 73y3m12d
/Ware,Felix Henry 1837-1897	/Ware,Irene P. 1 Jan 1884 3y
/Ware,Henry A. 1829-1900	/Ware,Mabel 9 may -24 sep 1878
Gergiana 1840-1904	/Ware,Walter 3 sep 1839 inf
/Ware,Kate Purvis 1847-1896	xWarren,Cora 1908
xWarner,Mrs,J.C. 1 mar 1911	xWarren,Douglas 29 Jul 1924
xWarren,B.A.--	xWarren,George 21 mar 1922
xWarren,Eva--	/Warren,Sarah 1877-78 d/BA&SV
/Warren,John Thomas 9 dec 1932	/Warren,Standard 1871 inf s/oBA&SV
xWarren,Spicey J.4 may 1930	xWarren,Sarah 10 feb 1914
/Warren,Walter,1859-1920	/Warren,Virgil Jackson 16 feb 1936 64y11m
xWarrick,Daniel 5 Jan 1927	xWarrick,Mary 1931
xWarrick,Mary 8 Jul 1928	xWarrick,Sarah 27 apr 1921
xWase,John 24 apr 1934	xWartenberg,Eleanor M.31 mar 1916
/Wash,Ada L. 1878-1920	/Wash,Addie Jr.1878-1923
/Wash,Alice C. 1860-1927	/Wash,Bettie E.1849-1906
/Wash,Geo.Sheldon 1880-1938	/Wash,George W.4 Jul 1889 36y
/Wash,Harry O.11 aug 1884CW&AC	xWash,Ida Lee 8 mar 1920
xWashington,Clint 1 mar 1924	/Washington,Bernard 8/1/1856-619/1891
xWashington,Eliza 21 aug 1916	/Washington,Geo.D.10 sep 1934 45y5m8d
xWashington,Ervin 19 Jan 1927	/Washington,Hershell 14 dec 1934 28y2m
xWashington,Fannie 27 may 191	xWashington,Helen 5 apr 1932
/Washington,Jack Sweeneys BN CSA	xWashington,James 19 apr 1939
xWAshington,Josephine 4 apr 1932	xWashington,Lucy 28 feb 1928
xWashington,Marhta A.22 oct 1920	xWashington,Milton 12 oct 1910
xWashington,Rosa 2 aug 1933	xWashington,Ruby 9 sep 1922
xWashington,Sarah 12 feb 1918	xWashington,Sheb 24 feb 1915
xWashington,W.M. 5 oct 1923	xWassum,Elizabeth 19 may 1933
/Waston,Morton Wall 1909-1929	xWatershed,inf 9 feb 1932
xWatkins,Henry 26 dec 1933	xWatson,James H.12 Jul 1922
xWatson,Johana 5 sep 1931	xWatson,John 23 feb 1914
xWatson,July 2 may 1920	xWatson,Morton 1909-1929
xWatson,Nellie 25 Jul 1913	xWatts,A.27 may 1924
/Watters,Wm.Abner 1853-1920	/Watts,Chas.Wellington 28Jun1867-18dec34
/Watts,Dr.A.J. 1865-1931	/Watts,Elizabeth Biggs 1875-1904
xWatts,Barter Lee 12 Jul 1923	/Watts,Clifford Goman 1907-9 nov 1927
/Watts,C.C. 1896-1923	/Watt,George W.26 may 1867-7 oct 1937
/Watts,C.F. 1865-1933	xWatts,Grace C.15 oct 1934
/Watts,Harrison 1842-1926	/Watts,Goble B.1887-1890 s/oAJ&Bettie
Sarah 1843-1906	/Watts,Harry 1875-1902
/Watts,Holly M 1897-1899	/Watts,inf s/o Hans & Jennie
/Watts,Jesse 1870-1916	xWatts,Julia Ann 9 oct 1936
/Watts,Laura Bell 1872-1939	xWatts,Lora 17 aug 1940
/Watts,Letha A. 1893-1918	/Watts,Mary 1869-1887
xWatts,Mary 1897	xWatts,Virginia 21 Jun 1930

/Watts,Mattie M. 1873-1899   /Watts,Ora Herbert 4 feb 1890-1 oct 1918
/Watts,Virginia 1870-1906   xWaugh,Dora 17 dec 1927
/Waugh,Florence J. 1860-1926   /Waugh,James P.1858-1923
xWaugh,Lelie boyd 14 dec 1927   xWaugh,Marhta 14 apr 1936
/Wayland,James G. 1924-25   /Weatherall,Leonard 9 oct 1934 WWI
/Weathers,Frank M. 1865-1912   /Weatherford,Robt 12 oct 1859-13 apr 1901
/Weathers,Harold Vernon 1891-1918 /Weaver,Bernard 1894-99
/Weaver,Edwin Jr. 1864-1916   xWeaver,John L.13 Jun 1928
/Weaver,L.J.7 mar 1924   /Weaver,Marjorie 1905 inf
/Weaver,Martha J.1850-1933   xWeaver,Otmer Lee 30 oct 1928
/Weaver,Pearl d1898   /Weaver,Rachel 1885-1906
/Weaver,Ruth 1897   /Weaver,Rozella C.5 Jul 1938 74y2m27d
/Webb,Ammie B.1866-1921   xWebb,Eliza Ann 21 nov 1935
xWebb,Foster 10 Jul 1925   /Webb,Job 1863-1910
xWebb,H.21 Jul 1922   Josephine 7 oct 1872 30y4m4d
xWebb,Harry 14 Jul 1914   /Webb,John Basques 9 Jul 1873 inf
xWebb,Lorena 24 oct 1889   /Webb,Margaret 1866-1936
xWebb,Nancy A.17 feb 1896   xWebb,Phillipina 4 Jan 1929
xWebb,Pluma E.31 Jan 1917   xWebester,Jessee 7 aug 1935
/Weiden,Alice E. 1893-1908   xWeed,Aaron 1856-1940
xWeekley,Fred 22 feb 1906   xWeed,Annas R. 22 nov 1920
/Weekley,Mary Green 1876-1935   xWeekley,Henry W. 16 dec 1912
/Weekly,Ida M. 1864-1925   xWeekley,Joe 18 oct 1918
/Weekly,Orpha 1887-1905   xWeekly,Rose 16 dec 1909
xWeeks,inf 27 dec 1917   /Wees,Elijah Fleet 17 Jul 1937 84y6m23d
xWees,Sarah J.29 Jun 1921   xWees,Walter E. 5 Jul 1917
/Weiden,Frank A. 1856-1922   xWeider,Alice E.1893-1908
/Weider,George 1883-1900   /Weider,James M. 1818-1891
/Weider,Harry H. 1863-1911sJM&M   Mary Hay 1835-1922
/Weider,James 1886-1888   xWeider,Mary H.9 Jun 1917
/Weider,May Lowe 1871-1926   xWeider,Mary J.3 dec 1922
/Weider,Paul 1891-1896   /Weider,Thelma Coreene 1898-99
xWeider,Thelma W.1896   xWeidle,James F. 5 sep 1919 inf
/Weigal,Aloys 1873-1925   /Weil,Anna 1871-1909 w/o L.H.
/Weiler,Bertha A. 1872-1920   /Weil,Edith Strauss 22 feb 1921 75y
/Weiler,Clara W. 1862-1927   /Welch,Gene 1933 inf
/Weiler,Fabion S. 1871-1938   xWelch,J.H.18 apr 1930
/Weiler,Francis d1927   xWelch,Thomas 1820-1880
/Weiler,James J. 1862-1933   xWelch,William 1886-1930
xWeiler,Mary Francis 17 Jun 1935xWelker,Vernon E.10 sep 1934
/Weiler,Wm.Geo.1910-1922   xWellen,Mary lee 20 Jan 1931
xWeller,Emeline 22 Jul 1934   /Welling,Imogene 1905-1923 w/o Frank
/Wellington,Noadiah 1828-1900   Frank 26 Jan 1957
    Elizabeth 1832-1871   xWelling,James T.30 mar 1921
/Wellington,Lucinda 1852-1921   xWellman,Adaline--
/Wellington,Rebecca F. 1847-1930xWellman,Addie 1 may 1859-27 sep 1891JD&M
/Wellington,Z.Taylor 1847-1923   xWellman,Allen 28 Jul 1933
xWellman,Amanda 24 may 1919   /Wellman,Elisha 1877-1936
/Wellman,Effie 1864-65d/oJD&MA   xWellman,Fannie 11 nov 1932
/Wellman,John D. 1831-1925   xWellman,Harry--
/Wellman,Jesse B. 1862-63JD&MA   /Wellman,Leona 1885-1917
/Wellman,Martha 1836-1919   xWellman,Minerva 29 oct 1938
/Wellman,Smylie 1894-1918   /Wellman,Ruth 1 Jul 1896-26 may 1903
xWellman,Samuel 5 Jul 1917   xWellman,William 9 mar 1937

```
xWells,Albert 25 Jul 1915           xWells,E.B. 20 feb 1930
/Wells,Anna 1861-1905               /Wells,Ann M. Beauchamp 1844-1915
/Wells,Elizabeth E.1835-1921            Granville G. 1842-1885
     Jesse A. 1838-1916            xWells,Elizabeth 18 dec 1912
/Wells,Eugene 1898-99               /Wells,Helen Wellman 6 dec 1913-25 feb28
/Wells,George 1867-1891             xWells,Harry 17 feb 1934
/Wells,John Marcum 1918-1920        xWells,Jesse A. 29 sep 1916
/Wells,Margaret 1866-1927           xWells,Kittie 2 Jun 1912
xWells,Margarette 19 feb 1937       xWells,Lawrence S.25 feb 1937
xWells,Mary M.24 Jan 1934           xWells,Sam 28 feb 1937
/Wells,Richard Lee 1913-1934        /Wells,Laura F.21mar1877-25nov1910JA&EE
xWells,Viloet 25 may 1915           xWells,William Albert 7 nov 1914
/Welsh,Dr.Thomas 21 may 1880 60y/Wells,Thomas M.21 Jul 1864-1 aug 1898
xWelston,Robert 15 may 1927         xWensel,Creola 2 feb 1934
xWentz,Myrtle M.15 mar 1934         xWescott,Henry Irvin 23 aug 1928
/Werninger,Anna B. 1855-1929        /Weser,E.Gerturde 10 sep 1890-11 may 1912
/Werninger,Mary R.G. 1847-1917      /Wesley,Harry 1914-1917
/Werninger,Wiliam 1811-1893         xWesley,Daniel 14 may 1925
xWest,Aletha 15 nov 1917            /Wesley,Nora M.1879-1906d/oJohn Mickens
/West,Clevy 14 Jun 1905             xWest,C.W. 23 may 1922
xWest,French 19 nov 1921            /West,Laura Molter 1867-1919
/West,Major J. 1870-1936            xWest,Lucille 5 sep 1937
/West,W.Edward 1862-1928            xWest,Vanie 14 aug 1925
xWest,W.H. 31 Jan 1921              xWest,William 20 sep 1923
xWest,William 24 mar 1928           xWestfall,Marhta 16 Jun 1923
xWetherall,John 22 nov 1880         xWetherall,Jamima 10 Jun 1826-1 dec 1912
xWetherall,Leonard 9 oct 1934       xWetherford,Robert 1859-1901
xWetzel,Louis 4 Jan 1920            /Weymouth,Emma 1868-1908
xWeymouth,H.B. 13 aug 1911             Fred Austin 30 dec 1938 77y10m14d
xWhalen,Michael R.5 aug 1928        xWhalen,Thelma Irene 21 aug 1928
/Wheatland,Wm.Goffey 1886-1921      /Wheatley,W.H. 8 aug 1875-22 aug 1911
xWheatly,Ella E.22 apr 1928         xWheatly,Henry W.14 sep 1927
xWheatly,William 24 aug 1911        xWheaton,Nettie H.10 aug 1920
xWheaton,W.C. 8 mar 1912            /Wheaton,Walter Paul 1909-1937
/Wheeler,Cora L. 8 apr 1939         xWheeler,Eldo Jane 5 aug 1929
/Wheeler,Edward 1844-1899           xWheeler,Harriet H.8 may 1924
xWheeler,Henry C.21 Jan 1924        /Wheeler,James A. 3 may 1926
/Wheeler,James R. 1906-1925         xWheeler,John A. 26 sep 1911
xWheeler,J.W. 6 nov 1912            xWheeler,Samuel 18 Jan 1925
/Wheeler,R.B. 1878-1934             /Whisman,William H. 1876-1930
xWhitaker,Joshua 21 Jan 1925        xWhitaker,Lou--
xWhitaker,Mary 22 sep 1912          xWhitaker,William 28 apr 1921
/Whitcomb,George N. 1844-1911       /Whitcomb,Alfaretta 1848-1928
xWhitcomb,Alice R. 29 mar 1935      xWhite--12 Jun 1919
xWhite,A.G. 1903                    /White,Carlos V. 1870-1937
xWhite,Carie A. 25 feb 1922         xWhite,Cecil C.4 dec 1939
/White,D.K. 1830-1906               /White,Emma Clark 1870-1921
xWhite,Elizabeth D.17 Jan 1913      xWhite,Isaac 4 Jun 1915
/White,Hala J. 1883-1916            /White,Henry Clyde 1896-1902
xWhite,J.G. 24 Jan 1911             xWhite,Julia 5 oct 1922
xWhite,Katie mar 1914               xWhite,Mary 16 mar 1920
/White,Mary A. 1836-1919            /White,Margaret Clark 1888-1937
xWhite,Mary L.9 may 1930            /White,Myrtle 1893 inf
/White,Myrtle, 1894-1922            /White,Okey Tracy 1894-99
```

xWhite,Ruby E. 4 dec 1939   /White,Otto 3 oct 1937 57y9m27d
xWhite,Mrs.R.E. 29 may 1915   xWhite,Sherman 24 may 1918
/White,Rufus 1864-1933   /Whitehead,William G.1866-1915
xWhitlock,Jack T. 21 dec 1912   xWhitmore,Belle 26 nov 1903
xWhitmore,Columbia 28 feb 1927   xWhitmore,George 2 feb 1922
/Whitmore,Eugene 28 mar 1933 12y   xWhitmore,Jesse 16 aug 1937
xWhitmore,Mary C.22 feb 1936   xWhitmore,Minnie 6 dec 1914
/Whitten,Maud B.5 aug 1938   xWhitmore,Thomas Franklin 29 nov 1921
/Whitten,John E. 1907-1934   /Whitten,John W. 1879-1920
xWhorley,Sallie 12 feb 1916   /Wiatt,Flora Roseberry 1825-1912
/Wiatt,Francis E. 1799-1874   /Wiatt,John Robert 1859-1902
/Wiatt,John Wm. 1807-1865   /Wiatt,Susan Turner 1865-1925
/Wiatt,Thomas Andrews 1857-1915   /Wiatt,Wm.Owen 1861-1931
xWibble,Dan 13 mar 1923   xWibble,James H.Jr.2 mar 1919
xWicke,Bessie 5 nov 1920   xWickline,D.M.10 feb 1920
xWickline,John R.4 dec 1939   xWickline,Wilson 12 mar 1921
xWigal,George Lee 24 may 1936   /Wigal,Josephine 1904-05 d/o LS&L
/Wigal,Lewis S. 1866-1916   /Wigal,Linnie S. 1868-1937
xWigglesworth,Berry L.6 feb 1929   xWight,Henry A.27 Jan 1939
xWike,Jacob 1892   /Wike,John Jr. 1916-1928 s/oJohn & Ida
xWike,Richard 15 may 1932   xWikoff,Curtis Lee 14 Jun 1925
xWilcox,Dorothy 22 Jun 1921   xWilcox,Mary M.30 mar 1912
/Wilcoxen,N.B. 1835-1900   xWilds,Gerturde May 2 Jan 1938
/Wilesek,Rosa 1848-1923   /Wilds,Blanche 1880-1918 w/o Wm.
/Wilesek,Samuel 1852-1924   xWiles,Rathimil 23 aug 1927
/Wiley,Ella R. 1858-1931   /Wiley,Macie 3 Jun 1938 38y11m
xWiley,John 9 may 1932   /Wiley,Thomas 18 nov 1875
/Wilkerson,Jo Ann 1925-26
xWiles,Anna 11 Jul 1923   /Wilkes,Bert 1873-1904
xWilkes,Charles B.27 feb 1917   /Wilkes,Ernest E. 1913-16s/oEM&L
xWilkes,Charles W.25 Jul 1917   xWilkes,Cora B.19 apr 1920
/Wilkes,James D.1867-1912   xWilks,John E.1903-1921
xWilkins,Jane 11 may 1917   /Wilkinson,Cassa B. 5 oct 1844-4 Jun 1894
     Thomas W.1 may 1917   /Wilkinson,George W. 1849-1916
xWilkinson,J.F.21 nov 1936   /Wilkinson,Mary V. 1854-1930
/Wilkinson,O.Jennings 1868-1931   xWilkinson,Viola Elizabeth 3 apr 1932
xWilkinson,Wm.E.1860-1893   xWilkinson,Wm.E.25 oct 1840-15 Jul 1893
xWilks,Earnest E.4 feb 1916   xWilks,Helen 24 Jul 1922
xWilks,James 7 mar 1921   xWilks,J.D.24 Jul 1922
xWilks,John E.12 feb 1920   xWilks,Levina 8 sep 1923
/William,Arthur 19 mar 1934 WWI   /Williams Ada L.13 dec 1882 inf/JH&EO
xWilliams,Andrew 18 Jul 1919
/Williams,Claude H. 1895-1929   xWilliams,Blanche 8 Jan 1913
/Williams,Andrew 1851-1919   xWilliams.Clarence 12 dec 1925
xWilliams,Cyntha Owen 9 Jan 1935   /Williams,E.O.1884-1910
/Williams,Edwin E.1869-1926   /Williams,Emma O. 1856-1938
/Williams,Ernest B. 1877-1925   xWilliams,Emley 15 mar 1912
xWilliams.Emma 6 mar 1914   /Williams,Fran.Catherine 1920 inf
/Williams,Frances C.1837-1919   xWilliams,George W.17 sep 1921
/Williams,Jonah B.1860-1916   /Williams,George C.4 sep 1935 60y3m6d
/Williams,J.H. 1853-1904   xWilliams,James 26 apr 1928
xWilliams,J.Clifton 12 aug 1924   xWilliams,John 27 Jul 1923
xWilliams,L.S.9 feb 1916   /Williams,Margaret 1835-1918
xWilliams,Margie Esta 5 aug 1937   xWilliams,Mary 14 Jul 1922

xWilliams,Mary E. 4 Jun 1910   xWilliams,Mary Jane 19 dec 1918
/Williams,Mary Jane 1857-1909   xWilliams,Mollie 12 apr 1924
/Williams,Nathaniel N.1902-1930 xWilliams,Nannie L.1852-1895
xWilliams,Nannie 26 apr 1926   xWilliams,pattie 15 apr 1937
/Williams,Richard 1874-1933   /Williams,Rebecca S.1810-18 aug 1862 52y
/Williams,Sarah Meeker 1887-1925   William M. 1799-26 nov 1862 63y
xWilliams,Sandy 27 may 1937   xWilliams,Sarah 1835-1888
xWilliams,Susie 6 oct 1930   xWilliams,Theodore 26 apr 1922
/Williams,Treldeen 1913 inf   /Williams,Wannie L. 1852-1895
/Williams,William C. 1835-1919 xWilliams,William H.22 sep 1918
xWilliamson,Alvery 18 mar 1915 xWilliamson,Dorothy 13 feb 1922
/Williamson,Eva 1903-09 d/o W&I xWilliamson,Ellen 23 oct 1918
/Williamson,Earl D. 1879-1932   xWilliamson,Francie L.1902 inf
xWilliamson,Belle--   xWiliamson,T.W.
xWilliamson,Eddie-   xWiliamson,Elizabeth--
xWilliamson,Lydia Viola--   xWiliamson,Mabel--
xWilliamson,Mamie 4 aug 1939   /Williamson,Minnie 16 sep 1877-10 Jan1933
/Williamson,Maine 1 aug 1939 41yxWilliamsoin,Marguarite 27 Jun 1916
xWilliamson,Martha 15 oct 1930 /Williamson,Robt.H.1860-9 may 1936 76y2m3d
/Williamson,Walter S. 1870-1916 /Williamson,William K.1877-1899
xWilliamson,W.S. 9 may 1916   xWilliamson,William E.19 may 1925
xWillis,Arthur 19 oct 191   /Willis,Cornelius 20 mar 1850-21 may 1898
xWillis,Eva 17 Jun 1924   /Willis,Homer W.13 Jan 1885-12 sep 1907
xWillis,Fannie 4 feb 1928   xWillis,Ivan Glenn 2 nov 1925
xWillis,Mrs.James 20 sep 1907   xWillis,J.C. 7 aug 1841-17 feb 1926
xWillis,Joe S.20 apr 1921   Jemima E.9 may 1843-2 oct 1918
xWillis,Robert 2 feb 1918   xWillis,R.T. 22 Jul 1924
xWillis,Sam J.2 aug 1909   xWillis,W,M. 16 apr 1930
/Willis,W.H. 1870-1924   /Willison,Margery J. 1900-1918
/Wills,Easter G.d1930   xWills,E.Gwendolyn 28 apr 1930
xWills,Ward H. 11 dec 1939   xWilmnick,George H.19 Jul 1916
xWilson,Ann 20 feb 1925   /Wilson,Asa L. 1 Jan 1817-21 Jun 1896
xWilson,Annid S. 15 dec 1916   Mary A. 27 sep 1822-7 feb 1897
xWilson,Arlis 16 aug 1924   xWilson,Asa P. 13 oct 1917
/Wilson,Belle 1862-1934   /Wilson,Ammie McMahan nov 1850-nov 1915
xWilson,B.J. 23 Jun 1927   John T. nov 1845-nov 1923
/Wilson,Carlin R.d27 sep 1916   /Wilson,David 27 sep 1845-23 sep 1918
/Wilson,David 1861-1929   CoK 178th OH Inf GAR
                                /Wilson,Charles R. 7 oct 1872-7 oct 1937
xWilson,Elizabeth 1862-1939   xWilson,Ellen 31 oct 1921
/Wilson,Ella S. 1839-1924   /Wilson,Erma M. 20 sep 1934 19y8m23d
xWilson,Elwood 13 apr 1925   xWilson,Gerturde 10 feb 1918
xWilson,Gideon 1933   xWilon,Gus 29 Jul 1912
xWilson,Hugh M.3 may 1934   /Wilson,Granville T.30 oct 1937 66y11m12d
xWilson,Ida 14 Jun 1921   /Wilson,Jane 1822-1892
/Wilson,John L. 1816-1902   /Wilson,Johnny 1900-1903
xWilson,John L. 3 dec 1939   /Wilson,Josephine 1862-1897
xWilson,James H.30 dec 1908   xWilson,Josie 1862-1897
/Wilson,Lottie B.1907-1932   /Wilson,Margarite 7 dec 1938 20y11m27d
/Wilson,Lon A. 1885-1922   xWilson,Margaret 11 apr 1909
/Wilson,Maxie B.1907-1932   xWilson,Mary Amazetta 20 nov 1915
/Wilson,Robert Burks 1908 inf   /Wilson,Ronald Leon 1913-1915
/Wilson,Reuben W. 1902-1936   /Wilson,Sarah D. 13 sep 1844-25 apr 1906
/Wilson,Ruth 1904-1907   /Wilson,Shirley Ann 27 feb 1939 7y

/Wilson,T.M. 22 feb 1886 29y1m1d /Wilson,Wm Walton 17 Jun 1939 41y8m29d
/Wilson,Will H. 1852-1925 xWilson,W.B. 21 dec 1923
xWilson,Wille 11 Jan 1929 xWilson,William 2 feb 1925
xWimbush,Marie 5 dec 1929 /Wimbish,Mary 3 apr 1938 62y7m15d
xWindsor,Thomas 1 Jan 1919 xWinford,John 1 may 1918
/Winget,J.Walter 1854-1908 xWingue,Laura 12 aug 1918
xWinget,Romina 27 aug 1927 /Winkler,Anna 1868 1937
/Wingett,Winniford 1889-1912 xWinkler,Boyd 8 Jan 1892
xWinkler,L.R. 17 sep 1918 /Winkler,Henry B.CoC 91st OH Inf USA
xWinkler,Lula M. 27 aug 1909 xWinkler,Willis 12 may 1896
/Winn,Elizabeth 1835-1914 /Winn,John W. 1853-1925
/Winn,Oley P. 1882-1913 xWinn,Wm.Edward 8 nov 1932
xWinsie,Criola 2 feb 1934 xWinson,Ady 17 mar 1924
xWinston,Alex 4 feb 1917 xWinson,Wm.Holderby 1916
xWinston,Belle 13 feb 1922 /Winton,Edward 1852-19 Jan 1892 40y
xWinston,George W. 24 Jan 1934 xWise,Averill 1 feb 1926
xWise,H.A. 14 Jul 1915 /Wiseman,Grover C. 1890-1918
/Wiseman,Lou Ida 1882-1907 /Wiseman,Louise C. 1871-1937
/Wiseman,William G. 1872-1938 /Wiseman, William H.1903-1922
xWishan,Hazel 9 oct 1922 xWisner,J.M. 15 Jul 1919
/Withers,Addie D.1890-1918 /Wisner,Theodore R.13 dec 1932
xWither,J.E. 14 apr 1921 /Withers,Mary Margaret 1909
/Withers,Dr.W.J. 1879-1930 xWithers,Mary M.14 oct 1920
xWithers,Mrs. 7 Jul 1917 /Withrow,Ambrose D. 1861-1936
/Withrow,Dora B.1866-1924 Sarah B. 1863-1917
/Withrow,D.H. 1894-1920 xWithrow,Garland 22 Jul 1912
xWithrow,Lydell 19 may 1930 xWithrow,Mary Ella 9 sep 1936
xWithrow,Ottie 8 Jun 1913 /Withrow,Scott 7 oct 1884-13 dec 1911
/Witwer,Charles R. 1895-1933 /Witzgall,Elizabeth 1866-1928
/Witzgall,Herbert J.1921 WWI /Witzgall,Lewis J. 1885-1920
xWoisawald,August 26 Jan 1913 /Wolcott,Amanda W. 1844-1931
/Wolcott,B.A. 1843-1918 /Wolcott,Annie 1874-1912 w/o L.A.
Sarah A.Cox 6 aug 1931 /Wolcott,Frank O. 4 dec 1872-7 apr 1909
/Wolcott,Charles 1873-74 /Wolcott,R.E.Lee 3 feb 1874 s/o LA&A
/Wolcott,Eugene 1872 inf xWolcott,R.Bruce 1844-1903
xWolcott,Mother 1835-1893 xWolbarger,inf/Nellie 25 Jun 191
/Wolfe,Benjamin 1834-1894 xWolfe,John Jr. 1907-1919
xWolfe,Bettie 1836-1895 xWolfe,Nellie May 22 aug 1920
xWolfe,William E. 1870-1891 xWomack,Alice
/Womack,Blanche Ferris 1888-1936 /George H. 1853-1911
/Womeldorff,Eliza K.1868-1917 /Woo,Willie 1866-1923
W.A. 1865-1933 xWoo,Yea 13 nov 1932
/Wood,Ambrose C. 1842-1921
/Wood,Bessie C. 1878-1931 /Wood,Cynthia A. 1 apr 1835-11 aug 1886
/Wood,Edwin L. 1876-1899 /Wood,Ellen 1854-1937
/Wood,Emily A. 1848-1916 /Wood,Geroge Corbin 12 feb 1939 83y9m2d
/Wood,Henry A.1843-1916 xWood,Henry Cambell 26 may 1918
/Wood,Hubert M. 1874-1931 xWood,John L.10 Jan 1933
/Wood,Ira R. 1856-1893 /Wood,Leroy B. 1869-1929
xWood,L.H. 11 may 1914 xWood,Mary Ellen 19 Jun 1937
/Wood,Mary J. 1844-1921 /Wood,Mary Virginia 1909-1914
xWood,Peter 14 Jun 1912 xWood,Rebecca H.Jun 1900
/Wood,William F. 1841-1891 xWood,William F. 15 oct 1931
/Woodrum,Robert L.1864-1937 /Woodrum,Lewis 23 apr 1862-20 mar 1936

/Woods,Annie Waldron 1842-1931   xWoods,Anna 28 apr 1931
xWoods,C.R. 20 feb 1927   xWoods,Dorothy 3 aug 1926
/Woods,Howard H.1872-1935   /Woods,J.L. 1846-1933
xWoods,Louisa 19 Jan 1912   xWoods,Robert 22 apr 1916
xWoodson,Ann E. 9 Jul 1916   xWoodson,ella Gay 23 feb 1937
/Woodson,James 1833-1903   xWoodson,M.C. 1913
xWoodson,R.A. 17 Jan 1920   /Woodson,Margaret 19 feb 1875-10 may 1913
xWoodson,Susie 17 Jul 1923   /Woodson,T.N.10 sep 1882-25 Jun 1903
/Woodward,Allen Bernard 1884-920 xWoodward,Mrs.Allen 29 sep 80
/Woodworth,Mary M.1850-1935   /Woodworth,Albert H.1 apr 1842-25 mar1904
xWoody,Athur 25 mar 1925   xWoolum,Ora L. 11 nov 1926
xWooten,Alfred V.24 Jun 1932   xWooten,Amanda 27 dec 1924
xWooten,Clarence 24 Jun 1932   xWooten,Elizabeth 19 Jul 1911 inf
/Wooten,Fred S. 1884-1926   /Wooten,Lectiscutie 19 Jan 1938 67y3m12d
xWooten,Phoebe Jane 21 Jan 1938   xWooten,Lucy L. 31 mar 1912
xWooten,Marshall 4 aug 1922   xWorden,Andrew 7 Jun 1917
xWorden,Charles 11 feb 1926   xWorden,Cora 29 Jan 1926
xWorden,Hattie 1903   xWorden,Ollie 1897
xWorden,Thelma 1903   xWorick,Mary 8 Jul 1928
/Worley,Clara E. d1928   xWorkman,-- 24 feb 1917
/Workman,Fredie 1901-1915   xWorkman,Frances 13 Jul 1921
/Workman,Lucian 1868-1924   xWorkman,harold 9 Jul 1921
xWorkman,Martha Ann 14 apr 1930   xWorkman,mary E. 15 dec 1918
/Workman,Stephen H.1832-1906   /Worley,Clara E. 18 apr 1928
/Wray,Eliza Jane 1824-1888   xWorley,George W. 15 nov 1938
xWray,Norman E. 10 may 1928   /Wren,Mary V. 1900-1920
      Sadie 27 oct 1918   xWright,Agnes 11 feb 1931
/Wray,Wilson, 1820-1908   /Wright,Albert 1864-1927
xWrught,Agnes Allen 1830-1897   xWright,Alfred A. 31 Jul 1928
xWright,Alfred A.8 Jul 1928   xWright,Allen 3 feb 1916
/Wright,Annie 1875-1876d/JM&G   xWright,Charlotte may 1934
/Wright,Bazzle 1820-1895   /Wright,Claud 1882-1884
xWright,Daniel 1889-1900   xWright.,Emily 31 Jan 1917
xWright,Frances 7 Jul 1919   xWright,Fred E. 22 may 1934
xWright,george 29 Jul 1915   /Wright,Georgiana 1847-1920
/Wright,Goldie M. 1891-1937   xWright,Ida 24 may 1927
/Wrigth,Helen B. 1898-1939   /Wright,Henry A. 25 Jul 1938 WWI
/Wright,James 1872-1917   /Wright,Jesse 1861-1920
xWright,Jacob 17 mar 1921   xWright,J.P.27 feb 1920
/Wright,James M.1848-1922   /Wright,John H. 30 Jul 1855-27 mar 1901
/Wright,Laura 1879-1930   xWright,Leona 4 apr 1913
xWright,Levinsen 3 dec 1913   xWright,Lottie 1934
xWright,Louise 1913??   xWrigth,louisa 8 Jul 1935
/Wright,Mauddie L. 1888-1889   xWright,Maxwelton 15 apr 1927
/Wright,Nannie L. 1853-1928   /Wright,Nancy Ann 1851-24 oct 1898 47y
/Wright,Phoebe 1820-1906   xWright,Pearl 27 may 1933
xWright,Robert Sr. 1828-1908   /Wright,Robert 12 feb 1883 3y s/o W&L
xWrigth,Robert 29 may 1911   xWright,Susie --
/Wright,Sallie E. 1847-1915   /Wright,S.O. 1872-1880
xWright,thomas P. 6 apr 1925   /Wright,W.G. 1877-1905
/Wright,Tressie 1884-1922   /Wright,Walter 1885 inf JM&G
/Wright,W.C. 1883-1931   xWright,Walter 27 Jul 1931
/Wright,W.P. 1840-1869   xWright,William 1856-1909
xWright,Wm.C.1867-1937   xWright,Winifred 3 Jul 1912

xWron,Virgil 18 sep 1925   xWroten,L.M. 1868-1903
/Wroten,Annie L. 1850-1927 xWroten,David J. 29 oct 1921
xWroten,Dora 1872-1894   /Wuchob,Mathew C.10 feb 1934 66y8m16d
xWyatt,Annie E.1843-1904   /Wyant,Inez 3 mar 1876-1 mar 1898
/Wyatt,Chas.Russell 1867-1913 /Wyant,Thelma Irene 1910-13
/Wyatt,Fannie Eliza 1843-1904 xWyatt,Ida Mae 1904
xWyatt,Joseph M. 1891   /Wyatt,Isabel Adelaide 1823-1898
xWyatt,mary 8 nov 1926   /Wyatt,Margaret Baynham 1856-1929
xWyatt,Virginia 27 apr 1916 /Wyatt,Margaret Catherine 1914 inf
/Wylie,Oliver B. 1829-1908 /Wylie,Rebecca A.1834-1903
xWyont,Vila A. 22 feb 1915 xWysong,Frank 24 oct 1918
/Yates,Elister D.15 Jun 1909 xWysong,Charle 1899
    CoA----- GAR   /Yates,Hattie C. 5 sep 1879
/Yates,Fredrick 1 Jan 1932 4y Roy M.10 Jun 1875-18 nov 1909
/Yates,Sadie M.1879-1899   xYaudas,Barbara 21 Jan 1923
xYingling,Marvin Geo 12 may 1936/Yeich,George W.25 mar 1858-23 Jun 1910
/Yon,Orfeo Angel 1916-1919 /Yeich,Steward Glenn 11 Jun 1933 35y1m2d
/York,Dr.A.B.1899-1936   /Young,Albert L.1868-1926
/York,Dr.James F.1866-1921   Emma 18 apr 1915
/Yorke,Minnie M.1888-1921   xYoung,Albert D. 2 dec 1930
xYoung,Allen P. 28 mar 1934 xYoung,Araninta 11 mar 1920
/Young,George D.17 Jan 1937 WWI xYoung,G.G. 15 apr 1922   GAR
/Young,Isabelle E.1854-1937 xYoung,Maria 6 apr 1912
xYoung,Muncie 12 feb 1934   /Young,Patsy lee 9 Jun 1933
xYoung,Virginia 22 Jul 1923 xZacara,Sammy 12 mar 1913
/Zeller,Margaret 1902-1919 xZihlam,Joseph 3 apr 1918
/Ziegler,Harry A.1867-1924 /Zihlam,Anthony 1842-1912
/Ziegler,Pauline E.1909-1910 /Zihlam,Margaret 1871-1931
/Zinn,Katherine Ann 16 nov 1935 /Zihlman,Wm.G.Jr.1922-1924
/Zintsmaster,Theresa 1905-1937 /Zihlmann,Mildred 1875-1926
/Zirkle,Alice A. 1913-14   /Zihlmann,Rose Ann 23 oct 1936
/Zirkle,Charles D.1937-38   /Zirkle,C.Bird 9 may 1935 49y20d
/Zirkle,G.W.1884-1905   /Zirkle,Ruben 1849-1913
/Zirkle,Myrtle P.1936   inf /Zirkle,Paul David 6 sep 1936 inf
xZommes,Elsworth 11 may 1921

Add to this list at least 200 inf graves which I did not record and
several mausoleums. It seems there is no record in the office of these
burials plus some of them have been torn down.

SPRING HILL
as of
1874

NORWAY AVENUE

⑥ 🏠

④

①

⑦

OLDEST

② ✝

OLDEST

⑦

⑦

③

③

⑤

④

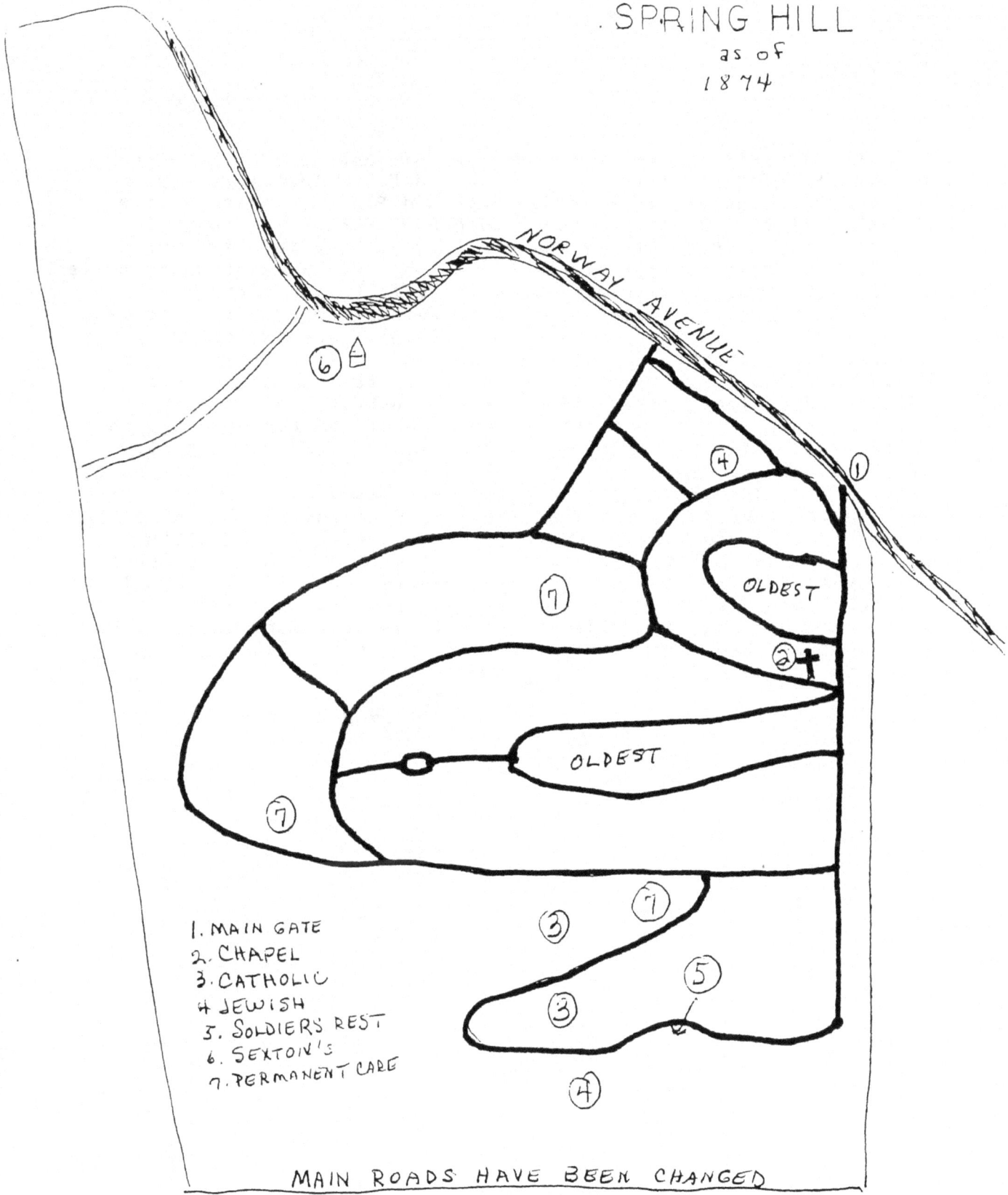

1. MAIN GATE
2. CHAPEL
3. CATHOLIC
4. JEWISH
5. SOLDIERS REST
6. SEXTON'S
7. PERMANENT CARE

MAIN ROADS HAVE BEEN CHANGED

193

Deed Book 16-540
Cabell County

W.P.Holderby
      to
C.S.Holderby(others)

        This indenture made this third day of January 1870 between
William P.Holderby of the first part and E.S.Holderby,Harvey
Poage,John Johnson,P.(W.M.)McCullough and P.C.Buffington of the
second part Witnessth thus the said party of the first part for
and in consideration of the sum of fifty dollars to him in hand
paid by the said parties of the second part the receipt where of is
hereby acknowledged hath bargained and sold to the parties of the
second part and their successors a certain piece or parcel of land
lying and being in the county of Cabell and state of West Virginia
between the turnpike and railroad and bounded as follows to wit:
Beginning at a beech about 11 feet west of the church now being
built on said land marked WPH church North to the turnpike and
south to the railroad with the south side of the turnpike and the
north side of the railroad to include all the land between said
road East of said land containing about one half of one acre be the
same more or less to have and to hold said land as trustees   for
the use and benefit of the Southern Methodist and the Southern
branch of the Presbyterian Church forever free from the claim of
the said party of the first part his heirs or assignees is further
understood that the church now being erected on said land should be
the joint property of the denominations of Christians above
mentioned and known as Holderbys Chapel. In testimony where of the
said party of the first part has herewith set his hand and seal
this day and date first above written   .

Seal   William P.Holderby

194

The Spring Hill Chapel

One of the pluses in doing a cemetery study is discovering the unexpected. The Spring Hill Chapel is one such surprise. This beautiful chapel was built in 1870 by William Holderby and sold for fifty dollars. The building is a two story brick chapel with vaulted windows and a slate roof. It is probable that the brick was made locally near present 16th Street.

About 1870 a group of men lead by P.C.Buffington and known as the Central Land Company,began buying land to build the city of Huntington.(backed by Collis P.Huntington) A deed from Book 16 page 540 is from William P.Holderby to this group of men. The deed identifies the church "now being built" as Holderby's Chapel and locates it North of the turnpike and South of the railroad. The reader must know the local history to locate this site. The "turnpike" refers to the James River Turnpike that ran from Richmond,Virginia to Lexington,Kentucky.This road is located today on the site of Norway Avenue to Gallaher Village then to Woodland Drive along 4 Pole Creek and eastward to Catlettsburg. The "railroad" as first built was present day US 60 along the Guyandotte River into Huntington on the south side of the river.

Holderby's Chapel's location made it very accessible to the community. The deed also states the chapel was to be used by both the Southern Methodists and the Presbyterians. Prior to this chapel, these groups had shared a church at Marshall Academy which was lost to them when the school when into private hands. Although small this chapel would have been able to provide for both congregations for the area population was small before Huntington. The 1860 census figure for Guyandotte was only 360.

Source:Map from 10.0 Deed for Spring Hill -Park Board
       Map-City of Huntington 1874-Court House
       Deed- Bk 16-540-Cabell County Court House
       History of Huntington

Heritage Books by the author:

www.ingramcontent.com/pod-product-compliance
Lightning Source LLC
Chambersburg PA
CBHW080239270326
41926CB00020B/4308